# SOPHIA

# SOPHIA

*Princess, Suffragette,
Revolutionary*

ANITA ANAND

BLOOMSBURY

NEW YORK • LONDON • NEW DELHI • SYDNEY

Published by Bloomsbury USA, New York
Bloomsbury is a trademark of Bloomsbury Publishing Plc

All papers used by Bloomsbury USA are natural, recyclable products made from wood grown in well-managed forests. The manufacturing processes conform to the environmental regulations of the country of origin.

LIBRARY OF CONGRESS CATALOGING-IN-PUBLICATION DATA HAS BEEN APPLIED FOR

ISBN: 978-1-63286-081-1

First published in Great Britain in 2015
First U.S. Edition published 2015

3 5 7 9 10 8 6 4 2

Typeset by Hewer Text UK Ltd, Edinburgh
Printed and bound in the U.S.A. by Thomson-Shore Inc., Dexter, Michigan

Bloomsbury books may be purchased for business or promotional use.
For information on bulk purchases please contact Macmillan Corporate and Premium Sales Department at specialmarkets@macmillan.com.

*For Hari and Simon, the two halves of my heart*

*&*

*For the wonderful women in my life who teach it how to beat*

*Arise! Ye daughters of a land*
*That vaunts its liberty!*
*May restless rulers understand*
*That women must be free*
*That women will be free.*

From 'The Women's Marseillaise' (1909),
words by Florence Macaulay

# CONTENTS

PART III

WAR AND PEACE, 1914–1948

# Prologue

Soprano and alto voices rose from the polished wooden floor and bounced off the plaster ceilings. They amplified, spilling from the high windows, slapping onto the wet, grey pavement outside. Startled commuters, with their thick coats buttoned high, broke stride, craning to see who was responsible for the jarring noise. But the building was giving little away. The Portland stone women, carved in relief above the grand entrance, were tight-lipped and serene, and the window panes were curtained by a thin film of condensation. Only the blur of bright colours behind gave a clue. Slashes of purple, white and green sliced through the otherwise monochrome November morning. The suffragettes had evidently taken over Caxton Hall again, and they sounded angrier than usual.

Inside, massive banners dominated every available space. Eight-foot slogans proclaiming 'Deeds Not Words', 'Strive and Hold', 'Arise! Go Forth and Conquer!' made the very walls seem as if they were shouting. Below them sat hundreds of women dressed in the muted blacks and browns of the season. From their clothing alone it was clear that they came from a myriad of backgrounds. Plain bonnets pushed up next to expensive wide-brimmed, feather-trimmed hats. Some had furs and kid gloves, while others wore patched, floor-length dresses. Irrespective of their armour, all of them were dressed for battle.

Thirty-eight specially chosen suffragettes sat in tightly packed rows on the stage behind the speaker. Their eyes were fixed on Emmeline Pankhurst's narrow back as she jabbed the air to emphasise her fury. Most of them could have single-handedly held audiences such as this in their thrall, but today they were the Praetorian Guard, and their stillness only seemed to accentuate the animation of their leader. At times it sounded as if Emmeline's voice might fail her – but she managed to keep going. Emmeline always did. Only her pale face broke the uniform blackness of her costume and her mood.

Elizabeth Garrett Anderson sat in the front row, to Emmeline's right. Shifting her gloved grip on the elegant walking cane in her hand, she listened to words she had heard many times before. At once England's first female surgeon, magistrate and mayor, Elizabeth had the ramrod straight deportment of a woman who was always ready to rise and speak. By 1910, long political rallies had become a trial for her seventy-four-year-old body, but she had no intention of missing the fight that day.

Also in the front row sat Emmeline Pethick-Lawrence and Pankhurst's firebrand daughter Christabel. Every so often, the two loyal lieutenants, bristling and determined, passed messages to their leader. Scrawled writing on folded pieces of paper shuttled through the hands of lawyers, scientists and social philanthropists. All of them had furthered the cause of women's rights, and all of them had come that day because Emmeline Pankhurst had summoned them.

Though she was doing her best to fade into the background, one face stood out among them all. It belonged to a quiet, bird-like woman seated right at the back of the stage. She was dressed in expensive Parisian couture and her brown face stared back fiercely at those who stared at her. Princess Sophia Duleep Singh was as close to an international celebrity as it was possible to be in 1910. Many had been reading about her for years in the popular press: daughter of a flamboyant Maharajah, goddaughter to Queen Victoria, champion dog breeder, and resident of Hampton Court Palace. Fashion pages frequently declared her one of the best-dressed women in the country and shops would boast about her patronage. There were less desirable facets to Sophia's fame, however. She was the daughter of 'that man', 'the traitor', 'the one who had lost everything'. Whispers followed Sophia wherever she went. She was the dark princess, granddaughter of the greatest ruler the Punjab had ever known, descendent of warriors.

Since childhood Sophia had lived her life watched by invisible eyes. She had been placed under surveillance by the British government, her movements, along with those of her family, diligently recorded, by spies. Thanks to her father's exploits, Sophia had experienced arrest and detention before even her tenth birthday. Her recent radical activities had earned her a special file of her own at the Political and Secret Department of the India Office, and it was getting fatter by the day.

Watched and judged by others for years, Sophia had been trained from an early age to maintain her poise and nerve no matter how uncomfortable the situation. Sitting stiffly in her chair at Caxton Hall, the Indian princess gave the impression of being much taller than she really was. At just a shade over five foot, she was usually the smallest person in a room. Her manicured fingers, heavy with emerald rings, drummed out the beat of the songs bellowed around her. Though she knew the words, Sophia refrained from joining in. She could play the piano better than most but knew that her voice was less than perfect; as was her custom, she sought to hide her imperfections. Though those all around her were absorbed by Emmeline's speech, Sophia's eyes had landed on a press photographer moving about on the balcony opposite. Sensing the exact moment his shutter would click, she peered out from behind the broad-shouldered woman in front and looked directly into his lens as he took his picture. In one of the only photos that exist of that historic morning, Sophia's gaze is calm, direct and confident, even though events all around her were building to frenzy.[1]

The princess was about to pitch herself into a violent street brawl which would leave many – including herself – bruised and bleeding in the shadow of the mother of all parliaments.

PART I

*Sophia's Childhood and
History, 1876–1898*

# Roots of Rebellion

Princess Sophia Duleep Singh's arrival coincided with the severe heatwave of 1876. Some parts of the country had not seen a drop of rain for more than forty days by the time she was born on 8 August, and temperatures soared to thirty-six degrees Celsius. From her nursery in Belgravia, a short walk from the gardens of Buckingham Palace, Sophia gasped the dry and sweltering air into her lungs for the very first time. The heat seemed to speak of India.

Sophia's emergence into the world coincided with a rebirth for her godmother. After fifteen long years in purdah, mourning for her late husband Albert, Queen Victoria had chosen 1876 to venture into the world of the living again. A solid testament to her enduring loss stood in Hyde Park. Though the main body of the monument had been completed years earlier, the statue of Albert at its heart had been shrouded until now. Freshly gilded, the unveiled figure gleamed in the relentless summer sunshine. With one hand resting carelessly on his knee, the Prince Consort sat quietly under a garish Gothic edifice, its golden spire rising 175 feet into the air. Solid granite steps led down from each corner of the memorial to four pristine white marble figures, representing Africa, Europe, America and Asia, the continents of the British Empire. They simultaneously guarded Albert and looked out upon London, the seat of Victoria's power.

Though she had agreed to be Sophia's godmother and watch over her immortal soul, it was an inescapable irony that the seizure of the child's inheritance had contributed to Queen Victoria's latest accolade. Her Majesty's government had bestowed the title 'Empress of India' on a delighted Queen, just weeks before Sophia's birth.[1] A visible reminder of all that Sophia's family had lost came on the very day that Victoria arrived to open Parliament, when at her throat she paraded the Sikh Kingdom's greatest talisman, the Koh-I-Noor diamond: 'Her Majesty's robe was of black velvet, trimmed with white ermine, over this was the dark blue riband of the Order of the Garter, clasped by diamonds . . . the Queen's necklet (the famous Koh-i-noor) and stomacher were of the same precious stones, and over her widow's cap gleamed the small crown of brilliants worn on these State occasions.'[2]

In the lifetimes of most of the peers and MPs who crammed into the chamber to hear the Queen's historic speech, the Koh-I-Noor had belonged to another potentate. Sophia's grandfather, Maharajah Ranjit Singh, had worn the vast gem strapped to his bicep as his north Indian Empire bowed to his will. To the British who watched and coveted his realm back then, the thought of possessing the diamond – the size and weight of a hen's egg – had seemed an impossible dream.

Ranjit Singh's Sikh Kingdom in the Punjab was hugely wealthy and expansive, extending from the borders of Tibet in the east to the craggy foothills of the Khyber Pass in the west. On old maps, before India and Pakistan were divided, if you were to slice off the top quarter of India, most of these territories were ruled by the Maharajah in Lahore. In a reign that lasted some fifty years, Sophia's grandfather managed to unite Hindus, Sikhs and Muslims under one banner and brought unprecedented prosperity to the region.

The Punjab itself had an even more illustrious history stretching as far back as the origins of mankind. Harappa in the Indus Valley was one of the earliest known ancient civilisations. Its ruins dated back to the Bronze Age, making the region hallowed ground for archaeologists. To Indians it was much more. It was a place where gods and demons once walked the earth. Legend has it that when Kuru, an Iron Age king, first came to the region the gods miraculously transformed the chariot on which he rode into a plough. Yoked to two terrifying beasts, the Bull of Shiva – lord of destruction, and the Buffalo of Lord Yama – sovereign of the underworld, Kuru tilled the land, compelled to do so by instructions from a voice that only he could hear. When he completed his final furrow, Vishnu, one of the three most powerful Gods in the Hindu pantheon, descended to earth and asked Kuru to sow the virtues of mankind. Given that his pockets were empty, the King decided to sacrifice one of his own arms, shredding its flesh into a thousand pieces and planting each dripping gobbet as a fleshy seed in the earth. Feeling he should do more, he then offered up his other arm, both legs and head. The gods were pleased, and they blessed him, proclaiming that henceforth the land would be named after Kuru. Anyone dying upon it would receive *moksha*, a state of grace, freeing the individual from an endless cycle of reincarnation.

Generations later, during the tenth century BC, new furrows were ploughed into the ground at 'Kurukshetra' and filled once more with human gore. During an epic battle lasting eighteen days, Kuru's descendants fought each other for his crown and kingdom, causing so many deaths in the process that sages claimed the heavens were almost torn apart with grief. Locals said that the spilled blood of heroes gave the Punjab the most fertile soil in all India.[3]

There was a less supernatural explanation for Punjab's golden fields of grain. Literally translated, *panj* means 'five' and *ab* means 'waters'. The region owed its bounty to the five mighty rivers running through it. The Sutlej, Jhelum, Ravi, Chenab and Beas stretched across Punjab like the splayed fingers of a hand.

Indeed, so burgeoning was the Punjab with crops and so rich were its mineral deposits that it became the prize that every invader wanted. Between 558 and 486 BC, the Persian Kings Cyrus the Great and his nephew Darius had ruled the Punjab's lands, using the area's wealth to finance their wars and its men to fill their armies. Soon after, Alexander the Great conquered Persepolis in 330 BC, and he too set his sights on India, thwarted in his ambition only by the men of the north. He described them as 'Leonine and brave people, where every foot of the ground is like a wall of steel, confronting my soldiers.'⁴ The mighty Alexander never managed to capture anything more than a small portion of the Punjab, and it too was lost soon after his death.

The greatest civilisations the Indian subcontinent has ever known, including the Mauryans, Kushans, Guptas, Hunas and Palas, all seized the lands in the north only to see them plucked from their grasp. In 1220, Genghis Khan, the Mongol leader of the largest contiguous empire in history, scythed through northern India on his way back to the Steppes. Crushing all resistance in his wake, he plundered the Punjab to the bone. Time and again palaces and temples rose and were crushed as victors sought to destroy any memory of what had gone before. In the flux, dark-skinned natives, pale traders and blood-stained invaders mixed. The tall, sharp-featured, caramel-skinned people who emerged over time were a genetic melding of Asia and Europe. Their beliefs and cultures had blurred edges, and Hindus and Muslims lived together in the villages, sharing a common language and culture. Though they prayed to their own gods, they danced to the same music.

Forged in a string of conflicts, Punjabis gained a reputation for ferocity; however it was nothing compared to that of their nearest neighbours. Tribes across the mountainous border were feared with good reason. Even though a series of mountains rose up between the Punjab and Afghanistan, stretching over 600 miles and soaring higher than 7,000 metres in places, they could not keep the two sides apart indefinitely. From 1451 to 1526, Lodhi Pushtun warriors from Afghanistan poured into the Punjab. Sikandar, the second sultan in the Lodhi dynasty, had little tolerance for the infidels of his new territory. He destroyed Hindu temples, built mosques and based the Punjab's laws on the Quran and Sharia code. The Lodhis permitted non-Muslims to practise their religion only if they paid a tax, or *jizya*, for the privilege. Despite the uncompromising subjugation, it was during this period that a new religion was born. In villages around the five rivers, a tiny minority began to call themselves the Sikhs. In doing so, they confused everybody around them.

The first Sikhs did not look distinct from their neighbours. They spoke the same languages and shared the same ancestors as those who toiled by their sides but they did not share their spiritual beliefs. Like Muslims, the new Sikhs scorned Hindu idolatry, rejecting the pantheon of gods and goddesses. They talked of one true God but refused to accept Muhammed as his prophet. Like the Hindus, they believed in reincarnation and karma, but they did not accept the caste superiority of the Brahmins, who enjoyed primacy among the Hindus. They bowed only to one man, referring to him as their leader and teacher. His name was Nanak, and he would change the Punjab for ever.

Nanak was born in 1469 in a village not far from Lahore. His parents, Mehta Kalu and Mata Tripta, were high-caste Hindus living a humble but comfortable life, at peace with their Muslim neighbours. Nanak was said to be a contented child, much coddled by his sister Nanaki who was five years older than him. His parents had hoped their son would follow in his father's footsteps, acting as the local inspector of land revenues, but it soon became apparent that the child was unusual. Nanak was given to long bouts of prolonged introspection. Instead of watching his father's cattle, as was his duty, he would slip into trances, leaving the cows to wander for miles, much to his father's irritation. Some believed that miracles occurred when he was near. One day the boy fell asleep on the ground beneath a tree. As he slept, villagers noticed that while all the shadows around him lengthened and shifted, the shade over the sleeping boy remained constant. On closer inspection they saw that a large poisonous cobra had spread open its hood in order to protect him from the sun.

More than the miracles, reports of his wisdom began to attract followers to Nanak. At around the age of eight, most Hindu boys of high caste were required to attend a sacred thread ceremony. A long piece of string, comprising three strands, was draped across the boy's left shoulder and tied in a knot at the hip. The strands represented the most powerful Hindu gods: Brahma, Vishnu and Shiva. The thread was a visible contract between the individual and his Hindu faith: it conferred the right of education and marriage and without it a boy would grow up out of caste. Since the caste system was such a powerful concept among Hindus at the time, those who had no thread were considered untouchable. Teachers would shun them, just as high-caste parents would ignore them as matches for their daughters.

Nanak was presented for his thread ceremony when he was nine years old. Friends and family gathered to celebrate his coming of age; however, as the priest approached him, the boy grabbed his hand and refused to let him tie his knot. To gasps of disbelief, Nanak announced that faith should not need physical symbols and that a relationship with God should be private, discreet and pure. To growing discomfort Nanak added that since women and members of the lower castes were not allowed to wear the thread it had no value to him. The priest was furious, but others marvelled at such reasoning from a child so young.[5] The boy left the ceremony without a thread, to the dismay of his own father.

Nanak had many such arguments with Hindu priests and Muslim clerics, infuriating them equally with his constant questioning. Even though he rejected both Hinduism and Islam, he preached tolerance and brotherhood: 'Whether Hindu or Turk (Muslim) or Sunni or Shia recognise the caste of all mankind is one . . . Let all serve the One. The Master of all is the One. All are the form of the One. Know in all the same life giving light resides. The Hindu place of worship and the Muslim place of worship are the same. The Hindu mode of prayer and Muslim mode are the same. All humans are one but superfluous misunderstandings are many.'[6]

As if to prove how easily the faiths could co-exist, in his thirties Nanak left his home accompanied by his Muslim friend, a minstrel called Bhai Mardana. Together, they undertook five epic journeys, or *Udasis*, which would take them hundreds of miles from home and last almost three decades. The companions travelled to Arabia, Iran, Iraq and Central Asia. Wherever they stopped, the friends broke bread with people of different faiths. Stroking the three strings of his pear-shaped rebec with his bow, Mardana filled the air with music while Nanak recited his poetry about 'One True God'. He spoke of a beneficent deity who watched over all his children no matter whether they prayed to him in a mosque, temple, field or forest.

Soon, word of the wise man and his minstrel began to spread. Nanak gained the title *Guru*, or 'honoured teacher', and his followers began to call themselves Sikhs, a derivation of the Sanskrit word for student – *sisya*. By the time of his death at the age of seventy in 1539, the Sikh religion was growing rapidly.

While Nanak preached, a descendent of Genghis Khan named Babur became the first Mughal emperor of India, sweeping across the Khyber Pass, crushing the Lodhis and swallowing the Punjab into his vast dominion. Some of the Mughals who followed him tolerated the proliferation of religions among the Punjabis. Others did not, and in the middle of the seventeenth century religious conflict became common, with Hindus and Sikhs battling to exert their identity under crushing Mughal rule. The sixth emperor, Aurangzeb, was particularly ruthless: he abhorred the Sikhs, finding them secretive and clannish and their beliefs subversive. Deciding they were a direct threat to his rule, his attempts to wipe them out led Sikhs to arm themselves and scatter across the Punjab; many were forced from the lands they had farmed for generations and into the forests and foothills. It was only after the death of Aurangzeb some fifty years later, and the decline of his Empire, that the Sikhs were able to emerge from the shadows, and take their place in the open once more.

As the Mughal Empire began to weaken, the Punjab became open to invaders. Mounted tribesmen from Afghanistan began to charge over the Hindu Kush again. Testing the strength of the region's defences, they raided Punjabi villages, looting all they could carry and leaving devastation in their wake. In 1778, the Afghan ruler Timur Shah Durani sent riders to take the Punjabi city of Multan. They returned with the heads of several thousand Sikhs dangling from their horses – a gruesome warning to all who would defy the will of the Afghans.[7]

Just a couple of years after Timur Shah's bloody lesson, Ranjit

Singh was born in 1780. His family were Sikhs in the richly agricultural area of Gujranwala in the north-west of the Punjab. Unlike the majority of young boys around him, it was clear that Ranjit would never grow up to be a farmer. His father had been the head of a Sikh warrior clan, known as the Sukerchakias, and from an early age Ranjit showed himself to be skilled on horseback and deadly with a sword. Charismatic, but not beautiful – smallpox had ravaged his face, robbing him of his left eye – the young *misldar*, or clan leader, inspired trust and loyalty among his peers even before he reached his teens. On horseback he was unstoppable. By his fourteenth birthday he and a group of loyal young followers had left home looking for adventure. On their travels, the band of boys started battles against much older, more powerful men. Ranjit was victorious every time and talk of his bravery spread quickly across the territories.

His followers swelled rapidly in rank and in just five years he had amassed a small army. He was just nineteen years old when he set his sights on Lahore, the fortress capital of the Punjab. It was a conquest warmly welcomed by the majority of Lahore's subjects, who were tired of corrupt and weak rulers and desperately sought change. When they heard the epic tales of bravery surrounding Ranjit Singh, they appealed to him to become their leader and rid them of their oppressors. He did so in 1799 without difficulty and promised to treat Sikhs, Muslims and Hindus as equals in his kingdom as long as they pledged unquestioning loyalty to him.

Lahore was the jewel of the north, and the pride of all the Punjab. Mughals had made the city their seat of power and created an environment of culture, opulence and architectural splendour. Gardens with intricate pools and fountains provided relief from the searing heat of summer. Great tombs erected in the memory of former emperors dwarfed the streets. Carved marble, inlaid with semi-precious stones, brought beauty to every quarter. At the heart of the walled city, Lahore Fort rose from the dust, spreading over twenty hectares and containing some of the finest examples of Mughal architecture, including the Sheesh Mahal, or Palace of Mirrors. Its five cusped marble arches soared up and opened into a cool and ornate courtyard. Gilded cupolas formed the roof of the palace and were decorated with thousands of intricately tiny mirrors. Within the fort stood the Moti Masjid, or Pearl Mosque, a seventeenth-century building designed by the creators of the Taj Mahal. Although he was tolerant of other religions, Ranjit Singh expelled Allah from the building and used its cool white rooms to pray to his own guru. His children played within the serenity of the Shalimar Gardens, darting between the trees and splashing in the waters.

Poets and musicians flocked to the city whose every inch seemed to be decorated with gold or embellished with stone that had been so finely carved that it looked like stiff lace. Yet Lahore was not enough for Ranjit Singh. With a strategic wisdom beyond his years, he wanted to unite all the disparate, minor kingdoms and fiefdoms that lay in an area of over 20,000 square miles between the Punjab's five great rivers, turning the land and its people into an unassailable empire. Ranjit proclaimed he would govern in the name of his spiritual master, Guru Nanak, for the benefit of all men no matter what their creed. He revoked the hated *jizya* tax of his predecessors and attended ceremonies for the Hindu, Muslim and Sikh religions, taking wives from all three faiths. Punjabi folklore has it that when a courtier once asked Ranjit Singh why he had one empty sightless eye socket, he answered: 'God wanted me to look upon all religions with one eye, which is why he took away the light from the other.' Out of a mixture of adoration, fear and awe, his people began to call their king *Sher-e-Punjab* – The Lion of the Punjab.

In 1801, two years after deposing Lahore's former rulers, Ranjit Singh was crowned Maharajah, or supreme king. Great tracts of land fell to him without resistance, while at the same time he harried the Afghan tribes until they retreated back to their own lands. The message was clear: the Sikh Kingdom was inviolable and no enemy would be allowed to breach its borders again.

Yet despite his hunger for conquest, the Maharajah seemed uncomfortable with the trappings of success, refusing to wear a royal crest in his turban and preferring not to sit on his throne. He was leaving it empty, some said, for the spirit of Guru Nanak himself. Moreover, when the Maharajah had coins minted, they bore the name and image of Nanak rather than his own. It was an act of humility never known before, or after, in the region.

Ranjit's peculiar mix of piety and power caught the attention of the authorities in London at a time when Britain was expanding its territories in the East. Not knowing what to make of the one-eyed warrior of the Punjab, they despatched a political agent, Captain William Murray, to assess the Maharajah's rise to power and identify his weaknesses. Murray's initial reports were fulsome in their praise: 'Ranjit Singh has been likened to Mehmet Ali and to Napoleon. There are some points in which he resembles both; but estimating his character with reference to his circumstances and positions, he is perhaps a more remarkable man than either. There was no ferocity in his disposition and he never punished a criminal with death even under circumstances of aggravated offence. Humanity indeed, or rather tenderness for life, was a trait in the character of Ranjit Singh. There is no instance of his having wantonly infused his hand in blood.'[8]

The British presence in India had been established as early as the 1600s through the trading activities of the East India Company. It was largely confined to the Surat in western India's region of Gujarat, the Coromandel Coast in the south-east of the country and Calcutta in the east. The white foreigners with their livery and long titles were known simply as 'the Company' to the Indians who watched them inch across their lands, setting down deep roots wherever they went. It was only in the early nineteenth century that the British came into direct contact with the Punjab, by which time Maharajah Ranjit Singh's dominance was firmly established. Recognising that he would make a formidable foe, the British sought an alliance with the Sikh ruler. A treaty of friendship was signed on 1 January 1806 in which it was agreed that everything to the north of the Sutlej River belonged to Ranjit Singh. The rest of India was up for grabs.

Although Ranjit's numerous conquests brought him ever more wealth, the greatest prize in his *toshakhana*, his treasure house, was the Koh-I-Noor, a 186-carat diamond. When a Persian potentate named Nadir Shah seized the gem from the Mughals in 1739, one of his consorts claimed: 'If a strong man should take five stones, and throw one north, one south, one east, and one west, and the last straight up into the air, and the space between filled with gold and gems, that would equal the value of the Koh-I-Noor.'⁹ The stone was also said to carry an ancient curse which condemned any man who owned it to a life of destitution, possible madness and the certainty of a terrible death. Women, however, were said to be immune to its dark power. As if to spite fate, Ranjit Singh wore the Koh-I-Noor as an amulet on his arm. His disregard of the superstition made him seem superhuman to his foes.

With a combination of martial dominance and good governance, by 1839 the Maharajah possessed lands and riches greater than any Punjabi before or since, and the mythology surrounding his name was such that his subjects believed he could not die unless he himself chose to do so. So it was on 27 June, Maharajah Ranjit Singh passed away peacefully in his sleep. At the age of fifty-nine, having ruled for almost forty years, he had brought peace and prosperity to the people of the five rivers.

Hours after his death, on the morning of 28 June, the funeral cortege of the Maharajah processed through Lahore, passing crowds of mourners, to the site that had been readied for his cremation. Here, four of the Maharajah's twenty wives and seven of his concubines, who had also been given royal titles, burned themselves alive on his funeral pyre. The ritual of *sati*, where living women would sit with their dead husbands while the flames rose to burn them both, was against Sikh teachings, yet still took place in some families. It was said to be the ultimate sign of fidelity because it meant that couples might be reincarnated as lovers again in their next life. Pressure on a woman to submit could be fierce and the honour granted to a *sati*'s family could be great. Not all *satis* went voluntarily to the flames.

One who refused to take part was the most recent of the Maharajah's wives, Maharani Jind Kaur, or Jindan, as she was affectionately know by the people of the Punjab. To any who dared to question her, she would simply say she owed a greater duty to her only son than to her dead beloved. Her steel prevented any further discussion and betrayed a rebellious spirit which was to define her in the years to come.

It was remarkable that one who had come from such humble beginnings as Jindan was prepared to defy those with power in the Lahore court. Born in 1817, she had been brought up in the palace kennels where her infant cries had competed with howls and barks. Her father, Manna Singh Aulakh, was the servant in charge of the Maharajah's hounds. Almost from the time of her puberty he had thrust Jindan at the Lion of the Punjab. A wily and ambitious man, Aulakh begged the ageing one-eyed king to take Jindan as his wife, tempting and teasing him with the prospect of a passion which might rejuvenate his old age. Despite resisting for some years, in 1835, when Ranjit Singh was fifty-five, and Jindan eighteen, he gave in and married the girl.

Jindan was a striking beauty. Fair in complexion with an oval face, strong aquiline nose, and large, intense, almond-shaped eyes, she moved with the grace of a dancer. By the time of their marriage, war and the pressures of kingship had taken their toll on the Maharajah: his long hair and chest-length beard were snowy white, and his tanned and pockmarked face was deeply scored with wrinkles. Jindan's youthful looks and his gnarled old age made the pair an incongruous couple, but there was a lot more to his youngest queen than appearances alone.

On 6 September 1838, Jindan gave birth to a son, Duleep. The Maharajah already had seven sons by his four senior queens. Though appearing to coexist peacefully, they were constantly plotting against one another. Vicious rumours, no doubt promulgated by the Maharajah's other queens, suggested Jindan's child could not have been fathered by the old man. To silence his court, the Maharajah publicly claimed Duleep as his own and elevated Jindan's position to that of one of his senior wives. The boy never got to know his father, however, for just nine months and twenty-one days after his birth, Ranjit Singh died.

The years that followed the Maharajah's death were marked by turmoil, murder, the break-up of his kingdom and the exile of his heirs. One by one, his family schemed to kill each other in an attempt to get their hands on the throne. First kingship passed to Ranjit's oldest son, thirty-nine-year-old Kharak. A notorious alcoholic and opium addict, he was cruel and debauched and despised in the realm. Having spent his four-month reign largely drunk, Kharak was poisoned with mercury by nobles of the Sikh court. When Kharak's son, a fine warrior and favourite of the Sikh troops, came to Lahore for his father's cremation, a large block of stone fell mysteriously from the palace archway, striking him on the head. Although apparently not badly hurt, and able to walk away from the scene unaided, two days later Nanihal Singh was found dead in the palace with his skull caved in. The explanation given was that he died from complications from the archway 'accident'.

The Sikhs then proclaimed another of Ranjit Singh's sons, Sher Singh, to be Maharajah, but it was not long before he too fell prey to the murderous ambitions of others. While he inspected his troops, a relative asked permission to show him how to fire a new gun. Sher Singh was later found riddled with bullets in what was claimed to be another tragic accident. Soon after, his ten-year-old son was found dead in a pool of blood outside the palace grounds. And so the violent assassinations went on, as one claimant after another was poisoned, stabbed or bludgeoned to death.

The resulting power vacuum created a climate of great instability in which the nobility and the army vied for control. After the last heir fell prey to yet another murderous plot, Jindan's infant son Duleep returned to Lahore. As the last one standing in 1843, the boy was placed on the throne and the steely Jindan, at just twenty-three years of age, was appointed regent of the greatly weakened state. At first, the powerful aristocrats of the Sikh Kingdom thought they could control Rani Jindan and play the child-king as they wished. However, it became clear that Jindan had ideas and advisers of her own, and murderous dissent began to ferment in the Lahore court once more. Controversially Jindan chose to leave the purdah of the women's quarters, where she had lived since the time of her marriage, and govern with her own voice. She sat in the throne room, with her child beside her, and formulated laws while surrounded by the fearsome generals of Ranjit Singh's army and those members of Duleep's extended family who had been lucky or clever enough to avoid being assassinated during the previous five years.

Jindan proved to be a controversial ruler. Her decision to raise the army's pay proved popular, as did the diplomatic truce which she negotiated between factions within the court. Others caused deep consternation, none more so than her decision to appoint her own brother, Jawahar Singh, as prime minister, or *vazir*. With his new powers Jindan's brother hoped to firm up Duleep's reign, and his own position, by neutralising potential rivals. His intrigues were tolerated for a while, but Jawahar Singh went too far when he decided to target a prince of the royal blood. The kennel-keeper's boy would pay dearly for his audacity.

Prince Pashaura Singh was Ranjit Singh's son. Although older than Duleep, his claim to the throne was weak. His mother Daya Kaur was one of Ranjit's nine *chadar andazi* wives; these were royal or aristocratic widows taken into the harem after the death of their husbands. A simple ceremony conferred rank and protection on the women who were otherwise left destitute by widowhood. A sheet was held over the woman as prayers were recited, symbolising the shelter her new lord would provide. *Chadar andazi* marriages were not deemed to be as significant as the traditional Sikh marriages. Only Kharak Singh and Duleep were the product of such traditional unions, and one of them was dead.

Pashaura Singh had attempted to take the throne from Duleep by force, but his army had been routed by Jindan's troops. A treaty was agreed between the victorious queen and her nephew. If he kept to his lands, he would be allowed to live in comfort, but Jawahar Singh wanted a more reliable arrangement. On 11 September 1845, Jindan's brother had the prince lured from his bodyguard and strangled to death. The act provoked outrage among the nobility.

Just ten days later, Jawahar Singh and Rani Jindan were summoned to a meeting of the Sikh council of elders. As they made their way to the appointed place, a group of soldiers surrounded Jawahar Singh's elephant, pulled the vazir to the ground and hacked him to death as he begged for mercy. Spattered in his uncle's blood, seven-year-old Duleep, who had been sitting on Jawahar Singh's lap, saw every brutal blow. The screams of his mother ripped through the air and mingled with his own. With the deed done, the soldiers bowed calmly before the hysterical child and vowed never to let any harm come to him. Memories from that day would haunt Maharajah Duleep Singh for the rest of his life. Despite her grief, Jindan agreed to continue as regent, acting with the counsel of the very men who had slaughtered her brother before her eyes.

It was now that the East India Company sensed its moment to act, having watched palace events with great interest. The Punjab was a coveted prize, yet with Ranjit Singh on the throne the British had found the north impregnable. Now they began increasing troop reinforcements close to the Sikh Kingdom and sent spies to secretly approach those closest to the throne. Their aim was to identify courtiers whose ambition outweighed their sense of loyalty. Promising kingdoms in a carved-up Punjab to those who were prepared to help them, the British then waited until the time was right.

Their efforts paid off within three months. Marching units of sepoys from as far as West Bengal more than a thousand miles away, the British were able to amass a sizeable army on the Punjab borders. The Sikhs took the unconcealed troop build-up as an act of aggression and on 11 December 1845 sent a contingent of riders south over the Sutlej River to confront the forces. With that move the first Anglo-Sikh War had begun. It would continue for months and claim thousands of lives.

As the battles raged, neither Rani Jindan nor Duleep Singh knew that two of the most powerful men at court had already struck deals with the East India Company. Lal Singh, the new vazir, had passed key military intelligence to the British, including gun positions, the numbers of troops and even the plan of attack. He would also later abandon his troops in the field at a crucial stage of the fighting, leaving them to be slaughtered. The treachery of Tej Singh, the commander of Duleep's armies, was more damaging still. The battle of Ferozeshah on 21 December 1845 was one of the hardest ever fought by the

British; after long and brutal clashes, the British had all but resigned themselves to defeat. The turning point came after what India's Governor General, Sir Henry Hardinge, described as 'a night of horrors'.[10] From the midst of the battlefield, surrounded by Sikhs, Hardinge was so convinced of his army's imminent defeat and his own death that he ordered the burning of all state papers and gave his most precious possession, a sword which once belonged to Napoleon Bonaparte, to his aide-de-camp.

As Tej Singh and his troops approached from the west, the Company armies, out of ammunition and exhausted, waited to be overrun. Under cover of darkness the Sikhs should have been handed a decisive victory; instead Tej Singh ordered his forces to pull back. The Sikh army which had fought so hard at Ferozeshah was mown down by British reinforcements with superior artillery. Tej Singh's withdrawal had given these fresh troops vital time to reach their stricken British comrades. Tej Singh would later claim that his decision had been a strategic one and an attempt to outflank his enemy, but most Sikhs saw his actions for what they truly were: the Maharajah's commander had been guilty of the worst betrayal.

So it was that the great army founded by Ranjit Singh met its end at a final battle on 10 February 1846. Following the heavy defeat at Ferozeshah, the Sikhs withdrew across the Sutlej River at every point except Sobraon, a settlement on the shores of the river some forty miles south-east of Lahore. There they dug in on the river bank, and from these defensive positions crossed bridges over the river, challenging the British to meet them in hand-to-hand combat. The formerly beleaguered troops of the British Army had been reinforced with fresh men and munitions. With superior numbers and firepower the British attacked the main Sikh bridgehead but found themselves fighting men who simply refused to give up. The warriors of the Lahore army wove their way through the endless barrage of cannon and gunfire, engaging the British soldiers and their sepoys with their swords. It was at this point that the bridges across the Sutlej collapsed. Eyewitnesses at the time swore that the traitor Tej Singh had ordered them to be destroyed. Without hope of reinforcements, the commander had trapped all his men on the wrong side of the river, but not before he himself had fled north to safety.

Despite the hopelessness of their plight not one Sikh soldier surrendered that day. With their backs to the swollen river, they fought until British firepower brought silence to the banks of the Sutlej. Sikh dead and injured are said to have numbered around 9,000.

The defeat at Sobraon effectively broke the Sikh army for ever. After their decisive victory, the British imposed peace terms on the Punjab which reduced the army to a nominal force. Knowing they did not have the martial strength to hold the kingdom if the Sikhs rose up against them, the British claimed to have acted out of friendship for Duleep Singh, protecting the boy-king from opportunistic attacks from rivals. The Maharajah's enemies now posed as his guardians. Signing the Treaty of Bhyroval with the child, they vowed to protect him until he reached the age of sixteen, at which point he would be old enough to govern for himself. Then they would leave as friends.

The ink was still wet on the treaty when the British began to garrison soldiers in Lahore, ostensibly 'for the Maharajah's protection'. This was a masterstroke. The boy's continued presence on the throne legitimised British control, ensuring the loyalty of potential resisters in the army and among the general populace. Ferocious Sikh warriors who had survived the war had no reason to rebel if Duleep was still on the throne. Slowly but steadily, the British began to infiltrate the whole of the Sikh empire, laying the ground for a final takeover. Anybody who showed a hint of defiance was removed – quietly, but permanently.

One of those was the Sikh regent, Duleep Singh's own mother, Rani Jindan. Enraged by the build-up of foreign troops and the erosion of her son's authority, she began to accuse the British of seizing the Punjab by stealth and talked openly of pushing out the usurpers. And it was not just the British who attracted her fury: she took the bangles from her wrists and hurled them at her own military generals, cursing them for acting like eunuchs and taunting them for their weakness and stupidity.

For his treachery, Tej Singh was richly rewarded by the British. They had promised him a kingdom of his own and drew up papers to grant him the throne of Sialkot, a district at the foot of the Kashmir hills. Yet for the gift to be recognised in the Punjab, it was still necessary for Duleep Singh, as Maharajah and supreme leader, to give his blessing. All the boy had to do to ratify the treacherous commander's new title was to place a mark of saffron and carmine on his forehead. But Jindan had other ideas. She told her son to refuse no matter what his new British advisers told him; at no point should he touch the traitor's skin. Obeying his mother, Duleep snubbed Tej Singh at the public ceremony which had been organised to ratify his accession. The child's defiance left his former commander humiliated and the British fuming. Henry Lawrence, the new British Resident of Lahore, blamed Jindan, whom he described to the Governor General as having 'turned vindictive . . . during the last day or two her whole energies have been devoted to win over the sirdars of high and low degree, and unite them all together in a scheme of independent government, of which she herself was to be the head'. The Punjab would be 'perfectly tranquil' he noted but for the 'perilous passions of the Queen-Mother'.[11] It was clear that the mother had to be dealt with.

On 14 August 1847, when Duleep was barely nine years old, Jindan was torn screaming from his side and banished from the palace.[12] She fought as she was pulled away, begging the Sikh men around her to wake up and fight, not just for her and her son but for the very survival of the Punjab itself. Not one man lifted a finger to help her.

Jindan was imprisoned first in Lahore Fort and later moved to a fortress in Sheikhupura, some twenty-five miles from the city. She was reduced to begging for the return of her only child. From her prison cell she wrote letters to General Lawrence, pleading for mercy: 'Why do you take possession of my kingdom by underhand means? Why do you not do it openly? . . . You have been very cruel to me! . . . You have snatched my son from me. For ten months I kept him in my womb.'[13] . . . 'In the name of the God you worship and in the name of the King whose salt you eat,' she implored, 'restore my son to me. I cannot bear the pain of this separation.

Instead you should put me to death.'[14] Jindan promised Lawrence anything for the return of her only child: 'My son is very young. He is incapable of doing anything. I have left the kingdom. I have no need of the kingdom. For God's sake, pay attention to my appeals. At this time I have no one to look to. I raise no objections. I will accept what you say. There is no one with my son. He has no sister, no brother. He has no uncle, senior or junior. His father he has lost. To whose care has he been entrusted?'[15]

Lawrence was made uneasy by her accusations. He had signed a treaty to protect Duleep's interests. Could the British really argue that it was best for Duleep to be kept from his own mother, miles away?

His superior, Sir Henry Hardinge, had no such misgivings. He warned everyone to harden themselves against the deposed regent: 'We must expect these letters in various shapes, which a woman of her strong mind and passions will assume as best suited either to gratify her vengeance or obtain her ends.'[16] He then wrote to Lawrence to congratulate him:

Nothing can be more satisfactory than the manner in which you have carried the removal of the Maharanee into execution. I entirely approve of the judicious terms in which the proclamation was worded. Her Highness's seclusion at Sheikhopoorah is, in my view, preferable to a more distant banishment. It avoids the national affront of parading the mother of all the Sikhs through Hindustan, and will reconcile the Sikh people to the step; and as we cannot publish all we know of her misconduct, but must justify the step on the expediency of the separation, the less any of the measures taken have the appearance of punishment the better. In this sense don't reduce her pension too low. It was granted at the time the treaty was signed . . . The resolution should not deprive her of any comforts and luxuries to which, as the Prince's mother, she may be entitled; on the other hand, she should not have the means of offering large bribes. Her Highness must be warned that on the first occasion of her entering into intrigues other and more serious steps must be taken.[17]

A year later, Lawrence was rewarded with a knighthood from Queen Victoria and replaced by Sir Frederick Currie, who was as little troubled by Jindan's plight as Hardinge. Currie decided that the Rani should be removed from the Punjab altogether and transferred her to Chunar Fort, hundreds of miles away in the north-western provinces of British India. By now the British had also realised that the old treaty left them vulnerable to challenge: they needed to free themselves of the promise to return Duleep's kingdom to him. Only a total and lasting annexation of the Punjab would do.

Jindan's treatment was beginning to cause agitation in Lahore. Her suffering had even moved some of those traditionally hostile to the Punjab and her rulers. Dost Mohammad Khan, the Muslim Emir of Afghanistan, openly condemned the British for their cruelty and petitioned for Jindan's release. The Governor General responded with a campaign intended to discredit the Maharani. She was a woman of low birth and even lower morals; he referred to her in his diplomatic despatches as no more than a whore, calling her the 'Messalina' of the Punjab, a reference to the third wife of the Roman Emperor Claudius who had a reputation for promiscuity.

By 1848, a year after they had disposed of Jindan, the British were ready to complete their formal annexation. The majority of the Sikh soldiery and senior nobles in outlying areas of the empire hated the spread of foreign control. Jindan's treatment and her dire warnings augmented their dismay. The British then provocatively increased taxes in the name of the boy-king Duleep, sparking insurrection in Multan, one of the Punjab's largest and oldest cities. When Sikh soldiers then began to defect from Lahore to join rebel armies in Multan, the British finally had the excuse they had been looking for. Declaring the uprisings in Multan acts of war against Duleep Singh's rightful sovereignty, the British retaliated with overwhelming force.

Troops from all over India converged upon Punjab. Too late the Sikh nobles realised their empire was being seized right out from under them. During the second Anglo-Sikh War (1848–9), Sikh armies were routed as British reinforcements continued to pour into the region. Confident in their power over the boy, the British then

forced a new legal document on Duleep. According to the Treaty of
Lahore, the child was told he must sign over his kingdom and his
fortune if he wished his British guardians to save his life from the
violence threatening to engulf his palace. And so it was that with no
one to counsel him, the Maharajah, aged eleven, signed away his
kingdom, his fortune and his family's future.

From her prison cell in Chunar Fort, Rani Jindan heard of her son's
fall with impotent rage. Her separation from Duleep had hastened a
rapid and dramatic collapse in her health. Yet even in a greatly weakened state Jindan managed to confound her captors. On 19 April
1849, eight months after her arrival at the British gaol, she made her
escape, dressed as a beggar, in the middle of the night. Before she fled
she had a last taunt for the British, throwing money over the floor of
the cell with a note explaining that she was paying for their 'hospitality': 'You put me in a cage and locked me up. For all your locks and
your sentries, I got out by magic . . . I had told you plainly not to
push me too hard – but don't think I ran away, understand well, that
I escape by myself unaided . . . don't imagine, I got out like a thief.'[18]

Jindan spent the next few months on the run from the British. She
gradually made her way to Nepal, over 300 miles away, where she
threw herself at the feet of its ruler, Jung Bahadur, and begged asylum.
Jung Bahadur agreed but on condition that she did not try to make
contact with her son. With no other choice, for almost ten years she
remained there, pining for Duleep, and at the mercy of Jang Bahadur,
a man capable of great cruelty. The British Resident in Nepal, Colonel
Ramsay, was appalled by the Maharani's treatment at the hands of
Jang Bahadur: 'a more unprincipled scoundrel does not tread on the
earth'.[19] She was held as a virtual prisoner; Jang Bahadur controlled
where she went and who she saw, all the while coveting the jewels he
believed she had hidden during her escape. She lived in miserable
isolation, fearful of her Nepalese benefactor and the white soldiers
who filled the land outside his realm. Colonel Ramsay described the
Maharani's rapid decline: '[she is] blind and [has] lost much of [the]
energy which formerly characterised her, taking apparently but little
interest in what was going on'.[20]

Having annexed his kingdom, the British now expelled Duleep Singh from the Punjab for ever. The streets of Lahore were lined with weeping men and women, lamenting the kidnap of their young king. Frightened but without complaint he was taken to Fategarh in the north-western provinces, hundreds of miles away from the only home he had ever known. There the British placed him in the care of John Spencer Login, a well-respected Scottish doctor, and his wife Lena.

The Logins were a kindly couple who always tried to do their best for their young charge. In return, Duleep tried to be a diligent child: he studied hard, played parlour games when invited, and was quiet and courteous. Lena Login kept a meticulous diary of her time with the deposed king, and often thought about all that had been snatched from him: 'One could not but have great sympathy for the boy, brought up from babyhood to exact the most obsequious servility.'[21]

It was under the Logins' tutelage that Duleep, still wearing the heavy, embroidered silks and jewels of his native land, learned to speak and act like an Englishman. He read the Bible, learned to play cricket and studied Shakespeare and the classics. In time he even took a blade to his long hair, cutting off the waist-length, jet black tresses – so sacred to the Sikh religion of his parents. The young Maharajah began to ask whether he might be able to rid himself of his old faith entirely and, at the age of fourteen, he was given leave to convert to Christianity by the new Governor General of India, Lord Dalhousie. News of his baptism broke the heart of an already grieving Punjab, and that of Rani Jindan too.

Far away in England, Queen Victoria rejoiced at the salvation of the Maharajah's soul. From the time of his exile, she had asked for regular reports about Duleep Singh's progress, which she had read with great care and building excitement. The more she learned about him, the more fascinated she became by the exotic young king with the impeccable English manners. Descriptions of the boy's beauty were the most captivating thing about the correspondence. His long lashes, dark eyes and strong straight nose were praised by all who saw him.

Victoria soon tired of the written descriptions and longed to see Duleep for herself. The Maharajah was also curious about the Queen across the water. When he turned fifteen, he asked his guardians if he might ever be able to visit England. Victoria enthusiastically granted permission and Duleep packed his belongings, and made the long voyage with his guardians, the Logins, by his side.

# Do Not Be Conspicuous

From the very moment he set foot in her court, Duleep became Queen Victoria's favourite. Her praise for him was frequent and full: 'he is extremely handsome and speaks English perfectly, and has a pretty, graceful and dignified manner. He was beautifully dressed and covered with diamonds . . . I always feel so much for these poor deposed Indian Princes.'[1]

Despite, or maybe because of, her pity, the Maharajah enjoyed the status of a senior aristocrat and was invited into all homes that mattered, featuring prominently at state occasions. 'His candour and straightforwardness made him a great favourite with Queen Victoria and the Prince Consort,' Lena Login wrote. 'He was frequently invited to Windsor and Osborne.'[2] There, in the bosom of the royal family, mutual love blossomed. The fifteen-year-old Duleep and the thirty-five-year-old Queen would sketch each other for hours, exchanging drawings they had made of one another. He dressed her children in his finest silks and jewels, and they put on plays together, filling Osborne with the sound of their laughter. When her youngest son fell behind in the games, Victoria watched Duleep scoop up her little Leopold and carry the toddler on his shoulders. She loved him for his kindness to the haemophiliac child.

Senior palace officials counselled Victoria against showing too much favour to a deposed Indian monarch. They warned that it might go to his head, it might set a dangerous precedent or open her to ridicule, but she resolutely ignored them. Victoria's gifts to her Indian king continued to be ostentatious and personal. She gave the Maharajah jewellery, precious trinkets, cameos of herself and even a thoroughbred horse. She indulged him at any opportunity, even going as far as to allow him to sit on the woolsack in the House of Lords, much to the dismay of her own politicians.[3] Prince Albert was also growing very fond of the Maharajah and personally designed a coat of arms for him. It comprised a lion standing beneath a coronet surmounted by a five-pointed star. He even chose the motto that went with Duleep's design: *'Prodesse quam conspici'* ('Do good rather than be conspicuous'). It was an odd standard to bestow on someone who so adored being the centre of attention.

It was hardly surprising that Duleep liked to be noticed, after all, the most powerful monarch in the world had put him on a pedestal, at times quite literally. On 10 July 1854, Queen Victoria fussed over 'her beautiful boy' as he posed on a specially constructed stage set up in the White Drawing Room of Buckingham Palace. She had asked the celebrated court painter, Franz Xaver Winterhalter, to capture his likeness for her on canvas.

Duleep enjoyed dressing in all his splendour and stood in silk pyjamas, a heavy gold embroidered shirt on his lean frame, a decorative sword hanging at his waist. On his feet he wore embellished slippers which curled at the toe, and on his head a turban dripping with emeralds – even though the hair beneath had been shorn away. In his pierced ears, Duleep wore thick gold rings, and his neck was heavy with magnificent pearls. One string was long enough to go around five times, and from it, at his throat, hung an ivory miniature of Victoria, set in diamonds. As the Queen recorded in her journal, 'Winterhalter was in ecstasies at the beauty and nobility of the young Maharajah.'[4]

There was, however, one item conspicuously absent from all Duleep Singh's finery: the most famous diamond in the world, the Koh-I-Noor. It ought to have been strapped to his arm like an amulet, just as his father Ranjit Singh had worn it before him.

However the Koh-I-Noor no longer belonged to the Maharajah and its loss filled him with pain. Although Duleep said nothing, Queen Victoria guessed the gem was on his mind. While Winterhalter worked, she beckoned Lady Login to follow her into a corner of the room where they could talk quietly. Lena recorded the conversation in her diaries: 'She had not yet worn it in public, and, as she herself remarked, had a delicacy about doing so in the Maharajah's presence. "Tell me, Lady Login, does the Maharajah ever mention the Koh-I-Noor? Does he seem to regret it, and would he like to see it again?"'[5]

There was urgency in the Queen's enquiry and she ordered Lady Login to find out before the next sitting. Lena said she would raise the matter with Duleep, although in her heart she already knew how he felt: 'There was no other subject that so filled the thoughts and conversation of the Maharajah, his relatives and dependents as the forsaken diamond. For the confiscation of the jewel which to the Oriental is the symbol of sovereignty of India, rankled in his mind even more than the loss of his kingdom, and I dreaded what sentiments he might give vent to were the subject once re-opened.'[6]

Despite her fears, Lady Login dutifully brought up the matter while she was out riding with Duleep in Richmond Park a few days later. How would he feel if he saw the Koh-I-Noor again? 'I would give a good deal to hold it again in my own hand. I was but a child, an infant, when forced to surrender it by treaty . . . now that I am a man, I should like to have it in my power to place it myself in Her Majesty's hand.'[7]

Lena knew it was an answer that would please the Queen, but was it the truth? The very next day, as once again Duleep posed for the German artist at the palace, a pantomime of sorts was enacted. Lena Login watched as an emissary from the Tower of London, escorted by yeoman warders, entered the drawing room with great flourish. The diminutive, frock-coated official carried a small casket. The Queen opened it and took out the contents. She showed it to Albert and together they walked to where Duleep stood on the dais. When she was beneath him, she cried out breezily, 'Maharajah, I have something to show you!'[8] Duleep Singh stepped hurriedly to the floor. Before he knew what was happening he found himself once more with the Koh-I-Noor in his grasp as she dropped it into his outstretched hand. Victoria stood within touching distance, asking him 'if he thought it improved, and if he would have recognised it again?'[9]

Prince Albert had sent the stone to Amsterdam to be re-cut, spending a fortune in transforming the rough diamond into the multifaceted gem which now caught the light along with the room's breath. The Maharajah walked towards the window, and held the diamond aloft: 'For all his air of polite interest and curiosity,' wrote Lena Login, 'there was a passion of repressed emotion in his face . . . evident, I think, to Her Majesty, who watched him with sympathy not unmixed with anxiety.'[10]

The minutes ticked by painfully. 'At last, as if summoning up his resolution after a profound struggle, he raised his eyes from the jewel. I was prepared for almost anything,' recalled Lena Login, 'even to seeing him, in a sudden fit of madness fling the precious talisman out of the open window by which he stood. My own and the other spectators' nerves were equally on edge – as he moved deliberately to where her Majesty was standing.' Bowing before her, Duleep gently put the gem into Queen Victoria's hand. 'It is to me, Ma'am the greatest pleasure thus to have the opportunity, as a loyal subject, of myself tendering to my Sovereign – the Koh-I-Noor.'[11] Neither Duleep, nor any of his family, would ever come so close to the diamond again.

On his sixteenth birthday, the Maharajah was granted an annual income of £25,000 (almost £2.5 million today) by the India Office. Such wealth placed him far above the average English nobleman in terms of income, although it was only a tiny fraction of what he would have possessed had he not lost his jewels and his kingdom: although the value of the Koh-I-Noor is today marked as 'inestimable and unknown', in the nineteenth century it was said to be worth 'two million pounds sterling' (almost £194 million today).[12] The money and the favour the Maharajah received from Queen Victoria made him one of the most sought-after men in court; as aristocrats opened their doors to him, Duleep was suddenly engulfed by London high society. He adored lavishing his friends with expensive gifts and inevitably attracted flatterers and hangers-on. He fell in love with unsuitable – and sometimes married – ladies in the Queen's court.

Women defied convention to flirt, accept his gifts and agree to secret liaisons with him, but they refused to accept his proposals of marriage. Wealth and patronage notwithstanding, Duleep was still regarded as coming from an inferior race, and not a single noble family would countenance a match with their daughters. Though the rejection hurt him deeply it did little to dampen the Maharajah's behaviour. Together with his great friend 'Bertie', the Prince of Wales, he happily gambled and whored his way around London. When news of Bertie and Duleep's exploits became the talk of the court, the Queen stepped in. She let it be known that she expected both her eldest son and the Maharajah to settle down immediately.

While casting around for a suitable match Victoria and her retainers also made strenuous efforts to shield the Maharajah from Indian matters, even though at times this was impossible. In 1857, Britain was stunned by news of an Indian uprising. It had started on 29 March on the parade ground at Barrakpore near Calcutta. For months tension had been rising in the ranks all over India since the Company had introduced a new type of rifle musket. Loading and firing the Enfield Pattern 1853 was a complicated affair. A soldier had to take a paper cartridge covered in grease, bite off the end, pour the gunpowder and metal ball contained within down the barrel and ram the mixture down tightly with a rod. Rumours were running wild that the grease was made from pig and cow fat. The former was unacceptable to Muslims as it was deemed *haram* and against their faith; the latter was an anathema to Hindus, who held the cow as a sacred beast and believed they would lose their caste if they bit into such a cartridge.

Although the British tried to reassure the soldiers that the grease was not made from animal fat, few believed them. At Barrakpore suspicion turned to anger, which in turn boiled over into full-blown mutiny when sepoy Mangal Pandey of the 34th Bengal Native

Infantry raised his gun and shot his British senior officer. Unrest spread quickly across India as sepoys followed Pandey's example and turned their weapons first on their commanding officers and then on British civilians. Ironically it was the Sikh soldiers who first rallied to British aid. Their actions came more from a sense of grievance against the Indian sepoys than a sense of loyalty to their new masters. They remembered well that these same soldiers from the east and the south had fought against them at the behest of the British in the first and second Anglo-Sikh Wars, and blamed them for the worst atrocities and betrayals of those times.

Approximately 1,500 British were killed during the violence of 1857, and many thousands of Indians were slaughtered in reprisals. In August there was moral outrage as details reached London of the 'Death of Sir Henry Lawrence . . . and the Massacre of the English'.[13] Lawrence – the former Resident in Lahore who had ordered Rani Jindan to be separated from her son – had become well known in England thanks to his authorship of *Adventures of an Officer in the Service of Runjeet Singh*. He had been sent to fortify the city of Lucknow in anticipation of a local uprising. Lawrence created a stronghold where all British military personnel, their families and staff could retreat should violence break out. Full-scale rebellion reached Lucknow on 30 May and 855 British soldiers, 712 loyal sepoys, 153 civilian volunteers and 1,280 non-combatants fell back to the safety of the improvised fort. Sir Henry was one of the first to be killed. On 2 July he was fatally wounded by a shell and died two days later from his wounds. The rest of his compatriots were besieged for six months, under near constant attack, and ravaged by hunger and disease.

Commentators around the world declared Britain's Eastern Empire to be teetering on the brink. Some blamed the turn in British fortunes on the 'malignant presence of the Koh-I-Noor', which had been recently displayed near Buckingham Palace in a 'golden prison' during the 1851 Great Exhibition. Others accused officers of the Raj of 'going native' – 'going soft' and letting their guard down in the face of Indian savagery. Even after the Mutiny was finally put down on 20 June 1858, the events left a deep and lasting wound on the psyche of the Raj. Indian governance was taken away from the East India Company and placed under the direct control of the Crown. There was disillusionment too with Britain's 'civilising' and Christianising mission in the subcontinent and a shift in attitudes towards Indians generally. No longer could they be regarded as friends; instead each was a potential traitor, to be ruled rather than 'improved'. Two years later, even Victoria's pet Maharajah appeared to be showing worrying signs of contamination.

In 1860, as he turned twenty-one, Duleep Singh attempted to make contact with Rani Jindan. He penned a message and sent a trusted servant to Nepal to investigate her wellbeing. However, the message was swiftly intercepted by the British. They had the power to stop his letter, but they could not prevent news of her plight from reaching the Maharajah in London. Duleep began to ask politely whether he might be permitted to see his mother again.

The British needed to tread carefully. Although the idea of Duleep being reunited with Jindan was unpalatable, the government could not risk re-igniting passions in India. Nor did they want to insult the Sikhs, who had proved indispensable during the Mutiny. The risk in the Punjab of appearing heartless and insensitive to a son's duty to his mother was too great. However, it was believed the bond between mother and son had been broken after the years of separation. In many  eyes, Duleep was making the request because he felt he had to, not because he was overly concerned about his mother's welfare. The Maharajah certainly did little to challenge that impression. As he prepared to return to India, he appeared more energised by the prospect of hunting tigers than seeing his mother again.

Permission for a meeting was granted, provided the reunion took place as far from the Punjab as possible. Rani Jindan, in Nepal, was informed by the British that she had leave to meet the child she had longed to hold for so long. In her mind he was still the shimmering and bejewelled boy-king who had been dragged from her side in 1847. Now blind, Jindan would never be able to see for herself the beautiful young man who had captured the heart of court painters, sculptors and Queen Victoria herself.

The place chosen for the rendezvous was the Spence Hotel in Calcutta, a grand building built by and for the British in the 1830s, and chosen by writers such as Jules Verne as an exotic location in novels.[14] The hotel would prove a magnificent backdrop for the epic reunion, scheduled to take place on 16 January 1861. Popular accounts describe how, when Rani Jindan was first brought to her son, she held him for the longest time, dry-eyed, silent, yet shaking with emotion. She is said to have run her hands all over his face and body, trying to get a sense of who her little boy had become. It was only when she reached his head and felt the hair that had been shorn away that the tears came. Jindan railed at her son, crying that she could live with the loss of her husband and the kingdom, no matter how much pain it brought her, but that her son had abandoned his Sikh faith was too much for her to bear.[15]

Yet once she had calmed, Jindan was determined never to let Duleep go. She refused the government's offer of a house in Calcutta, where it was suggested she might spend the rest of her days in more comfortable surroundings. Wherever her son went, Jindan resolved to follow, even if that meant having to leave India and moving to the country of her enemies.

The British, who had tried for so many years to keep Jindan away from her son, were oddly pleased by the turn of events. To them it meant a totemic figure, who might still have power in the Punjab, would fade away quietly and insignificantly in England. The government returned many of Jindan's confiscated jewels and even offered the Maharani a comfortable pension of £3,000 a year to convince her to go quietly.

If the settlement seemed a high price to pay, the British were soon reminded of the blind Maharani's potency, and in dramatic fashion. While mother and son were meeting at the Spence Hotel, a troopship filled with Sikh soldiers returning from fighting in the Second Opium War was sailing up Calcutta's Hooghly River. Rumours spread of the presence of the Sikh Maharajah and the Queen Mother, and soon hundreds of exhausted and emotional soldiers had gathered around the hotel to salute their deposed rulers. They bellowed the unique Sikh call – '*Bolo So Nihal, Sat Sri Akal!*' – 'Whoever says these words will know true joy. Eternal is the Lord God!' Their voices shook the walls of the Spence Hotel and quickened the beating of Jindan's heart. After that, the British could not get the Maharani on a boat fast enough.

Back in London, at the end of January 1861, Duleep found a home for his mother and her servants close to his own residence at 5 Lancaster Gate, facing Hyde Park. The Maharani Jindan's residence at number 1 fascinated the local inhabitants with its odd aromas. The smells of Indian cooking wafted out of the house and over the inquisitive folk who gathered outside to peer through her windows.[16] Mostly, however, the front door remained closed to the outside world. Lady Login recalled a rare visit to 1 Lancaster Gate, where she describes finding Duleep's mother 'sitting huddled on a heap of cushions on the floor, with health broken and eyesight dimmed, her beauty vanished, it was hard to believe in her former charms of person and conversation! However the moment she grew interested and excited in a conversation unexpected gleams and glimpses and the torpor of advancing age revealed the shrewd and plotting brain of one who had been known as the "Messalina of the Punjab".'[17]

Soon mother and son were again inseparable. Duleep took her everywhere with him, even up to Mulgrave Castle in Yorkshire, a 16,000-acre estate which the Maharajah had leased since 1858. Duleep wanted Jindan to see that, even though he was thousands of miles from home, he still conducted himself as a king. The aristocracy did indeed hold him in high regard, although the same could not be said of his mother. Everywhere she went Jindan was the subject of vicious gossip. Lady Normanby, whose family had leased Mulgrave Castle to the Maharajah, poured scorn on her house guest: 'She keeps herself very much within the house with her attendants,' she told her son, and 'sometimes dresses in a dirty sheet and a pair of cotton stockings, sometimes decked out in Cloth of Gold and covered with jewels . . . It rather seems to me when I see queer Indian figures flitting about that "The Heathen are come in to mine inheritance".'[18]

As mother and son drew closer, Duleep seemed to change under Jindan's influence. He began to consult his mother on all important matters, much to the concern of his former advisers. More worrying still for the India Office, he started to ask direct questions about his inheritance. 'I very much wish to have a conversation with you about my private property in the Punjab and the Koh-I-Noor diamond,'[19] he wrote to Sir John Login as he and his mother prepared to leave Mulgrave. It was the first time that the Maharajah had raised such matters formally. Jindan was clearly driving the questions, which caused a good deal of discomfort in the India Office.

From the moment of their reunion, the Queen Mother reminded her son of the mighty kingdom that his father had created and which should have been his. She steeped her tales in the supernatural, telling Duleep of a prophesy which predicted that he would one day return to reclaim his throne and his place in the pantheon of Sikh saints. As Duleep would later explain to the Queen, 'Shortly after I ascended to the throne of the Punjab it was found written in the book of Sikh prophecies called *Sakhean* that a man of my name would be born, who after becoming entirely disposed of all he inherited and residing alone for a long period in a foreign country, would return to be the eleventh gooroo of the Khalsa, or "Pure"'[20]. Queen Victoria did not enjoy such conversations at all.

In September 1861, Duleep once again wrote to Sir John Login. This time he expressed himself in an Indian voice which may have been entirely alien, and indeed possibly hurtful, to the man who had done so much to anglicise the young Maharajah. 'My mother begs to send her best *salaam* to the kind Doctor Sahib,' he began, before going on to ask who he might commission to achieve 'a good likeness of my mother in oils'.[21] Through gritted teeth, and ignoring the provocative, traditional Indian salutation, Sir John now made arrangements for George Richmond, a renowned court painter of the day, to capture the ailing Maharani's image for her son. The portrait shows a frail but proud woman, seated on the ground, draped in heavy silks and jewellery, with a hawkish gleam yet in her eye.

Duleep's former guardian was becoming more and more unsettled by what he saw as his former charge's increasing infatuation with his mother. His discomfort was expressed in letters to the Palace, in which he advised immediate action. Queen Victoria had just lost her beloved Prince Albert, in December 1861, and was in no fit state to challenge Jindan's passionate play for Duleep's heart. Deep in mourning, the British Queen had lost all interest in that which had brought her joy in the past; even concern for Duleep could not rouse her. Instead it was left to her close adviser and Keeper of the Privy Purse, Sir Charles Phipps, to deal with Login's concerns: 'I am very sorry to hear what you say about the Maharajah – nothing could be so destructive to him as that he should succumb to his mother's, or any other native influence. He is too good to be lost; and, if I were in your place, I should certainly not, at such a moment, forsake any position which gave me any influence over him, or could possibly tend to prevent him doing anything foolish.'[22]

Apart from urging Login to reassume his role as Duleep's de facto father, Phipps suggested two other strategies. The first involved having the Maharajah married off as soon as possible, giving him a wife and children of his own to worry about. To that end a suitable bride was sought, and Elveden estate, a country house on the Norfolk–Suffolk borders, was suggested as a possible home in which the Maharajah might put down uncorrupted roots. The second strategy involved putting some distance between Duleep and his mother. Arguments raged in the India Office about whether it would be prudent to send Jindan back to India, taking her far away from the Maharajah, but closer to those who might be inspired by her to rebel. It was a difficult decision, and letters went back and forth on the matter. In the end, just as she had done so many years before at Chunar Fort, Rani Jindan took the decision out of the hands of the British. On 1 August 1863, she died at her home in London. Though she looked decades older, she was only forty-six years old.

Even in death, Jindan caused the British a great deal of inconvenience. They had made careful plans to have her discreetly buried in London at a dignified ceremony at which her son and a few select guests could bid a quiet farewell. However, when two of her Sikh former servants found out what was to happen to their mistress, they wrote a letter of protest to *The Times* in which they insisted that the Maharani's body must not be desecrated in the dirt.[23] She must have a Sikh cremation, officiated by a Sikh holy man. Fearing the Indian response if they were perceived to have dishonoured her, the British authorities acted quickly to remedy the situation. Two days later, Jindan was removed from her home and laid in the Dissenter's Chapel, an unconsecrated vault in Kensal Green cemetery, until her remains could be transported back to India to be burnt with all relevant ceremony. There was one stringent condition: neither her body nor her ashes would be permitted to enter the Punjab. Even though, as tradition dictated, her remains would be scattered in a river, the fear was that the very river bank might become a place of pilgrimage for those Indians entertaining thoughts of rebellion.

Forbidden from taking his mother home to Lahore, or indeed anywhere within the state of Punjab, Duleep instead took her body to Nasik in the Bombay Presidency for cremation. Although Duleep did not know it when he departed for India on 16 February 1864, this would be his last voyage to his homeland.

Duleep was twenty-five when his mother died. Two months later, his guardian John Login also passed away. Despite Jindan's efforts to poison her son against the British, Duleep Singh was heartbroken at the loss. As Lena Login recounted in her memoirs the young Maharajah's 'grief at my husband's death was indeed most sincere and unaffected, and many at the graveside spoke afterward of the touching eloquence of his outburst there, when he gave vent to the words, "Oh I have lost my father! For indeed he was that – and more – to me!"'[24]

With Jindan and Login gone, an isolated and lonely Duleep found he could no longer ignore Queen Victoria's pleas to settle down. Victoria had tried over the years to arrange a marriage, much as Jindan would have had she been allowed to have a say in his life. Victoria had even handpicked another of her Indian favourites, a princess who, like Duleep, had been brought to England as a child after the forfeiture of her own father's kingdom. Princess Victoria Gourama of Coorg was the only other Indian in England who had enjoyed the personal patronage of the Queen. Victoria had become her godmother upon the insistence of the Raja of Coorg, who had hoped – mistakenly as it turned out – that the relationship might restore him to his lands and fortune. Like Duleep, Gourama had also converted to Christianity, and knew the etiquette of court life. They were the only two people of their kind in all England and it seemed logical to Queen Victoria that they should marry. Small-boned, light-skinned and with pretty round cheeks and even rounder hips, there was a sensual quality to Gourama's beauty which it was thought might appeal to the pleasure-seeking Maharajah.

However, Duleep would have none of it. He politely advised the Palace that he found Gourama too flighty and flirtatious for a wife. He assured royal courtiers that he would find his own match in his own time.

In spring 1864, on his way back from his mother's cremation, Duleep approached Presbyterian missionaries in Cairo and asked them to help him. The city was a stop-off point on voyages between India and England, and he had visited some of the mission schools and churches almost a decade before, when he had first left his homeland. Duleep begged them to help him find a wife: he wanted an unsophisticated young woman who was pretty, virginal, knew her Bible, and would be an outsider like him. The missionaries were surprised by his overture but admitted that they knew of just such a girl.

Aged just sixteen, Bamba Muller was young, devout, unspoiled and malleable. She was also beautiful, with skin the colour of honey, large dark brown eyes and jet black hair that flowed all the way down her back. But there were obvious drawbacks to the union. The girl was the 'bastard' child of a wealthy German merchant and an Abyssinian slave. She had been left in Cairo by her father to be brought up by Christian missionaries behind the high walls of the cloister. Her father, Ludwig Muller, was not a heartless man, and had paid an annual sum to the church to take care of his indiscretion. He also paid for her mother, Sofia, to be taken in by the missionaries. The girl had grown to be a valued part of mission life, studying her Bible with such zeal that she became a teacher at the church school when she was barely more than a child herself. The Reverend Dr John Hogg, who was the head of the mission in Cairo, had grown particularly attached to his young ward, describing Bamba as 'extremely winning in all her ways, and graceful, even queenly, in her movements'.[25]

The more he heard about her, the keener Duleep was to meet the girl and pressed for an introduction. Even though they had suggested the match, the missionaries arranged it with some trepidation, worried in case they bore responsibility 'of being in any way instrumental in transplanting a young, tender flower from its native soil, in which it was growing in vigour and beauty every day, to a region and climate where it might pine away and die from withering blasts'.[26]

After just one brief meeting Duleep was besotted. He assured Dr Hogg that he would treasure their ward, and then wrote to Bamba's father asking if he might legally acknowledge his daughter, granting her legitimacy before the wedding and therefore lessening the shock he was about to deliver to Queen Victoria. Herr Muller was delighted to do so, and with his blessing Duleep and Bamba were married less than four months later, on 9 June 1864, in an understated ceremony in Cairo. The bride needed an interpreter since she spoke not one word of English and Duleep no Arabic at all. She was one month away from her seventeenth birthday but looked even younger.

After a short honeymoon in Cairo, the couple sailed to England on 25 July 1864, and were immediately plunged into the potentially scalding scrutiny of Queen Victoria's court. Confounding all expectations, Duleep's young wife was well received and instantly liked. Word of the Maharani's delicate good looks spread quickly, as did the existence of an additional, disarming characteristic: attention made her blush deeply. It was a childhood trait that had earned her the name 'Bamba', the Arabic word for pink. Nobody knew her by any other name. Although Duleep had been nervous about the Queen's response to his unusual choice of bride, she too was charmed by the pious, shy girl at his side.

Duleep's friends could not help but notice that Bamba was unlike any of the women he had been drawn to before. She spoke quietly with a heavy Arabic accent and showed a halting lack of self-confidence. He revelled in her beauty, however, parading her around in outfits designed by his own hand: colourfully outlandish full skirts, or ballooning culottes, with heavily embroidered short jackets. He also made his new wife wear her long black hair in numerous thin plaits, like Cleopatra. As if such costume were not dramatic enough, he topped every creation with a jaunty pearl-encrusted Turkish cap, from which long jewelled tassels hung down upon her shoulders.

Most were enthralled by Bamba's exotic appearance, but some took pity on the vulnerable young woman. Lady Leven, a Scottish aristocrat, begged her dear friend Duleep to tone down his costume ideas for his wife. Writing to a friend, Lady Leven complained that the Maharajah was beyond reason: '[he] will interfere with everything concerning his wife's attire, and has the most absurd notions about the matter . . . You can fancy how it is now, with two dressmakers in the house, and he finding fault if she does not look like other people, and yet insisting on her dresses being cut short, and no trimmings of any kind, and choosing colours irrespective of the becoming!'[27]

All would share Lady Leven's sense of pity towards the blushing Maharani in the years that followed.

# 3

# The Suffolk Mahal

Having remodelled his young wife, the Maharajah spent the first decade of his marriage on a relentless mission to refashion his country estate. Purchased in 1863, the year his mother died, Elveden was a sprawling and expensive affair near the market town of Thetford. Comprising 17,000 acres of East Anglian flatlands, interspersed with windbreak plantations of Scots pine, oak and larch, the estate had long been celebrated for its abundance of game.[1] Duleep raised the purchase price of £105,000 (more than £11.5 million today) through a government loan of £110,000, plus interest at four per cent.[2] But he would need much more than the surplus £5,000 for his vision. He wanted the hall and the estate to be the talk of the realm, and there was much competition.

The year before, Duleep's friend Bertie, the Prince of Wales, had purchased Sandringham, half a day's ride to the north. The Earl of Leicester, Lord Albemarle and the de Grey family, all notable members of the British aristocracy, owned vast estates within thirty miles of the Maharajah's new home, placing him exactly where he most liked to be: at the centre of great influence and wealth. Although the geography and calibre of his neighbours pleased him, the bricks and mortar of his new home did not. Elveden's original house dated back to the early fifteenth century, when it had been appropriated by Bury St Edmunds abbey, one of the richest Benedictine monasteries in all England. It was large, solid, square and grey. In the

1500s, when the Church failed to grant Henry VIII a divorce from Catherine of Aragon, the King seized Elveden and presented it to the Duke of Norfolk, uncle to Anne Boleyn.

The duke did not have it for long, falling out of favour after the execution of his niece. Two centuries later, the estate became the property of Augustus Keppel,[3] first Lord of the Admiralty. Keppel had fought during the Seven Years War and the American War of Independence. He adored Elveden Hall and the clear flat landscape which surrounded it. Having constructed special gangways on the rooftops, he would stride high above his property, telescope in hand, surveying the estate as if he were on the deck of one of his battleships. It was said that even death could not part him from his beloved home, and for many years locals spoke of a spectral figure hovering above the house with spyglass pressed to an empty socket.

Yet neither history nor a resident phantom could stop Duleep ripping the place to pieces. In place of the grey sobriety of old Elveden Hall, he ordered his builders to create a modern design in red brick and white stone. Arranged over three storeys, the front of the house was dominated by forty windows which stretched from ceiling to floor. In the evenings, when the lamps were lit, the mansion gleamed in the darkness like a jewel. A white ornamental balustrade ran around the top of the house, skirting the ostentatious bay windows. As a result, Elveden Hall had the appearance of an intricately iced cake.

However, nothing on the outside could prepare visitors for what lay within. The house brimmed with jewelled ornaments, exquisite rugs, marble carvings and the finest works of art from both India and Western Europe. Once through the grand entrance, guests were ushered through lines of liveried footman into an imposing hall, where decorous arches and elaborate carved columns soared high above their heads. They were confronted by a magnificent newly installed marble staircase which twisted up to the top of the house, each hard white step engraved with the Maharajah's monogram and that of his Maharani. The whole space was lit by sunlight which came in through a huge glass dome above the stairs; Elveden had a luminous quality that was altogether alien to the age. As with many of the house's architectural flourishes, Duleep had personally designed the staircase at a rumoured cost of £3,000.⁴ (The sum was wildly extravagant, in an age when a good family home cost £10 a year to rent.⁵) The staircase accounted for a tenth of the total cost of the redesign, not including the bill for his highly extravagant drapes and furnishings.⁶

*The Field* magazine, a publication which often filled its pages with breathless descriptions of stately homes around Britain, could barely contain itself: 'the large drawing room with its silken hangings and mirrors, its gilded ceiling inlaid with stars and Crescents of silvered glass, was divided by an elaborate screen in gold and silver tracery, and its windows opened onto an enclosed lawn on which dozens of peacocks, gold and silver pheasants and other rare birds strutted about as if quite conscious of the gorgeous effect their colours added to the scene'.⁷ Dinner guests – frequently royalty and the most powerful members of British imperial society – were entertained in a room in which gold leaf covered the walls. Overhead a ceiling with 400 or so convex mirrors inlaid in raised reliefs of green foliage caught the sun, making the room dazzle both in the daylight and by the reflection of lamps in the evening. Throughout the house, gilded French candlesticks stood in front of heavy embroidered Indian cloth. On the walls hung paintings by the Hungarian artist August Schoefft, who had spent time in Duleep's homeland and painted scenes of his father, the Lion of the Punjab, and his court at Lahore.

Elveden was a collision of Eastern and Western decadence, and the man tasked with realising Duleep's eccentric and eclectic dream was the celebrated English architect John Norton. The Maharajah had sent Norton to study the contents of the India Museum – one of London's greatest attractions – for inspiration. The museum's most famous exhibit was Tipu's Tiger, an eighteenth-century mechanical toy created for the much-feared Sultan of Mysore. It comprised a carved and painted life-size tiger crouching over a supine figure. Dwarfing the unfortunate victim with its heavy paws pinning his chest, the tiger's jaws clamped onto the man's throat; concealed mechanisms in the creature's wooden body enabled the beast to chew the life out of its prey – a uniformed white-skinned soldier, who cried out in pain as the mechanical tiger grunted with satisfaction.[8]

Elveden itself had no need of clever toys to remind the Maharajah of Indian wildlife. He built large pens in his grounds which housed real leopards and cheetahs.[9] Positioned just beneath the nursery, their low growls were the first thing Duleep's growing family heard every morning; that and the tramp of numerous workmen who were constantly revising the estate, turning it into a peculiar Mogul palace in the heart of the English countryside. Duleep Singh's desire to spend money on improvement extended to Elveden's little parish church to which he donated a small fortune for much needed renovations and expansion.

For the first ten years of her marriage Maharani Bamba was almost constantly pregnant. Her first child, a son, died only a few days after he was born, but the other five princes and princesses – Victor, born in July 1866; Frederick, born in January 1868; the namesake Princess Bamba, born in September 1869; and Catherine, born in October 1871 – were strong and healthy. With every birth, however, Bamba grew weaker and more agitated. The constant squabbles in the nursery did not help her nerves. With so small an age gap between the siblings, they all developed uncompromising personalities. Victor was imperious, Freddie obstinate, Catherine secretive, and Princess Bamba had the worst temper of all and was prone to fits of fury. By the time of Sophia's birth the Maharani had enjoyed five pregnancy-free years and felt stronger and more rested than she had during her entire marriage. Luckily, Sophia was a very easy baby. Plump and pretty, she fed and slept peacefully, showing no sign of the independent and headstrong young woman she would one day become. Bamba was finally free to enjoy motherhood in tranquillity. Even though she had numerous staff to look after her children in London and Suffolk, the Maharani was able to tend to Sophia. In a letter to her closest confidante, Mrs Lansing, the wife of an American Presbyterian missionary based in Alexandria, she confessed her delight at being able to breastfeed her youngest daughter instead of resorting to a wet nurse: 'the baby is a dear little pet . . . She is a healthy little thing, you will be glad to hear that I have been able to nurse her. I enclose some photographs that were taken here last October.'[10]

The images were probably taken by Sophia's father. The Maharajah was a passionate photographer, keen to embrace all the latest technological developments, such as the 'gelatin dry-plate' process which gave 'instantaneous photographs', and allowed him to indulge his passion for photography at home among his family. With her increasingly chubby cheeks, her thatch of thick wavy black hair and her intense dark eyes, Sophia made a delightful subject. Not only was she an attractive child, she also sat obligingly and unusually still on her mother's lap as the Maharani gave the faintest of smiles in an otherwise formal Victorian pose.

Sophia's birth also coincided with the end of the Maharajah's great rebuild. Thirteen years after he had begun to remodel the house, carpenters and masons had all finally left and Elveden's now mature gardens were beginning to flourish. And there were more than just flowers to look at in the summer beds. Huge eagles and sleepy-looking vultures chained to posts watched as the Duleep Singh children played amidst enclosures filled with ostriches, rare parrots and monkeys. Laughter echoed throughout the house, as the family was treated to the spectacle of servants chasing dangerous escapees across the grounds.[11] Footmen were regularly called on to capture jewel-coloured birds out of the trees, and the unluckiest were ordered to break up fights between a bad-tempered baboon and a sadistic local jackdaw.[12] The estate had an air of surreal but pleasant madness.

The nursery, in the south wing of the house, was a particularly happy place to be. Perhaps in consequence of the age difference between Sophia and her next oldest sibling, she found herself treasured by her brothers and sisters, and never had reason to develop their uncompromising survival instincts. She brought calm to the nursery, distracting the siblings from their arguments as they cooed over her crib. The children shared four enormous bedrooms, and nestled between them, a plainer smaller chamber served as bedroom to their nanny, Miss Date, with whom all the children formed a close attachment.

Like his wife, Duleep reserved a special affection for his youngest daughter. He showed his partiality by asking Queen Victoria to be Sophia's godmother, an honour she had already bestowed on his eldest son, Victor, but on none of the other children. It was a general custom that all the Queen's godchildren were named after her: the boys were called 'Victor' and the girls either 'Victoria' or 'Alexandrina', the monarch's other name. Duleep decided, not for the first time, to throw convention to the wind. 'Sophia', the child's nursery name, was made official and echoed that of her slave grandmother on her mother's side. It was spelt differently and pronounced with stretched vowels according to the fashion of the day – '*So-fire*.' For her middle name, Duleep acknowledged the Queen, but twisted the traditional Alexandrina into Alexandrovna. The unlikely interpretation of tradition bothered no one. Duleep seemed above reproach.

Grand titles held no place in the nursery, however, and Sophia was known by her brothers and sisters simply as 'Saff' or 'Sophie'.[13] Her bossy sister Princess Bamba gave her her own title, 'Little Asa', which only she was allowed to use. Sophia seemed to be blessed with beauty, fortune, favour and happiness; the Maharani had many reasons to be happy, chief among which was the state of her baby girl's immortal soul.

For many years the Maharani had fretted over whether her children were going to hell. Although their father was a church-going Christian who knew his Bible, Bamba was aware that his religious conversion had happened only after a childhood in which, in her opinion, he had been brought up amongst heathens in India. Although she knew little about her husband's Sikh roots, she knew that she feared them and was constantly worried that his former faith might somehow taint them all. Anxiety made Bamba ill, and she confided the depth of her concern to her friends at the Cairo mission: 'the Lord's mercies have been great to me in restoring me to health and strength again. May my heart be quietened more and by his Holy Spirit, that I may serve him as I ought. Our little ones are on the whole dear good children, still one sometimes sees the old nature rising up.'[14]

'The old nature' was a wild and unfettered spirit which all Sophia's siblings seemed to share. The Maharani Bamba attributed these negative traits to her husband's 'godless' past, but with the arrival of Sophia, who presented evidence of no such torment, she seemed reassured.

Before Sophia's first birthday, the family idyll at Elveden was beginning to show cracks. For some time Queen Victoria had been receiving reports about the Maharajah's expenditure; not only had he sunk a fortune into the bricks and mortar of his house, but also he was haemorrhaging funds as he continued to try to turn Elveden into the greatest estate in Britain. The India Office handled his annual budget of £25,000 a year, but the Maharajah was sending them invoices to settle as if there were no limit to his income. Apart from the expense of his hunting estate, he had a terrible gambling habit. The debts were building faster than the India Office could pay them. After hearing yet another complaint from her Secretary of State, the Queen sent a series of representatives to advise His Royal Highness to temper his spending, and his behaviour. He ignored them all.

At colossal expense he hired the best gamekeepers for Elveden, stocked rabbits, pheasants and grouse, so that the estate was teeming with targets. He also installed an enormous glass mews in which to keep his hawks. As a boy in the Punjab, Duleep had become a skilled falconer, and he now collected birds with the zeal of an unrestrained schoolboy. His Icelandic silver-plumed gyrfalcons, for centuries the preferred bird of kings and nobles, were suited to the British climate; his Indian hawks, however, were not. Though they dropped dead from the cold each year, the Maharajah insisted on restocking them. He would send for more every year, giving no thought to the cost of catching, crating and shipping the birds from the Punjab.

This passion, which may have seemed like a mania to his family, won him many international plaudits. France's Champagne Hawking Club, set up in the wine-growing region in 1865, was the oldest association in the world. Hundreds of hunters would gather in the plains of Chalons-sur-Marne to show off their skills every year under its aegis.[15] However, when the Franco-Prussian War was declared in 1870, the club shipped its entire stud of hawks to Elveden;[16] there was no greater compliment that could be paid in the world of falconry. The Maharajah took great pleasure in training the birds himself. He tied small brass bells to their feet, upon which he had inscribed the words, '£2 reward for safe return. If caught alive put the Hawk in a hamper, give it some fresh meat or birds, not salt meat, send it as addressed.'[17]

The hunting grounds of Elveden soon became the place to go for unfettered carnage and the Maharajah enjoyed the shoots more than anyone. Sophia was only four months old when the Prince of Wales made a particularly bloody visit to her home. As Bertie wrote in a letter to one of his friends, all were flushed with the excitement: 'We had the most extraordinary day's shooting having killed yesterday and today close on 6,000 head, nearly 4,500 of which were pheasants! It is certainly the most wonderful shooting I ever saw, and I doubt whether such bags have ever been made before.'[18]

In order to knock the greatest number of birds out of the sky in the quickest time, the Maharajah would sit upon the ground, on a specially designed low stool, and wheel himself around, shooting as he spun. The method was effective, if not elegant. By the time of Sophia's infancy, her father was beginning to lose his hair and run to fat. He looked like a rotund spinning top as he blasted the skies. Yet despite his comical appearance, few could rival the Maharajah's deadly aim. The year Sophia was born he held two separate sporting records: the first for bagging 780 birds for a thousand cartridges expended, making it the largest hunting haul achieved by one gun in England; the second for shooting 440 grouse in one day in Perthshire,[19] an astonishing ratio of bullets to carcasses.

Sophia's brothers were encouraged to follow in their father's foot-steps from an early age. Both Victor and Freddie learned to handle guns before their teens and became talented marksmen. As their guns thundered away outside, Sophia gurgled in her crib, while the other girls spent their time playing with their dolls on the third-floor nurs-ery, on the sunny south side of the house.[20] In time, Sophia and Catherine learned to hate firearms. Princess Bamba, perhaps affronted at being left behind while her brothers accompanied their father, maintained a jealous fascination towards them.

By 1877 the British government had begun to issue far blunter warnings to the Maharajah about his spending. Duleep was indignant. He believed that as a king, albeit a deposed one, he was entitled to live any way he pleased; the great fortune that he had as a boy and which he had signed over to the British guaranteed it. Duleep's anger was further fuelled when he saw the way in which other deposed Indian monarchs, who had given up far smaller kingdoms than his own, were receiving more lucrative settlements. The Maharajah began to question whether the Queen and her imperial agents had taken advantage of him when he was just a child.

He started to delve deeper into his past, his mother's imprisonment and the period leading up to his exile. Turbaned strangers began to mysteriously appear in Suffolk, filling the Maharajah's mind with stories of his father, the Lion of Punjab, and of the great kingdom which the British had stolen from him. They also reminded him of the words of Jindan's prophecy: that he would return to India as a mighty ruler and a Sikh saint. Gradually, but inexorably, the ideas spread through the Maharajah's mind like a drug. More and more Duleep showed signs of bitter disillusionment. For weeks on end he would be morose and irritable. Sophia and her brothers and sisters were ushered away from their father who was spending most of his time behind closed doors, writing and researching. The Maharani Bamba, in whom he felt unable to confide, became nervous of her husband's moods.

On 9 January 1878, the Queen's bankers, Coutts, wrote to inform the Maharajah that he was heading for financial disaster.[21] India Office representatives visited the Maharajah, telling him to cut back on his excessive spending with immediate effect or face repercussions. Duleep responded by going on a spending spree and publicly challenging the India Office to return almost half a million pounds-worth (more than £50 million today) of family jewels, which he insisted were never subject to the 1846 Treaty of Lahore, along with over a million pounds-worth (£100 million today) of ancestral lands.[22]

Though the children sensed their father's anger they were far too young to understand the precise cause. Victor and Frederick confidently strode about Elveden in formal tweed suits, like miniature versions of their father. The Princesses Catherine, Bamba and their toddler sister Sophia were protected from the worst of the tensions by Miss Date, and the thick walls of the nursery.

Though bankruptcy loomed, Duleep defiantly paraded his children in front of a constant stream of aristocratic visitors throughout 1877 and 1878, as if he had not a care in the world. The Prince of Wales continued to visit, as did the Lords Huntingdon, Walsingham and de Grey, and the Maharani hosted ladies' tennis parties, entertaining the likes of the Duchess of Atholl and the Ladies Fitzroy and Leicester. Photographs record tableaux of richly adorned and powerful guests posing in front of the main doors of Elveden Hall, the little Duleep Singh princes and princesses sitting cross-legged in front of them. Though Bamba said nothing, she wore her stress like a mask. In faded photographs, the Maharani sits awkwardly at the centre, casting forlorn looks at her husband behind the camera. Oblivious to his wife's unhappiness, Duleep seemed to believe that his photographs were a clear message to the watching world: his family remained at the apex of society, regardless of being chased by creditors.

The children too look awkward and out of place in almost all of these photographs, their brown faces and bodies at odds with the country jackets and starched lace petticoats. The boys' jet black hair had been allowed to grow until it was almost as long as their sisters', and left untied it flowed all the way down their backs. This is how Queen Victoria liked the children to be. In August 1878 she wrote to Duleep, asking after his 'dear children' and requesting a new picture of her godson Victor: 'I hope he still has his beautiful hair?'[23] There was an irony in her desire, for in India such long hair on a boy would have denoted a commitment to the very Sikh religion Duleep had forsaken.

In the same letter, the Queen also gently chided the Maharajah for his intemperate spending: 'You know how deep an interest I have ever taken in you, and how much I feel for the trying position in which you were and are placed by circumstances over which you had no control – but as an old friend, excuse me for saying that I think you are considered a little inclined to extravagance which may act unfavourably on the settlement of your affairs.'[24] Duleep heeded the Queen's warning only reluctantly. For now, he cut back on his expensive diversions in London, his clubs, the Garrick and the Marlborough, and some of his more superfluous friends, and he tried to spend more time in the country with his family. In August 1879, Bamba gave birth to her sixth and final child, a son. In line with his new attempts to defer to the Queen, the boy was named Prince Albert Edward Duleep Singh in honour of the late Prince Consort. To his family, the child would be known as Edward. To Sophia, who would love him most of all, he would be 'Eddie'.

# 4

# The Fall

Not only were Sophia and Edward deeply fond of each other, they also bore a strong resemblance. Edward had large soulful eyes, which turned down at the corners. Like Sophia he was quiet and shy, although altogether more serious. He had, like his sister, a broad, square forehead and a long aquiline nose, although hers was slightly crooked at the bridge. Both children had thin, downturned mouths, which could make them look deeply unhappy, even when they were not. In Edward's case, his eyelids did not help. Heavy and hooded, they gave him a perpetual look of world-weariness. From the beginning the prince was thin and physically fragile, but when Edward caught up with his sister's height, the two looked almost like twins. The most marked difference came in their pigmentation, for Edward had dark brown skin, while Sophia was much fairer.

Despite the arrival of her sixth child, by the end of 1879 it had become clear to Bamba that she was trapped in a sham of a marriage. For the first few months of Edward's life the Maharajah was almost entirely absent from home. He took to spending most of his time, and money, in London, leaving Maharani Bamba isolated and downcast in the countryside. Her misery only increased when the salacious gossip from the capital made its way as far as remote Elveden. Rumour had it that not only had the Maharajah's gambling taken on ruinous proportions, but he was also very publicly cheating on his wife.

In fact, Duleep had been unfaithful throughout his marriage, though these were usually low-key dalliances involving housemaids, or women from the local villages who were no more tempted to trumpet their affairs than he. These indiscretions remained in the shadows, allowing the Maharani the façade of a happy marriage. If any children resulted from these liaisons, Duleep would pay for their education, even going as far as to employ some of his offspring on his estate. It was not until Sophia was older that she would notice that there were various youths working around Elveden with dark skin and features not dissimilar to her own. A few of his illegitimate children even had 'Singh' noted as middle names on their birth certificates. One, Kate Singh, was born in the nearby Norfolk parish of Swaffham in 1876, the same year as Sophia's birth, and grew up to be a domestic parlour maid.

After the birth of Prince Edward, the Maharajah made no attempt to hide his infidelities. He was regularly seen in the company of Polly Ash, a singer and *danseuse* at the Royal Alhambra Palace in Leicester Square, a place known for its 'reckless liberality' and 'where wantons expose their shame'. Numerous wealthy men would come nightly for the theatre's attractions – not the shows themselves, but the barely clad young dancers. A huge basement canteen was open to the public, and the richer patrons mixed with the performers while the champagne flowed. It was not unusual for young women to seek out the most generous benefactors and leave with them at the end of the night. It was here that the Maharajah first met Polly and became transfixed, to the extent that he was soon to be seen escorting Miss Ash around town in the full glare of public attention.

Queen Victoria's private secretary, Sir Henry Ponsonby, was alarmed by the very public poor conduct of the Maharajah, and by the amount of India Office money he was prepared to lavish on his dancing girl. Duleep submitted bills for expensive hotel rooms and perfumes, and even badgered the government to pay Polly Ash a stipend of £2,000 a year. Ponsonby wrote to the Prince of Wales hoping that, despite his own playboy reputation, the heir to the throne might prevail on his friend to see sense. But no amount of persuasion could sway the Maharajah from his indulgence of his mistress. Duleep continued to strut about London with Polly and a bevy of Alhambra regulars in tow. The spectacle led the press to mock the Maharajah openly in caricature and editorials. By 1880, Duleep presented an easy target. He was no longer the beautiful boy whom Victoria held up as 'a bright example to all Indian Princes, for he is thoroughly good and amiable, and most anxious to improve himself'.[1] The youth who had exuded such beauty and nobility was now a stout, balding, middle-aged man who spent almost every night at the Alhambra, 'graciously accepting the homage of *houris* in the green room, and distributing 9-carat gimcracks with Oriental lavishness'.[2] The Maharajah was making a laughing stock of himself, and his family, and never more so than when he was caught waving small jewels above the heads of the Alhambra throng crying out, 'What nice little girl is going to have this?'[3]

Humiliated, and with only her servants and very young family for company, Bamba slipped ever deeper into despair, so alarming friends with the speed of her decline that they urged the Maharajah to return home and take care of his wife and children. Lord Hertford, a friend, and former Lord Chamberlain under Benjamin Disraeli, wrote to Duleep warning of the disastrous effects of his absences. In reply, the Maharajah did not deny his neglect, but took no responsibility for it. Instead he blamed his actions on the British government, which had robbed him of his fortune: 'The accompanying statement will show you the state my affairs are in and explain my apparent neglect of my wife and family. The fact is I cannot afford to bring them up to Town but if thru' the kindness of the Queen, the government of India treat me in a liberal spirit none of my friends will ever be able to bring against me such a charge.'[4]

Photographs taken at the time show how almost overnight, the pretty young Maharani had become a hollow-eyed matron, dressed always in black, with her hair swept severely back off her face in a taut and joyless bun. The children's nanny, Miss Date, did her best to fill the void left by the withdrawal of their mother, but it was largely up to the children to comfort themselves. It was during this time that the senior sisters became very protective of Sophia and Edward, who, in turn, held firm to one another. With Edward, Sophia knew where she stood, behaving like a little mother to him, providing him with a constancy and a warmth that the Maharani had become less able to give. Victor and Frederick had been sent to Eton soon after their tenth birthdays, and only returned for the holidays during which they were preoccupied with outdoor pursuits. Princess Catherine and Bamba spent their days absorbed by governesses and lessons. The girls were both bright and interested in learning; like most well-bred young ladies, their father had wanted them to be educated at home, though not excessively. Sophia was too young to join them and so, gradually, she was left behind.

As the decade turned, their father's behaviour worsened, and the British government decided enough was enough. A lasting solution to the Maharajah's financial situation had to be found. What the civil servants finally came up with set him on a collision course with Queen Victoria. In the early months of 1880, more than two years after Coutts had called in its loan, the government agreed to pay the Maharajah an interest-free sum of £57,000, enough to pay his debts and save him from bankruptcy. The loan came with one stringent condition: Elveden would have to be sold upon his death and all proceeds paid back to the British government. The Maharajah was left devastated by the proposed terms: it meant he would neither be able to leave his beloved Suffolk palace to his eldest son Victor, nor settle any pensions on his other children. The creditors were now closing in on him fast. He had only one roll of the dice left: Duleep wrote directly to the Queen.

Since Victoria was godmother to Victor and Sophia the Maharajah felt sure that she would not allow her godchildren to be left destitute after his death. He scribbled a plea for help, adding that since the British were responsible for much of the current misery in his life she was morally obliged to help him: 'As the bankers are pressing for the repayment of the advance made by them I have no alternative but to accept the accommodation thus offered – as that or nothing. Nevertheless it breaks my heart to think my eldest son will have to be turned out of his house and home and leave the place with which his earliest associations in life are connected,' he wrote. 'No one knows but myself, my Sovereign, the agony that I suffered when I was turned out of my home and exiled from the land of my birth and I shudder to think of the sufferings my poor boy may undergo.'⁵

Queen Victoria's reply was warm, but offered little remedy:

Dear Maharajah,

I have to acknowledge your letter of the 13th which has pained me so much. You know how fond I have always been of you, and how truly I felt for you, knowing how completely innocent you were of the unfortunate circumstances which led to you leaving your own country. I have at once written to Lord Hartington [the Secretary of State for India] to see what can be done to ensure your own comfort and a proper position for your children. As I once or twice mentioned to you before, I think you were thought extravagant and that may have led to a want of confidence as regards the future . . .

Trusting that the Maharanee and your dear children are well . . . ⁶

Victoria's 'told you so' reply proved a watershed in their relationship. Duleep was so angered by it that for the next two years he shunned the royal court, locking himself away in the British Library, in an attempt to find documentary evidence to overturn the original treaty he had been forced to sign as a child. The result of his endeavours was a book entitled *The Annexation of Punjaub* which he wrote in association with a well-known critic of the Raj, the retired Indian Army Major Evans Bell.

Bell was an ardent secularist and scholar of Indian history. He had grown to despise the conduct of the British in India, and advocated an end to imperialism. The leather-bound volume Bell and Duleep Singh created was circulated among the press, politicians at Westminster, and courtiers at the palace. Though it was supposed to be an irresistible argument against the legality of British conduct in the Punjab, the volume was clumsily written, inelegant, hastily compiled and full of factual inaccuracies. Predictably the publication met with a hostile reception in Britain, and the Maharajah was forced onto the back foot by numerous calls to correct factual errors. The main thrust of his argument was all but ignored. The book was also deeply insulting to many of the most powerful figures in the history of British administration in India. Particular venom was directed towards Lord Dalhousie, the former Governor General of India who had presided over the annexation of Duleep's old empire, whom Bell and the Maharajah described as 'a violator of treaties who abused sacred trust'.[7]

When it became clear that his book would not move the establishment directly, Duleep Singh took his grievances to the British newspapers, writing ever wilder letters to *The Times*: 'Generous and Christian Englishmen, accord me a just and liberal treatment for the sake of the fair name of your nation, of which I have now the honour to be a naturalised member, for it is more blessed to give than to take.'[8]

Far from eliciting sympathy, this public appeal made Duleep look ridiculous; the papers now accused the Maharajah of whinging venality. The reversal in their attitude marked an unbearable change in fortune for the family as a whole. Maharani Bamba and the children withdrew entirely from public life, as the aristocratic families who had once been so well disposed to the Duleep Singhs now chose to avoid them. The Maharani was forced to deal with the ostracism alone, while the Maharajah stayed away in London, and she began drinking heavily.

By 1883, Duleep was reduced to pleading with the government for more money. On 1 March, he wrote to Lord Kimberley, the Under Secretary of State for India, beseeching him to reconsider the final settlement and terms which would force him to sell Elveden. Gone were the claims for jewels and lost land, replaced only with the repeated request for 'such provision as will enable me to maintain the high rank confirmed to me by my Gracious Sovereign during my life and by my Children after my death, worthy of the magnanimity of this great just and civilised Nation'.[9] He was, he explained, not asking for much:

> 1st. I would venture humbly to request that if no greater generosity can be bestowed upon me at least my present life stipend of £25,000 per annum be continued to my male heirs at my death.

2ndly. That the £138,000 in which I am indebted to the Indian government together with the £105,000 given to me for the purchase of an estate in this country may be considered as full compensation for the loss of gold and silver plate and Palace jewels, thus relieving my stipend of the heavy charge of interest deducted from it.

3rdly. That the Premiums on the Policies of Life Insurance effected for the benefit of my younger children and widow paid by me out of my life stipend of £25,000 per annum be discharged from the surplus arising out of the unexpected balance of the sum allotted for the maintenance of myself my relatives and servants of state at the annexation.[10]

For a proud man like Duleep, such a compromise was humiliating, but he was determined to leave some kind of legacy to his children: 'My Lord, I feel very deeply the hardship to which my children will be subjected, viz., being brought up in the position which I occupy in this country through the graciousness of my Sovereign on being compelled to relinquish it at my death for a lower sphere of life.'[11]

The reply from Lord Kimberley was cold and uncompromising: 'I regret to be under the necessity of informing your Highness that I am entirely unable to entertain the request which you have now put forward.'[12] Friends of the Maharajah were appalled at the government's intransigence and wrote personally to the Queen asking her to do something on his behalf. Some went as far as to argue that they had forced him to sign away his empire contrary to British law and Christian morality. One such was Lord Hertford, the venerable statesman and former Lord Chamberlain who had previously tried to intervene in Duleep's affairs. Hertford informed the Queen that the Maharajah was facing certain ruin, due to the new settlement that the India Office was imposing upon him. He also alerted her to the fact that Duleep was selling jewels and family silver in order to pay for the basic upkeep of Elveden. As a result, Hertford warned, the Maharajah was being pushed into a volatile state of mind and was talking privately of quitting England for good.[13]

It was the first time since his arrival in England that Duleep had suggested he might want to live in India again. 'Surely this is not only suicidal for himself, but may be productive of immense mischief to England,'[14] wrote Hertford to the Queen's private secretary. Victoria had for many months watched with dismay the developing stalemate between her Maharajah and her government. Memories of the Indian Mutiny were still very raw. Duleep's presence in Punjab might be the catalyst for another armed revolt. Victoria dispatched her courtiers to calm the Maharajah and personally pressed the India Office to show more generosity towards him. The Secretary of State, however, would not be moved. Duleep was left with little option but to come up with funds himself.

After neglecting his family for almost two years, the Maharajah returned to Elveden Hall shamefaced, in order to plunder its riches. Sophia and her siblings watched in confused horror as their father stripped the house of some of his most treasured belongings in order to collect them for auction. Jewels, rare Indian carpets, silver teapots, embroideries and '25,000 Oz of Chased Plate'[15] – ornately engraved silver platters – were carried out in crates by the London auctioneers Philips, Son & Neale. The lot that would cause the greatest excitement was 'a magnificent centrepiece, 39 inches high, composed of a large and finely modelled figure of an elephant carrying the Maharaja of the Punjab, surrounded by several equestrian groups'.[16] Duleep had been reduced to selling himself.

Not even a sympathetic editorial in *The Times* could persuade the India Office to think again:

> The news of his Highness being compelled to sell his jewels and other valuables will excite a deep feeling of sympathy among all who are acquainted with the history of the 'Lion of the Punjab' . . . There is very good reason for the complaint on his part that he has practically been deprived unfairly of a large share of the income which was guaranteed to him . . . Although the government, from a purely business point of view might be justified in believing that the Maharajah has 'partly brought his pecuniary difficulties upon himself', it could be said in extenuation that the

ways of Oriental potentates are not as those of modern English princes . . . A golden bridge might, with generosity and dignity, be built for retreat from a position which is embarrassing the both parties.[17]

No such bridge materialised, and on 23 July the auction went ahead, raising in excess of £20,000. As it did, Duleep threw down the gauntlet: the catalogue which accompanied the sale stated that he was raising money 'preparatory to his leaving for India'. If the British threatened his children's inheritance, then he would return, with his children, to his homeland, no matter how it might stir the Punjab. The auction of the Duleep Singhs' belongings triggered feverish debate, and questions were raised in the House of Commons. The Maharajah wrote in unsparing terms, accusing the Queen and her government of setting out to destroy him from the very start: 'From childhood I have been absolutely in the hands of the government without a will or independent action of my own – trusting implicitly to their good faith. Now there appears to have been a deliberate intention from the first, merely to do what least might suffice to answer my urgent demands and leave my children and family to gradually sink in the world.'[18]

Duleep now thought only of vengeance, wanting nothing less than to smash the Raj's hold on his former kingdom. His family saw little of him during this time. He remained almost entirely in London – where he rented a townhouse at 53 Holland Park – plotting his next move or drinking away his frustrations. The more he fulminated about his past, the more he convinced himself that Queen Victoria, whom he had once loved, was at the heart of a conspiracy to impoverish him and his children. He took to referring to her as 'Mrs Fagin',[19] after Dickens's fictional receiver of stolen property.

In a letter to Sir Henry Ponsonby, the Maharajah made dark threats: 'there is a terrible storm gathering in India and I hope to render such service as to compel the principal ministers of the Crown to recognise my just claims which perhaps under the present circumstances they may have been disinclined to admit. I know that the advent of Russia is hailed with intense joy both by the people and

Princes of India in their secret hearts whatever they may outwardly say and they are all prepared to rebel as soon as that Power advances a little nearer.'[20] In the same letter, he penned the words which would wound Victoria even more. He wanted the Queen to know that he was thinking of abandoning his Christianity: 'I may re-embrace the faith of my ancestors and eventually take up my residence in India, but I will not take the latter step without laying before her Majesty my reasons for doing so.'[21]

Victoria was taken aback, having always considered herself to be Duleep's 'best friend'.[22] Her reply, one month later, was an appeal to these bonds of friendship and sentiment. Her youngest son, Leopold, Duke of Albany, had died two years before from a fatal brain haemorrhage caused by a combination of a fall and his haemophilia. The Queen reminded Duleep of his affection for her youngest boy: 'You were so much attached to my dear Leopold from his earliest childhood, that I thought you would like to possess a recollection of him, and therefore send you an enamelled photograph of him.' Victoria then came to the crux of the matter: 'You mentioned the possibility of returning to your own old faith. Now, considering what a fine and fervent Christian you were for between 30 and 40 years, I cannot believe you would forsake the blessings of what is your religion – for one which offers none of its comforts and blessings . . . I am sure the Maharani (to whom I wish to be kindly remembered) and your children would feel the same. Believe me always, your affectionate and faithful friend, Victoria R.I.'[23]

Duleep Singh's response was cutting and to the point: 'My Sovereign . . . I embraced Christianity because those by whom I was surrounded at the time happened to be so consistent in their conduct. We Sikhs though savages by nature, implicitly act up to the (such as it is) morality of our faith. We do not profess one thing and do the other.'[24]

As Victoria anticipated, the Maharani found her husband's threat to abandon his Christian faith devastating. Bamba spent her time locked away in her room weeping. On the occasions Duleep did return to Elveden, he ignored his wife but spoiled his children with expensive gifts and attention. Sophia and her siblings loved hearing tales about India and the kingdom he promised to restore to them. The girls in particular wanted to know about their grandmother, the beautiful and formidable Rani Jindan.[25] Duleep's eldest and youngest daughters received their father's stories in very different ways. For Princess Bamba they were a reminder of her father's dispossession and they inflamed in her a sense of anger and vulnerability. For young Sophia they were merely exotic fables – fairy tales. Catherine's reactions lay somewhere in between. The Maharajah's visits were all too fleeting and soon he was on the train back to London again.[26]

The sense of disorder at Elveden deepened. Sophia, who turned eight in 1884, was coming to the age where her education ought to have been taken in hand. But with her mother locked in her sadness and her father absent, there was no one to instruct teachers or look after her interests. Her lessons, if they happened at all, were haphazard and Sophia's education was severely set back. Her poor beginnings were reflected in her poor penmanship: Sophia's handwriting remained messy and difficult to read for the rest of her life.

Elveden too began to show signs of neglect. Three years of unseasonably hot weather and poor rainfall caused crops on the farms to fail. The Maharajah's continuing absence meant that the sporting part of the estate was allowed to run to ruin. Without the great hunts to check numbers, rabbits took over the fields. Without the supervision of gamekeepers, many of whom had been let go as the debts mounted, the stock of grouse and partridge was allowed to dwindle. Elveden's pheasant eggs, which once sold for 9d a dozen in London's finest shops, were no longer boxed up and sent to Mayfair, and were left to poachers instead. Everywhere young Sophia looked, she saw decline and despair.

The only real change in the three years that followed the first Elveden auction came when Duleep Singh transferred his amorous attentions from Polly Ash onto a mysterious and even younger new mistress.

Ada Weatherill had been acquainted with the Maharajah since the mid-1880s. From an impoverished upbringing in Lambeth, south London, Ada went straight into domestic service at the age of thirteen. Within a couple of years she had worked her way up to a slightly more elevated role, as chambermaid at Cox's Hotel in St James's, a discreet establishment that was well known for providing wealthy men and their mistresses with rooms. It was there that Duleep Singh first met Ada.

Few failed to be moved by the sixteen-year-old's youthful good looks. Long-limbed, with thick chestnut brown hair, bright eyes and creamy complexion, Ada attracted the attention of many men, but the Maharajah pursued her with a degree of obsession which surpassed the rest. Duleep and his 'Marini' – a nickname Duleep used for Ada in a play upon the word 'Maharani' – became inseparable. On meeting them together about town, one of Duleep's old Alhambra companions, the playboy and playwright Julian Osgood Field, commented that Ada's manifest charms were only spoilt by her 'unmistakable Whitechapel [*sic*] accent . . . her pronunciation and the expressions she used were, to say the least, abnormal'.[27] As long as she remained silent, Ada was admired by all.

When news of his new infatuation finally reached Bamba the atmosphere at Elveden became even more suffocating for the children. Sophia spent increasing amounts of time outdoors, as far as she could from her mother's worsening depression. The princess developed a great love for the many hounds kennelled on the estate, which had been bred for locating prey and retrieving carcases. By talking to the kennel keepers she began to learn about dog rearing and breeding. She also ventured further than ever before, exploring her surroundings on the back of a small pony which had been bought for the children in better times. Sophia had been taught how to ride almost as soon as she could sit up straight in the saddle and she quickly became fast and fearless on horseback, surpassing her sisters in skill and daring. It became something of a joke between Catherine and Bamba that Sophia was at her happiest out in the fresh air, regardless of the English weather.[28]

On one of his rare visits home, in 1885, their father announced that he was planning a trip for them all, but kept the destination secret. When it emerged he had commissioned one of London's leading dressmakers to design hot-weather outfits for the children, his intentions became clearer.

Duleep submitted the bill for the children's clothes to the India Office (a preposterously high £1,102 5s 6d,[29] which was returned unpaid) and then informed the government that he and his family intended to sail for India in the New Year. Though the Queen sent her courtiers to try to broker a last-minute deal, it soon became clear that no amount of pressure would change the minds of her ministers, for the India Office simply did not believe that the Maharajah would carry out his threat. They advised the sovereign to wait out the storm. They were wrong.

Sophia spent the days before Christmas packing her belongings for a long voyage to a country she had only heard about on her father's knee. By January 1886, the Maharajah had put the entire contents of Elveden Hall up for sale. Everything from the fixtures in the house, to the few remaining pheasant eggs in the hatchery, was priced up and catalogued. In the end the items would only realise a fraction of their true value at auction. The exotic style of the Maharajah was no longer fashionable in the country. As *The Times* noted tartly, any future sale of Duleep's unique home by the India Office might itself prove challenging: 'Elveden Hall has been so transformed from an old red-brick mansion into a sort of Oriental Palace, that it would have to be considerably restored back to its English garb to suit most tastes.'[30] It seemed that every trace of the Suffolk Maharajah would be erased after he left the country.

If Britain had lost its taste for the Maharajah, the feeling was mutual. Duleep stopped pleading for kindness and finally found his roar. He emptied his Coutts safety-deposit boxes of all his jewels, leaving behind just his debts. He then booked passage for his entire family, the nanny, an ayah and a valet to sail on the SS *Verona* at the end of March the following year.

The mere purchase of the tickets caused immediate ripples in India. Raj intelligence reports nervously described the popular excitement in the Punjab at the prospect of the Maharajah's return. 'Wild rumours are current regarding the powers that will be conferred on him,' a report of 20 March 1886 warned. Without even knowing it, Sophia and her sisters were at the heart of the furore. One of Duleep's cousins, Thakur Singh Sandhawalia, was 'said to have sent letters announcing that the Maharaja has re-embraced the Sikh religion in England, and has betrothed his daughters to the Buriya Sardars in the Ambala district. The Sikhs are elated.'[31] Buriya was a minor, yet populous principality in Punjab, where Sikhs retained the reins of power. Though they were surrounded by British-controlled territory, Buriya support in any possible future uprising was considered a real threat.

Finally waking up to the trouble on their horizon, the Viceroy of India and the Secretary of State looked for ways to head off the problem. As the date of the Duleep Singhs' departure loomed they offered the Maharajah £50,000 as a one-off payment, in return for a promise that he would never again attempt to return to India.[32] Ten days before the *Verona* was due to weigh anchor, at a fractious meeting at London's Carlton Club, Duleep threw the offer back in their faces.

The Maharajah then broadcast his defiance to a wider audience. In an open letter to the London *Standard*, peppered with Punjabi words, the Maharajah addressed his 'beloved Countrymen':

It was not my intention ever to return to reside in India, but Sut-Gooroo [The True Guru-God], who governs a destiny, and is more powerful than I his erring creature, has caused circumstances to be so brought that against my will I am compelled to quit England . . . I now, therefore, beg forgiveness of you Khalsa-ji, or The Pure, for having forsaken the faith of my ancestors for a foreign religion; but I was very young when I embraced Christianity.

It is my fond desire on reaching Bombay to take the *pahul* again. But in returning to the faith of my ancestors I have no intention of conforming to the errors into Sikhism by those who were not true Sikhs such as wretched caste observances or abstinence from meats and drinks, which Sut-goroo has ordained should be received with thankfulness by all mankind, but to worship the pure and beautiful tenets of Baba Nanak and obey the commands of Gooroo Gobind Singh. Sut-gooroo's Will be done. With Wah Gooroo Jee ki Futteh, I remain, My beloved countrymen, your own flesh and blood, Duleep Singh.[33]

The letter, which would have baffled the average reader, carried its message far beyond the breakfast tables of Britain. With its references to the *pahul* ceremony – the baptism of the Sikhs, through which they are inducted into the faith – this was a proclamation to the Punjab itself. The Maharajah was asking his 'countrymen' to forgive him for abandoning his faith. Directing his words particularly towards the Khalsa, the body of fully initiated Sikhs, he vowed to become one of them again. Elsewhere in the same letter he loftily informed the Khalsa that although he would be happy to rejoin them as their leader, he would have no time for their teetotal, vegetarian lifestyle.

When the family reached the SS *Verona* docked at Gravesend, Duleep appeared to be in buoyant mood and chatted animatedly with crew and passengers alike. But as they made their final preparations to leave England, thoughts of Queen Victoria filled the exiled Maharajah's mind. In a letter that recalled their former mutual love, Duleep addressed 'My Sovereign'.

> Before quitting England I humbly venture to address your Majesty in order to convey to your Majesty the inexpressible gratitude I feel for all your Majesty's graciousness both to me and mine during my stay in this country now extending over some 30 years. I could not face the pain that such a[n] event would cause me if I ventured to take my leave of your Majesty in person and therefore I humbly implore your Majesty's forgiveness for not paying any last homage before starting for India.
>
> Your Majesty's heartbroken subject – Duleep Singh.[34]

# Scramble for India

At almost four hundred feet long, forty feet wide and over 3,000 tonnes, the SS *Verona* was a great beast of a vessel. It had been designed by celebrated shipbuilder Robert Napier for the Peninsular & Oriental Steam Navigation Company. Constructed on the banks of the Clyde,[1] with its sleek black hull, four towering masts and billowing central funnel, the *Verona* sat in the water like a long slick of ink,[2] underlining the fact that in 1886, Britannia still ruled the waves.

Steam travel was a relatively recent advancement and the *Verona* was one of the first passenger and cargo vessels to stretch its capability. The speed of the ship, 12.5 knots, was still a novelty to most passengers, not least the younger Duleep Singh children. They watched in delight as the rushing waters sluiced past the great hull, making their trip seem even more like a magical adventure. After getting over their initial seasickness, Sophia and Edward loved their experience of first-class seafaring. The Maharani Bamba, meanwhile, had locked herself away in her cabin, tortured by worry. On 15 April, in a letter to her friend Mrs Lansing in Egypt, she tried to put a brave face on her predicament:

Thank you so very much for all your kind letters and I know that you forgive my not having written to you for so long which is so kind of you, I cannot tell you how I appreciate your kindness. I am thankful to say that all the dear ones here are in good health. We were poorly only one day, since then we have enjoyed our voyage so far. The Lord has been very merciful to us His loving Kindness has never failed us! I know he will not leave us at any time.[3]

Unlike their mother, the children knew nothing of the brewing political storm, and several of the ship's passengers remarked on their joyous laughter. Yet not all of Sophia's siblings were enjoying the voyage as much as she. Victor spent his time on the *Verona* simmering with rage. He had no desire to journey to a land that he had never seen, let alone reclaim a kingdom that meant nothing to him. The Maharajah's heir took to referring to his father as 'my idiotic parent'.[4]

Victor might have been a little more circumspect had he known that spies travelled with them on the *Verona* and that such outbursts from him, and indeed every word his father uttered, were being reported back to London. Duleep Singh was keeping the agents busy as he held court in the ship's dining room, telling his captive audience all about his grievances and plan for a glorious return to his kingdom.

Meanwhile, strict instructions were issued by the Viceroy of India Lord Dufferin at his summer capital in Simla and wired to British officials at the next port of Yemen: 'Duleep Singh left with wife and six children. A warrant will be prepared and sent to you. Viceroy hopes Maharajah's removal may be so managed as to cause no excitement. We ought to include wife and three sons and three daughters in arrest warrants if possible.'[5] The Gulf of Aden was a gateway to the Suez Canal and ultimately the Indian Ocean. The British had taken control of the narrow channel four years before and therefore had the authority to stop the Duleep Singhs travelling through it.

General Adam George Forbes Hogg, a genteel man who had been the British Resident in Aden for two years, left for Egypt immediately, wondering how difficult the confrontation with the Maharajah might be. On board the *Verona*, as the ship steamed its way closer to the Suez Canal, Duleep was also preparing himself. He had anticipated they would be stopped. He might even have hoped for a dramatic arrest. A potentially unedifying scene, involving handcuffs and tears from the youngest children, might cause outrage in England

and therefore shift the position of the India Office. However when they came, the arrests were altogether more civilised.

Hogg was sent to wait for the ship to drop anchor at Port Said. In preparing for the showdown, the Maharajah wore his most opulent Indian robes, jewels and a Sikh turban. His children too were dressed in their finest clothes. The jetty, where the ship docked on 21 April, stood at one end of the Suez Canal. Hogg had desperately wanted the arrests to be low key and after boarding the vessel with his police escort implored the Maharajah to go quietly. His Highness, however, 'refused to leave the ship unless arrested, so in presence of the captain I told him he must come with me, and touched him on the shoulder. He complied at once and the rest of the party came voluntarily,' Hogg reported by telegram to Lord Dufferin.[6]

Sophia felt a combination of fear, confusion and humiliation as she and her family were led down the gangplank. Amidst a phalanx of officers in the searing heat, they left the *Verona* to the cheers of fellow passengers. As they were taken away, Duleep shouted: 'I leave this ship unwillingly – my case will be the subject of a great state trial – before the House of Lords!'[7] There would never be a trial.

For two weeks the family kicked their heels at the British residency in Aden, waiting to see what Duleep would do next. The Maharajah was trapped in diplomatic limbo: the British would not let him go forward, and he himself did not want to go back. If he wished to return to England he would have to swear loyalty to the throne and give up any notions of trying anything so foolhardy again. The British hoped that by making him sweat in Aden he would see the error of his ways. Sophia watched her mother grow increasingly desperate as she attempted to keep her head and those of her six listless children.

The days were long, tedious and swelteringly hot. If she had hoped for some comfort or support from her husband, the Maharani was to be disappointed. Sophia's father was even more remote and distracted than usual. Maharani Bamba's persistent entreaties must have eventually moved or at the very least bored Sophia's father because, on 6 May, he relented and put his children and their mother on a ship destined for England. Sophia did not know it then, but this was the moment her father would abandon them for good.

In Aden, Duleep stood his ground and volleyed a series of telegrams to the Viceroy in Simla. These telegrams, which contained increasingly infuriating demands, hit the Raj's otherwise cool and pleasant summer hill station like a gust of unwanted hot air. Duleep said he would give up all attempts to go to India if they paid him £250,000; when that offer was rejected, he asked for the seventeen servants who were waiting for him in Bombay to be sent to Aden and that the British government pay all their expenses. The communiqués continued, with the Maharajah showing no sign of compromise. The Viceroy despatched urgent missives to the India Office and to the Queen's advisers. Even now, Victoria was inclined to defend Duleep, who she felt must be gripped by madness or sinister influences. She was also deeply worried about the fate of his innocent wife and children. 'The Queen Empress thanks the Viceroy for his last kind letter of the 5th May about the poor Maharajah Duleep Singh,' she wrote in reply to Lord Dufferin:

> He was so charming & good for so many years, that she feels deeply grieved at the bad hands he has fallen into and the way in which he has been led astray, & the Queen thinks it will have a very bad effect in India if he is ill-used & rather severely punished & especially if the Maharanee (an excellent pious woman) & their six children especially the two boys, quite Englishmen, are in poverty or discomfort. In the Maharajah's present state of excitement nothing can be done but he is sure to quiet down & then the Queen is ready herself to speak to him. Some money should be settled on his wife & children & a good man of business be placed about him & enough given him to enable him to live as a nobleman in England. The Queen wishes he or his son could be made a Peer & then they could live as any other nobleman's family. It is most important that his Indian advisers & relatives should be kept from him for they are those who have brought him to this pass.[8]

The coterie of 'advisers & relatives', whom Queen Victoria blamed for Duleep's imbalanced state of mind, were at that time travelling from India to reach the Maharajah. On 8 May, his cousin Thakur Singh Sandhawalia arrived in Aden with his associate Attar Singh. Duleep now wrote to the Viceroy in Simla in provocative terms: 'I desire to take advantage of my cousin's presence here and to be re-initiated into Sikhism.'⁹ This was a move that few – especially the British – believed he would go through with. There was very little they could do to stop him. The Lieutenant Governor of the Punjab, Sir Charles Umpherston Aitchison, tried to put the best possible spin on the government's inevitable acquiescence to Duleep's wishes: 'Refusal would be misunderstood and might cause irritation as interference with freedom of religious conviction . . . As long as he does not return to India consent will do little if any harm.'¹⁰

The conversion would cause tremendous harm. Quite apart from raising further the expectations of India's Sikhs, it damaged beyond repair Duleep's relationship with Queen Victoria. She had tolerated Duleep's excessive spending, his promiscuity and even his defiance of her government, but now he shunned Christianity. She had never truly believed that Duleep would turn his back on salvation, yet here he was preparing to become a Sikh once more. Never again would Queen Victoria cross her ministers for his sake.

The *pahul* baptism ceremony which Duleep had vowed to undertake was one that dated back to 1699. It was the lasting legacy of the tenth guru of the Sikhs and served as an unbreakable covenant between a Sikh and his religion.

After the death of Guru Nanak in 1539, a line of nine successors had successively taken his place at the head of the faith. All of the gurus practised their religion against the backdrop of Muslim dominance in India, and two would lose their lives because of their beliefs. In 1606, Emperor Jahangir sentenced Guru Arjan, the fifth guru, to a brutal death: he was made to sit on a hot metal plate and burning hot sand was poured on his body for five days. Despite the torture, he refused to comply. Dragged to the river to wash away the old scabs so that new wounds might be inflicted, he disappeared under the waters, never to be seen again. Jahangir's grandson Aurangzeb would be just as intolerant.

During the time of the ninth guru, Tegh Bahadur, forced conversions to Islam were gaining pace in Kashmir, and a group of high-caste Hindus fled to the Punjab and begged for protection. Tegh Bahadur heard their petition and agreed to act as their shield: he told them to send a letter to Emperor Aurangzeb offering unconditional conversion if he managed to convince the Sikhs' ninth guru to embrace Islam. Deliberately, Tegh Bahadur focused Aurangzeb's ire on himself.

The full wrath of the emperor descended on Guru Tegh Bahadur in July 1675. He was arrested and tortured for more than three months before finally being brought before the emperor in Delhi in an iron cage. Still he refused to renounce his religion. He was mocked by the Mughal court and told to perform a miracle so that he might save his life and prove that his God was real. He refused, saying he had no need to do so: the truth was the truth and needed no trickery to prove itself.

It came as no surprise then, when Aurangzeb sentenced the guru to death by public execution. Tegh Bahadur was beheaded before a large crowd of spectators in Chandni Chowk, Delhi's busiest bazaar, on 11 November. The spectacle was supposed to serve as a warning to any who would defy the will of the emperor.

Before his death Tegh Bahadur had appointed his young son Gobind as his successor. The boy vowed to continue his father's defiance of the Mughals. He spent his adolescence training as a soldier and other young Sikhs followed his example. Very soon, Guru Gobind Singh had assembled an irregular army. He also decided that the time had come to give his followers greater discipline and structure.

The Sikhs usually assembled at the guru's headquarters at Anandpur Sahib[11] for the annual harvest festival of Vaisakhi. In 1699, Guru Gobind Singh encouraged Sikhs from all over India to gather and hear him speak, and they came in their thousands. Emerging from a tent in the middle of the field, he addressed the crowds, asking whether any of them was willing to give up his life for his religion.

After initial hesitation, one man stepped forward from the crowd. He bowed before the guru, who motioned towards the tent. The crowd did not know what to expect as the guru led the volunteer into the darkness, his hand tightening on his long sword. Only those closest heard the swish of metal through air and the sickeningly dull thud which followed. What had the guru done? Had he killed the man who only moments before was standing among them?

An anxious murmur radiated through the crowd as the Sikhs tried to make sense of what they had just seen and heard. Their worst suspicions seemed to be confirmed by what happened next. The guru emerged from the tent with his blade dripping with blood. Again he asked if any man was willing to step forward to prove his devotion. To gasps a second man stepped forward. The guru led him into the tent, his sword swung and a thud rippled the thick silence which had now settled over the field. Three times more, the guru came out and three times more a young man offered his life for his religion while thousands held their breath outside.

After what seemed like an age, Guru Gobind Singh emerged from the tent leading out 'the five beloved ones' or *panj pyare*. Far from being killed, they had been blessed by the guru for their unquestioning devotion and trust. The men had been bathed and dressed in fresh clothes symbolising their new lives as the first members of the Khalsa. After their initiation, the guru told each man to find five others who were as worthy. So it was that the Khalsa grew until eventually it became the bedrock of Ranjit Singh's Sikh Kingdom.

The baptism of Duleep Singh on 25 May 1886 did not take place before any crowds. Five Sikhs, representing the *panj pyare* of 1699, and a *granthi*, or scripture reader, were needed to re-initiate him into the faith. Thakur Singh Sandhawalia and two of the Maharajah's menservants, Aroor Singh and Jawan Singh, stepped forward to play their part. Hogg, the British Resident, found a *granthi* and had him brought to his home. This still left the ceremony short of two Sikhs. So a couple of turbaned merchant seamen, whose ships happened to be anchored in the port of Aden, found themselves summoned to attend.

The Maharajah, wearing the five symbols of the Khalsa initiate,[12] knelt on the ground holding his hands together in supplication. The officiants blessed the *amrit*, a mixture of sugar and water, as they stirred it in an iron vessel with the tip of a double-edged dagger. They poured it into his cupped hands so that he could drink and sprinkled the remainder onto his head until the vessel was dry. Then they distributed *karah prasad*, a sanctified mixture of cooked wheat, sugar and butter among the small group. Only when it had been consumed in silence did Duleep Singh rise to his feet. He was a Sikh once more.

Aden with its intense dry heat soon became too much for the Maharajah and he fell gravely ill. In late May 1886, two weeks after putting his family on a ship to England, Duleep was given permission to leave the British residency and depart for wherever he wished, as long as it was not India. Failure to obey would result in drastic action. Left with few options, on 3 June Duleep boarded a French mail steamer bound for Marseilles. Almost as soon as he reached France, Duleep began to plot again. At his side, according to the spies sent after him by the British, was a mysterious young English woman who had travelled to Paris at about the same time Duleep left Aden.

Duleep and his pretty young companion were soon seen cavorting around the most exclusive parts of Paris. More worryingly, they were also seen meeting with known Irish Republicans. It was a nexus which alarmed the Foreign Office. A particularly successful British spy, Charles Tevis, was now sent to befriend the Maharajah. Duleep, who had never been the best judge of character, welcomed Tevis into his inner circle. Soon his every move and intention was being reported in detail back to both England and India.[13]

The mysterious woman with the Maharajah was Ada Weatherill, the chambermaid from Cox's Hotel who had swept all the dancing girls from Duleep Singh's bed. The Maharajah and Marini now took the city by storm. They attended glamorous parties and socialised with political radicals. Paris played host to a nest of anti-British activity. As well as establishing links with Irish Fenians, Duleep Singh consorted with Russians, who promised to introduce him to the Tsar. Duleep started to dream of an international army that would scythe its way through British troops stationed in Punjab and put him back on his throne. He had now graduated from a major irritant to a full-blown traitor.

*       *       *

Even before their return to England, Bamba understood immediately how bleak their futures might be. With no husband, no money and no home, the Maharani and her children had nowhere to go and nothing to live on. It was only thanks to Queen Victoria that they were ushered into one of London's grandest hotels. A suite at Claridge's was prepared, which would be their home while the Queen and her government discussed what should be done with them. Victoria felt a moral obligation towards Duleep's children, particularly those whom she had sworn before God to protect, and it was decided that the family should be allowed to move into Duleep's old London residence at 53 Holland Park, a place he had previously abandoned to his creditors. A handsome, white-fronted townhouse, it nestled among some of the most fashionable homes in the capital. Clean lines and a quintessentially English appearance provided an antithesis to the colourful eccentricity of Elveden. Yet not even the drastic change of scene could pull Sophia's mother back from what had now become an abyss of depression. Her mood was made worse by the fact that 53 Holland Park had hardly any furniture in it, beyond a few beds. It fell to Victor, the eldest, to write to his father asking for help. The Maharajah's venomous reply left the children in no doubt as to where they stood:

> I am delighted to see your handwriting but what a fool you are, my son, to write such a letter . . . how dare you tell me to write and ask for money said to belong to me at the Indian Office . . . You will soon be of age and will consequently be able to settle your debts. Let the Trustees sell the pictures or the jewels if they please, for I cannot be bothered afresh with matters connected with England. All that is over as a dream and I have awakened to a new life and the destruction of the British power. But if you wish to retain my affection for you, childie, do not mention again to me such matter, nor ask me to humble myself to my bitterest enemy. Look upon me as dead. But I will never be swerved from my purpose or I would not be the son of the Lion of the Punjab whose name I dare not disgrace . . .

P.S. I could see you starve and even would take your life to put an end to your misery, but will never return to England. I am entirely changed since you last saw me.[14]

As if such a homecoming were not traumatic enough for young Sophia, a couple of months later, the family was dealt another hammer blow. Duleep placed a startling notice in the personal columns of *The Times*: 'I, the undersigned Maharajah Duleep Singh, having resigned all the property professed to me in England for the benefit of H. H. the Maharani Duleep Singh and my children, and hereby declare that I am no longer responsible for their debts or for articles ordered for them in my name.'[15]

Overnight the Maharajah relinquished any responsibility for his family. Fatherless, abandoned and broke, the children became near urchins, living in a shell of a house, surrounded by packing crates, in a city where their misfortune was the source of much gossip. Moreover, their mother was seeking consolation elsewhere: Queen Victoria was informed that the Maharani 'whether from despair or being neglected, had taken to drinking alcohol to an injurious extent'.[16]

Sir Henry Ponsonby was dispatched to find out if rumours about Bamba were true. He found that there was nobody to supervise the servants, the younger children were unkempt, and the Maharani rarely left her bed. The situation was becoming desperate for the family and Ponsonby sent urgent letters to the India Office asking: 'Who is looking after her and can the Queen take any steps to save her?' Maharani Bamba was trying to save money, he wrote, 'by the entire neglect of the health and education of her children'.[17]

Letters began to be exchanged between the Palace and the Secretary of State, and the India Office swiftly settled a pension of just over £6,000 a year on the Maharani. It was also decided that the two eldest sons needed immediate order and stability. To that end, twenty-one-year-old Victor was enrolled at Sandhurst Royal Military Academy, and Freddie, two years his junior, returned to Eton to finish his final year before going up to Cambridge.

It seemed prudent to remove Victor from London as soon as possible. He was fast developing a gambling habit to rival that of his father's; he had also run up huge debts during his time at Cambridge. By enrolling him at Sandhurst it was hoped that he would learn some much-needed self-discipline. After graduating, Victor was to embrace a military life under the benevolent yet firm watch of some dependable British officer, yet to be appointed. Ordinarily foreign princes were forbidden from entering the British Army, but Queen Victoria was willing to bend the rules for her godson. Victor's future, at least, seemed settled.

As for Queen Victoria's other godchild, eleven-year-old Sophia had been plunged into chaos with her remaining family. Hearing disturbing reports that the princesses were running wild in the overgrown gardens of Holland Park, the Queen refused to stand by any longer. Arthur Craigie Oliphant was chosen to keep an eye on the family and make sure things were not getting out of control.

Arthur Oliphant was a decent man with a strong sense of fair play, as well as extensive experience of the civil service in India. It was a peculiar irony that he was the son of the well-respected Colonel James Oliphant, former director and chairman of the East India Company. Oliphant senior, the figurehead of the very organisation that had swallowed great swathes of India, had been appointed by Queen Victoria to attend to the young Duleep Singh when he first arrived in England, and served the Maharajah as equerry and comptroller of the household at Elveden. Now, it was left to Oliphant's son, Arthur, to save the Duleep Singh children from their wretched fall from grace.

Not only was Arthur delighted to carry on the family association with the Duleep Singhs, he was also happy to act as an amateur spy. Every word the children uttered about their father was reported back to the government, and the contents of letters passing between Victor and Duleep in France were also conveyed. Oliphant's assessment was damning: 'From the letters I have had from the Maharajah, all of which you have seen and are at your disposal, and from all the circumstances which have come to my knowledge about him, I have long since arrived at the conclusion that he is a traitorous and dangerous lunatic.'[18]

Lord Henniker, Queen Victoria's lord-in-waiting, was formally named the children's legal guardian, but it was Arthur Oliphant who took care of their day-to-day needs. He made sure there was food in the pantry, furniture in the rooms and linen in the cupboards at 53 Holland Park. In a letter sent to Sir Henry Ponsonby in July 1887, Arthur expressed relief that his father had not lived to see the predicament faced by a once illustrious family: 'It is all a sad sad story, and I feel most thankful that my dear old Father was not spared to know him [the Maharajah] as he is.'[19] Oliphant had little or no help from Bamba, on whom drink and depression were taking a toll. The Maharani had been particularly devastated by a terrible experience at Queen Victoria's Golden Jubilee celebrations that summer.

Victoria marked the fiftieth anniversary of her accession with a magnificent banquet. The guest list included fifty kings and princes from around the world and the following day the sixty-eight-year-old monarch participated in a procession that, in the words of the American writer Mark Twain, 'stretched to the limit of sight in both directions'.[20] Later, she attended a thanksgiving service in Westminster Abbey. Victoria made sure that the Maharani was prominent on the guest list. However, when Bamba arrived in the abbey to take her seat for the service she found it had already been occupied by someone who would not move, and she was forced to withdraw in embarrassment. Some of those who had watched her leave hissed at her as she passed. They called her the 'thief's wife', and her face flushed hot with the humiliation.[21] The Maharani Bamba would never venture out in public again.

Moved by the wretched plight of his charges, Oliphant quickly decided that the place which offered Sophia, her siblings and their broken mother the greatest stability was not London but rather his own home in the coastal town of Folkestone in Kent. The house at 21 Clifton Street with its cheerful white façade was just moments from the sea. With large sash windows and broad bays letting the sunlight stream in, it seemed the perfect place for the family to regroup and convalesce in private. The first thing Arthur Oliphant did was try to recall the children's nanny, Miss Date. After many years of service at Elveden and having returned to the children in London, she had quit the unhappy home at 53 Holland Park when the Maharani's behaviour became too erratic to cope with. She had since taken a position looking after the children of the Crown Princess Gortschakoff in Russia. Arthur Oliphant begged the governess to come back to England to take care of the Duleep Singh children again. To his delight she agreed, but shortly before setting off on the trip home, Miss Date contracted a virus. She died before even setting foot on the boat back to England.

Oliphant sheltered the children from the shocking news for many months, until he felt they were less fragile. The death of Miss Date dealt a terrible blow to his plans for the children's rehabilitation, of which there was clear and urgent need. Neglect had left its mark. As Arthur wrote in one of his reports to the Palace, the princesses 'did not know how to walk like young ladies';[22] 'the poor Maharani was also going to give them lessons in calisthenics, and always going to take them to church, but these intentions, as indeed all others, were never carried out . . . [The] poor little things have had no play with other children for a long time . . . [They are] too shy to touch the piano . . . they have never had books.'[23]

Queen Victoria began to show much more of an interest in her goddaughter. She sent Sophia gifts, including a miniature dinner service and cutlery fit for a toy banquet.[24] On another occasion, she sent her a large doll with a fine bisque face and exquisitely painted features. It was more of a masterpiece than a plaything. 'Little Sophie', as she came to be known, had real blonde human hair glued to her china head, delicately blushing cheeks, rosebud lips, bright blue eyes with distinct black pupils and long, curling lashes.[25] Such was the detail that even the cuticles of the doll's toenails were painted with a light pink blush and her lifelike porcelain ears were pierced by tiny jewelled earrings. But what made Little Sophie truly special to Princess Sophia were the accessories she came with. Queen Victoria sent the finest Parisian outfits for the doll: costumes for the opera, grand balls and glamorous garden parties; jewels, kid gloves, hats and tiny opera glasses, as well as a fine leather valise in which to keep them. The stitching on the doll's clothes was perfect, right down to her bloomers and corsets, and in a splendid added detail which would have delighted any young girl of Sophia's age, Little Sophie even had her own little china-faced doll to play with. Sophia would treasure the gift all her life.

Queen Victoria sent the toys to amuse and distract her young goddaughter from her awful reality, but also to inculcate her with some refinement. As Arthur Oliphant reported, the older girls were becoming increasingly feral under the neglect of their mother, and were dragging Sophia down with them. Arthur enlisted the services of tutors and governesses to 'civilise' Sophia and her sisters. They included a drill sergeant from Thorncliff army camp, who taught the princesses how to walk with decorum by marching them up and down the house[26] and a tutor who attempted to show the princesses how to curtsy and sit correctly.[27] Finally there was a German governess engaged; the kindly young Lina Schaeffer would become a particular favourite with the children.

It seemed as if some structure and semblance of normality was being brought into the turbulent lives of the young Duleep Singhs. But then, as so often in Sophia's life, events threw her into chaos once more.

Industrialisation, the very thing that was bringing Victorian England power and prosperity, was also killing it with dirt and disease. London's population had surged from one million in 1800 to six million by the dawn of the twentieth century. The picture was similar in towns and cities up and down the country. Everywhere people crammed into substandard housing in order to feed the hunger for labour in the mines, mills and factories. Overflowing drains and cracked pipes leaking sewage were commonplace. Human excrement and the corpses of decaying animals were left to mingle with the mud of the unpaved, slimy streets. A public health catastrophe was inevitable. Disease favoured those living in the slums, but it had no regard for rank and social standing. Rivers running through quarters of poverty and affluence alike were sluggish with tonnes of raw sewage. As a result, contagious diseases like cholera, typhus, influenza and typhoid fever laid waste to towns and cities. As early as 1843 it was estimated that for every person who died of old age or violence, eight died of specific diseases caused by the lack of sanitation.[28] Thanks to the new rail networks, the disease could spread to the very edges of England.

In Folkestone, during the first week of September 1887, Sophia began to feel unwell. At first the symptoms were fairly mild, a slightly raised temperature, an intermittent cough, a general malaise. The sea air of the Oliphants' home ought to have given the young girl rosy cheeks and rude health, yet she was pale, exhausted and suffering constant throbbing headaches. Her joints ached and her stomach was upset and sore. The princess's condition deteriorated rapidly and by 17 September, Sophia was diagnosed as being in the full grip of typhoid fever, the illness which had killed Queen Victoria's husband, Prince Albert, some twenty-six years before.

Sophia drifted in and out of delirium, passing from periods of calm exhaustion to serious agitation, numerous times a day. Tender rose-coloured spots appeared on her chest and abdomen and she found it difficult to swallow or keep down water. Slowly she lost awareness of her surroundings as she battled dehydration. When the news of her goddaughter's illness reached the Queen, she sent her own physician, Dr William Gull. It was a generous gesture but a futile one, since by the time the doctor reached Folkestone events had already taken a tragic, if unexpected, turn.

On 17 September, Maharani Bamba, distraught and weeping, stayed by her daughter's bedside all night, praying for her fever to break. As Sophia drifted in and out of consciousness, her mother chose to dismiss the other servants and tend to her alone, just as she had when Sophia was a baby. It was a long and frightening night during which it often seemed as if her child might die.

There is no record of who came into Sophia's bedroom first the next morning, although the Queen received a comprehensive report of the scene that was discovered. Sophia, whose breathing had been so laboured the night before, was sleeping peacefully, her fever having broken at some point in the night. On the floor by her bed lay her mother, cold and dead. Sometime during her long vigil, the Maharani Bamba had collapsed and slipped into a coma. She had stopped breathing just before dawn. Dr Gull reported that the Maharani had suffered comprehensive renal failure brought on by an acute case of diabetes, exacerbated by her drinking and the stress of her daughter's illness.

When Queen Victoria received a telegram at Balmoral later that same day informing her of the tragedy, the Duleep Singhs were already foremost in her mind, thanks to the Maharajah's latest public denunciation of the British sovereign's reign. The Queen noted in her journal for that day: 'The unfortunate Maharajah Duleep Singh has published a most violent, crazy letter, speaking of being "the lawful Sovereign of the Sikhs" and "England's implacable foe"!! Heard this evening that his poor abandoned wife, the Maharani Bamba had died quite suddenly yesterday. How terrible for the poor children, who are quite fatherless and motherless!'[29]

When Duleep heard the news of his wife's death, he wrote a simple one-line telegram to his eldest son: 'Heart-broken – can't realise – will write next week.'[30] But his words came as scant comfort to his 'childies', whom he had so resolutely abandoned, along with their mother.

Queen Victoria voiced the feelings of many when she wrote about the tragedy to her daughter, Princess Beatrice: 'The poor Maharani died of all the worries she went through and his desertion of her. The children (of whom there are 6!) – will be well cared for, have good guardians and allowance and kind people with them and I shall see them whenever I can. Would to God! I had done some more of late with the poor Maharajah! But really the family had become so large and so much to do about them that it was difficult to do and besides the extreme shyness of the Maharani made it more difficult to see much of them.'[31]

# The Old Nature Rises

Bamba was buried on 23 September 1887. Dressed in the black of mourning, and heavy with despair, Sophia watched as her mother was transported by a special train from Folkestone to her final resting place, a churchyard in Thetford, across the road from their old home of Elveden. Her coffin was borne on the shoulders of men who had until recently toiled in her husband's fields. Within view of the old house, in the shadow of the unprepossessing St Andrew's church, the Maharani was given a simple funeral. The engraving on her plain headstone read: 'In Memory of Bamba Duleep Singh, Maharanee. Born July 6th 1848 died September 18th 1887. The Lord gave and the Lord hath taken away. Blessed be the name of the Lord. God is Love.'[1] Sophia and Edward placed small bouquets on the coffin.

Duleep, whose ambitions had now taken him to Russia, did not return for his wife's funeral. Even though Queen Victoria let it be known that she would not have stopped him from paying his final respects, the Maharajah insisted he could not travel to the land of his mortal enemy. There was, however, another, less grandiose reason preventing him from leaving the shabby Moscow guest-house which now served as his home. Marini Ada was six months pregnant.

The Maharajah's absence was made all the more intolerable when on the very day of the funeral, the estate manager at Elveden received a letter asking him to retrieve Bamba's old saddle from the stables. 'Setting aside all political affairs for some time to come, I am going to indulge in some splendid sport in the Caucuses, the sportsman's paradise,'[2] he wrote. Presumably Duleep thought Ada might now get some use out of it after having her baby. He would later insist that his letter was sent before he knew of his wife's death.

Sophia withdrew completely into her own world after the death of her mother. Already weak from her illness, grief only drained her further. Her mother left behind a modest estate worth just over £2,000,[3] most of which had only survived Duleep's withdrawals because it had been invested in long-term interests.

Soon after the funeral, Victor and Freddie returned to Sandhurst and Cambridge and it was left to Arthur Oliphant to once again step into the parental breach. He gathered up Sophia and Eddie and took them back home with him to Folkestone. Although he felt no great bond with Catherine and Bamba, at sixteen and eighteen respectively they had nowhere else to go, so they too became part of his household. As Oliphant would soon explain to the Queen's private secretary: 'The poor children have really no friends to whom they are attached. They exhibited considerable pleasure when I told them two days ago that Mrs Oliphant and I had consented to continue to take charge of them, and they told nurse afterwards that they did want to express how pleased they felt, but that they did not know how to express themselves – I think perhaps their pleasure was because they were not to be handed over to strangers rather than owing to any feelings of real attachment to us. It is early days to judge of them, for they are not communicative or demonstrative.'[4]

Arthur knew that the Oliphant family home in Folkestone could only be a temporary residence for the children; the place would be for ever associated with their mother's death and it held a particular horror for Sophia. While a more suitable home was sought, he tried to handle his wards' grief with a light touch and sensitivity. He would suggest rather than demand, whisper rather than shout. It took many weeks to break through the children's defences, but finally in January, Arthur was able to deliver some good news:

19th January 1888

My dear Sir, I think Lord Henniker explained to the Queen the reason why I did not write last month. I am glad now to report for the information of Her Majesty that the Elder Princesses Duleep Singh have continued their studies with unabated interest and diligence. They, by their own request, have added Latin to their other subjects of study, and their Governess reports that they are making satisfactory progress generally. In music they are particularly persevering and painstaking. Princess Sophy and little Prince Edward, together with our own little son, have for several weeks past had a daily Governess to themselves and we could not desire that they should make faster progress. The dancing lessons of which they have had some 3 dozen are stopped for the present: They have all made excellent progress in dancing, and all enjoy it.[5]

The Oliphants' gentle patience was working. Not even when their brother Victor urged a stricter approach to his wayward sisters did Arthur resort to imposing more rigid discipline: 'Victor is evidently a little disappointed that Bamba and Catherine have not yet been persuaded "to do up their hair" and to adopt the wearing of corsets. Mrs Oliphant has of course lost no opportunity to put before them these little matters but she has not attempted to coerce them. We think it better to give plenty of time and the prejudiced views they entertain for these things will dissolve when we get them to associate with us and our friends and young people of their own ages.'[6] Only on one issue did Arthur insist on being obeyed. Sophia and Edward had a habit of sleeping with their bedroom windows wide open, no matter how inclement the weather. Arthur believed that this was the cause of their seemingly continual coughs and colds. 'The Doctor has at last positively forbidden open windows when there's a frost and a biting east wind,'[7] he declared triumphantly.

The scrutiny the children received under the Oliphants' care fitted wider Palace and government schemes very well; throughout, the Duleep Singh offspring were kept under careful watch. Early in their association, Arthur Oliphant had identified worrying traits in the elder daughters, which he reported in his letters to the Queen. 'I am very sorry to find,' he wrote, 'that they certainly hold some of their father's views with respect to his grievances and wrongs he believes to have been inflicted on him by the British government.'[8] All the children expressed resentment towards the country in which they lived and their hatred of the English. 'Even the youngest girl Sophy in her play with Edward and our own boy speaks of "those horrid English who would not let them all go to live in India, but stopped them at Aden"'.[9]

The 'old nature' that their mother Bamba had worried about in Sophia's infancy seemed to be taking over, and that Arthur could not allow. The desire to Anglicise the children was as strong in Oliphant as it had been in Sir John Login when he first took charge of Sophia's father as a boy back in India in 1849. Finally, after much careful consideration, it was decided the children needed a new start, a move to Brighton was approved. Arthur was convinced that the clean air, sea views, peace and quiet might allow the children to regroup without distraction. Only when he could promise them a life away from Folkestone and its terrible memories did he finally break the news that their beloved nanny Miss Date was never to return. The older sisters wept bitterly at the news of her death, but Sophia registered no response. Grief, it seemed, had numbed her.

Once Brighton was established as their new home, Arthur Oliphant felt the best way to rehabilitate his youngest charges was to plunge them into their education and separate them from the older girls. Sophia would be sent to a nearby girls' day school, run by a kindly but strict mistress, Miss Parkinson. Edward would be prepared for the rigours of Eton by way of a small boarding school, Sandroyd in Suffolk. Both Bamba and Catherine were swiftly enrolled at Somerville College, Oxford – an institution which had recently and controversially been established to educate girls to the same level as undergraduate boys – even though, at seventeen, Catherine was rather young to be sent to university. It was decided that the princesses might otherwise negatively affect the impressionable young Sophia. Arthur also hoped that the experience might humble the haughty senior sisters.

Sophia would need far closer attention and careful care. She was regressing into a pronounced state of infantilised insecurity. She craved physical contact with her family, sitting so close to them that her body was almost welded to whoever was next to her. In photographs from the time, she leaves no space between herself and her brother Edward. She also struggles to look directly into the camera, tilting her head down or else looking away to the side, as if attempting to disappear entirely from view.

The separation from her sisters, when it came, was as painful for Catherine and Bamba as it was for Sophia. Before the girls left for university, they promised to bridge the distance with regular and detailed correspondence. Letters from Sophia would provide great solace for them in the difficult months that were to follow, for at Somerville, Catherine and Bamba were accorded no significant favours. If Arthur Oliphant's aim had been to cut them down to size, it worked: photographs taken at Somerville College in 1888 show Bamba and her sister looking diffident. Visibly marked out by their ethnicity and their diminutive size, they struggled to fit in with the more assured young women who surrounded them. Catherine and Bamba looked and acted more like grave and suspicious children than students eager to learn.

Catherine found the change in her circumstances hardest to bear. When she was not with her sister, she spent her time with Lina Schaeffer,[10] the young German governess who had been appointed to look after them when they became wards of the Palace. Although her teaching duties were no longer required, Arthur Oliphant sent Miss Schaeffer to settle them in at university, and Lina rarely left Catherine's side.

Meanwhile in Brighton, Sophia struggled to keep up with her lessons. Her guardians were kind, but there was little intimacy, and she had few friends of her own age. After school, she would return to the Oliphant house in Brighton where tutors tried to polish off her rough edges. She was given intensive lessons in music, dance and deportment, in an attempt to transform her from an odd, ungainly child into a refined young lady. Despite her late start in learning, Arthur was delighted to discover that Sophia had a gift for music.

She made swift progress at the piano and pleased her tutors with her diligence.

With all her siblings now living away, Sophia found that she had somehow become the very centre of her family. All of her brothers and sisters would write to her, expecting her to disseminate important news to the other Duleep Singhs.[11] Sophia was relied upon to keep everyone up to date with family matters and to deal with the tedious practicalities that none of the others could be bothered with. In particular she became indispensable to young Prince Edward.

'Dear Sophy,' he wrote from his school in Suffolk,

Do not forget to send me the things I am going to ask you for, these are the things. My Butler's book, my music, 6 worth of pink blotting paper, one B pencil, two HB pencils, and a pile of India rubber, and send them as soon as you can and I will send you the money which I think the things will come to, if it comes to any more please tell me. I will keep account of the postage and everything else . . . I will write again soon. This letter is for Bamba and Catherine, give my love to the girls and Miss Schafer [sic].

I remain yours ever, Edward Duleep Singh.

I have begun my riding. Please send me some stamp paper if you can because a boy is collecting it.[12]

Sophia became the anchor in Edward's life, and matured quickly to live up to his expectations. At a time when other young girls' heads were filled with thoughts of storybooks, sweets and playthings, Sophia fretted about her eleven-year-old brother, who by his own admission, suffered frequent ill health:

Dear Sophy,

. . . I and the chap I sleep with are not going to church because we have got colds my cold never properly went and last Wednesday I got another cold.

The compasses which I exchanged with the stamp album were much better . . . I am sending Bamba the canary book so when it comes tell her that I sent it please.[13]

Despite his frequent bouts of sickness, Edward excelled at school. His report card showed the little prince achieving top marks for Latin, history and divinity.[14] His masters and the other boys liked him immensely, and when the warden was required to sum up the school's impression of Edward, he described him as: 'a hard worker and most excellent boy'.[15] With his place at Eton a certainty, the future looked bright for the prince.

Even Bamba and Catherine were receiving praise at last. Lord Henniker, who with Arthur Oliphant served as guardian to the children, was proud to pass a glowing progress report to Queen Victoria: 'They are very much improved in every way and are nice presentable young ladies. Catherine is a very pretty child and the eldest, Bamba, is nice-looking. I have great hopes that the management of them, poor neglected children, will turn out well.'[16]

While the Duleep Singh children began to find some stability their father, in contrast, was crumbling in France. The British spies who remained in his shadows were reporting a dramatic decline in England's self-styled 'implacable foe': 'Duleep Singh is constantly drunk. This pretender is now, under the influence of his wife, fast becoming a besotted swine . . . He is drinking very hard and his head and face is like that of the defeated prize-fighter from a fall while intoxicated.'[1]

His campaign to reclaim his throne had brought Duleep nothing but sorrow. After abandoning his wife and family, taking up with Ada and consorting with anti-British elements in Paris, Duleep had tried to pursue an alliance between the Punjab's Sikhs and the mighty Russian army. Intermediaries from Moscow had convinced him that together, he and the Tsar could pincer the British forces out of north India and trigger a rebellion larger than the Mutiny of 1857. Duleep trusted that his mere presence in Russia would seal the deal. He was wrong.

Tsar Alexander III was not interested in the Maharajah, and refused even to grant him an audience. Duleep was forced to wait for almost a year for an imperial invitation which never came. Such was the maelstrom of surveillance around him that he slept every night with a loaded revolver under his pillow. Duleep and Ada were stuck for months in the down-at-heel Billoi Bolshoi boarding house, a draughty and inhospitable hole situated close to the neoclassical grandeur of the Bolshoi Theatre. It was all the Maharajah could afford, having been robbed on the journey between France and Russia. Suspecting that Queen Victoria's spies had taken his belongings to thwart his mission, his resulting financial hardship gave him yet another reason to hate the British.

On Boxing Day 1887, in the bleak misery of the Billoi, Sophia's half-sister was born. Duleep's illegitimate daughter entered the world only three months after his former wife, Bamba, had left it. Her life seemed blanketed in destitution and frustration from the start. The Russian winter dragged on interminably and even though Duleep was living more modestly than ever before, his meagre cash reserves were running out. The Maharajah took so little interest in his newborn daughter that he left Ada to select her name. There was nothing regal about the resulting 'Pauline', but then, this child was not destined to live the life of a princess.

Her parents scraped together money for food and rent, relying on mysterious political connections to get them from day to day. They drank to while away the long hours of darkness, unable to visit the ballet and the great restaurants that surrounded them, and resenting the baby and each other for it. Despite Duleep's preoccupations, he did at least manage to give the infant her middle name. Perhaps Pauline Alexandrina was so christened in an attempt to flatter Tsar Alexander and get him to change his mind about meeting. Or it might have been a nostalgic nod to his old benefactor, Queen Victoria.

Less than two years later, a second daughter, Princess Ada Irene Helen Beryl Duleep Singh, entered the world in a different country but in similarly bleak circumstances. The names chosen for her came entirely from the streets of Lambeth, showing just how much Duleep had disengaged from his new family as well as his old. Irene, as she became known, was born on 25 October 1889 in Paris, after Duleep had amassed enough funds, largely borrowed from friends, to get out of Moscow. He had finally been forced to accept that Russian help would never be forthcoming and it left him bitter and angry. Although there may have been little joy at her arrival, Irene's birth at least was legitimate. Duleep had chosen to marry Ada soon after arriving back in France. With Maharani Bamba dead, there was nothing to stop the union. Ada was keen on the status and recognition that came with being a queen, albeit a penniless one.

The family moved from boarding house to boarding house, attempting to keep one step ahead of their creditors. The stress of living that way often drove Duleep and Ada into alcohol-fuelled rages. While they fought with one another and blamed the world for their hardships, the girls were forced to grow up without roots, play-mates or competent parents. Quiet, introverted and fearful, in their father they saw only an old tottering drunk who barely noticed them and a mother who seemed more interested in escape than giving them care. The girls shuttled between their parents like unwanted packages.

Ada was struggling in her own way too. She could neither bear her financial situation, nor her depressed and needy husband. Instead she chose to feign the life of a Parisian socialite, running up bills that could never be settled and attending parties where she was always the subject of gossip. Duleep stayed in his half-lit rented accommo-dation while Ada whirled around town without him.

In 1890, when Irene was just a few months old, Ada decided she could tolerate Duleep no longer. Gathering up her children and most of her belongings, Ada moved out to the western outskirts of Paris. There she set up home with a new and mysterious female friend, Madame Parraton, whom London spies concluded must be a Russian agent sent by the Tsar. Ada, her children and Mme Parraton moved into an expensive villa situated in Le Vesinet, an exclusive tree-lined suburb of Paris. It was left to the Maharajah to pay for both his accommodation and Ada's new address, despite having the reserves for neither. Hunted by creditors, he was forced to sell what remained of his ancestral jewels.

Angry and lonely, the Maharajah was often seen out, drunk and insensible by lunchtime. It was only a matter of time before Duleep's body began to fail. Having had to move his lodgings again, he was now living in a small attic room in the Grand Hotel at the heart of

Paris. On the morning of 13 July, as he roused himself to face yet another miserable day, Duleep suffered a stroke. Alone, he had no idea what was happening to him and in terror managed to stagger out into the Boulevard des Capucines, gesticulating wildly to passersby. When nobody came to his aid, he managed to hail a cab and slur directions to his doctor's house. Finding him out for the morning, he panicked and begged the driver to find another physician, 'so then drove about Paris in search of another – all this motion, aggravated the attack'.[718]

The second doctor confirmed Duleep's fears. He had suffered a massive stroke, paralysing his left side and leaving his functioning right arm to tremble uncontrollably. He could barely speak and could not walk more than a few steps unaided. Even the British government's spies began to feel sorry for him, and sent back reports filled with his frailty. 'He's on his last legs,' commented one, and it seemed the Maharajah knew it too.

Faced with his own mortality, Duleep was frightened, exhausted, and desperate to live out the rest of his days in some semblance of peace. Encouraged by his eldest son Victor, Duleep made the first of several furtive approaches to Queen Victoria's officials. He wanted to come home and he wanted her forgiveness. Letters shuttled between Victor, his brother Frederick, the Palace and the India Office, negotiating the terms of his supplication. If such a pardon were to be granted the Crown wanted nothing short of full and unconditional obedience from the Maharajah. Duleep agreed to all their conditions. After nearly two decades of defiance and crushing failure, he felt that God himself had turned his back on him. Summoning Victor, he told him to write what would be one of the most painful letters of his life:

> May it please your Majesty, my son Victor is writing this letter from my dictation – I have been struck down by the hand of God and am in consequence quite unable to write myself – I have been disappointed in everyone in whom I have been led to believe and now my one desire is to die at peace with all men – I therefore pray Your Majesty to pardon me for all that I have done against You and Your government, and I throw myself entirely on your clemency.

It seems to me that it is the will of God that I should suffer injustice at the hands of Your people. I can find no one to curse Great Britain and in spite of all her faults and her injustices God blesses her and makes her great and when I look at her, I feel that in fighting against Your country I have been fighting against God – I would return to England, were I assured of your free pardon. I am your Majesty's obedient servant.[19]

Duleep's once bold signature was reduced to a spidery, tentative scrawl across the bottom of the letter. This and Victor's subsequent petitions were considered for some months at the highest levels of government before the Queen became involved in the matter. Between the Palace, the India Office and Westminster it was decided that only a complete and public capitulation would facilitate Duleep's return to England. He would have to state his loyalty to Britain and repudiate any plans to unseat the Raj. He would also have to apologise without reservation to the Queen Empress and pledge his loyalty to her for as long as he lived. He agreed to all of the above and told his son he was longing to see her Majesty so that he might make an account of himself to her face.

While he was waiting to hear whether Victoria would see him, in August 1890, Duleep suffered a further stroke. Victor now pleaded with the British government to allow the Maharajah to come immediately to England, for at least a short spell of convalescence; the sea air might revive him, and his children could look after him. Permission was granted and the British watched carefully to see how this dress rehearsal for his (permanent) return might run.

Victor rented a house at 6 Clifton Gardens in Folkestone for the Maharajah, who arrived with his second family, Ada and their two daughters, in tow. Ada, it seemed, had grown tired of her fugitive life in Paris and was more than a little frightened of the domineering Mme Parraton. She too was ready to come home. Alarmed at the extent of their father's decrepitude, Victor and Freddie also moved in and engaged a nurse for Duleep's care. After a week or so, with some trepidation, Arthur Oliphant allowed Edward and Sophia to visit their father. It was the first time they had met their stepmother and little sisters, and Arthur did not record their reaction in his letters to the Palace. However he did note sadly that there was no room for Sophia and Edward in the house, forcing them to stay at a nearby hotel with their nanny.

Bamba and Catherine were away in Germany with Lina Schaeffer when their father arrived in Folkestone and it was decided that they should not be called back early for Duleep's sake. Instead, they would be allowed to see their father only when they returned to England in September, on their way back to Oxford. The prospect of even a brief meeting between Duleep and his elder daughters was causing concern in some quarters. Lord Cross, the Secretary of State for India, feared corruption. 'I do not want these young ladies to go to D. Singh,' he wrote to the Palace. 'They are much better off at Oxford. At the same time if their father insists upon it, I am not sure that we can prevent it.' The Queen noted in the margin of his letter 'Think we cd *urge* strongly agst it.'[20]

In the end, the Maharajah only stayed in Folkestone for less than two months. He longed for warmer climes, and in late September left for the spa town of Aix-la-Chapelle in North Rhine-Westphalia. The Romans had believed that the hot sulphurous waters possessed miraculous healing powers, and for centuries invalids had gone to the town in the hope of curing rheumatism, gout and scrofulous disorders.

Palace and government officials were satisfied: Duleep Singh was not the rebel king he once was, and the damage he might do to his children could be contained. They now set out to arrange the final part of his penitence, a reunion with Queen Victoria herself. The date was set for 31 March 1891, when Victoria would be holidaying in Grasse on the French Riviera. The Maharajah would be brought to her in order to apologise personally.

Queen Victoria was staying at Grasse's Grand Hotel under the name of the 'Countess of Balmoral'. Prince Frederick had already travelled from England in order to escort his father from Aix-la-Chapelle to the meeting place. With his decreased mobility and heightened state of anticipation, the journey was hard on the Maharajah. Queen Victoria in contrast was in a calm and pleasant mood on the day of his arrival. She had spent her morning among the flowers in the fabulous gardens of her friend Alice de Rothschild and after a pleasant lunch, she settled to receive Duleep in the small drawing room of the hotel. Victoria recorded the event dryly and factually in her journal, but in a letter to her daughter Victoria, the Princess Royal, Empress of Germany and Queen of Prussia, the Queen gave vent to her true feelings:

> The poor Maharajah Duleep Singh came to see me yesterday having driven over from Nice with his 2nd son Frederic. He is quite bald and very grey but has the same pleasant manner as ever. When I came in I gave him my hand which he kissed, and said; 'Pardon my not kneeling' for his left arm and leg are paralysed tho' he can stand and walk a little. I asked him to sit down – & almost directly he burst out into a most terrible & violent fit of crying almost screaming (just as my poor fat Indian servant Muhammed did when he lost his child) – and I stroked & held his hand, & he became calm and said; 'Pray excuse me & forgive my faults' & I answered 'They are forgotten & forgiven.' He said; 'I am a poor broken down man' & dwelt on the loss of the use of his left arm as a great trial. I soon took leave & he seemed pleased with the interview – but it was very sad –; still I am so glad that we met again & I could say I forgave him.[21]

Duleep returned to Paris, comforted by the meeting. Ada was less happy. She had been snubbed by the Palace and forbidden to travel to Grasse with her husband: Queen Victoria could forgive Duleep, but not the woman who had caused him to abandon Maharani Bamba and their children. The Maharajah promised Ada that better days were around the corner, and soon they would be able to leave Paris for England where life would be easier.

One of the very few visitors during that period was Raja Jagatjit Singh of the princely state of Kapurthala in the Punjab. The fathers of Jagatjit and Duleep Singh had been close confidants during their lifetimes, and it was out of deference to the old order that Jagatjit, who had managed to hold on to his minor kingdom, decided to pay his respects while travelling through Europe. What he saw so appalled him that he begged Duleep to hasten his planned return to London, where at least his grown-up children might minister to his needs. The Raja wrote later in his journal, 'he gives me the impression of a man whose mind is affected'.[22]

Victor and Frederick increased the intensity of their negotiations with the British government, helped in their cause when Queen Victoria let it be known that she had no objection to the Maharajah's permanent return. Arthur Oliphant, however, was alarmed at the prospect. Having worked so hard to settle the children and wean them off their antipathy to the Crown, he worried about the impact of Duleep's return. It was a fear echoed by Sophia's other guardian, Lord Henniker: 'I shall be very sorry for them if they have to return to their father's house, but, if he insists, I don't know that there is any course for us to pursue than that of yielding to his wish.'[23]

Oliphant was less sanguine about the situation. He set out to build a case against the man he felt was morally bankrupt and physically incapable of looking after the children. He travelled to Paris to visit Duleep himself and see whether he could be convinced that Edward and Sophia were better off in his care. Arthur's assessment was not promising: 'I was in Paris a fortnight ago and saw the Maharajah. He is still very weak and unable to walk much. I did not like the appearance of his face – he looked bloated and unhealthy. In speech he was very humble and grateful for all God's mercies; but he did not touch on the subject of his children, tho he was pleased to hear from me of their well doing.'[24]

Her guardian's fears notwithstanding, Sophia began to allow herself the hope that her 'papa' would finally be home. Christmas 1891 passed with a sense of great anticipation for all the Duleep Singh children, both in England and in France. Sophia, surrounded by her family again, felt enveloped and safe. However her sense of happiness was fleeting. Edward had to return to his school just a week after Christmas for the spring term. The Princesses Bamba and Catherine were also packing to go back to Oxford, and Victor and Frederick left soon after the festivities to resume their lives in the army and at Cambridge.

Alone in Brighton just two weeks after they had all been celebrating together, Sophia received distressing news. One of Edward's numerous colds had turned into pneumonia. In the days that followed, his condition deteriorated swiftly. Within a week he was sent back by the school, deemed too sick to be cared for by the nurse. Edward's health declined to such an extent that physicians advised him to give up his place at Eton.

By late April, Edward was battling a secondary condition as well as pneumonia. He had developed tubercular swellings in his stomach which rapidly increased in size and were filling with pus. Sophia looked on in horror as her brother sank deeper into feverish sickness. Just as Maharani Bamba had watched her deteriorate some years before, Sophia was powerless and could only pray for her brother. It was determined that the young prince would receive the best care at a private hospital in Hastings in East Sussex. There, Edward was placed under the care of Dr Cecil Christopherson, a young medic who was something of a local hero, famed for his skill in treating conditions like the prince's.[25] Christopherson battled valiantly to arrest the progress of Edward's illness, but not even he could save the stricken prince. He advised the family to gird themselves for the worst. Sophia and Bamba and Catherine spent all their time at Eddie's bedside, trying to keep him comfortable and calm as he drifted in and out of consciousness.

Once more the sisters had to rely on each other for support in the absence of their eldest brothers. Victor and Frederick had been called away earlier that same month to attend to their father, who had become seriously ill. Failing to find his miracle cure in Aix-La-Chapelle, Duleep had travelled to Algiers in the hope that the heat might restore some mobility to his frozen left side. No sooner had he arrived in the French colony than he suffered a major heart attack. Ada wired Duleep's sons urgently, telling them to come to their father's bedside. The Duleep Singh men were all together in Algiers when news of Edward's plight reached them.

As he later informed Queen Victoria, Arthur Oliphant was the one who broke the news of Prince Edward's decline: 'When the little boy's illness commenced I was commissioned to send a telegram daily to the Maharajah as to the little one's condition. I mention this to show that the Maharajah has some sort of feeling for his children, though not quite as much as one would like.'[26] Arthur was being unduly harsh. When it became clear that Edward's condition was terminal, the Maharajah found the strength to make the journey to England, reaching Hastings on 21 April 1893. His once proud and mercurial bearing was reduced to that of a distraught and shattered old man. Victor warned his father to hold back his tears in Edward's presence, so as not to scare the boy.

Duleep sat by his son's bedside struggling to contain his emotions. Edward drifted in and out of consciousness, wondering whether he was hallucinating when he saw his father by his side, his breathing laboured. Any joy Sophia might have felt at seeing her father again was made leaden by the cause of his return. After only three days, the Maharajah became too sick to remain by his son's bed. Rather than becoming a second patient for his family to nurse, Duleep returned to Paris and awaited the inevitable. The doctors had told the Maharajah that Edward would die in a matter of days.

Before parting, Duleep had quietly pressed a piece of paper into Edward's hand. On it, in trembling handwriting, he had written five words from Psalm 23: 'The Lord is my Shepherd'. It was perhaps a clue that despite his baptism into the Sikh faith, the Christian teachings he had received at John Login's knee as a boy, around the same age as Edward was now, still meant the most to him.

One week after his father's departure, thirteen-year-old Edward Duleep Singh, the most beloved brother of Princess Sophia, died. Sophia was at his bedside the whole time. The family decided that the best place to lay the boy to rest was at his mother's side. Sophia was forced once more to make the trip up to Elveden for the interment of another she had loved dearly. With memories of the Maharani Bamba's death still fresh in her mind, so it was that Sophia watched as the little coffin was lowered into the Suffolk earth where she and Edward had played in infancy. Sophia could not have guessed that in less than six months, the soil of St Andrew's graveyard would once again be churned by her misery and grief.

*　　*　　*

The Maharajah returned to Paris alone. The hotel in which he lodged was an airless gloomy place, which darkened further with news of Edward's death. When Duleep had made the voyage to France he had given up any hope of seeing his youngest son alive again. More than that, he had given up his own will to live.

The rooms he rented at the Hôtel La Tremouille were shabby and unloved. Just two minutes' walk from the Champs-Elysées, Tremouille's nineteenth-century exterior spoke of Napoleonic grandeur. Inside, however, the fabrics and paints were faded and a musty smell of neglect hung heavy in the air. Duleep knew that his mind and body were failing as he shambled about the cluttered suite. His latest heart attack had been devastating, and at fifty-five, his diminished mobility and lack of independence were hard for him to bear. The Maharajah now lived as a social pariah. His infirmity and humbled situation embarrassed those who had formerly vied to be seen in his company. Invitations had long since dried up, and very few of his friends either called on him or wrote. Ada, meanwhile, was in England, planning their new life with the help of her stepson Prince Frederick. Once again she had found it easier to leave little Pauline and Irene behind in Paris, in the care of their nanny.

For years the Maharajah had been able to close his eyes to the plight of the family he had left behind in England, taken up as he was with Ada. In his mind, his greater aim, the all-consuming obsession to reclaim the Sikh Empire, absolved him of any sense of guilt for his betrayal of Bamba and their children. Those dreams of the Punjab now lay in ashes, and over the course of the past twelve months he had seen with his own eyes how much his sons and daughters had missed him and how much they had suffered.

On the night of 21 October 1893, Duleep suffered a catastrophic fit in his bedroom. He remained unconscious and undiscovered until the next day. For hours he lay cold and powerless to move on the floor, until eventually his heart gave up. He died, quietly and alone. It was impossible to know how quickly death had come to Duleep. He was only found when the hotel proprietor, Monsieur Lafond, grew anxious that his chambermaids could not get access to the rooms. 'A physician was summoned without delay, but was only able to pronounce life extinct.'[27]

Arthur Oliphant managed to assemble a fuller picture of the Maharajah's last day by piecing together reports from the nanny, hotel staff, Victor, friends in Paris and the Reuters news agency. As ever, he passed on everything he knew to Queen Victoria:

> On Saturday the 21st (on the night of which he was taken ill), he had the two little girls to see him three times, and gave them each a hawk's bell which on other occasions they had been allowed to play with and then only when they were good . . . The elder little girl told her father that she had heard from mummy and was writing to her. The Maharajah told her 'to give his love to her mother and ask when she was coming back'.[28]

The Oliphants did their best to comfort the distraught Sophia. Having barely recovered from the loss of her mother and brother, she was plunged into grief once more. Those around her had seen how much she had looked forward to being reunited with Duleep and worried about the long-term effects on the young princess. Frederick and Ada immediately left London for Paris to arrange the Maharajah's funeral, while Victor, who had been visiting his best friend Lord Carnarvon in Germany, arrived soon after.

Queen Victoria wrote to Victor, the son and heir, to express her condolences and to reaffirm her commitment to the late Maharajah's children:

> I need hardly say how I like to dwell on former years when I knew your dear father so well, saw him so often & we were all so fond of him. He was so handsome so charming. But I will not dwell on the few after years which followed, which were so painful. It is however a great comfort & satisfaction to me that I saw the Maharajah two years and a half ago at Grasse & that all was made up between us...
>
> Pray accept this expression of my warmest sympathy in your heavy loss & convey the same to your brothers and sisters. Be

assured that I shall always take the deepest interest in the welfare
and happiness of yourself and your Brother and Sisters. Believe me
always, your affectionate friend and Godmother. Victoria R.I.[29]

Arrangements were made for Duleep's body to be brought back to
England. Before his death, their father had expressed a desire to be
buried wherever he might die, but his children collectively overruled
this final wish. His Royal Highness the Maharajah Duleep Singh
would receive a Christian burial in the shadow of Elveden Hall, next
to his first Maharani, Bamba, and their son Prince Edward. Ada
voiced no objection.

The Maharajah's body was returned on the midnight boat from
Dieppe to Newhaven on 26 October, and from there was transported
to St Pancras station where a special train took him, for the last time,
to Thetford. Workers from the old estate waited at the station for
their former master to arrive, their caps clutched to their chests. The
body was taken to lie in the very church which the Maharajah had
remodelled in happier times.

Early the next day, Sophia and her family followed on a train to
Thetford, and from the station they departed for the church in a
sombre procession of carriages. They were followed by Lord Camoys
and Colonel Stanley Clarke, distinguished representatives sent by
Queen Victoria and the Prince of Wales. In the churchyard Arthur
Oliphant stood inconspicuously in the shadows, keeping a close eye
on his youngest charge, wondering whether Princess Sophia had any
tears left to weep.

Before the Maharajah's body could be lowered into the ground,
the abundance of wreaths and flowers had to be moved from the top
of the coffin. A large and ostentatious cross, fashioned from white
flowers and woven through with violets spelling out 'ADA' dominated the pile.[30] In contrast, a beautiful and understated wreath
bearing the words 'from Queen Victoria' gave away little of the
intense feelings which must have stirred in the heart of its sender. The
Prince of Wales, despite his estrangement from Duleep, was more
emotional in his tribute. The note accompanying Bertie's wreath
read, '*For Auld Lang Syne*, Albert Edward'.[31]

The small church where Duleep's coffin stood was crammed with officials and starchy looking strangers. Most of those who had enjoyed Duleep's friendship in life did not attend in person, for even though the Queen of England had forgiven him, they had not. With the last of the dirt shovelled onto the grave, the British must surely have believed that their troubles with the Duleep Singhs were also dead and buried.

# Polishing the Diamond

As Princess Sophia was gently guided away from her father's grave-side, it seemed unlikely that she would ever take up the mantle of radical political dissent. At seventeen years old, Sophia was seen as a docile little thing, damaged by the tragedy of her short life. She had grown into an awkward-looking young woman. Thicker about the waist than either of her sisters, Sophia had neither the fine-boned elegance of Catherine, nor the full pouting mouth and fiery glint which made Bamba such a fierce beauty. The only vaguely rebellious thing about Sophia was her long hair, with curls that constantly escaped from numerous pins and combs. Her teeth had shifted during her adolescence, leaving her with a slight overbite which she exacerbated with her strained, tight smiles. She spoke little and was barely audible when she did.

Once again, on Palace instructions, the princess's guardians attempted to build up her confidence. Her deportment lessons increased in frequency and tutors who had worked with members of European royalty were drafted in to work on her posture. Yet despite their efforts, and her natural talent for music and dance, Sophia spent most of her adolescence hating the attention. She spoke in a breathy, alto voice, barely audible to all but those close to her. When having her photograph taken, she preferred not to look into the lens at all, instead standing in profile so that she could gaze off into some middle distance. Acutely sensitive about her appearance, Sophia looked to her sisters for reassurance, sending them portraits for their approval and never truly believing them when they called her beautiful.

Yet, much as it had for her mother, Sophia's charm and fragility endeared her to all who came into contact with her, whereas the other Duleep Singh princesses rarely failed to provoke irritation. Even before the Maharajah's death, Sophia's eldest sister Bamba had been causing much annoyance with her constant questions about the type of treatment she might expect when she reached the age of majority. At twenty-one, unmarried women in England could inherit money and property; though it was not yet clear what remained of Duleep's estate for her to inherit, Bamba demanded that her legal position be acknowledged.

Even though Princess Bamba, like her sisters, was entirely dependent on the British government, she found it impossible to moderate her imperious tone. She made it clear that she expected all titles and honours to be bestowed upon the Duleep Singh princesses, as befitted the heirs to the Sikh Kingdom. At no point did she acknowledge that they would be destitute without Queen Victoria's patronage, who she also referred to as Mrs Fagin, like her father before her.[1]

While Sophia showed polite gratitude, Bamba fired off questions to the Palace and to the India Office in so brusque a manner that she succeeded in alienating all who had power over her. Sir Henry Ponsonby, the Queen's private secretary, was particularly exasperated and referred the matter up to the sovereign herself. In 1889 he wrote: 'Princess Bamba is 20 and may wish to go to Court next year. Should she be allowed to come? And as a Princess? She is very particular to be so treated.'[2] Her other guardian, Lord Henniker, vetoed the move: 'I do not think that Bamba should come out in society yet. She is 20 but her early training makes it difficult for her to join in general society at present i.e. she is very young for her age.'[3]

The snub came as a bitter blow to the headstrong princess. With her letters either ignored by the government or rebuffed by her guardians, Bamba was left in limbo, which only succeeded in souring her disposition further. It was only in 1893, when Sophia, the Queen's clear favourite, neared the age of her own majority that there seemed any impetus to decide the future of the Duleep Singh princesses. Despite her advisers' reservations, Queen Victoria ordained that the time was right to settle the girls' financial *and* social positions. Their father's transgressions notwithstanding, the girls would be granted a full debut in society alongside the highest members of British aristocracy. The ritual of 'coming out' was considered integral to the establishment of a young woman's place in society, and usually took place when a girl turned eighteen, rather than twenty-five and twenty-three, as in the case of Sophia's sisters.

Meanwhile, the India Office found itself being pressured gently by Sir Henry Ponsonby to decide how much money the princesses might be given to live on. Sir Owen Tudor Burne, a former private secretary to the Viceroy of India, laid out the amounts the Government of India was willing to settle on the children: 'The five girls, (Bamba, Katherine, Sophy and two of the second family) will receive about £22,000 each, or about £600 a year each, and the two elder ones £10,000 on marriage. As to the three elder girls, the trustees remain on a special arrangement until 31 March 1894 . . . and the India Office will pay their expenses up to that date, as a gift, to the extent of £800. After that, they will have to make their own arrangements on their own income which they receive from the dates of the MR's death (22 Oct 1893).'[4]

Sir Owen made it clear that the amounts were non-negotiable and any calls for greater generosity would be met with resistance: 'On the whole, this is, I think, a fair provision for all; more than I expected, and as much as can be done without a strong remonstrance from the Indian Govt!'[5] Burne's letter also revealed the date Bamba, Catherine and Sophia would be free of their guardians. It was a time the two eldest sisters looked forward to with impatience. However, at seventeen years of age, and never having experienced any degree of autonomy before, Sophia found the prospect daunting. The Oliphants had always shown her great kindness, and she in turn had fond feelings for them. There was never an explanation from the Government of India why Sophia would not, like her sisters, be provided with a dowry; perhaps it just implied that she was more anglicised than the others and unlikely therefore to settle with an Eastern potentate.

The financial settlement also placed Ada's children on a largely equal footing with Sophia, Catherine and Bamba, however they were only referred to as 'the two of the second family'. Moreover, seeing Pauline and Irene mentioned in the same legal document forced Sophia and her siblings to confront their own relationship with Ada's daughters. The princesses responded in very different ways. Bamba was resentful, having over the years come to the conclusion that Ada was a British spy, sent to wreck her parents' marriage and spoil her father's chances of regaining his throne. Catherine, on the other hand, maintained a cool indifference, her mind on affairs of the heart. Her intense friendship with Lina Schaeffer had become the only thing that mattered to her, and she longed to escape England for ever, for a life with Lina in Germany.

Of the three girls, Sophia alone welcomed her half-sisters. In the thrall of Bamba when it came to most issues, in this matter she was fiercely independent. Although Pauline and Irene were just six and four and still living in Paris with their mother, Sophia wrote them friendly letters. Victor already enjoyed a good relationship with Ada, though showed no interest in her children. Only Freddie shared Sophia's warmth, welcoming the girls and Ada into his life and his home, whenever they wished to stay.

Freddie and Victor were far better placed to lend support in family matters. The Maharajah's sons had received more favourable financial settlements than the girls, who had been granted just £600 a year to live on, compared to Victor who had been promised £5,000 a year and Freddie £2,000.[6] Whereas Victor frittered away much of his fortune on gambling and high living, Freddie opted for a quieter life and would become known for his philanthropy and loyalty to the throne. He offered Ada help to find a home in England and would remain a source of financial stability for her and the children throughout their lives.

Ada opted to stay on in France for a few years more. She had no reason to hurry back. Besides, the glamour of the single life in Paris and the draw of the roulette tables of Monaco were too appealing. The modest India Office settlement and the access to more generous funds for her daughters provided an independent income at last. For the first time in her life, Ada was solvent and free and she wanted to celebrate. Her young daughters had no choice but to remain with her. Throughout their time together in France, Irene would later recall, she never received the maternal attention she so desperately craved.

Back in England, Sophia decided to face her future away from the Oliphants head-on. The months in Brighton passed in a crucible of intense study. The princess threw herself into her academic lessons and tutorials with more zeal than ever before, and as the date of her formal release from her guardians – 31 March 1894 – approached, she began to walk with a straighter back, and sit with her chin up. Sophia learned to override her shyness and make polite conversation, never saying anything that might cause offence but always having something to say. She learned to be proud of her musical abilities and friends found they could at last persuade her to play the piano at small social gatherings. It might have been fear of the impending coming-out ceremony which drove her to improve herself, or the realisation that her transition to adulthood was likely to prove a jarring experience. Whatever the motivation, she practised everything she turned her hand to and worked with extreme diligence. Reports from the princess's headmistress were more than satisfactory and all who met her remarked on her metamorphosis.

As Sophia was being congratulated for her success, Bamba and Catherine were graduating from university with far less fanfare. Arthur Oliphant informed the Palace in his final report on his charges: 'I feel sure that the Queen will like to hear of Princess Catherine Duleep Singh having taken honours (III Class, in French and German) at the close of her Oxford career. Princess Bamba (the elder of the two) has not been successful I am sorry to say. As these Princesses are no longer under our charge, I fear my reports for the information of Her Majesty must now cease.'[7]

Although he was, as ever, lukewarm in his appraisal of the senior sisters, Oliphant betrayed a degree of pride when relating news of 'Sophy'. 'I am glad to say she is doing very well at Brighton,' he reported. 'She will terminate her four years stay at Miss Parkinson's school there next month – and her desire is to go to reside in a German family for six months to complete her education in German.'[8]

This last was a surprising wish, since Sophia had shown very little sign of an adventurous spirit before. As her family and guardians knew only too well, the princess enjoyed nothing more than staying at home, finding strangers too taxing and her shyness too difficult to overcome. But Catherine's close relationship with Miss Schaeffer had made Sophia curious about Lina's homeland and she wanted to see it with her own eyes. Neither Sophia nor Bamba ever reproached Catherine for her unconventional closeness with their governess. Lina and Catherine were devoted to one another; Sophia would later describe their relationship as 'intimate'.[9] Catherine found her little sister's acceptance especially valuable, as Sophia was usually far from tolerant when it came to matters of sexuality. Any hint of impropriety made her feel prudish and uncomfortable. She, like her mother, had a deeply Christian view of the world, and personally showed no interest in men or women at the time. Permission to visit Germany for a long stay was granted by the princesses' guardians and, with the encouragement of the Palace, a wider Grand Tour was suggested. The proposed itinerary would allow Sophia and her sisters to stay in Germany for four months, with a further two months' travel around the Mediterranean on their way home. They would visit Greece, Egypt and Italy, studying the classics and improving their knowledge of the world. The arrangement suited Queen Victoria, for it gave her valuable time to decide what to do with Sophia in the long term.

Arthur Oliphant dutifully made all the arrangements. He would not be accompanying the princesses and so Miss Schaeffer was chosen to act in loco parentis. Arthur also hired two ladies' maids to ease their journey, one of whom was the daughter of the old gamekeeper at Elveden, John Mayes. Mayes had been particularly loyal to the family and named his son after Prince Frederick. His daughter, Margaret, had grown up around the Duleep Singh princesses and was just as devoted as her father. With a practical head on her shoulders, she seemed a wise choice.[10]

The romance of the European Grand Tour gripped Sophia completely. The women began their travels in Holland which, according to Margaret Mayes, in the meticulous yet discreet diary she kept of the trip, they found flat and boring.[11] They then made their way to Germany which they loved. Lina Schaeffer revelled in showing them the very best of the country, and inspired them with tales of history and folklore. Italy enchanted the princesses, and they devoured the delights of Florence, Naples, Milan and Venice. Sophia, in particular, soaked up the culture greedily. Her tutors had taught her about music and art, she had learned to paint and play instruments, but she had never until now *felt* how these skills might connect to human emotion. When she went to Egypt, the birthplace of her mother, she saw the Sphinx and the Pyramids, became lost in the bazaars and was dazzled by the dance of the dervishes. Such rapid and intense experience of a wider world opened Sophia's eyes and broadened her horizons. She returned from the Grand Tour with an appetite for adventure which would never leave her. She also returned with no idea where she might live or what she might do with the rest of her life.

For Queen Victoria and her court, deciding the fate of Sophia and her sisters had been no easy feat. Their incomes had been settled but there was little hope that they would marry well and settle down with an English family. There were no British aristocrats willing to bring Indian brides into their homes, and royal titles and pardons notwithstanding, the Duleep Singh daughters were still thought of by many to be the progeny of a traitor. Cartoons which satirised Duleep's betrayal of the realm were still circulating. One depicted the Maharajah, wide-mouthed and dressed in a waistcoat embroidered with shamrocks, jigging while waving a shillelagh in the air. A Russian bear played the tune that made him dance.[12]

Realising the difficulty, Queen Victoria felt a particular obligation to provide for her goddaughter. Upon her return to England, Sophia was granted a residence at Hampton Court where, on the Crown estates, she, and Catherine and Bamba, could reside for the rest of their lives.

With its magnificent gardens and maze, Hampton Court had once been the pride of Cardinal Thomas Wolsey, the most senior cleric in the realm of Henry VIII. Building work began in 1514, and in the years that followed, Wolsey spent a fortune on improvements. However, when the Cardinal failed to persuade his Pope to grant the King a divorce from his first wife, Hampton Court was seized. Later, during the reign of King William III and Queen Mary in 1689, the palace was transformed from its previous Tudor splendour into one of the finest examples of baroque architecture in Britain, perching like a mini Versailles on the banks of the River Thames. Despite becoming the principal residence of the Crown for more than a hundred years, by the 1800s King George III had grown tired of the place. He decided to break with tradition and spurned Hampton Court Palace, instead dividing his time between Kew, Windsor Castle and his newly purchased home, Buckingham Palace.

As a result, Hampton Court was left empty and available for any whom the monarch wished to reward. The palace's apartments were divided and given their own separate entrances. These 'grace-and-favour apartments' were allocated to those who had done great service to the country. Since most died giving that service, more often than not it was their dependants who came to live at Hampton Court. By the nineteenth century, the rooms were largely inhabited by widows, unmarried sisters and daughters of heroes of the British Empire. Such was the scale of the place that by the mid-1800s as many as 300 residents lived at Hampton Court with a retinue of around 250 servants.[13]

When Princess Sophia was granted her grace-and-favour, contemporaries at Hampton Court included a certain Mrs Charlotte Slade,[14] cousin of the former Governor General of India, Lord Dalhousie, whom Sophia's father had despised. The apartments were also dotted with relatives of Hodson's Horse, a fearless cavalry regiment which was regarded as one of the bravest Britain had ever produced. During the 1857 Mutiny, young men carried messages over vast tracts of India, flailing their swords on horseback through areas swarming with hostile natives. Other prospective neighbours included the formidable Lady McPherson,[15] widow of the distinguished general Sir Herbert McPherson. He had also served during the Mutiny and was awarded the Victoria Cross for bravery during the battle for

Lucknow. Another resident was Mrs Constance Barrow,[16] daughter of Major Frederick McDonald Birch who had also served and been badly wounded at Lucknow in 1857. The sacrifice of her family had spanned generations and Constance's husband too had almost lost his life during the siege. Nobody would have blamed her if she were less than comfortable around Indians.

Sophia, whose father had tried so desperately to raise a Russian army to crush British forces, might have received a frostier reception had it not been for her status as the Queen's goddaughter. She moved in to her grace-and-favour, and tried to ignore the potential for ill feeling all around her. Sophia's sisters were not nearly as immune to the whispers. Even though the Lord Chamberlain included Catherine and Bamba's names on the lease, the prospect of living in such a place, amidst people who despised their father, appalled them. Although they moved their belongings into the grace-and-favour house, they had no intention of staying. Catherine had resolved to live with Miss Schaeffer in Germany and Bamba was desperate to get out of England too, although her sights would be set much further than Europe.

Sophia's grace-and-favour, Faraday House, lay opposite the front gates of the palace at 37 Hampton Court Road. A large private property arranged over four floors, it had once been the home of the Master Mason who had presided over the great rebuild of 1689. The Astronomer Royal, Sir Christopher Wren, had owned and lived in a near identical building next door. It was Wren's vision that had shaped the vast and expensive transformation of the main palace during the eighteenth century. The residences bore the flourishes of men proud of their craft. The façade of number 37 was divided into two distinctive halves. On the left side, five enormous rectangular windows looked out on to the gates of Hampton Court, while on the right, a large canted bay window nestled in cheery red brickwork. Large panes of glass gave it the look of a punchbowl.

The house had been renamed in the late nineteenth century after Michael Faraday, the great physicist who had lived and died at the address. Faraday had been granted the grace-and-favour in recognition of his work in the fields of electromagnetic induction and electrochemistry. For many years after his death in 1867, the house became a shrine for his acolytes, but even after they stopped coming, it continued to bear his name.

The ground floor of Faraday House consisted of a dining room and Blue Room, a large formal sitting room which looked out on to the palace. A spacious hallway bisected the house and led to a back sitting room, bathrooms, conservatory, informal drawing room and the more sombre Panel Room, which Sophia quickly converted into her music room, filling it with a variety of instruments and an abundance of sheet music. She was particularly fond of Liszt, Schübert and Ravel, and her regular purchases from Chappell & Co. Ltd, the music publisher on Bond Street, betrayed a romantic sensibility and advanced skill.

A central staircase twisted like vertebrae from the lower ground floor to the attic. Above, five bedrooms varying in size and grandeur took up the upper two floors. On the lower ground floor modest servants' quarters led off to a cavernous kitchen. At the side of the house, a narrow path led to a private mews with a four-bedroom cottage at the end of it. These served as quarters for the housekeeper and chauffeur,[17] and next door stood a small stable. From 1902 a small garage would also nestle next to the hay bales, large enough to park an elegant Morgan automobile.[18]

The 'motor', as Sophia referred to it, was more for Bamba's infrequent use than Sophia's. Bamba loved the speed and noise of modern automobile travel, whereas her younger sister preferred to ride her horse, a feisty mare called Kathleen, around town.[19] The horse, cart and footmen all bore the same Duleep Singh crest designed by Prince Albert many years before, a starred coronet. The motto that went with it, *Prodesse quam Conspici*, had been dropped by the sisters. Being inconspicuous at Hampton Court was not an option.

Sophia could never have afforded such a home were it not for her godmother's generosity. She was expected to pay a token sum of £4 10s[20] per year for the house, its gardens and additional mews buildings. In her neatest handwriting, on behalf of all the sisters, Sophia diligently made out cheques in six-monthly instalments to 'Number 1 Whitehall Place',[21] the Department of Land Revenues. This was the first independent act Sophia had undertaken since leaving the care of

Arthur Oliphant. Her second act was to fill the place with animals. Pairs of parakeets and brightly plumed lorikeets brought life and noise to the house, and an assortment of dogs brought mud and warmth. Her brother Victor, who had also developed his love of dogs at Elveden, helped his sister choose the best breeds. His extensive knowledge of raptors, passed down by his father, was less useful.

Sophia revelled in her new freedom. A high wall around the front of the house kept her far from the prying eyes of those who lived across the road in the palace, but she still had free rein to go where she wished in the grounds. To the dismay of some of the older residents, she took to walking her dogs through Hampton Court Maze.[22] Though falling foul of some of the palace's conventions, Sophia cherished the house's rich history, and became fiercely protective of one particular tree in the gardens, under which she insisted Professor Faraday must have had many inspirational ideas. When groundskeepers later threatened to cut the tree down the princess launched an energetic but ultimately doomed campaign to save it from the axe.[23]

With the question of Sophia's long-term residence and finances settled, attention was now turned to her introduction to society. The date for Sophia's coming out had been set for 8 May 1895, almost a year after she moved into Faraday House. Around 150 debutantes would appear before Queen Victoria over three days at a 'Drawing Room' at Buckingham Palace. The ceremony coincided with the Season, which ran from April to the start of the grouse-shooting season, 'the glorious twelfth' of August.

For the presentation each girl would dress almost as if it were her wedding day, and having 'come out' would find herself eligible for invitations to social functions with the most important families in the realm. Her Majesty's Drawing Rooms were among the most formal occasions in England's annual society calendar. Steeped in ceremony, and governed by strict rules of eligibility, the debutantes who attended were almost always young, aristocratic, and in search of a husband. Although Bamba and Catherine were much older than the other 'debs', and had no interest (or desire in

Catherine's case) in finding a husband, they entered into the spirit of the occasion for their sister's sake. Sophia's presentation at court was the most exciting thing ever to have happened to her. Only those formally presented to the Queen could receive invitations to court functions, parties, dinners and balls, and Sophia wanted to attend them all.

High-born ladies hoping to come out before the Queen required sponsors – suitable aristocrats who had already been presented at court. They would not only vouch for their debutantes but also become their mentors and chaperones. These distinguished women would teach their young ladies how to behave, and what to expect. The loftier the social rank of the sponsor, the better the debut of the lady in question. Despite the Maharajah's ignominious fall from grace, there were still a few important families in Britain who retained affection for Duleep Singh and his children. Victor's friend, the Earl of Carnarvon (who would later go on to discover the tomb of Tutankhamen) was one such. He asked his sister Lady Winifred Gardner[24] if she might sponsor Sophia and her sisters for their presentation. Their father had been a former Secretary of State for the Colonies under both Benjamin Disraeli and Lord Derby, and even though she was just a few years older than Bamba, at thirty-one years old Winifred had the pedigree and poise to coach the girls through their big day. (It was ironic that while she schooled Sophia in the importance of finding a suitable man to marry, Winifred's own daughter would, some thirty years later, wed a man she detested, the writer Evelyn Waugh.)

While Sophia and her sisters discussed what to wear and how they might fashion their hair, other conversations of greater import were taking place at Buckingham Palace. The Duleep Singh princesses were to be granted access to high society after their debut. However, the question remained to be settled, when it came to the state balls and banquets to which Queen Victoria was keen to invite Sophia, in what order would she enter and where would she sit? Such matters were not trivial, as they signalled the importance of lineage to the world. Lord Henniker dealt with these questions in the days leading up to their presentation:

It was settled some time ago that they were to be called Princesses, but not Highnesses. This was Her Majesty's decision, and if I may venture to say so, I think a wise decision. I spoke to a great friend of the family today who may be able to do much for the young people, and he says there is some difficulty as to precedence – how to send them in to dinner etc. etc. I said I thought they would possibly not mind one way or another, but suggested they should go after Duchesses, or greatly distinguished people. If the Queen would give me a hint as to Her Majesty's wishes, I will see to this being carried out.[25]

Yet Lord Henniker was wrong to believe that the sisters 'would possibly not mind one way or another'.[26] As the granddaughters of Ranjit Singh, their relegation behind duchesses rankled with them greatly. They came from a royal family that once held greater dominion and boasted more wealth than many of the monarchies of Europe put together. Even Sophia, usually the most sanguine of her sisters, felt insulted by the decision and would do so all her life. Nevertheless, the princesses were in no position to bargain and even Bamba managed to hold her tongue. In the run-up to their coming out, they had other preoccupations.

Lady Winifred explained that they would be expected to dress in white gowns, preferably off the shoulder with just the hint of décolletage. Their hair was to be pinned up and crowned by flowing trains up to twelve feet long. Regulation dictated that three white ostrich feathers should be arranged in the hair, as a tribute to the Prince of Wales, and long white gloves and white satin slippers should be worn. Young ladies were also required to hold bouquets of flowers and delicate white fans. The constant fear of tripping gripped each deb like a vice, whilst tightly boned bodices pinched the breath from their bodies. If the weather was hot on the day of a Drawing Room, which traditionally began at three in the afternoon, the whole experience would be an ordeal. Fighting fear, nausea and suffocation, the young debutantes were expected to navigate their way up a long staircase and through the crowded Throne Room where the Queen and her courtiers awaited them. There they had to curtsy.

A full court curtsy looks much like a ballet plié. With her knees bent, her feet pointing out and her back straight, Sophia practised lowering herself evenly and elegantly to the floor. Unlike ballerinas, however, she would be wearing a heavy and elaborate dress trailed by yards of fabric. Without losing posture, Sophia then had to bend forward from the waist, without listing, and kiss Victoria's hand. With her hands holding the fan and flowers, and her head dragged back by the weight of her long veil, the princess knew that her every move would be scrutinised by the most powerful courtiers in the realm. The room would be filled with Palace officials and dignitaries, making the air thick with heat. So much could go catastrophically wrong. Tales circulated of former debutantes fainting, or else disgracing themselves with gown slips, fan drops and wobbly curtsies. Sophia had more to worry about than most. As a goddaughter to the Queen she could not merely withdraw, as the other debs would, after her curtsy. Instead she had to rise gracefully and receive a kiss on both cheeks from Victoria. This honour added to the scrutiny and duration of her appearance. She would then be expected to rise and walk backwards without tripping, elegantly holding the flowers and the fan while a nearby attendant gathered up the ample train and placed it over her left arm.

Bright sunshine greeted the morning of 8 May, but it was not what anyone would call a lovely day. As Queen Victoria noted in her journal, 'the atmosphere [was] very thick',[27] and the humidity would only get worse as the day progressed. Unlike the debs, who had almost certainly spent a fretful, sleepless night, the Queen had rested well and had woken early to have a leisurely breakfast with her son Arthur and an assortment of her grandchildren at Buckingham Palace. 'Georgie's little boy was brought in. He is a fine strong, big child,'[28] she remarked of the future Edward VIII, who was coming up to his first birthday. Despite the presence of her loved ones, the Queen was not in the best of spirits. Her loyal and trusted private secretary, Sir Henry Ponsonby, had been ill for some time and with heavy heart Victoria had decided to replace him with Colonel Arthur Bigge, the future Lord Stamfordham. In addition to her sadness at losing a trusted aide, the Queen was also coming to terms with the loss of a much loved friend. As the *London Standard* informed its readers on 8 May, 'The Queen received yesterday, with deep grief, the news of the death of the Dowager Duchess of Roxburghe . . . one of her Majesty's dearest, most valued, and most devoted friends, for over thirty years a Lady of the Bedchamber.'[29] Victoria attempted to compose herself by walking among the profusion of flowers in the palace gardens.

Some thirteen miles away at Hampton Court, there was no sign of such serenity. The florist had arrived early at Faraday House to deliver three enormous white bouquets. An atmosphere of hysterical activity reigned behind the heavy front door, as dress fitters, ladies' maids and hairdressers from London's finest salons all fought for space to do their work. Lady Winifred, who had arrived early, attempted to calm the mounting chaos. Once Sophia, Catherine and Bamba had bathed, like all debutantes, they struggled to consume breakfast, torn between the knowledge of the unforgiving whalebone corsets and the thought that this might be all they would eat all day. With no refreshments served at the palace, they were unlikely to get as much as a glass of water until later in the evening.

Breakfast was dealt with quickly and without relish, as the sisters fussed over their accessories. Each had an ornate Chinese fan in a delicate cream silk, embroidered in silver and white filigree. All would wear pearls, although in very distinctive styles. Sophia opted for two chokers, one of which contained a central pearl the size of a gooseberry, sitting tight at her throat. Catherine and Bamba selected long, loose ropes of smaller pearls, which wound extravagantly around their throats and hung low over their bosoms. All three wore white satin shoes on their uniformly tiny feet.

By ten o'clock the three sisters were in their gowns, great voluminous dresses whose starched and embroidered silks billowed out at the waist and stretched down to the floor. Just as their jewellery and bouquets were unique, so too were their dresses: Sophia's was cinched tightest at the waist and a white rosette of silk sat on her right hip. In the last year she had grown in height and shed the remnants of childhood plumpness. Her waist was now the tiniest of her sisters and her arms and legs were slender and graceful. Sophia's dress was embroidered with beads and sequins which caught the light and made her shimmer when she walked. Great puffed and pleated sleeves which capped her upper arms were also ornamented by thin silken gauze decorated with white beading. Diaphanous fabric flowed down her bodice like water. Bamba's dress in contrast was made of heavier, more luxurious fabric and had exquisite cream embroidery. Intricate pleats of satin ruched across her chest and upper arms. Catherine's dress, the plainest of the three, had fine touches of delicate detail. Gossamer-like lace ran across her chest and onto her heavy white skirts. Silver embroidery and beading crept down alternate panels of her tight bodice, giving her the look of a mermaid disappearing into waves of white foam.

Each of the princesses had a high and ornate headpiece pinned to the crowns of their heads. These comprised great puffs of gathered lace, silk, ostrich feathers and fresh white roses, with long veils flowing down their backs to the floor. Their hairdresser, who had been at work since dawn, had neatly pulled back their long dark tresses, securing them in tight and tidy chignons which disappeared beneath a welter of white. Not even Sophia's unruly curls had a chance of escaping. Long white gloves stretched up over each of the girls' elbows and they practised walking up and down the hallways of Faraday House in nervous rustles, clutching their fans and flowers, attempting as much grace as they could muster in the clammy heat of the May mid-morning.

They had followed the guidance issued to debutantes faithfully, and as the photographer charged with capturing their image for an official portrait that morning revealed, all three princesses felt themselves beautiful. Sophia looked fearlessly down the lens of the camera, exuding confidence.

The rented landau which would take them to Buckingham Palace arrived just after eleven. Together with Lady Winifred, they crowded in, consumed by the voluminous layers. As the carriage clattered its way across London, Sophia knew she would have to sit like this for hours. Even when they reached the palace, the carriage would have to wait at the gates for a considerable time until the guests were allowed in. It was uncomfortably hot by noon and

Lady Winifred dabbed furiously at the beads of perspiration gathered on top lips and temples. The sweet smell of talcum powder mixed with acrid sweat as nervous stomachs churned. After what seemed a lifetime, Sophia heard the sound of the band of the 2nd Battalion Scots Guards drifting down The Mall. The music cheered and revived her, although progress to Buckingham Palace was painfully slow. The length of the wide avenue was jammed with carriages, horses and footmen, jostling for space.

As they drew closer, the Duleep Singh coachmen, dressed in their vivid livery of deep maroon with golden flashes, leapt off the landau and rushed to the police constables on duty at the gates. Producing their invitations from the Lord Chamberlain, they waited to be welcomed into the quadrangle. The gates opened on the stroke of two and the crush to get in began. Although Sophia had taken tea with the Queen at Buckingham Palace before, never had the great arches seemed so intimidating. As they entered, the guard of honour of the 1st Battalion Coldstream Guards lined the route, their scarlet coats and heavy bearskin hats making them every bit as hot and uncomfortable as the arriving debutantes.

The Queen's Mistress of the Robes, the Dowager Duchess of Atholl, waited in the Grand Hall beside other ladies-in-waiting. A frequent guest at Elveden, the duchess had been photographed with Sophia's mother at the staid tennis parties which the Maharani Bamba had come to dread. The duchess and the other older women who waited on the Queen were dressed in gowns of white, ivory or black. Pageboys darted between them in their uniforms of red and gold.

Sophia girded herself, looking at the crimson carpet of the Grand Staircase, which, in her tight bodice and heavy trailing gown, she would soon have to scale. She and the other debutantes were then informed that the Throne Room was filled with dignitaries: the day had been billed in the London newspapers as 'a Drawing Room which promises to be the most brilliant Royal function of the Season'. As well as the Prince and Princess of Wales, the Duke and Duchess of Saxe-Coburg, the Duke of Connaught, and the Duke and Duchess of York were all present. The ambassadors of Russia, Germany, Turkey, Austro-Hungary and the United States, along with the heads of twenty-two other diplomatic missions, had assembled round the Queen.

The afternoon was proving difficult for the seventy-six year old Queen too. Her health had been fragile for the last few months, and she found long periods of time in the public eye an ordeal. It was with a clear sense of relief that she noted in her diary that it was her last Drawing Room of the season.

Shortly after three o'clock Victoria entered the Throne Room accompanied by the Prince of Wales, his wife and children. The future King George V and his wife Queen Mary followed behind and took their positions around the monarch. The Queen looked tired and older than most people remembered her. The court reporter for *The Times* refrained from commenting on her frailty, instead describing her dress in detail: 'Her Majesty wore a dress and train of black brocaded grenadine, trimmed with lace and fine jet and bows of satin riband. Headdress and a veil of Honiton lace surrounded by a diadem of diamonds. Ornaments – diamonds and amethyst. Orders – The Star and Riband of the order of the Garter, the Victoria and Albert, the Crown of India, the Royal Red Cross, and the Coburg Family Order.' Slowly and painfully, the Queen made her way to the centre of the Throne Room and awaited the first of her debutantes.

Victoria later wrote in her journal: 'I remained for an hour, but could not stand beyond a few minutes.'[30] A chair was brought for her to sit in, which meant the debs brought before her had to stoop even lower than usual to kiss her hand. On the outskirts of the royal circle, silent and deferential, stood the stern and dark-suited figure of the Secretary of State for the Home Department, the Rt Hon. Herbert Henry Asquith. Next to him was the Rt Hon. H. Campbell-Bannerman, the Secretary of State for War.[32] When it came to her turn, Sophia walked as delicately as she could, through the heat and scrutiny of the room, to her godmother. Curtsying low, as she had been taught, Sophia rose and kissed her godmother on both cheeks. Then, without a word, she backed out of the room. Like all the debutantes who went through the ordeal that day, Sophia was carried out on a wave of euphoric relief.

Sophia's Drawing Room was clearly a success, for the weeks that followed were filled with one glittering engagement after another. Heavy, embossed invitations came in thick and fast. The parties and balls thrilled Sophia as she began to drink in the rarefied atmosphere of high society. In the years that followed, Queen Victoria made sure the princess was included on all important social lists, and Sophia's life became an endless round of balls, parties and banquets. Often she would be accompanied by her brother Frederick, who enjoyed the pomp and pageantry of such occasions every bit as much as his sister.

It was now that Sophia developed an appetite for attention; she positively revelled in the spotlight. In photographs taken after her debut Sophia no longer looked away from the camera but directly and challengingly into the lens. As the society columns began to notice her it was not long before newspapers were dissecting her developing sense of style. As the century drew to a close, Sophia became an integral part of the circles that had once embraced and then shunned her father. The princess spent her nights dining and dancing with the aristocrats of England and her days furnishing Faraday House. At first, Sophia relied on her brother Freddie's tasteful cast-offs for her furniture and décor, but soon she learned for herself all the places where a stylish young lady might procure the latest trends. She commissioned bespoke furniture from the exclusive shops in Grosvenor Square, and bought linen and crockery from Harrods, which had just opened its most impressive store on London's Brompton Road.[32] It was while she examined their wares that Harrods unveiled one of the world's first escalators. The experience proved so invigorating for some customers that they were offered a brandy at the top of the moving staircase to revive them after the ascent.[33]

Sophia bought her butter from the exclusive White's, the gentleman's club (which Freddie belonged to) and which prided itself on giving its coveted label only to the finest luxury items. Her drapes and silks came from D. H. Evans, an exciting new department store which had just opened in Oxford Street, and flowers came from Gerard and Pie Ltd, 'Florists to the Queen'. Sophia also ordered tartans and woollen weaves from the Highland Tweed and Tartan

Warehouse, which declared its royal patronage proudly on its masthead.

Desiring the best of everything, Sophia subscribed to the new breed of fashionable ladies magazines to ensure she knew what the best looked like. As a result her tastes became dangerously expensive. From the moment she was given rein of her own budget, Sophia began to spend vast proportions of it on clothes and accessories. She bought only the finest: her ballgowns and more ostentatious hats were designed and made for her by Marescot Soeurs on the Avenue de l'Opéra in Paris. It was an establishment with links to Mme de Pompadour, the stylish eighteenth-century mistress of Louis XV. Her day wear came from the 'Maison Valerie Urner' on the rue Saint-Honoré; gloves from a variety of exclusive and expensive boutiques around Paris; and her shoes from the American Shoe Company in London's Regent Street. Sophia spent a fortune in Madame Mole's boutique on the Avenue de Friedland, buying accessories and embellishments for her more dazzling evening creations.

Sophia also took great pains to ensure that her servants were the best dressed in London. Her maids wore distinctive uniforms of deep burgundy, with starched, snowy white aprons and caps. Her male servants wore tailcoats in the same colour, with embroidered gold and burgundy waistcoats and gold flashes at the neck and collar. All buttons, brassy and gleaming, were engraved with the princess's monogram, 'SDS'. Sophia also paid for her stationery to be printed with the Prince Consort's design of a five-starred coronet as the letterhead and her initials and address underneath. She had similar paper printed for both her sisters, personalised in their names, but omitted the Hampton Court details, knowing how little time they intended to spend with her there. They had already made clear their disdain for the place by moving most of their belongings to Freddie's house in the country.

Sophia's endless extravagances made her sisters despair, and they constantly urged her to wear clothes for longer than just one season, but it did little good. She had developed a taste for expensive furs and quickly acquired an impressive collection, including a striking long, white, fox fur coat with matching hat and muff. The papers soon began to notice and praise the distinctive style of the Indian Princess of Hampton Court. At the height of Scotland's social season, the papers toasted the 'brilliant success of the Northern Meeting Ball' and under the headline 'Some Pretty Girls' described Sophia's unusual use of traditional jewellery: 'Princess Sophie Duleep Singh was in white satin with a rope of pearls twisted in her hair.'[34]

Sophia and her sisters possessed an impressive collection of spectacular jewels inherited from their grandmother Jindan, including pearls, large diamond rings and a number of ruby and spinel necklaces. Sophia also had intricate earrings and chokers which contained emeralds 'larger than scarab beetles'. An American publication went as far as to credit the princess among a handful of women who made the emerald a popular gem in fashionable society. If Jindan had lived to see Sophia's rise in society, she might have been struck by the irony of her granddaughter's situation. Sophia's gems, which now drew the gasps of British aristocracy, had been seized from Jindan along with the boy-king Duleep in 1847. It was only Jindan's stubborn refusal to bow down to the British which led to her ultimately reclaiming both her jewels and her son.

## PART II

# The Revolutionary Years, 1898–1914

# A Thoroughly English Girl

In the spring of 1898 preparations were under way for the marriage of Sophia's brother Victor to one Lady Anne Blanche Alice, the youngest daughter of the 9th Earl of Coventry. The capital was abuzz with excitement: the event would attract some of the world's most celebrated aristocrats and their very best jewels would be on display. The Princesses Sophia, Bamba and Catherine were to be bridesmaids, and Prince Frederick was to be the best man.[1] The sisters sifted through the finest items in their grandmother's collection, deciding who should wear the diamonds, and whose dress would best offset the emeralds and rubies. That Victor was at last to find some stability was a huge relief to them all, not least because the previous ten years had seen him lurching dangerously from one embarrassment to another.

Echoing his father's behaviour, Victor had spent a fortune on drink, gambling and doomed love affairs. In 1887, Queen Victoria had made attempts to turn her godson towards a more settled future by sending him to Sandhurst after his graduation from Cambridge. However, reports of his conduct thereafter had been lukewarm at best. After leaving, Victor had served as a lieutenant with the 1st Dragoon Guards, but his persistent gambling and astronomical debts had led superior officers to seek a post for him far away from temptation. In consequence the army had sent the prince some 3,000 miles away to Halifax, Nova Scotia, where the prince was made an aide-de-camp. Yet even in this damp and sparsely populated outpost of the British Empire, scandal was never far from Victor's door.

In Halifax, Victor had continued to carouse, playing high-stakes card games with his fellow officers and courting glamorous women. Then, while on leave in New York, he met a pretty American heiress and wooed her. Jeanne Turnure reciprocated and a romance blossomed. After a brief but intense period, Victor proposed, but any joy was short lived. Jeanne's father Lawrence Turnure, a prominent Wall Street banker, forbade his daughter to marry. The Indian prince had a bad reputation and little fortune, and so determined was Lawrence Turnure to end the affair that he went to the *New York Times*, giving them an interview in which he emphatically denied that there had ever even been a relationship between his daughter and Victor: 'He said that it was absolutely untrue, and that it had caused his daughter and himself much annoyance. The Prince had been his guest at his house in Newport last summer for a few days, but nothing had occurred to warrant any such report.'[2]

If Turnure had any doubts about wrecking his daughter's romance, by February he felt vindicated. An article appeared describing Victor as an absconding debtor who had escaped the authorities and was fleeing to England. He owed money for goods or gambling debts and creditors had been chasing him around the wastes of Nova Scotia for months. The sum he owed was around $50: 'This state of affairs has provoked much talk, and society is greatly shocked and surprised, as it was generally believed the Prince was well off. Among his unpaid bills are those of a tobacconist and confectioner.'[3]

Unable to pay for even his sweets and cigarettes, Victor returned to London in disgrace. During the seven miserable years that followed, he found himself mocked and unhappy. The prince borrowed money only to drink and gamble away his cash in a pattern of self-destruction. His English creditors also began to lose patience and bankruptcy loomed. However, just as matters seemed to be reaching the point of no return, a chance reunion with an old flame saved Victor from his trajectory towards total insolvency and disgrace.

Victor had enjoyed a brief entanglement with Lady Anne Coventry after his time at Sandhurst. The relationship had ended amicably after he received his orders to travel to Canada. Her father, the Viscount Deerhurst, who sat on the Conservative benches in the House of Lords, was a well-respected member of the British establishment and of the royal household. Much like the New York banker before him, Viscount Deerhurst was aghast when his daughter took up with Victor again, forbidding her to have anything to do with the prince. Unlike the American heiress, however, Lady Anne refused to give up so meekly. A gentle and refined woman with a halo of curly, strawberry blonde hair, Anne had a quiet strength. Despite her father's objection, when Victor proposed at the end of 1897, she agreed to marry him.

It was only thanks to the intervention of the Prince of Wales himself, who spoke to the viscount on Victor's behalf, that the marriage was finally accepted by Anne's family. The future King Edward VII felt a nostalgic obligation to the Duleep Singhs because of his friendship with the late Maharajah. Even though he had been unable to save his father, the prince seemed determined to do his best for Duleep's heir.

Sophia was overjoyed when the engagement was formally announced, having been immediately drawn to her brother's fiancée, who was only two years her senior. Struck by both her independence and her elegance, she found in Anne the role model she had been yearning for. Sophia began to emulate Anne's style and study her interests. Their friendship was made easier thanks to their mutual love of dogs, horse-riding and clothes.

The morning of 4 April 1898, the day of the wedding, was bright and crisp. By eleven the streets around Eaton Square in Belgravia were filled with onlookers, eager to catch sight of dignitaries arriving in their carriages. Among those who came to St Peter's church were Victor's old friends, the swashbuckling Egyptologist Lord Carnarvon, whose son was Victor's godchild,[*] and Lord Rippon, a former Viceroy of India. There were also representatives from the

---

[*] There were rumours that the boy had in fact been fathered by Victor.

de Rothschild, Albemarle and Buxton families, some of the most powerful aristocrats in Britain. Sophia and her sisters glowed in their gowns and jewels, while Freddie stood proudly at his brother's side. The last time that the siblings had been together in such a formal setting was to watch their father being lowered into the ground, six years before.

After the ceremony, festivities carried on well into the night. Champagne flowed, friends toasted the couple, and there was much dancing. The prize amongst the lavish gifts for the bride and groom was a bust of Her Majesty the Queen, sent by Victoria herself to grace the newlyweds' home. Since the death of Prince Albert, Victoria rarely attended such events herself, but the statue was a valuable personal gesture and seemed to cement the couple's good fortune.

With the sound of the effusive toasts still ringing in their ears, Victor and Anne set off for their honeymoon. Although he knew a trip to the Punjab was prohibited, Victor thought he might be able to show his wife something of his eastern heritage, even if it was from the distance of British Ceylon (now Sri Lanka). However, when they arrived at the port city of Colombo, they were prevented from disembarking. The imperial authorities had decided that having Ranjit Singh's grandson and heir anywhere near their Indian territories was too dangerous. Even the neighbouring country was too close for comfort. The episode was acutely embarrassing for Victor, who returned to England boiling with silent rage. To calm the waters, Queen Victoria invited the couple to a state ball at Buckingham Palace. Sophia and Freddie were also invited; Catherine and Bamba were not.

Princess Victor, Anne's title after marriage, soothed her husband's temper by reminding him what an honour it was to be so favoured by the Queen. She seemed vindicated when, soon after the ball, Anne was asked to Buckingham Palace for a private audience with Her Majesty. It was an invitation she was thrilled to accept, which made what followed even more distressing. The Queen told Anne that she must never have any children with Victor. She offered no explanation but made it clear that these were her wishes. She also strongly advised Anne to take Victor away from London and live

Princess Sophia Duleep Singh, *c.* 1900. A rare photograph of the princess in Indian dress. She preferred Western fashions.

Maharajah Ranjit Singh (*far right*), the 'Lion of the Punjab' and Sophia's paternal grandfather.

Rani Jindan, Sophia's paternal grandmother.

Sophia's grandparents on her mother's side: German merchant Herr Ludwig Muller and his Abyssinian slave mistress, Sofia (*far left*).

The submission of the Maharajah Duleep Singh to the British Governor General, Sir Henry Hardinge, *c.* 1850. Separated from his mother, Rani Jindan, the Maharajah was forced to sign away his kingdom, his crown and the Koh-I-Noor diamond.

Sophia's father, Maharajah Duleep Singh. His youthful beauty captivated Queen Victoria.

Sophia's mother, Maharani Bamba, whose name means 'pink'. From childhood she blushed at any attention.

Queen Victoria, who described herself as Duleep Singh's 'best friend' and took a maternal interest in him. She became Sophia's godmother and principal benefactor.

The Maharajah's coat of arms, designed by Prince Albert. The motto translates: 'to do good rather than be conspicuous'. Sophia would use the starred coronet above as her own crest.

The drawing room at Elveden Hall. The
Maharajah Duleep Singh wanted his Suffolk
home to look like a Moghul palace.

The Maharajah's profligacy led to squabbles
with the British government over money, and
increasingly he became a figure of fun.

The Royal hunting party, including 'Bertie', the Prince of Wales (*seated, sixth from left*). He was a regular visitor, as were other members of the English aristocracy. This photograph was taken at Elveden in 1876, just weeks after Sophia was born. The Maharajah's (*seated, fourth from right*) increasingly extravagant lifestyle was already driving him to bankruptcy.

Maharani Bamba and her children, (*from left to right*) Frederick, Sophia (*on her mother's knee*), Victor, Catherine and Bamba, outside Elveden Hall. Queen Victoria liked the boys to keep their hair long.

With Frederick and Victor sent away to school, Catherine (*standing, left*), Bamba (*right*), Edward (*seated, left*) and Sophia (*right*) relied on each other for support.

The strain of her husband's infidelities and financial difficulties took a terrible toll on Maharani Bamba. She took to 'drinking alcohol to injurious extent'.

Catherine and Bamba Duleep Singh (*seated centre front*) attended Somerville College, Oxford. Sophia's education was not such a priority; her guardians wanted to distance her from what was deemed to be the bad influence of her sisters.

Sophia (*centre*) and her sisters, Bamba (*left*) and Catherine, at ease on their brother Frederick's Old Buckenham estate. The three sisters would be devoted to each other all their lives.

*Left to right*, Princesses Bamba, Catherine and Sophia Duleep Singh at their debut at Buckingham Palace, 1894.

Princess Sophia (*centre*) with her half-sisters, Princesses Pauline (*left*) and Irene (*front*), and her stepmother 'Marini' Ada. Catherine and Bamba detested their stepmother; only Sophia attempted a relationship.

Princess Sophia surrounded by her beloved animals – her 'houndses' meant more to her than most people did. She became a champion dog-breeder at the Ladies' Kennel Club and was a formidable horsewoman.

abroad in peace.⁴ There is no record of Victor's reaction when his wife told him what had passed, but the couple never did have any children. There would never be another Duleep Singh heir to challenge for the throne of the Punjab.

Since her coming out, newspapers all over the world had been diligently recording Sophia's movements, often in minute and tedious detail. Publications such as *Colonies and India*, a weekly journal widely read throughout the British Empire, regularly commented on Princess Sophia's comings and goings. The observations made by the paper were bloodless and factual. Luckily for the more sensational newspapers, the princess had some rather unusual interests that appealed to their readership too.

A prominent article in the *Hackney Express and Shoreditch Observer* noted in October 1895: 'Cycling is certainly the fashion of the hour and it is generally annexing the royalty and nobility of Europe. It is patronised by Czar and Kaiser, the King of Greece and the King of Portugal, the King of the Belgians and the Grand Duke Cyril the Crown Prince of Sweden . . . The Maharanee Duleep Singh has just been completing a series of lessons in Battersea Park.'⁵ The newspaper may have incorrectly promoted Sophia to the title of Maharani, but they were right about one of her growing obsessions. From the moment she took ownership of her shiny new 'Columbia Model 41 Ladies Safety Bicycle' from the American Columbia bicycle shop in London's Baker Street, Sophia was hooked; and without knowing it, she was throwing in her lot with the burgeoning women's suffrage movement.

The year after Sophia purchased her Columbia bicycle, in America the suffragette, Susan B. Anthony, was so inspired by the growing cycling craze there that she was moved to state that the bicycle had 'done more to emancipate women than anything else in the world. It gives women a feeling of freedom and self-reliance. I stand and rejoice every time I see a woman ride by on a wheel . . . the picture of free, untrammelled womanhood.'⁶

Not everybody was as enthusiastic. Physicians Thomas Lothrop and William Porter argued that the practice of sitting astride a bike would damage women's reproductive organs,[7] and male undergraduates in Cambridge hung an effigy of a woman on a bicycle in the city's main square. Sophia either did not know or did not care about the controversy. She equipped her own bike with the very latest accessories, including a 'Vigor and Co. pneumatic anatomical cycle saddle', which claimed never to get hot, due to its V-shaped ventilated design. It was the saddle favoured by Victorian ladies of distinction since it promised to deliver 'no vibration, no shock', and presumably nor would it cause unnecessary excitement.

Soon Sophia became a poster girl for a growing and evangelical cycling movement. She was photographed with her Columbia 41 in Richmond Park, and in Battersea, where the most fashionable 'wheel people' tended to congregate. Publications such as *The Sketch* featured photographs of her posing stiffly but proudly with her bicycle, declaring that she was very fond of the outdoor life 'and simple amusements which are felt to be the birth right of every happy, healthy girl, be she Princess or peasant'.[8] The article went on to describe Sophia as a 'first-rate cyclist'.[9]

A publication called *Wheelwoman: the Lady Cyclist* regaled its readers with reports of 'famous devotees of the wheel'. Sophia featured in its pages, as did the writer Sir Arthur Conan Doyle, who was described as 'a good friend of the wheel'. 'He says:- "When the spirits are low, when the day becomes dark, when work becomes monotonous, when hopes seem hardly worth having, just mount a bicycle and go for a spin down the road, without thought of anything but the ride you are taking . . . I can only speak words of praise for the bicycle".' The magazine added as a postscript: 'Perhaps one of these days the famous storyteller will give us a modern romance of the road, with a wheel woman for a heroine.'[10]

Sophia was now as passionate about her bicycle as she had once been about her pony at Elveden. Cycling afforded her the life she cherished: fresh air and exercise, but also a sense of solitude and freedom. Her new craze caused deep suspicion among the so-called 'non-wheel people', whose objections were due in large part to the un-chaperoned liberty that cycling afforded impressionable young women. The thought of hot sweaty females ranging freely across the fields of England was abhorrent to many.

Influenced by sophisticated friends, Sophia also took up smoking in her twenties, a habit both Catherine and Bamba deplored, but one which Sophia embraced with considerable dedication. Predictably, the princess's taste in tobacco was expensive and exotic. Apart from the regular brands widely available in England, Sophia ordered large batches of speciality cigarettes straight from the manufacturers, Isherwood Brothers in Cairo;[11] the *yenijee* leaf of the Isherwood No. 5s had a resinous quality and gave off a sweet perfume which drove Catherine to distraction whenever she was visiting Faraday. It was not long before she was hopelessly addicted. Sophia seemed forever cloaked in the smell of Turkish tobacco and Verbena-scented talcum powder. In 1900, Sophia placed orders for 800 of Isherwood's finest cigarettes, spread across a period of eight months. By 1903, her order would swell to 600 cigarettes in one month alone.[12]

Another of Sophia's passions was driving Catherine equally mad. Slowly but surely, Sophia was filling her Hampton Court home with dogs of all shapes and sizes. Catherine disliked animals in general and dogs in particular, finding them needy, dirty and selfish. Sophia loved them, with a particular soft spot for the working breeds she had known at Elveden. Now through her sister-in-law, Anne, a successful breeder of exotic hounds, Sophia discovered a whole new world in which dogs were appreciated for their beauty as well as their utility: the newly flourishing dog show.

Late Victorian England was very fond of its competitive exhibitions. The phenomenon at once provided education and filled the increasing leisure time of the upper classes. The Kennel Club had been set up three years before Sophia was born, in 1873.[13] Anne had been exhibiting her award-winning Pomeranians at its annual exhibition since she was very young. Immediately competitive, Sophia decided to throw her hat and her hounds into the ring. At first she chose the Borzoi as the breed she would show. These large hunting dogs, which had been bred by the Cossacks to hunt wolves in the deep snows of Czarist Russia, had strong, independent demeanours, and were almost silent by nature. Weighing about a hundred pounds, and around seventy centimetres tall, they were almost the size of the princess herself.

With advice from Anne and Victor and the groundskeepers on their Norfolk estate, Hockwold Hall, Sophia found the best sires for future champions. She went about her ambition with organised zeal and before long was the owner of five magnificent Borzois. Almost immediately they started winning best-in-show prizes at dog fairs up and down the country. Sophia found the experience, and the sense of achievement, exhilarating. The press interest only encouraged her. Reporters loved the idea of an Indian princess challenging the nobility of England in their own competitions and beating them.

The princess and her dogs soon became regular features in illustrated journals such as the *Lady's Realm* and *The Sketch*. 'Princess Sophia exercises her dogs daily herself, and loves walking on the moors with them in Scotland,' one article described. 'She is devoted to any that are ailing, and nurses them most carefully if they get injured. The Princess, who does not care for motoring, is a clever horsewoman . . . Among her pets are also a French poodle and a fox terrier, and she much admires toy Pomeranians.'[14] The same article noted that Sophia was also 'fond of hockey', a sport which gave the princess another way of venting her competitive urges. The world's first women's field hockey clubs were emerging at the turn of the century, and Sophia was a keen and talented sportswoman. She competed regularly – one of the first ladies' hockey clubs in Great Britain was on her doorstep in East Molesey and the team regularly played fixtures against Ealing and Wimbledon.[15] Sophia revelled in her victories, sometimes drawing criticism from her siblings, who thought she ought to show more feminine modesty. Catherine once warned her little sister that she risked losing an invitation to Christmas dinner at Victor's house if she continued to boast about her sporting prowess.[16]

The timid girl who used to squirm before the camera was now an unabashed show-off. She would strike absurd poses for newspaper photographers, marrying her two greatest loves: high fashion and dog breeding. One photo feature showed Sophia seated on a bench wearing a long dress with elaborate collar and large flat velvet hat, dwarfed by her award-winning Borzois.[17] In *The Sketch* she posed with horse and hounds together, demurely casting her eyes to the ground while holding the reigns of a gleaming chestnut thoroughbred in one hand, and the leashes of four enormous dogs in the other.[18] Catherine found the whole thing preposterous, and teased her little sister mercilessly.

In time, Sophia switched her breeding efforts from Borzois to Pomeranians. The tiny fluffy dogs, with their fox-like faces and feathery manes, had been a favourite of aristocracy and royalty since the eighteenth century, when they were favoured by George III's wife Queen Charlotte. Queen Victoria had been the owner of a particularly small example, which had triggered a surge in the dog's fashionability and a breeding trend which saw the size of Pomeranians decrease by fifty per cent in the monarch's lifetime. Some dogs achieved celebrity status in their own right. Former prime minister William Gladstone was often photographed with a beloved black pom called 'Petz', which travelled with him everywhere, even on state visits. The dog's death in 1898 made national headlines. Gladstone died a few weeks later.

In her efforts to rear the perfect Pomeranian, Sophia attracted plaudits and awards, and was soon regarded as being among the best breeders in the country. Of all her spoilt and pampered dogs, a spirited black pup named Joseph captured her heart the most, and every prize in the national Pomeranian categories. Sophia documented Joe's lineage, and treated her little dog like a prince, despite the derogatory names of his ancestors: in handwritten family trees, which she kept locked away among her most treasured papers, the princess noted lovingly that Joseph's 'grandparents' were called 'Liebling and Lulu' on his mother's side, and 'Nigger II and Topsy' on the other.[19]

Sophia and Joe featured in a popular book of the times, *Dog Shows and Doggy People*, which included photographs of the pair accompanied by page after page of genuflecting prose:

I am pleased to be able to give an excellent portrait of Princess Sophie, who will be known to many of my readers as an occasional exhibitor at some of our leading shows, and her charming little Black Pomeranian Joseph . . . the writer has been assured that their mistress has always been extremely fond of dogs, and likes them not only from a show point of view, but also for themselves. The above sentiments warrant the hope that we may see more exhibits forthcoming from Her Highness's kennel, and that the Princess may long be numbered amongst the ever increasing ranks of Doggy People, who are honoured by her presence and personal patronage.[20]

In an attempt to encourage their sister into more refined pursuits, Catherine and Bamba badgered Sophia to start taking piano lessons again. Their father had enjoyed music – Duleep had once composed an opera for one of his mistresses – and Sophia was said to have inherited many of the Maharajah's musical talents. One of her most expensive purchases at Faraday House was a Steinway grand piano which cost £136, almost a quarter of the princess's entire annual budget.[21] Sophia also vigorously pursued another of her father's great passions – that of photography. Space and independence at Faraday House allowed her to practise her art, and she became a regular client of the Eastman Kodak Company which had just opened its doors at 115 Oxford Street. The huge number of surviving bills and receipts for equipment, film and development show the extent of her commitment.[22]

As she embraced her twenties, Sophia revelled in her newfound pursuits and glamorous, if not slightly unconventional, lifestyle. Catherine too was happy, spending all her time with Lina in Germany. For the eldest sister Bamba, however, life was becoming unbearable.

For as long as she could remember, Bamba had loathed the country which she believed had robbed her of everything. She blamed the British for betraying her father and the press for vilifying her brother, Victor. She had never felt as though she belonged in England, nor did she have any desire to be accepted. Unlike Sophia, Bamba did not enjoy the company of the British aristocracy, and her direct and challenging manner provoked fierce reactions from those she met.

She also decided that Britain was a country fit only for crushing her dreams. Despite failing at university, Bamba declared that she wanted to become a doctor. It was a surprising ambition and also a very difficult one to achieve. In Victorian England the opportunities for women to study and succeed in medicine were almost non-existent, despite the trailblazing work of individuals such as Elizabeth Garrett Anderson, the first woman in Britain to qualify as a physician and surgeon. Shunned by medical schools and teaching hospitals, Garrett Anderson had been forced to enter the profession through the back door by getting her medical licence in 1865 from the Society of Apothecaries. After she did so, the society changed its rules, and no other woman was admitted. Garrett Anderson only gained membership of the British Medical Association in 1873, and remained its sole woman member for almost twenty years. Disheartened at the number of doors slammed in her own face, Bamba planned to make her way across the Atlantic in order to investigate medical colleges there. America had granted a medical degree to its first woman in 1849. Elizabeth Blackwell then went on to found a medical college in New York with her younger sister who also qualified as a doctor. Similar schools were opening up in other cities, despite voluble opposition from the male establishment. Bamba would have been aware of Elizabeth Blackwell's memoir *Pioneer Work in Opening the Medical Profession to Women*, which had been published just a couple of years before. It had proved to be inspirational to many would-be women medics around the world.

Although her desire to qualify was real, Bamba had one eye on an ambition that burnt more deeply still. She wanted to get to India and live out her days in the Sikh kingdom of her ancestors. Knowing how the British had stopped her brother Victor from travelling there, and aware of the government's surveillance and monitoring of her family's movements, Bamba felt trapped. Never known for her good manners, she became even ruder to the Hampton Court neighbours and less tolerant of the servants. Only her sisters truly understood the depth of her torment. They realised that they had to get Bamba out of England before she lost her mind.

With Catherine and Sophia's help, Bamba looked for a more

circuitous passage to India. The sisters announced that Princess Bamba was looking at medical colleges in America but first planned to take a holiday to prepare for the hard years of study which lay ahead of her. On 30 January 1900, Bamba booked tickets on the *König Albert*, a majestic new German ocean liner bound for China via Ceylon. The plan was for Bamba to travel as far as Yokohama in Japan, all the while pushing to see how close she might get to India without provoking the ire of the British government.

Sophia agreed to accompany her sister on the liner as far as Japan, and prepared for the long months ahead. Freddie could not believe that his little sister was happy to leave England for such a length of time. To him, everything abroad was 'horrid' and 'unnecessary'. To Sophia, Bamba's needs were obvious and overwhelming; only the idea of being parted from her pets made her hesitate, especially her beloved Joe. She did not wish to leave her animals in the care of indifferent servants, but neither did the princess wish to let her sister down. From Germany, Catherine realised Sophia's torn loyalties and offered to come back to look after the menagerie at Faraday House. Even though Catherine made great play of her antipathy, Sophia knew that nobody would take better care of her dogs and birds, for her sake. She also promised to write to Sophia regularly and update her on Joseph's health and happiness, even though she and the dog had taken an immediate and intense dislike to one another.

From the moment they embarked on the voyage, the Duleep Singh princesses attracted attention from fellow passengers and the press. Bamba hated the spotlight almost as much as Sophia enjoyed it, and ferociously ignored all approaches. She treated crew and staff with either brusqueness or outrageous bad manners. The sisters tensed as the *König Albert* approached the coast of Colombo. Would they be turned back just like Victor? In the event they were given permission to disembark and they spent shore leave shopping and sampling local cuisine, before rejoining the ship with the other passengers. The India Office sent favourable communications to London: the Princesses Sophia and Bamba were keeping a dutifully low profile and the authorities had no complaints to make against them. Bamba's far-off dreams of settling in the old Sikh kingdom no longer seemed impossible.

At Faraday House, Catherine monitored her sisters' adventures with relish. Sophia, ever the diligent correspondent, wrote to her at least once, often twice, a week. Catherine reciprocated, forwarding post and gossip, and paying bills on Sophia's behalf. On 2 February 1900 she wrote: 'Dear Saff, I am sending those of your innumerable letters which I think will amuse you ... There was some Pug Dog Chat rubbish.'[23] Knowing that Sophia would be pining for news of Joseph, Catherine jokingly refused even to use his name, referring to the beloved pet only as 'the piece of goods'[24] or 'that little horror'.[25] 'Your most precious piece of goods is perfectly well,' she announced in one letter, 'but do not flatter yourself that he misses you. On the contrary I should say he is very happy to be able to stay in the kitchen in peace, I have heard him bark once for the front door bell, which we will suppose was for you, but only once! There is a nice piece of faithlessness and indifference for yourself!!'[26]

No piece of Joe news was too trivial to pass on: 'I just picked him up a few steps towards the hall, which caused no end of growling; having teased him sufficiently I let him go ... I tell you all this Joe-ish nonsense knowing it interests you more than anything else.'[27]

These weekly letters between the sisters were heavily laced with mutual affection. Catherine frequently addressed Sophia as 'Dear little Saff'. On occasion Catherine would refer to her as 'Zwaff', and herself as 'Caswen' (the private joke being that this was how Joe the dog would say their names if he could speak). 'I am glad you seem to be enjoying yourself all right – all the dogs are all well – Joe quite happy! One morning he set off howling in the kitchen ... I don't think the howl was for you; whenever I say, do you want Zwaff, he pretends he wants to go to the door.'[28]

Freddie missed Sophia terribly and was dismayed to learn that his youngest sister had enjoyed the voyage to the Far East so much that she had decided to extend her time away. Sophia informed her brother that she was now en route with Bamba to the other side of the world. From Japan they sailed for America on the steamship *Nippon Maru*, arriving on the east coast in July 1900. The trip would keep Sophia from her brother and England for a further two months. Freddie complained bitterly in letters to his sister, imploring her to come back.

Travelling in such close quarters and spending all their time together fostered a new intimacy and understanding between Bamba and Sophia. The women's friendship baffled the rest of the world. To the outsider's eye, they could not have been more different: Sophia was graceful, languid and friendly; Bamba was aloof and irascible. The international press were fascinated by the odd couple, as an article in the *Boston Daily Globe* revealed. 'Princesses Bamba and Sophia Duleep Singh recently arrived in San Francisco from Tokyo,' the paper announced on 17 July. The reporter wanted to know whether the ladies liked America. He was surprised by the answers Sophia gave:

'We have met many Americans and think the women charming,' said Princess Sophia.

'And American men – you like them?'

'Not so much. They work too hard and are not the women's equal,' said the representative of the most aristocratic caste system in the world.[29]

The interview was not going well. The *Globe* reporter persisted.

'With you, are the women also superior?' But the Princess Dhuleep Singh declined to answer further than to say that the 'Indian colleges are open to women'.

'We in San Francisco have been trying to do something for your starving people in India.'

'Indeed,' said the princesses, but without one spark of interest, and playing indifferently with the diamonds on their slender fingers – ransom of innumerable lives in that death-stricken country.[30]

Bamba had barely spoken to the journalist and now Sophia turned her back on him too. As the interview ground to a painful halt, the *Globe* reporter was left to make his final observations alone:

They visited in San Francisco the medical department of the University of California and were much pleased with what they saw. They are travelling *a la Americaine* – almost – with a French maid only, these princesses of the oldest and most aristocratic race known today. With a marked English accent and a decided Spanish appearance it would be indeed difficult to determine their nationality without the Hindoo name. But those slim fine brown, tapered fingers are only 'made in India' – and beautiful they are![31]

After touring many of the colleges, Bamba applied for a place on a course at Northwestern University in Chicago, and was accepted. Sophia fretted about her sister being alone in America, without a loved one to protect her or translate her idiosyncratic ways to an often hostile world. Knowing that she would be lonely in her inevitable isolation, she convinced Bamba that when she returned to start the course in a month she should do so with a couple of Sophia's dogs for company.

Bamba's relationship with the American press, which had started badly, got progressively worse. Reporters waiting to catch sight of the royal visitor were given short shrift:

A dark, timid-looking woman of small stature, who was the object of much attention on the pier, was the Princess Bamba Duleep Singh. She is from the Punjab India. She had a large assortment of baggage, besides two fine dogs, one a Great Dane named Leon, the other a beautiful cream colour Russian wolfhound, the name of which she refused to divulge. When asked by the newspaper men to say something for publication, the princess turned her back on them and refused to say a word. When one of them asked her if she would not tell them the names of her dogs, she turned around and said: 'Leave the dogs alone, and don't you put anything in the paper about them either.'[32]

Newspapers from Maine to Oregon reported the princess's career aspirations with a degree of opprobrium. Although several universities were admitting women medical students, many Americans found the practice distasteful, believing like their British counterparts that women doctors were an affront to the natural order. Yet despite their disapproval, readers were hungry for news of their royal 'freshman' and papers up and down the country obliged:

> The Women's Medical College has a new student – the Princess Bamba Duleep Singh. If fate had not been against her, Princess Singh might have perhaps today been a queen of India instead of a humble medical student. Her grandfather was the last ruler of that Empire, the kingly Runjeet Singh, from whom Great Britain wrenched the crown, and also the famous Koh-I-Noor diamond. The princess has taken it into her head to become a doctor. Her home is in England, but it is said she harbors no special love for the country that took away her hereditary possessions . . . of course she is dark and has wavy black hair, and eyes that flash blackness from under long, silky lashes. If she was a queen of India she might with a wave of her slender little hand, order a head chopped off as easily as she now turns a page in her anatomy books. But those days are over in India, so the princess is going to be a life-saver, instead of a life-taker.[33]

Bamba's discretion was simply fuelling the interest: 'The young women students were nearly thrown in to hysterics by the coming of the dainty Indian princess, who made her first appearance at the college in a carriage.' Other papers actively invaded Bamba's privacy, stationing reporters on the street outside her home and in her lecture halls. Without Sophia to shield her, Bamba was entirely exposed: 'As soon as she arrived the princess took apartments in the residence of Miss Palmer at 404 West Adams Street and presented herself for matriculation . . . The princess keeps generally in the seclusion of her rooms, her maid serving her meals there. On Sunday morning she went out for a walk with two dogs which crossed the ocean with her . . . On the street she wore a short blue skirt with an Eton jacket of fur and a brown felt hat. Her dress is European, her speech a quaint, lisping English. The maid she brought from England is as reserved in speech as she is.'[34]

Meanwhile, Sophia quickly resumed her place on the British social scene, once again proving to be very popular. The press there were altogether less intrusive than the Americans, keeping her pleasingly in the public eye without violating her privacy. 'Christmas sees the Riviera at the beginning of what promises to be a really good season,' reported the *Daily Mail*. 'There has this year been no scare of epidemics, no anti-English feeling, to keep away those who can leave the cold and murky north to enjoy brilliantly sunny days. The tables at Monte Carlo are crowded daily, and so is the Opera House . . . Lord De la Warr and Baron Arthur de Rothschild are both staying at Monte Carlo, and the Princess Duleep Singh drove over to Nice the other morning from Beaulieu to do some shopping.'[35]

Everything Sophia did seemed to endear her to them, and the British press was now even claiming her as one of their own. 'Notwithstanding her great Oriental name, which marks her to those cognisant of Indian history as a descendant of the famous founder of the last Sikh Empire, the princess is to all intents and purposes, a thoroughly English girl'.[36]

Sophia might have continued to live her life in a comfortable bubble were it not for the news of Bamba's continuing difficulties. Not only was Bamba battling to maintain her privacy while at the same time keeping up with the punishing workload at her medical school, but the locals were also being unkind to her. As usual the press were never slow to report on Bamba's tribulations: 'On her daily trips between her home on West Adams Street and the University, the daughter of the Maharaja of Lahore has been pelted with lumps of snow. "Such a thing would not be permitted in England,"[37] she said. "I shall leave Chicago . . . I have never encountered such rude people in all my life."'[38] Bamba was not the only person who was finding the winter difficult.

After spending Christmas at her beloved Osborne House on the Isle of White, Queen Victoria, now eighty-one, felt weak and unwell. She was already frail, with eyesight diminished by cataracts and mobility curtailed by severe rheumatism. The demands of the festive season took a further toll on her health. For some time the Queen had become almost entirely dependent on one of her Indian servants,

Mohammed Abdul Karim, who she fondly referred to as her *Munshi*, the Hindi word for secretary.

Karim had served Victoria faithfully for the last fifteen years of her life, feeding her unquenchable desire to learn more about India. He cooked curries for her, taught her to write in Urdu and Hindi and filled her head with exciting tales of his childhood. Victoria's devotion to the Munshi was absolute and she ignored warnings from her close circle to distance herself from what they regarded as another 'malign influence'. To many at the Palace, the relationship echoed a past and ultimately doomed obsession. When she had been besotted with the Maharajah, however, advisers had cloaked many of their misgivings. Now that a mere native servant enthralled her, there was no attempt to hide hostility. Despite widespread disapproval Victoria kept Karim close at all times. She signed letters to him with 'your loving mother', and 'your closest friend', and even placed kisses below her signature. The Munshi watched helplessly as the Queen's condition deteriorated through Christmas into the New Year. On 22 January 1901, at half past six in the evening, Victoria died in her bed at Osborne House. Her son and successor, King Edward VII, and eldest grandson, Emperor Wilhelm II of Germany, were at her bedside.

The nation was plunged into a period of intense mourning. People went about their business dressed in sober black and banners of black and purple were draped on shop fronts and from the gates of houses. It was as if a dark bruise had settled over the country. Victoria's reign had lasted for almost sixty-four years, during which Imperial Britain had swallowed as much as a fifth of the world's land mass. The new king gave the nation three months to grieve, after which time the official period of mourning ended and Britain and the Empire awoke to a new, modern, Edwardian era.

If the loss of her godmother affected Sophia in any way, she did not show it outwardly, throwing herself into the unending tidal movements of high society. In the early 1900s she spent autumns on the French Riviera, Hogmanay in Scotland and divided the rest of the year between London and the country, staying either with Victor at his Norfolk home, or nearby with Freddie at his impressive new country estate at Old Buckenham Hall in Suffolk. Both brothers had chosen to live within a few miles of Elveden. Their father's sprawling old home had been sold to the Guinness family soon after his death and though Freddie maintained a good relationship with the new masters of Elveden, Victor remained aloof.

Sophia's country breaks allowed her to draw breath before the next exhausting round of social engagements. Prepared to go wherever the most important parties were being held, she dedicated herself to the pursuit of her own pleasure. Her father's dear friend and frequent visitor to her childhood home, Bertie, was on the throne and she was the belle of most balls she attended. Life was good and beyond that Sophia had little connection with what was happening around her, even though so much of the world was changing.

The Empire bubbled with talk of insurrection, and calls for Home Rule from the newly formed Indian National Congress were getting louder and more insistent, echoing the situation in Ireland. A second Boer War had been raging since 1899 and the Sultan of the Ottoman Empire was dragging all of Europe to the brink of conflict by sending 50,000 troops to the frontiers of Bulgaria. Although she seemed to close her eyes to all of it, not everyone in her social circle was as immune to politics as Sophia. Talk at aristocratic tables would often stray to trade unions, which were becoming more organised and influential, and Keir Hardie's newly formed Labour Party was gaining support among the workers in the industrial towns and cities.

One of the most unsettling changes for the conservative post-Victorians came from an organised movement of middle-class women which was growing in rank and file. One of the most influential, Millicent Fawcett's National Union of Women's Suffrage Societies (NUWSS), with its central tenet of 'Votes for Women', was gaining traction. The patricians in the higher social orders had many reasons to grumble. Even though some of the women she mixed with were showing an interest in Fawcett's manifesto, Princess Sophia had little time for such matters. It was only when Bamba suffered direct discrimination that Sophia began to take notice.

During the summer of 1902, the authorities of Chicago's

Northwestern University, quite without warning, changed their minds about the propriety of training women to become doctors. One university trustee, Paul Raymond, was particularly scathing when called upon to explain the unexpected cancellation of Bamba's course: 'Women cannot grasp chemical laboratory work or the intricacies of surgery. Fifteen years ago the graduating class of men and women signed a memorial saying that coeducation was a failure. Then we conducted the college exclusively for women, and it has been worse than a failure.'[39] Having terminated the course mid-term, Raymond and his board left all the women medical students stranded, and crushed Bamba's hopes of ever becoming a doctor. Sophia waited anxiously for her sister to return to England, knowing how hurt and angry she must be feeling.

The journey home was a struggle for Bamba. It was June and every berth on every ship seemed to be taken up by the hordes travelling to England for the upcoming coronation of King Edward VII. There were even reports of crew members illegally renting out their own bunk space. Once Bamba secured passage, the crowded, week-long voyage was tense and depressing. She had had to listen to the excited chatter of passengers talking about a royal family she despised. Her avenues of escape from England were closing one by one, and she longed, more than ever before, to get to India and make a life for herself there. It may have felt as though she was asking for a ticket to the moon, but within a matter of months her dream would become a reality.

# The Cubs Come Home

After Bamba's doomed American adventure, and her unceremonious return to London in late June 1902, the days seemed painfully long for Sophia. She had attempted to make Faraday as welcoming as possible for her dejected sister, ensuring that her room was beautifully furnished and the house was stocked with all the things Bamba liked. Catherine too had rallied for her sister's sake: returning to England from Germany, she moved temporarily into the dog-ridden home she hated. As always, in times of emotional hardship the princesses enveloped each other, hoping that their mutual love would heal whatever wound had been inflicted.

Despite their best efforts, Bamba's mood only continued to darken. She loathed the idea of being back in the house that the Queen Empress had given them. Bamba found fault with the neighbours, the accommodation, the weather, and the meaningless social engagements which, in her opinion, cluttered Sophia's life. She spent her days picking fights with everyone, from the household staff to the Lord Chamberlain himself. When she discovered that the sisters were not to be given their own royal pew in the chapel at Hampton Court, Bamba fired off a volley of complaints and refused to attend services until the situation was rectified. As always, her belligerent ways became the source of gossip, and the more the residents of Hampton Court talked about her behind her back, the worse her behaviour became. The situation put a considerable strain on Sophia's own carefully cultivated relationships within the palace community.

Like her older sister, Catherine too was listless at Faraday House. Apart from Sophia's dogs and tobacco, which vexed her constantly, she longed to return to Miss Schaeffer and Germany. It became evident that Sophia would have to do something to lift both her sisters' spirits, but she had no idea what. Bamba talked incessantly of her desire to go and live in the Punjab, leaving Sophia feeling both powerless and nonplussed. Quite apart from the practical difficulties of returning to their homeland, Sophia had little empathy or understanding of India.

Only the trip they had taken together as far as Ceylon provided any optimism. They had behaved so well, and the Secretary of State for India had been untroubled by communications about them. Their only hope was that one day the Duleep Singh princesses might be rewarded for their invisibility. The prospect of waiting years, however, for the travel ban to be lifted was almost too much for Bamba to bear.

Had anyone known that during this time Bamba had somehow got hold of a gun, and kept it loaded in her bedside table, they would have had a deeper sense of her crisis. Then, as luck would have it, the British Crown inadvertently gave Sophia and Catherine a chance to save their sister.

On 9 August, only weeks after Bamba's return, Edward VII was to be crowned at Westminster Abbey, becoming simultaneously 'King of Great Britain and Ireland and all the British Dominions beyond the Seas, and the Emperor of India'. The country had been waiting for the announcement of the coronation for weeks. It had been planned for June, but an acute attack of appendicitis meant emergency surgery for Edward, leaving him bedridden for weeks and setting celebrations back by almost two months. With a sense of growing impatience Britain and her empire waited for their new king to take his place on the throne. In London a spectacular coronation was planned, to which Sophia and Frederick were invited, seated with senior royalty and aristocracy in the choir stalls of

Westminster Abbey. Thousands of miles away, representatives of the Raj were also keen to make the most of Edward's succession. The Viceroy of India, Lord Curzon, 1st Marquess of Kedleston, had planned an extraordinary celebration in order to unveil Victoria's son to his Eastern Empire. The world would never have seen a show like it before.

Curzon commandeered vast tracts of land outside the north Indian city of Delhi. These were cleared of inhabitants, flattened, and in a matter of months a magnificent tent city was erected. It stretched for miles across the dusty plains. Thanks to an excellent civil administration, British engineering ingenuity and the vast Indian workforce at Curzon's disposal, he was able to give the former scrubland its own telegraph system, light railway, shops, hospital, magistrates' court, electricity grid and complex drainage system. To the inhabitants of Delhi it seemed as if a whole new civilisation had sprung up overnight. In contrast to the sprawl of the old walled city, Curzon's creation was orderly, clean, and shimmered white in the intense Indian sunlight.

The Viceroy billed his royal celebration 'The Delhi Durbar', a nod to the historical Mughal courts which had controlled most of the Indian subcontinent during the seventeenth and eighteenth centuries. As reports of the elaborate preparations reached England, important families scrambled to get tickets for the event. More than 150,000 people were expected to attend, and Catherine, Bamba and Sophia itched to join them.

Curzon's coronation city was divided into quadrants, or 'camps', to accommodate numerous Indian kingdoms and principalities, as well as British dignitaries and government officers of the Raj. The corralling of so many Indian potentates in one place, at one time, was unprecedented. Even before the Coronation Park was completed, flunkeys buzzed about the site with measuring tapes and maps, tasked by their royal masters to ensure that no reigning chief received preferential treatment. Petty squabbles were frequent and had to be mediated by the durbar committee, a group of overworked British civil servants whose job it was to mollify, contain, and if necessary cajole, rival Indian royals to be more reasonable. As well as dealing with their demands, the office also had to sort through and accommodate sacks of invitation requests and replies from England every day.

The cost of constructing the temporary durbar accommodation alone was over a quarter of a million pounds (the equivalent of almost £25 million today[1]). This did not include the considerable fortune spent by Indian royals themselves. They competed to make their quarters more luxurious than their rivals, hauling in expensive silk canopies, statues and jewelled ornaments to decorate their camps. One Maharajah even insisted on installing a complicated ornate fountain which was somehow plumbed in, despite being in the midst of a dust bowl. Each area was uniquely styled to represent the region of its royal. While crossing from one end of the camp to the other, with the changing languages, styles of dress and smells of regional cooking, it felt like traversing India itself.

Although money seemed to be no object, India could ill afford such expenditure for such fleeting festivity. A devastating famine between 1896 and 1897 had caused a human and financial catastrophe. Crops perished because of the lack of rain, and starvation and disease ravaged the country. The British-controlled dominions of the United Provinces, the Bombay Presidency, Madras, Bihar and the Central Provinces had been brought to their knees. Bubonic plague, malaria and cholera swept through cities, towns and villages, leaving populations decimated.[2]

Barely had India begun to recover when a second famine hit in 1899. Poor monsoon rains resulted in harvests failing completely; millions of heads of livestock died in fields of dust. Without the bullocks there was no way the farmers could till their land; and milk ran dangerously short for already undernourished children. Wave upon wave of disease hit the survivors. *The Lancet* estimated that around 19 million people died of famine-related deaths between 1896 and 1902.

The Viceroy was well aware of the problems. He had personally visited the worst-hit areas. Curzon, however, felt he had more pressing concerns than the daily death tolls. Politics in India was changing rapidly, and it threatened the very existence of the Raj. Even

moderate Indians were demanding radical reform and greater participation in government. Political leaders such as the Punjabi nationalist,
Lala Lajpat Rai, advocated a boycott of British goods and institutions. More ominously for Curzon, other firebrand leaders, including
Bipin Chandra Pal, Aurobindo Ghosh and Bal Gangadhar Tilak,
were calling for direct action. These men were rousing India's youth
to rise up and violently overthrow the British.

Curzon knew how outnumbered the British were and felt
compelled to remind Indians just who was in charge. The durbar
was a very visual way to make his point. As his grand finale, Curzon
planned to have every one of India's rulers bow down before their
British King Emperor. The symbolism would be unmistakable and
lasting.

There was just one problem with Curzon's masterful idea. The
very man he wished to honour, King Edward VII, refused point
blank to travel to India. Some speculated that his health remained
precarious after his appendectomy; others suggested, less kindly, that
the former playboy prince simply could not be bothered with such
tiresome duties of state. Whatever his reasons, the new king dele-
gated the visit to his younger brother, the Duke of Connaught. Lord
Curzon refused to scale back his ambition just because he was missing a king emperor.

Like many in their social circle, Sophia, Bamba and Catherine
applied weeks in advance for durbar passes, and initially their
requests were ignored. A squabble ensued with the India Office
about 'misplaced' paperwork and the three sisters bombarded the
Secretary of State, the India Office and the durbar committee with
complaints. If they were to be refused permission to travel, the
Duleep Singh princesses demanded to know, in writing, the reason
for it. The India Office's Political and Secret Department, responsible for intelligence and difficult diplomacy, suggested in internal
communications that it might be wise to tell the princesses they had
simply applied too late to be accommodated. It was hoped the tortuous process of British bureaucracy might put them off. Lord George
Hamilton, the Secretary of State for India, wrote personally to the
princesses informing them that due to lack of time it would be

'impossible to provide suitable accommodation for them or to arrange for their proper reception'.[3] Hoping that they might be discouraged by the polite rebuff, 'his Lordship strongly urges the postponement of the visit'.[4]

Far from being despondent, Sophia, Catherine and Bamba were jubilant. The very fact that the Secretary of State had accepted that the sisters could travel to India at a more convenient, later date, meant that they were no longer banned from the country. Unlike Victor and Freddie, who had not even bothered to apply for durbar passes, the Duleep Singh women were free to visit their homeland. The timing of the visit seemed to be the only thing up for debate. In a risky strategy, and perhaps calculating that all government departments were too severely stretched to notice them, the sisters opted to ignore Lord Hamilton's advice and booked passage on a ship to India. They needed to move quickly, just in case the Secretary of State decided to issue further missives.

Since no record of their booking can be found on ships' manifests, it is possible that the princesses travelled under aliases. Bamba and Catherine ventured out first, and Sophia followed soon after on another ship, accompanied by her faithful Faraday housekeeper Margaret Mayes. When they reached Delhi, the princesses found that their durbar 'home camp' was indeed closed to them. The heirs of the greatest ruler of Punjab could not find a corner of canvas to sleep beneath. Nevertheless the name Ranjit Singh still carried enormous weight, and thanks to the nostalgic respect of others, the women were discreetly absorbed into accommodation far away from royal enclosures.

As a curtain-raiser to his durbar, on 29 December 1902, Lord Curzon, in full vice-regal splendour, led a glittering parade through the streets of the old Mughal capital. The Duke and Duchess of Connaught rode at his side, and fifty of the most notable Indian kings and princes followed, seated on elephants in howdahs made of silver. Studded with precious jewels and heavy in their gold, they caught the light like a sparkling stream, meandering to the pounding sound of military marching bands. The procession took hours to snake its way through the city and signalled the start of two days of garden parties, polo matches and balls. All were designed to build anticipation for the durbar itself, due to take place on 1 January 1903.

From first light on New Year's Day the streets and rooftops of Delhi were crammed with spectators, anxious to see all they could. Most were not allowed near the durbar site itself, since those spaces were reserved only for the richest and most powerful guests. Provision had been made for 10,000 in the specially constructed amphitheatre at the edge of the tent city. Tens of thousands more who did not get a space in the enclosure were forced to stand on the plains beneath a rocky ridge, the sun beating down upon their heads. Some 34,000 troops took their places in what seemed like an endless patchwork of uniformed strength, stretching as far as the eye could see. Among them were more than 300 British and sepoy veterans of the 1857 Mutiny; white-haired and bent with age, they marched forward to the tunes of 'See the Conquering Hero Comes' and 'Auld Lang Syne'. 'It was a sight which moved many spectators to tears,' the English newspapers said, 'especially those whose memories could carry them back to the great struggle which decided the fate of the Empire.'[5]

As more than a thousand musicians from various regimental bands struck up, the Viceroy, the Duke of Connaught, and a selection of the most important dignitaries took their places. Curzon cleared his throat and read the royal proclamation, declaring the absent King 'Supreme Ruler of All India'. The valley shook with the pounding of gun salutes as more than a hundred of India's maharajahs, rajahs and nawabs, as well as the chiefs from almost all the princely states, approached the King's proxy and bowed before him. The ceremony took so long that shadows were lengthening by the time the last of them got to pledge their loyalty. Then, with the sun setting, British and Indian voices joined together in a crescendo of 'God Save the King'.

Festivities lasted a further eight days, with numerous fairs and banquets. Sophia and her sisters were not invited to any of them and the experience of being snubbed, on top of seeing other Indian potentates still in possession of their lands, titles and wealth, wounded all of Duleep's daughters. They consoled themselves in the fact that the durbar had never been the main aim of their visit. They had come to see the Sikh kingdom, and they had come to find Bamba a home.

The sisters made their way north to Lahore, their father's former capital, while the rest of India continued to revel in Delhi. As they travelled, and even though they were attempting to keep a low profile, they found the country still rang with stories of the Lion, Ranjit Singh. Those who stumbled upon their identity fell at their feet, remembering the day when their father was thrown out of his kingdom, and Jindan was dragged away screaming. With the echoes of her ancestors ringing in her ears, Sophia finally reached Lahore and saw a city that neither her grandfather nor her father would have recognised. Amidst the minarets, temples and palm trees, there were now Victorian clock towers, grand European churches and numerous British barracks. Sombre European Gothic architecture filled spaces between the colourfully inlaid Mughal city gates, its solid grey a stark contrast to the teeming streets below.

New Lahore was bisected by a recently constructed road, named 'The Mall',[6] after the approach to Buckingham Palace. As her eyes adjusted to the throbbing human sea, Sophia looked upon the newest monument to rise up from the dirt. Only months before, an imposing new statue in honour of her godmother had been unveiled in middle of the city; under a vast white stone cupola sat a gleaming, bronze Queen Victoria.[7] In one hand, she held the orb representing her global dominion and across her lap, the sceptre of power. There were no statues of Sophia's father to be seen anywhere.

As unhappy as the British were at the princesses' presence in Punjab, there was very little either the Viceroy or the Secretary of State could do about it, short of arresting them, and that would mar Anglo-Indian relations at a time when Curzon was fighting so hard to redefine them. The Duleep Singh women were scrupulously careful to adhere to the rules, denying anyone the opportunity to detain them. Instead the authorities decided to make things as awkward as possible. Sophia, Catherine and Bamba were openly shunned by senior British officials and were denied diplomatic support, normally extended to British subjects of rank. It was usual for senior officials to open their doors to travelling dignitaries, throwing parties for them and escorting them to see the sights; however no such courtesy was offered to the Duleep Singhs. They were on their own and the gesture was designed to humiliate.[8]

The impact of their slight was offset somewhat by the enthusiasm of the Punjab chiefs, aristocratic Sikhs with lineages inextricably tangled with those of Ranjit Singh. One of the first to take the sisters into his protection was Sardar Gurcharan Singh, a distant relative of their father. He would become a close friend to Sophia and Bamba and would attempt to steer them away from political controversy. Even though Sophia and her sisters spoke no Indian language, and had manners and dress which seemed outlandishly European to many of the elders, they were welcomed as daughters into the homes of complete strangers. For the first time in her life, the colour of Sophia's skin made her part of a majority, and not the visible outsider.

Also keen to open his doors to the sisters was Harnam Singh, uncle of the Maharajah of Kapurthala, a princely state which had remained loyal to the British ever since the first Anglo-Sikh War. Harnam Singh's family were great favourites of the British. They had sent troops to support the Raj during the Mutiny and had been richly rewarded for their service. Harnam Singh's use of the word 'mutiny' to describe the events of 1857 enraged many Punjabis, who preferred to call it 'the first war of Indian Independence'. Punjab was riven by its perception of history and although fifty years had passed since the bloodshed, differences in opinion continued to divide families as well as the communities they lived in. Some felt the British had brought order and continuity to the region while others believed they had been made slaves in their own country. Despite his controversial views, Sophia was charmed by Harnam Singh's refinement and courtesy. His nephew, the Maharajah, had visited her exiled father in Paris at a time when nobody else wanted to know him. Bamba, on the other hand, rarely let her guard down in his presence.

In contrast, all three Duleep Singh sisters were united in their unreserved fondness for Umrao Singh Sher-Gil, a slender, elegant aristocrat, who loved books and hated bad manners. Umrao Singh was also held in high esteem by the British, but unlike the royal from Kapurthala, he never believed in the British right to rule his country. Because he had kept his misgivings largely secret, he had been invited to attend Queen Victoria's Diamond Jubilee in England, as well as the more recent Coronation Durbar in Delhi. Nothing he saw eased his doubts and his home became a haven for subversive conversation. It was one of the few places where anti-Raj sentiments could be aired without fear the conversation might get reported back to the British. Umrao Singh was an elder of the Majithia clan, a prominent family whose ancestors had served as loyal generals in Ranjit Singh's armies. He had an interest in photography, like Sophia, and spoke five languages. Out of respect, the girls referred to him only by the honorific title *Sirdar-ji*,[9] meaning 'honoured Sikh'. His wife, Narinder Kumari, they addressed as *Sirdarni*; she was generous, kind and maternal and her ancestors had been imprisoned by the British for attempting to help Jindan. Sophia would soon become devoted to the couple.

Umrao Singh Sher-Gil was a passionate member of the Theosophical Society, a movement founded in the United States in 1875. The Theosophists believed in clairvoyance and reincarnation and were ardently non-sectarian.[10] Their gatherings traditionally centred on philosophical debate. However, at the turn of the century the movement became overtly political. The English theosophist Annie Besant was causing tension for the British Raj, having already made a name for herself in England as a troublemaker. A leading speaker for the Fabian Society and the Marxist Social Democratic Federation, Annie had actively supported Irish Home Rule, finding herself at the heart of the Bloody Sunday demonstrations of 1887. In central London, over ten thousand protesters had demanded Irish autonomy. When they reached Trafalgar Square, violent clashes with police left three dead and hundreds injured. Besant, as one of the organisers of the march, offered herself to the police for arrest if they would let others go, but they refused to make a political martyr of her.

Just one year later, Besant organised the London match girls' strike, leading a predominantly female workforce to walk out of the

Bryant & May match factory in Bow, East London. They were protesting against the use of white phosphorus in the manufacturing process, which caused painful and debilitating conditions like 'phossy jaw'. Workers developed unbearable abscesses in their mouths, facial disfigurement and sometimes fatal brain damage. The protest attracted many idealistic young women. One of them was a twenty-eight-year-old from Manchester. Her name was Emmeline Pankhurst, and she would describe her experience with Besant as life-changing: 'I threw myself into this strike with enthusiasm, working with the girls and with some women of prominence.'[11] Thanks to Annie's rabble-rousing, Britain eventually banned the use of white phosphorus in all its factories.

Much to the dismay of the British government, a decade after her victory with the match girls, Besant threatened to light a bonfire under India. Soon after her arrival, groups were spending less time debating the hidden mysteries of the universe and more time talking about practical steps needed to free the country. Through her new friends, Sophia moved in the same circles where whispers of treason against the Raj were circulating. Not since the banishment of her father had the potential volatility of the Punjab been of such concern to the British authorities. In ever greater numbers, intelligence files were opened.

Against this backdrop of growing political discontent, in 1903 Sophia embarked on the steepest learning curve of her life. She searched for information about her heritage and about India itself. Ranging widely across the former Sikh Empire on horseback, Sophia attempted to get a feel for the homeland her father had been so desperate to take back. For a while Catherine and Bamba accompanied Sophia, but eventually the rigours of her long rides proved too much for them. Sophia loved the intense heat of the Indian afternoons, but her sisters suffered terribly. Bamba in particular needed frequent ice baths to soothe her irritated skin.

Overcome by the climate, Catherine and Bamba announced their intention to escape to the cool of the Simla Hills. Sophia elected to spend the sticky monsoon months with her new Indian friends in Lahore. Moreover, English acquaintances who happened to be in

India at the same time gave her additional reason to stay. The Harlands were an upper-class family from East Sheen whom Sophia had known since she moved to Hampton Court. They made eminently suitable chaperones for the princess in Lahore, so Catherine and Bamba gave their permission for her to remain in the city. For seven weeks Sophia was free to explore Punjab without the opinions of her sisters constantly ringing in her ears.

When the weather in Lahore became more manageable, Catherine and Bamba returned to discover their sister much changed. She was by now quite at home, and was even attempting to learn the language. They found to their amusement that Sophia had been making a mark on all who met her. She spoke politely to the servants, which set her apart from the brusque Indians who employed them, and went as far as to write letters of thanks to those who particularly impressed her. Bamba found it hilarious that one of Harnam Singh's servants seemed utterly smitten: 'Boota Singh has been so amusing keeping me in fits of laughter. I asked him how beautiful he thought he was. He said "middle-class!!" You will be glad to hear he calls you 1st class.'[12]

Boota Singh was not the only man to admire Sophia. Kedar Natu, a humble clerk whose knowledge of English had become invaluable to the sisters during their stay in Lahore, came to dote on the youngest Duleep Singh princess. He served as a fixer and translator and Sophia had dropped him a letter of thanks for his efforts. She included a photograph of herself as a keepsake and it became one of Natu's most prized possessions. To receive such a gesture from a lady of Sophia's lineage prompted Natu to offer his eternal service, even if that meant leaving India and his own family: 'In case you don't get a suitable teacher there and that if it is quite convenient to you and not too much costly I can come over to England for as long time as you may desire.'[13]

Sophia declined his offer but accepted all that he could teach her about life in the Punjab, both the dark and the light. He told her about the destructive force of malaria, the indefatigable annual and deadly visitor to the region. He also educated her about the Hindu religious festivals, like Diwali, where under a moonless sky, millions of little lamps were lit all around India to guide one of the Hindu gods home after his years of exile in the wilderness. The skies exploded in a frenzy of fireworks, and Natu told Sophia of the travelling bands of actors who would fill the darkness with the glow of kerosene lamps, enacting scenes from scripture as well as tales from the life of Sophia's grandfather, Ranjit Singh.

Sophia cherished anything that shed light on her past. Among her most treasured papers, she kept a letter written to her by the wife of one of Duleep Singh's long-dead servants, Sheo Ram. When Ram's widow, Jumuna Bai, heard in 1903 that Duleep's daughters were in India, she hired a *chaprassi*, or translating clerk, to write to Sophia. The clerk was tortuously formal, and his English was not as good as advertised, but the warmth of feeling was clear: 'most respectfully and humbly I venture to encroach upon your valuable thoughts and time by submitting these few lines . . . The letters your Royal father sent to my husband will lend to throw light on the extent of our relations to your interest.'[14]

It transpired that Sheo Ram had served Duleep Singh when he too was just a boy. When the Maharajah was exiled to Fategarh, Sheo Ram went with him, leaving behind his own family in the Punjab, knowing that he might never see them again. Over the next five years the loyal servant never left Duleep's side. He would have stayed with him until death, had he not been forbidden to travel to England with the Maharajah in 1854. Sheo Ram was left behind, alone and unsure what his duties were. Believing that Duleep would one day return, he took to protecting his young master's private property. He never left his post, and his loyalty almost cost him his life. During the terrifying violence that swept the state during 1857, the faithful servant stood his ground until Fategarh was overrun by rebels intent on burning out the British and all who sympathised with them. Chased from Duleep's home, instead of melting into anonymity like many servants at the time, Sheo Ram made a perilous trip to the British garrison stationed in Cawnpore (Kanpur) and begged them to return with him, bringing men and arms to save his master's property.[15]

The British had more to worry about than the fortune of some spoiled child, and instead convinced Sheo Ram that if he gathered much-needed intelligence for them he might help end the conflict, allowing them to come back to Fategarh with him. Sheo Ram found himself in some of the worst arenas of battle during 1857. As Major General Outram, the commanding officer at Camp Alum Bagh in Cawnpore testified in his report from the field, Sheo Ram 'was present at the first relief of Lucknow, and afforded ready assistance during the time of our being besieged there'.[16] Sheo Ram was proving himself to be a great asset, but all the while he kept begging the British to come and save Duleep's home from looters. The commanding officer of another regiment in Ferozepur, Captain T. Brusfer, described both Sheo Ram's bravery and also his preoccupation: '[He] shewed much anxiety, about his employer's property which he had been obliged to abandon at Farrukhabad, he has always been very respectful and on several occasions attended me in the field, more particularly whilst in Lucknow where he had volunteered to take up and did actually carry arms for my protection.'[17]

It seemed from the papers Sheo Ram's widow passed on to Sophia that Duleep had kept in touch with his most faithful servant during his early years in England. The few letters that he had penned to Sheo Ram had an almost religious significance to his family: 'I have been left no medium except these holy relics (a copy of which I herewith attach) by which I could have any access to your noble and gracious feet ... Though we are such insignificant creatures as were never destined to pay our most humble respects personally to the late Maharjah yet (thanks to that art which immortalises the likeness) the photo your Royal Father sent to my husband in 1884 is as sincerely and adoringly loved as if the Maharajah in person.'[18] Sophia would treasure Jamuna Bai's letters till the day she died.

In late August 1903, after nine months in Punjab, Sophia decided it was time to go home. The timing of her decision vexed her sisters greatly. Catherine and Bamba were planning a dramatic trip across the snow-capped Pahlgam Mountains into Kashmir, and were sure that the journey would appeal to their adventurous little sister. It was the kind of trip that usually filled Sophia with excitement, involving as it did horseback riding along treacherous ridges, camping in the open air and walking for miles in the wind and snow. They were incredulous that Sophia would pass up the chance to go with them, and Bamba was appalled that she was choosing Hampton Court over Kashmir.

Sophia took the first sailing she could in September, travelling in the company of the Harlands, who were also heading back to England. The family from Sheen might have noticed a profound change in the princess. She was quieter, more serious and seemed preoccupied on the voyage home. Sophia had seen poverty and depravation on a scale that overwhelmed her. Also, for the first time, she had come face to face with all that her family had lost. Never would she find life as a socialite fulfilling again. Looking into the deep waters over the side of her ship she thought about what her life was actually for. The answers would not be found at dog shows and in fashion magazines. Not since the days she had acted as a little mother for her brother Eddie had she felt such a calling to protect someone more vulnerable than herself. It was more than a duty, it was a compulsion. She needed to be useful again, but who exactly needed her?

As her ship reached the British coast, Sophia would find her answer. Shivering on the docks, thin, dark and hungry, were lascars awaiting the ship from India, ready to unload its cargo. They had no idea that one of the passengers on the vessel would have a profound impact on their miserable lives.

# Patron of Lost Souls

Most people in Britain had never heard of the lascars. The word itself was exported to India by the Portuguese, thanks to the adventures of the explorer Vasco de Gama. His ships reached the Indian coast at Calicut on 20 May 1498, opening up one of the most lucrative trade routes the world would ever know. Over the course of two centuries the Portuguese word for 'soldier' – *lachar* – morphed into the Hindi word *lashkari*, but held the same meaning. It was only when the British arrived that the word and its meaning were transformed. Agents of the East India Company began to use the word *lascar* to describe the ragged merchant seamen they recruited to transport cargo.

Even though the number of lascars increased dramatically with the growth of the Raj, few knew anything about them. Of those who recognised the name, many owed their knowledge solely to literature. Sir Arthur Conan Doyle, in his short story *The Man with the Twisted Lip*, described his lascar as 'rascally' and a 'scoundrel'. In the words of Sherlock Holmes himself: 'The lascar was known to be a man of the vilest antecedents,'[1] and readers were encouraged to fear and loathe him.

In reality the lascars were among the most wretched and exploited underclasses in British society. Formerly peasant farmers, the majority had been recruited from Punjab, East Bengal and India's west coast, with the rest coming largely from China. Initially, in the 1700s, the East India Company had been reluctant to hire them, thinking them poor replacements for a British crew. However traders often had no choice. Thanks to desertions and indiscipline from their own men far away from home, by the 1800s, the practice of hiring lascars had grown common. Writing in 1855, a Colonel Hughes, who was then conducting an audit of seafaring personnel, suggested that 'at the lowest computation' the British merchant service employed 10,000–12,000 lascars for service in the East Indian, Chinese and Australian trade,[2] and about half of these men were brought to Britain every year. Despite the fact they were hired hands and not slaves, the lascars were often treated appallingly on their gruelling ocean voyages.

Christian missionaries were the first to pay attention to the stories being murmured in the East London docks. Tales of sadistic cruelty and even murder were filtering back thanks to British seafarers who hated what they had seen. So concerned were missionaries, they began to collect evidence of mistreatment. Their findings painted a grim picture of life for the Indian sailors on the high seas.

Lascars were frequently starved on inferior rations and given summary beatings on board their ships. In some of the more extreme cases, lascars were punished by their superior officers by being 'hung up with weights tied to their feet, flogged with a rope'.[3] Devout Muslim lascars had been forced to eat pork even though it was strictly against their religion, and 'the insult carried further by violently ramming the tail of the pig into their mouths and twisting the entrails of the pig around their necks'.[4] The act was designed to cause greater suffering even than physical violence. Joseph Salter, a 'Missionary to the Orientals and Africans', became the chief collator of evidence and searched the London docks for lascars who had been subjected to such treatment. They were not that hard to find, and Salter diligently recorded what he saw. One lascar had most of his teeth knocked out after being whipped repeatedly in the face with a chain. Others were left crippled from bone-shattering beatings. One of the most gruesome stories in Salter's files involved nine lascars who had been flogged to death by a ship's captain. He had then ordered their bodies to be tossed over the side of the vessel.[5] Writing in 1873, Salter said he found it almost impossible to believe that there were people who thought that 'the coloured part of mankind existed only to be used like brute beasts, and to have the most insulting names language can supply heaped upon them'.[6]

As terrible as their treatment on the ships could be, for many lascars the voyage to England was not the worst experience they suffered. As far back as 1782, complaints were reaching the East India Company of ships casting their lascars adrift in British ports. In one letter to the president and council at Fort St George in Madras, headquarters of the East India Company, the London office complained that several lascars had found their way to their building in 'great distress'. The office had therefore been forced to hand over money to the starving, homeless men, 'from motives of compassion and humanity as well as policy'.[7] However, humanity and policy only went so far. It was strenuously pointed out in the same letter that the expense incurred by any acts of charity ought not to be borne by them, and colleagues were actively discouraged from giving lascars the company addresses in the future.

While the East India Company quibbled about responsibility, the lascars themselves were fighting to survive on the cold and inhospitable streets of London. As one editorial in the *Morning Chronicle* put it, the men had been: 'Enticed, perhaps, from their native country where the climate is mild and tepid . . . brought to one more cold . . . without clothing proportional to conciliate them thereto . . . they are at present permitted to roam about this opulent city [London] unnoticed and unrelieved without a coat to shield them from the extremity of the weather, a shoe to preserve their feet from disaster, or even money to purchase sustenance sufficient to allay the gripping pangs of hunger.'[8] There is no way of knowing how many died due to the cold and malnutrition.

As the volume of exported goods from India increased, more lascars were employed, and the complaints multiplied. Some shipping companies simply refused to pay the sailors anything at all, threatening them with violence if they pressed for their meagre wages. In the early 1800s, the problem of destitute lascars had reached such a level that the East India Company was embarrassed into action. Grudgingly, arrangements were made to provide the lascars with board and lodging when they arrived. These dwellings were of the meanest kind, mainly in the slums of east London.

It was not long before locals started to complain about the 'nuisance' from the foreign presence, and so the lascars were moved out of the city to Shadwell, a swampy area on the north bank of the Thames. Tales of lascar suffering began to attract the notice of local Christian missions. Church groups unearthed tales of flogging and starvation in the boarding houses, but even though the missionaries seemed to be the only ones who cared about the lascars' plight, they too could take a dim view of their humanity: 'They are the senseless worshippers of dumb idols, or the deluded followers of the licentious doctrines of a false prophet ... ignorant, darkened, and deceived through the blindness which is in them ... They are the enemies to God by wicked works; they are practically and abominably wicked. They are a prey of each other and of the rapacious poor.'[9]

In one fact-finding mission in 1814, at a boarding house near Wapping, a member of the newly created organisation for the 'Protection of Asiatic Sailors' found 'nearly two or three hundred of them ... ill-fed and badly treated by a person (a superior lascar) who had command of them, both as to food, clothes and settling disputes among them. He frequently whipped them.'[10]

The buildings the lascars lived in were not fit for human habitation; most were cold and cavernous warehouses, designed and built for storing cargo, 'very dirty, and ... without pavement – the floor consisting of earth'.[11] At the back of the warehouse were rows of tall, narrow cupboards, where dockworkers stored their gear. When one of the missionary inspectors asked for these to be opened, 'out came a living lascar' who had been 'put into confinement for quarrelling and bad behaviour'.[12] How long he had been there, the missionary did not say.

Unlike most people in England, Sophia had grown up vaguely aware of the lascars' plight. Her late father, at the age of eighteen, just two years after his arrival in England, had provided finances to build and run a house for 'Oriental Seamen'. For Duleep's sake, Prince Albert had laid the first stone of the 'Strangers Home for Asiatics, Africans and South Sea Islanders'. But as her father's attentions wandered, the lascars trapped in the West also drifted from his mind. By the time Sophia returned from her trip to Punjab, the Indian sailors had been neglected for decades. Duleep Singh's safe haven for them in East London's West India Dock Road was falling apart, stretched well beyond its capacity. The number of lascars hired to handle cargo had grown exponentially since her father's day. On her return to England, Sophia found the Indian sailors clustered in their poverty around the foetid grime of London's three main docks. Shunned by society, the lascars stuck close to the River Thames, along which warehouses and cramped cheap accommodation blistered from the dank and stinking marshland.

The place was steeped in toxic industrial waste, dumped just outside the city limits. Opium dens and brawling bars dotted the landscape, and shivering lascars would often spend what little they had attempting to escape their appalling realities at the bottom of a bottle or in the curling smoke of a drug haze. The stranded sailors gave up hope of ever seeing their homes or their families again.

Sophia had found her cause and she threw herself into it. She began to evangelise among her rich friends, raising both awareness of the lascars' plight and funds to support them. Her social circle was bemused by her behaviour. When had Sophia ever cared about such things? Despite their confusion, Sophia galvanised support. Money started coming in, bulwarked by her own sizeable donations. Eventually Sophia's ambitions would dwarf the lascar provision created by her father and the East India Company. Together with two friends she would build and furnish a new lascar safe haven in London's Victoria Docks. In only a matter of five years, almost five thousand lascars would pass through its doors seeking and receiving urgent help.[13]

Although she was oblivious to such trends in her small circle of party-hopping aristocrats, Princess Sophia's embrace of social philanthropy chimed with the times. Recent decades had seen a flowering of women's charity work in fields of poverty and welfare. From the mid-nineteenth century it had become increasingly common for women of the upper-middle classes to concern themselves with the hardship of those less fortunate. Although charitable organisations were still run by men, it was becoming socially acceptable for women to use their 'maternal instincts' to work for the poor under such aegises. Acting as patrons of schools and hospitals, they devoted their time and money to the dispossessed in the city slums. What they saw made them angry. A radical form of women's politics was emerging. It centred on the belief that women were the key to family prosperity. They were less likely to drink away wages, and more likely to put the interests of their children before anything else. An unassuming house on Nelson Street, in the Chorlton-on-Medlock area of Manchester, became a particularly vibrant hub of activity. It was the family home of Emmeline Pankhurst.

Born in Lancashire, in Manchester's Moss Side, Pankhurst had witnessed the difficulties rapid industrialisation had caused, particularly for women and children. Between the turn of the nineteenth and twentieth centuries, the population of Moss Side exploded from 151 to 26,677.[14] Row upon row of cramped red-brick tenements scratched through the landscape as the city of Manchester swelled to accommodate the growing working class. They had been drawn to the area by the proliferation of textile mills. The city became the place where most of the cotton, transported by the lascars from India, was converted to cloth. Textile manufacturing so dominated Manchester that it became known as Cottonopolis.

Pankhurst watched as overcrowding brought poverty, disease and brutality to her city. Hunger was driving the poor to desperation, and Emmeline was horrified by the number of young girls she saw being pushed into prostitution. In 1894 she became a Poor Law Guardian and would regularly visit workhouses. During Queen Victoria's reign, the general attitude to the poor had been hardening. Previously the destitute were looked after by the state and provided with food and clothing paid for by funds levied from the wealthy. The Poor Law Amendment Act of 1834 changed all that. It ensured that no able-bodied person could get financial aid unless they went to live in special institutions where they would have to work for their food and lodging. The most vulnerable found themselves living cheek by jowl in the most basic, crowded accommodation on subsistence rations. In the workhouse, people were expected to labour for up to twelve hours a day. Soon, orphans and children whose parents were just too poor to feed them were abandoned on the doorstep. Anyone who fell on hard times could find themselves in the workhouse, but perhaps the worst treatment of all was meted out to unmarried mothers. They not only had to keep up with the harsh demands of the regime while nursing their babies, but also had to deal with sexual violence and the unforgiving judgement of their peers.

Moved by their plight, Emmeline Pankhurst decided that women needed to have a voice in the way society was run. Without the vote, she believed her sex would never truly be able to change anything. The men in the House of Commons, she argued, had little interest in or knowledge of the suffering of women. Emmeline was not the first to seek political empowerment for her sex. Millicent Fawcett, leader of the National Union of Women's Suffrage Societies (NUWSS), and sister of Elizabeth Garrett Anderson, had politely and persistently been asking politicians to extend the franchise to women for years. Fawcett had enjoyed a close relationship with the Liberal Party, and had assured her followers that by putting pressure on them, the shape of politics would eventually change to include them. However, Fawcett had put her faith in a party which was deeply divided on the issue. Every time she pushed them towards electoral equality, the Liberals pushed back. They bickered amongst themselves and backtracked on any commitment. Emmeline Pankhurst had initially supported Fawcett's efforts but by the turn of the century her patience had worn thin.

Pankhurst explored other political options beyond the NUWSS. She became a leading light of the Women's Franchise League, an organisation which supported the newly formed Independent Labour Party; but even Keir Hardie's progressive party moved too slowly for her liking. Pankhurst decided to take matters into her own hands. As they huddled around the table at her house in Manchester on 10 October 1903, a small group of women, including Emmeline's daughters Christabel, Sylvia and Adela, decided that only a militant organisation, prepared to break the law, could break the deadlock. The Women's Society for Social and Political Union

(WSPU) was born. It was an organisation which would reshape the political map of Britain by force and ultimately dominate the life of an Indian princess living at Hampton Court, even though she had no idea at the time.

It had long been Sophia's custom to receive her breakfast in bed. Her lady's maid brought up a large brass tray, one of her purchases from India, with a small silver teapot, two boiled eggs, toast, fruit and some goat's-milk curd.[15] The last item was an exotic addition to her menu, a habit formed from her time in India. Previously it had been Sophia's habit to wake just before noon, her nights having been filled with parties and dances. However, since her return from Lahore, she rose earlier and liked to start the day by reading the newspapers in bed. In 1903 it felt as if the world was changing so quickly. Pages were filled with stories of women defying their subordinate role in society. It was the year that scientist Marie Curie became the first woman to be awarded a Nobel Prize. Mary Howarth not only became the subject of headlines, she gained the power to write them, becoming the editor in chief of the one-penny *Daily Mirror*. The newspaper, 'for gentlewomen by gentlewomen', immediately caused a storm in Fleet Street. A one-time glamorous secretary called Dorothy Levitt gave the papers plenty to write about too when she became the first woman to take part in a public motor-car race in 1903. She went on to cause deeper consternation still by taking water- and land-speed records, leaving the men in her wake.

Although such stories caught Sophia's eye, they were not the first thing she sought out in the headlines. The newspapers of 1903 were also peppered with the latest disgrace facing her eldest brother. While Sophia had been discovering India, Victor had found himself teetering on the edge of financial ruin again. Though he had tempered his wilder excesses after marriage, he still managed to grossly exceed his allowance. Coupled with the historic debts that were catching up with him, Victor was faced with liabilities in excess of £100,000. When moves were made to collect on the debts, Victor argued that the bailiffs had no right to seize his belongings. In anticipation of the gathering storm, he had signed over the house and most valuable items to Anne soon after they wed. The creditors argued that the prince had deliberately hidden assets and an acrimonious court case ensued which dragged on for months and was widely reported in the national press. The *Daily Mail* was among those publications that covered the extent of Victor's problems in detail: 'It appeared that in 1899 His Highness made a free gift of the contents of Hockwold Hall to his wife. In 1902 he became bankrupt, and the question raised was whether the gift was a valid one, and whether, considering his financial position at the time, it was rendered void under the Bankruptcy Act . . . His pension is £8,000 a year from the Indian Government, and could not be assigned or anticipated. The reason given by him for his bankruptcy was that he was unable to live on the allowance made to him.'[16]

Victor was furious that his financial troubles were being laid bare and lashed out the only way he knew. Like his father before him, he made his own aggressive counter-claim against the British government. He argued that the late Maharajah's personal assets were worth many times more than the settlement imposed upon the Maharajah's children. Furthermore, Victor insisted that if he were given his fair inheritance then he would have no problem paying off his debts like a gentleman. The move was as futile as any launched by Maharajah Duleep Singh. In the end the courts judged the prince to be bankrupt, and told him that the only way he might save himself from total disgrace was if he could pay his creditors ten shillings of every pound he owed. Powerless to do anything else, Victor accepted the verdict, while squirreling away as much as he could from his creditors. For two years, Prince Freddie and Sophia became entangled in Victor's complex financial arrangements. Sophia even became complicit in hiding some of Victor's jewels, helping to spread them around family strong-boxes, to be returned at a later date.[17] It was a worrying time, made all the more so with her sisters away because she had nobody there to confide in.

Sophia attempted to distract herself with friends, fundraising, and a regular correspondence with Catherine and Bamba, in which the sisters filled pages with the minutiae of their days and amusing anecdotes. But it was getting harder to cheer Sophia up. Most of the pursuits which had previously absorbed her seemed empty and unimportant now. Her life at Hampton Court was beginning to grate and she found the routine stifling. Sophia relied on Bamba to provide the odd diversion, and even from as far away as Lahore, her sister did not disappoint. One day Sophia had been stunned to find the loaded pistol Bamba had hidden in her bedside cabinet at Faraday House. Wiring India, she asked what she should do. Bamba immediately telegraphed back warning her not to touch it herself, but to get a footman to deal with the gun's disposal.[18] Bamba was aware that depression was filling her little sister's head with dark thoughts. The last thing she needed was access to a firearm.

For months Sophia had been writing increasingly sullen letters to Catherine and Bamba. At first both of them perversely revelled in her Faraday House unhappiness: 'So you are beginning to have enough of the vulgarity of H. C.!'[19] wrote Catherine cheerfully; 'I should somehow make you come here and not go near that detestable dog-kennel vulgarness called Faraday House.'[20] And as if to rub salt into her sister's wounds, Catherine added at the end of her letter: 'How I pity you in that filthy climate.'[21]

Catherine and her governess were now living happily together in Cassel, a town in northern Hesse. The Brothers Grimm had written most of their fairy tales there and the landscape formed a chocolate-box backdrop for their happiness. Vast parks with ornamental fountains, canals, lakes and statues provided the women with beauty and tranquillity. The odd couple pursued a simple life together. They went for long bracing walks, pottered around old shops in remote villages and while Catherine tended the garden, Lina Shaeffer spent her days in the kitchen cooking all the things Catherine liked to eat, as she wrote to Sophia: 'I am having a very good time of it and enjoying myself thoroughly.'[22]

In India, Bamba too seemed content for the first time in her life. Refusing to return to Europe with either of her sisters, she was realising her dream. She moved from temporary accommodation at the luxurious Braganza Hotel to her own house near the Shalimar Gardens, where her father had played as a boy. She called her new Lahore home 'The Palms', and set about furnishing it with as much love and care as her youngest sister had lavished on Faraday House.

Sophia kept writing in vain, asking when Catherine and Bamba might come back to her. London made her feel unbearably lonely and to escape the silence of her grace-and-favour home, she had taken to spending long stretches of time with her friends, the Mackenzies, in Inverness. It was as far away from Hampton Court as she could get, but respite was only ever temporary.

Eventually Catherine stopped teasing and felt the depth of her sister's feelings. She tried to explain as tenderly as she could, why she could not bring herself to return to Faraday House: 'It was delightful for you to be so long in Scotland. You ought to come out here. What Scotland is for you, this is for me. I have such an appetite and have got such red cheeks. In fact I am just "bursting" and feel quite a different being to what I felt [in England] . . . You know how dead tired I always was even after doing nothing at H Court. You had better come out! The air is so delightful here and then Miss S's excellent German food is too good for any words.'[23] Sophia did not take up the offer, and instead remained in London where depression pushed her further under.

Bamba was the first to become truly alarmed by her youngest sister's condition. Sophia had admitted to her in a letter that she had stopped taking music lessons and hardly touched the piano any more. Bamba begged her to make time for her music since it had always brought her joy in the past. When she saw the latest pictures Sophia had commissioned of herself, Bamba realised that there was something gravely wrong. What looked out at her from the photograph was a pale and fragile version of her little sister, with none of the old spark in her eyes. She wrote to her, addressing Sophia with the childhood nickname she had used in the nursery: 'Thanks to little Asa for the delightful surprise of a photograph . . . But it is not Asa. It is much too serious and she looks very thin and ill. The eyes are the only nice part and they are much too sad . . . Be quick and look better.'[24]

Sophia's brother Frederick was blithely unaware of her suffering. He threw himself into his local branch of the Duke of York's Own

Loyal Suffolk Hussars, a volunteer cavalry unit which collected and drilled regularly near his home. Prince Frederick's involvement with the Yeomanry was more out of a fervent loyalty to the Crown than either a desire or an ability to be a soldier. By the turn of the century he had become a round and avuncular figure with his sharply tailored clothes camouflaging an ever more generous belly. His moustache was twirled and tipped with wax, and hereditary baldness had robbed him of the hair Queen Victoria had once so loved. The only battles dapper Freddie was fit to fight were those with the weeds in his vast estate, and he seemed to be losing them too. 'Nothing goes right, the garden is a failure ... it is disgusting ... people's borders are gorgeous – mine are in swarms.'[25]

Freddie was spending more time and energy than ever living the life of a true-blue English gentleman. He was a fervent supporter of the Primrose League, a political organisation inspired by the beliefs and values of Benjamin Disraeli, the former Conservative prime minister. The Primrose credo was a total anathema to Sophia and her sisters; members swore: 'I declare on my honour and faith that I will devote my best ability to the maintenance of religion, of the estates of the realm, and of the imperial ascendancy of the British Empire; and that, consistently with my allegiance to the sovereign of these realms, I will promote with discretion and fidelity the above objects, being those of the Primrose League.'[26] Freddie seemed untroubled by the polarity of his beliefs and those of the rest of the family. He was a conservative of both the big and small 'c', unquestioningly loyal to the throne and to the idea that Britain reigned supreme. There were few royalists as ardent as Sophia's brother; he even procured a valuable portrait of Oliver Cromwell just so that he could hang it upside down in the toilet of his Suffolk home.[27]

Freddie never concerned himself with issues of his Indian heritage, lost empires or sub-continental politics. In letters he wrote to Sophia he made no secret of his intense dislike of foreign places and the 'simply dreadful people' who lived in them. Freddie preferred to live in places anchored firmly in British history and filled his days collecting Jacobean art and studying the coats of arms of East Anglian aristocracy. Impeccably polite, chivalrous and refined, the once obstinate child was now the spirit of kindness and generosity loved by all. To the locals, the 'black prince' was a quintessentially English country squire with confusing dark skin and a cumbersome foreign name. The bachelor lived his life in a bubble, where modernity was the enemy and change was to be avoided at all costs. At times his olde-worlde quirkiness tipped into downright eccentricity. Prince Frederick was lost and perplexed by the modern age. Electricity was just beginning to make its way into British homes, and Freddie hated it. It was a new-fangled intrusion he would eschew for most of his life, even though all around him lit up gratefully. He was also in the dark about the extent of Sophia's malaise.

Freddie had always been deeply fond of his sister. They shared an even temper and stoic quality that made them dependable. Freddie appreciated beauty and since her coming out Sophia had been praised for her looks and poise. He had loved to chaperone her around the aristocratic balls of England. Lately, however, Sophia seemed unwilling to make the effort: her appetite for society had dwindled, as had her appetite for food. Reflecting her change of outlook, Sophia's shopping bill at the fashion houses of Paris went into steep decline as she accepted fewer invitations. Freddie had no idea how to make his sister happy again.

The simple truth that escaped them all was that Sophia needed to be needed. Since the time of Eddie, Sophia had taken responsibility for somebody more vulnerable than herself. She was only able to pull herself from the whirlpool of grief after the deaths of her brother, mother and father by turning her attention to her sisters, who, despite being older than Sophia, seemed ill equipped to deal with the world. Now that they had left her behind to pursue their own happinesses she did not know what to do. Sophia was uncomfortable and awkward again. Recent Indian experiences had soured her view of England. Victor's tribulations mirrored her father's problems which had blighted their childhood. Everywhere she looked, she saw greyness.

It was a desperate call for help that brought Sophia back from the brink. In the autumn of 1906, quite from nowhere, Bamba begged her little sister to come immediately to Lahore. Somebody, she said, was trying to kill her.

# The Princess and the Madman

As early-rising children put finishing touches to Guy Fawkes effigies, ready to drag them through London for pennies, Sophia scrambled to dress within the cold, lamplit bedroom at Faraday House. She was uncharacteristically tetchy, filled with dread for her sister.

The urgency of Bamba's letter[1] left Sophia very little time to prepare: her passage, booked for 5 November 1906, could not come soon enough. The maid had woken her while it was still dark; Sophia had rarely seen that time of the morning and was feeling harried. First she had to take a train from London to Southampton, leaving hardly any margin to catch the ocean liner leaving for India. All in all, the journey to Lahore would take about two months. Stressed and tired, she marshalled her hastily collected belongings. The task was made no easier by the numerous noisy dogs, excited by the change in their usual regime. Hating the upheaval, Sophia barely managed to catch the 9.25 train to Southampton docks. As she noted in her diary, she was feeling hungry and unhappy, 'having had not one mouthful of breakfast'.[2]

The train from London was busy and uncomfortable but Sophia struggled more than most thanks to a puppy just weeks old wriggling constantly in her lap. The shivering little creature was so new to the world it did not yet have a name. Well aware that the runt was ill-suited for the long voyage ahead, Sophia took it with her anyway, considering it too feeble to leave behind. Newspaper articles had written many times about her ability to look after sick and fragile animals, as if she possessed mystical abilities. Vanity had convinced her that what they wrote was true, even though the puppy was already showing signs of incontinence.

The whimpering bundle was not the only four-legged companion being jostled along with the luggage that day. Clinging to her side, like a tiny, twitching shadow, was the princess's beloved black Pomeranian, Joe. Sophia's last long trip had taught her that she could not live without her favourite dog. Since she had no idea how much time it would take to convince Bamba to come back to England, the princess had decided Joe must this time accompany her. The dog failed to appreciate his mistress's devotion and snapped and yapped. Sophia instructed her valet to dose him with magnesium in order to keep him calm, while her own nerves remained on edge.[3]

Stormy weather delayed the first crossing and Sophia's thoughts were just as unsettled. She and Catherine had been worried about Bamba for some time but they had never guessed that she was in fear for her life. Until the strange letter from her sister arrived at Faraday House, they just assumed that India was making her a bit out of sorts. As Sophia thought back on recent months, she realised that there had been many worrying signs. Once the most punctilious of correspondents, Bamba had for the past few months been missing the post on too many occasions. The sisters always had a strict code of conduct when it came to letter-writing: scattered in different corners of the world they relied on regular correspondence for reassurance. It was normal for the sisters to write to each other twice weekly and failure to do so was met with overwhelming disapproval. Traditionally, Bamba had been more unforgiving than anyone if the post yielded unsatisfactory news from her sisters. Nevertheless, her own correspondence had been erratic, bland and cagey for some months. When she wrote, she gave little away and sometimes her handwriting was shaky, verging on the illegible. The scrawl suggested the letter had been dashed off absentmindedly and in haste.

When, in the middle of 1905, their teasing yielded no improvement in Bamba's demeanour, Catherine and Sophia grew concerned.

She had been alone in India for almost a year, and Sophia decided it was now time to summon her back to England. When Bamba failed to respond and Sophia turned to nagging, she was met with a tidal wave of scorn: 'There were these pages of wrath from you at my remaining here rather more than I anticipated, but still I continue to survive it.'[4] . . . 'Many thanks for your letter but why always so much about my staying here?'[5] . . . 'I am once more in this paradise while you both are suffocating in Hampton Court – Why when a paradise is so easily obtainable, sit on earth! . . . Why do you particularly want to know whether I am coming back next year, and you know I never make such promises.'[6] 'Don't be surprised if I stay here another year! . . . How I pity you in Faraday.'[7]

Not even an act of God could persuade Bamba to return to England. On 5 April 1905, the deadliest earthquake in modern Indian history left almost 20,000 people dead in the north of the country. The epicentre of the quake was located in Kangra, a district nestled in the Western Himalayas, bordering Punjab. Measuring 7.8 on the Richter scale, the earthquake caused widespread devastation spreading through Dharamshala (more recently the mountain home of the Dalai Lama in exile) all the way down to the major Punjabi cities of Lahore, Jalandhar and Amritsar. Such was the force of the quake that even Calcutta, almost 250 miles away, felt the tremors.

Though the newspapers in England were filled with alarming stories of damage and loss of life, Bamba described the experience with infuriating flippancy, writing to Sophia a day after the quake: 'My experiences were only minor but it was a tragedy in the city and in other places. I was just having, or rather had just had my *choti huzari*[8] when it began and I thought it[s] only an earthquake I will stay in bed but it began getting worse. In a few seconds the whole room seemed to rock and the ceiling seemed to be cracking so I left my bed and went out into the garden . . . The crows were making such a noise, I certainly will tell you the rest later. There was a Purdah party yesterday at the Shalimar and it was very lovely.'[9] When Sophia questioned the flippant tone of her sister's account, Bamba again responded tersely: 'Did you really think the earthquake would frighten me back!!!'[10]

By late October 1906, however, the swagger had gone from Bamba's letters. Something or someone had definitely frightened her. She had been violently ill, poisoned, she believed. Her sister's terror was real enough to persuade Sophia to drop everything and rush to her side.

The SS *Barbarossa* was designed to soothe and pamper even the tautest of travellers. The upper decks stretched out like vast wooden boulevards and the cabins which led off them were decorated in the height of fashion. Cream and gold panelled ceilings were filled with frescos and in the capacious dining room, heavy, polished walnut and mahogany furniture gleamed. The smoking room, in which Sophia would spend a significant amount of time, had leather armchairs and leather-covered walls and smelt darkly of mink oil and tobacco. Those seeking privacy could find it in the numerous and discreet booths that had been created for games of cards and sensitive conversations.

Such luxury was only enjoyed by a small proportion of the ship's passengers. In total, the ship could accommodate around 2,500 passengers, though most of these travelled as steerage,[11] a population all but invisible to Sophia and her fellow passengers. Some evenings, the atmosphere on the upper decks could feel hedonistic and uninhibited: Sophia attended a fancy-dress party for the whole of first class, though did not go in costume herself: 'Mrs Howlett was a milk maid, quite good, she had a little stool and a toy cow which was splendid. Miss Reid as a Greek statue was excellent, quite the best as she had dressed herself in sheets. But only got 2nd prize. There was a lady in Frangi Chrysanthemums who was very good . . . an excellent Chinaman and one man as an Arab woman was very good.'[12]

Though Sophia adored the ambience of the *Barbarossa*, some of the passengers immediately grated on her, being a little too vulgar for Sophia's prudish disposition. Miss Stewart, travelling as far as Egypt, drew her particular disapproval: in Sophia's opinion, the young woman would make a fool of herself with any handsome chap who caught her eye: 'She is a shocker, she is good hearted and really nice, but very crude, no manners at all and an awful flirt. She goes too far . . . and it gives such a wrong impression.'[13] Sophia was more than a little amused by the frisson she herself was creating, however. 'The Balfours are very nice, Miss Stewart went up to them and said I wanted to know them, so up they come and he has "your highnessed" me ever since . . . Rather awful!'[14] Her objections were not convincing. Sophia rarely corrected anyone who used the title which had been forbidden to her by her godmother.

As one of the most distinguished guests on board, Sophia was invited to the captain's table every night to dine. The princess particularly approved of the formal evening meals, which often comprised seven courses, and throughout the voyage she relished the attention, along with the constant bowing and scraping from the crew and passengers. It would take a tiny four-legged creature to prick her dangerously inflating ego.

By the time the *Barbarossa* reached Aden, Sophia was on her hands and knees clearing up copious amounts of excrement and vomit: her puppy had become violently ill. To make matters worse, Joe, the Pomeranian, was also finding seafaring difficult. The nights in the princess's luxurious cabin were too hot and stuffy for the dog,[15] and the princess was kept awake by incessant panting and the overwhelming smell.[16] Sophia refused suggestions that she might put the dogs in steerage with her maid; still adamant that she was the best person to care for them, she fed the dogs on fine cuts of meat and the occasional nip of brandy.[17]

Eventually, after days without sleep, Sophia was forced to reconsider her position. She paid a young boy from steerage to help her care for the dogs, giving her time at least to sleep. The arrangement helped her mood but not the puppy's health, and it continued to deteriorate, although the princess refused to believe it: 'He will eat nothing of his own will, I have to pour everything down his throat in spoonfuls. I am giving him thin eggs and brandy and milk today – the owner of the dachshund [a fellow passenger] says he is not better and thinks he will die. As a matter of fact he is slightly better whatever he says.'[18]

Sophia took to sitting on the windy top deck, exhausted, with her listless dogs in her lap, in the hope that the sea air would revive them all. Seeing the forlorn figure, passengers would come and offer her unsolicited advice. Most were well meaning, but one young man seemed to take perverse pleasure in mocking her predicament. She recorded her first impressions of him in a diary she had purchased for the trip, a handsome, black leather book with a brass lock and catch for privacy. 'Lots of people came and spoke to me, including a man I could not stand as he said he hated dogs . . . besides I could not stand him by the way he talked,'[19] she declared. In the days that followed, the unnamed passenger kept up a flirtatious teasing of the exhausted princess.[20]

The brazen behaviour turned from irritating to charming in a short space of time. Sophia began to record in her journal even the smallest interactions with the fellow she would eventually come to refer to as 'The Madman'.[21] His presence filled her thoughts as the ship passed Port Said, where she and her family had been humiliatingly evicted from the SS *Verona* many years before, though she made no mention of it. Sophia was too distracted: 'Very odd, I am beginning to like the man I at first hated. But he does talk nonsense. We had a dance this evening, it was rather fun. I had 2 dances with that man. I like him . . .'[22] Recording her emotions with the self-awareness of a girl with a crush, she wrote: 'The Madman came and talked to me for a time, it's curious how he fascinates me, because I think he is really a devil. He imagined me about 21, so I have in the end to tell him my age [thirty]. It was a great shock to him.'[23] His flirting and flattery were intoxicating.

Sophia had so much experience of London's social life but she had little experience of romance. At home there had been no question of courting: the opportunities simply had not presented themselves. Victor and Freddie were too absorbed in their own lives to play matchmaker for their sister. Even if they had, an Indian princess whose father had been a traitor and whose brother was a notorious bankrupt did not make Sophia much of a catch. Moreover mixed-race children were looked down upon and judged as inferior. Only two years later, in 1908, a journalist would speculate on the whereabouts of Sophia and her siblings, referring to them as Duleep Singh's 'dusky tadpoles that drove about the King's Road at Brighton'.[24] It would never have entered the minds of the British aristocrats who danced with Sophia all night to fall in love with her. Bamba knew this and had previously tried to lure her little sister to India with talk of handsome and eligible Sikh suitors in Lahore. She even included badly sketched portraits in her letters; however Sophia had never taken the bait. These men with their turbans, beards and foreign manners did nothing to excite her. The Madman, on the other hand, was more like the men she had grown up around. The moments where their paths crossed were the best part of Sophia's day. Their flirtation would last the entire duration of the voyage.

Four weeks passed blissfully, but as she neared her destination, Sophia's mood began to change. She confessed to her diary that the end of her time with the Madman was distracting her from everything else: 'writing and pretending to study Urdu etc. . . . we arrive late tonight. Shall be able to go off ship early tomorrow morning . . . Madman now comes to walk . . . after dinner while I was sitting alone on my chair talking to Joe, suddenly he appeared, talked his usual nonsense . . . The lights of Colombo quite plain before I went to bed.'[25]

In the morning, as the passengers bustled in preparation to disembark in Ceylon's largest port city, Sophia looked out for the Madman to say her farewells. But he was nowhere to be seen. She spent the day glumly dealing with her luggage and her dogs, as she was transferred to a seafront hotel for the night. The puppy provided a sad but welcome distraction. It had taken a turn for the worse sometime during the night and was clearly very ill. The next leg of Sophia's journey would be long and arduous, taking her from Ceylon to the southern tip of India, from where she would have to make her way north to Bamba in Lahore. With heavy heart, Sophia found a local vet who agreed to take the puppy and look after him while she travelled.

That evening, with only little Joe at her side, Sophia looked out from her hotel window on to the ink black sea and watched the anchored *Barbarossa* bob gently in the distance, its lights prickling in the darkness. Returning to her diary she noted with a tone of sadness: 'The Madman never said good bye to me.'[26] Sophia never mentioned him again, or disclosed his identity. Nor did she speak of her puppy, which died just a few days later. Over the years it had become easier for Sophia to block out the pain.

# The Blood is Up

Sophia took a boat from Colombo to the bustling port of Madras the very next day. Noise, heat and sweat hit the princess as soon as she walked down the gangplank, clinging to her like a second skin. The port was crawling with chaotic industry and the air was thick with salt and the smell of fish and hot metal. Glistening men attempted to bring their catches in, navigating through stevedores bellowing orders at men carrying cargo. The British engineer Sir Francis Spring, pioneer of the Indian railways, was attempting to reshape Madras. He wanted to protect British freight from the frequent cyclones which slammed into the Coromandel coastline, and work was well under way. Huge machines on the waterside chewed up great sections of the docks, while wiry, dark-skinned men wove their way in between showers of sparks and rubble, balancing baskets of dirt and rock on their heads.

Anxious to leave the sensory assault behind her, Sophia departed Madras almost as soon as she arrived, embarking on the first of many bumpy rail and road journeys north to Lahore. As she watched the changing landscape with its blurring, vibrant colour, she scribbled in her diary, the train jogging her handwriting: 'Very delighted to be in India once more.'[1]

Every day, Sophia set aside time to write and always included – in extraordinary and often painstaking detail – her mealtimes: what times he ate, what she was served, how much she consumed . . . Having dealt with the contents of her stomach in tightly packed lines of spidery writing, she would go on to describe what she had seen. There were very few crossings out in Sophia's diary. She was as free flowing on the page as she was circumspect in her speech.

In contrast to her first visit to India this trip had been rubber-stamped by the India Office. As a result, the princess was met with great civility by the Residents of the states she passed through. The Raj Residencies acted as intermediaries between the Viceroy's office and the numerous princely states. When nawabs and rajahs heard that the granddaughter of Ranjit Singh was travelling through their territories, they asked their local Residents to bring her to them. Welcoming her warmly, they allowed her access to places no white man was usually allowed to go. Sophia spent time in the *zennanas*, the female quarters, which were closed off to the outside world. There she was presented with rare silks and priceless gems to inspect by *ranis* and *begums* who lived their lives in purdah. Because Sophia was an unusual visitor, a hybrid of East and West, kings and princes invited her to dine with them too, treating her like an equal. There were usually British officials present during these meals, ostensibly there to offer Sophia assistance. In reality they noted down every word that passed her lips.

It was what she learned of fallen empires which inspired Sophia to write most vividly. The earliest of her journal entries are peppered with notes about her father's lost lands; she was fascinated to learn of other dynasties which had also faded under conquest. When Sophia reached the fourteenth-century city of Daulatabad in the western state of Maharashtra, the ancient ruins there whispered to her of a once-great empire.[2] Daulatabad had been the capital of the mighty Tughlaq dynasty, a line of rulers who had their origins in Turkey. Muhamed bin Tughluq had in 1327 forcibly uprooted his people from Delhi and moved them to the middle of an alien central-Indian landscape. There, under the gaze of a mighty fort high up on the Deogiri, or 'Hill of the Gods', he commanded his people to flourish.

Sophia marvelled at the fortress, unable to understand how such a once-mighty edifice had been reduced to rubble. Perhaps thinking of her own family's decline, she imagined an invisible enemy had breached its walls: 'How anyone would ever have penetrated it I cannot think, it must have of course been taken through treachery.'[3]

Muhamed bin Tughluq proved to be a despotic and ultimately ridiculous man. He had moved his people from an area of comfort to one of great hardship. For two years he watched them struggle fruitlessly in the arid heat. Eventually they abandoned the place due to the lack of water, leaving to rebuild their lives in Delhi. Their ruler's authority disintegrated along with the homes and fort they left behind. Medieval India had once cowered before the Tughluq's mighty sultanate; however nothing remained of it but vine-covered stones. Like braille, the history of India could be read in the rocky ruins left by a succession of victors and vanquished.

Before leaving Daulatabad, Sophia heard that a stranger had been looking for her. Bamba had promised to send a man to help her on the journey weeks ago but nobody had materialised, and Sophia had given up hope of an escort. Someone called Pir Kareem Baksh had left his calling card in numerous locations hoping to find her.[4] She had been expecting a muscular footman to aid her with her bags but was met instead by a diffident young man who was not even strong enough to lift her lightest luggage. Baksh was Bamba's tutor and personal secretary, an acknowledged scholar in Persian, Arabic and English, and of practically no use at all.

Bamba, however, relied on him for everything, addressing him with the honorific 'Pir-ji', even though he was well below her in social status. Sophia noted grumpily in her diary: 'Bamba thought it might be amusing to have a travelling history lesson.' Karim Baksh settled in the train compartment and, as they set off for the final ten-day leg of the journey, he pointed out landmarks and told stories. Sophia was less than grateful, grumbling in her diary about having 'no servant to help with baggage etc.'[5] – although she should have known that such practical considerations rarely occurred to her sister.

Sophia's irritation dissipated as the train neared its destination. 'Getting quite excited as we near Lahore now,'[6] she scribbled on 17 December. There were numerous porters waiting for her when the train pulled into the colonial grandeur of Lahore station. As they hauled her luggage from the carriage like a line of busy ants, her sister arrived with great flourish, looking every inch the Indian princess. Unlike Sophia, who sweated in her tailored European clothes, Bamba had thrown herself into native costume, arriving in a stylish sari. Despite her recent troubles, she looked cool and beautiful, even though Sophia would only admit it grudgingly: 'B arrived in a sari, of course I had feared that, but she was looking very well. Had a very smart buggy and cream horse. We drove to her home, which was about where I expected . . . a very nice house, very big.'[7]

Bamba's sprawling bungalow, The Palms, stood on the Jail Road, on an affluent outer belt of the city. As the address suggested, the house was also near one of Lahore's three main prisons. It stood close to the Upper Bari Doab, a canal which provided a corridor of cool air and greenery, and near Lahore's great racecourse and polo fields.[8] These were playgrounds of the British sahibs, and Bamba was surrounded by Englishmen, despite having moved thousands of miles away to escape them. The proximity of the twenty-two-acre Birdwood Barracks made the area one of the safest in the city.

Sophia marvelled at how quickly Bamba had put down roots. Her home was filled with artefacts from all over India, and was both warm and welcoming. Special attention had been given to Sophia's accommodation: 'She had bought such a lot of furniture to make my room nice . . . such extravagance for so short a time.'[9] Pir-ji lived in an annexe to the main house. ('I do not quite approve myself,' wrote Sophia in her diary, 'but he is very nice and B is more obstinate than me.'[10]) It was perhaps Bamba's stubbornness that prevented the sisters from discussing the real reason for Sophia having been summoned to India in those first few days.

The morning of 25 December started in a disconcerting manner. Bamba woke early and told Sophia she was going off on her own, to visit 'friends'. When Sophia asked if she could come too, finding it strange to be abandoned on Christmas morning, she was told in no uncertain terms that she had to stay at home. It would not be the only time that her sister 'went all alone and would not let me go with her'.[11]

The hours ticked by and Bamba finally returned in the late afternoon. Sophia noted in her diary that soon after a local fabric pedlar arrived with a delivery of material for Bamba's new saris. Knowing that Christmas was important to his client, he had also brought boxes filled with edible treats. But Bamba did not seem happy at all, seeing this as another attempt to kill her: 'The silk man came and brought some Indian food which looked excellent, but which B wouldn't let us eat for fear of poison. B is quite of the opinion that she was poisoned last winter when she was so ill and it certainly seems suspicious.'[12] Feeling sorry for the baffled pedlar, she watched him go, leaving the untouched boxes behind him.

The strain of being at Bamba's house surrounded by what at best was paranoia and at worst mortal danger soon began to grate: 'I don't know why she remains in this horrible unsafe country when she is in fear of her life all the time,' Sophia confided to her journal. 'But in the moving of her, I don't know how I am going to get her away in the spring.'[13] Sophia was right about the difficulty facing her. Despite Bamba's conviction that someone was trying to kill her, she resolutely refused to leave India. A ferocious row threatened to erupt between the sisters for the rest of the day, but neither of them would begin it.

In an effort to rescue their first Christmas together in years, Sophia did not ask the questions that plagued her, and Bamba did not volunteer any explanations. The silent standoff stiffened an already awkward atmosphere as the two went through the motions of decorating the house and preparing a festive evening meal. Ironically, a bout of breathless choking saved the day: 'We had a real Xmas and in the evening had the Christmas tree, and cake for tea and mince pies for dinner. And then B got something stuck in her throat . . . and she was sure they are trying to kill her . . . so made herself sick and then found out it was just something unfortunately hard in the vegetables . . .'[14]

Sophia wondered if the threat of assassination was largely in her sister's mind. Whatever the truth of the situation, the spluttering fit diverted attention sufficiently. Despite Bamba's self-induced vomiting, Sophia concluded in her diary that they had had a 'perfectly lovely evening'.[15]

Bamba took to escorting her little sister to as many social engagements as she could. Lahore had a scene that could fill any socialite's calendar, although it soon became clear that Bamba herself hated the endless round of parties and those who attended them. At one reception Sophia noticed her sister bridle upon the arrival of the most important Englishman in Punjab. The Lieutenant Governor, or 'LG' as she referred to him, was a man most people threw themselves at. Sycophancy followed him wherever he went, but Bamba stayed well away, even avoiding the traditional line-up to meet him. 'B hardly knew anyone and we did not stay long – the LG was there . . . B does not bow to him ever.'[16]

The LG was Sir Charles Montgomery Rivaz, a long-serving British civil servant who had worked his way from mid-level Raj bureaucracy, up through the Viceroy's office and into the most powerful position in the Punjab. It was clear that Bamba loathed him and it was not long before Sophia understood why. Sir Charles and his wife, Lady Rivaz, had humiliated Bamba on several occasions, either snubbing her at social events or blocking her entry to them altogether. Their behaviour angered Sophia greatly. Her rage would have been considerably worse had she known what they said about Bamba behind her back. At the very highest levels of the Raj, Sophia's sister was being painted as a morally bankrupt character, unsuitable for refined company. Bamba was widely maligned by the British, much in the same way that her grandmother Jindan had been during her lifetime.

A document in the Political and Secret Department described an episode which had cemented Bamba's reputation: 'From the time the daughters of the late Maharaja Dulip Singh first arrived in the Punjab until the occasion of Lord Curzon's last visit to Lahore in 1905, the Lieutenant Governor and Lady Rivaz asked them to the periodical entertainments at Government House, Lahore and Barnes Court, Simla. On the occasion of Lord Curzon's last visit to Lahore the Princess Bamba, who had then adopted Indian dress, was invited to a garden party to meet Their Excellencies and appeared in an oriental costume which, to say the least of it, was distinctly improper.'[17]

Another note in a Duleep Singh classified file went into greater detail about Bamba's apparent fashion faux pas: 'A very puzzling case – it seems to be admitted that the lady was wearing a native dress – and that too an ordinary native woman's dress, with an "anjou" structure across the breasts and the body naked from that down to the navel.'[18] The outfit was said to have so offended the guests that later, in 1905, when the Prince of Wales (the future King George V) and Princess Mary visited Lahore, Bamba was shunned from all banquets and garden parties. She was even barred from the ladies-only 'purdah party' to which all her friends had been invited. For the granddaughter of Ranjit Singh, former ruler of all of the Punjab, such a slight was hard to bear: 'Sir Charles Rivaz felt that if the Princess Bamba were to come to either the garden party or the purdah party in the costume I have alluded to, it would be an insult to Her Royal Highness. The Princess, therefore, received no card of invitation. Previous to this I should have said that Lady Rivaz wrote to Sirdarni Umrao Singh, who was a friend of the Princess Bamba, and begged her to persuade the latter to adopt a more fitting costume, Indian or otherwise. The Sirdarni replied that she had already spoken and this had provoked such an outburst that she dared not approach her again.'[19] Bamba was mortified, particularly by Rivaz's decision to involve her friends in her censure, and never forgave the LG or his wife.

Rivaz with his stern moustache and aloof airs swiftly succeeded in alienating Sophia too when on Boxing Day he gave the keynote speech at Punjab University's degree ceremony. What Sophia heard made her feel distinctly uneasy: 'He made a long speech . . . and it was more or less advising the students not to try and govern for themselves except very much under his boot.'[20] Although Sophia was perturbed by the idea of Indians living as second-class citizens in their own country, she did not identify herself as one of them. When Punjabi friends of her sister asked her if she was happy to be 'home' in the 'mother country' she was bemused. Sophia simply did not feel for India the way her sister Bamba did. Whenever Bamba slated the

British in her company, Sophia would defend them passionately, reminding her how kind her friends were, and how much she liked them. There seemed to be a new level of friction between the sisters which had never existed in England.

In the weeks that followed, Bamba tried to make her sister understand why she would not leave. She set out to make Sophia love India and hate Britain as much as she did, arranging for folk singers and musicians to come to the house, ordering her cooks to create complicated menus of spicy food. Sophia was a lover of heat, both in the weather and her cuisine. Despite her previous bland diet in England, she took her curries as spicy as the kitchens could make them.

As soon as the festive season was over, Bamba planned to take Sophia to see some of the old Sikh Kingdom, convinced that if she could show her little sister the injustice of British rule she would come to feel as she did. The lesson began as soon as the train pulled out of Lahore station. Bamba took Sophia on a short trip to Jullunder, a city some eighty miles away. The city had been wrested from its rulers in 1807 by their grandfather Ranjit Singh and before that formed the easternmost of Alexander the Great's territories. The British guard on the train insulted the Duleep Singh party repeatedly. As Sophia wrote in her diary, he was 'first rude to Pir-ji and then came to give us the tickets and was disgustingly rude to B'.[21] Bamba had become immune to such slights from the British, but Sophia was not prepared to tolerate them: 'I intend to write to the LG about it and have him dismissed. I shall not put up with that sort of thing.'[22]

Things only got worse when Sophia and Bamba attended the New Year's Eve celebrations back in Lahore. The day began with an afternoon at the races, one of the few occasions where Indians were allowed to compete directly with the British. Still bruised from her train experience, Sophia cheered on the Indian jockey: 'We saw the Patiala man win with one of his horses which was very nice. I do not think they were favourites; however it was delightful to see an Indian win something.'[23] Later that night there was a ball, the pinnacle of the Punjab's social calendar, thrown by Sir Charles Rivaz for all the dignitaries in his jurisdiction. Sophia had been invited, and for once, so had her sister.

Sophia chose a Parisian ballgown of finest pink silk which she had brought with her from England. As she preened in the mirror, Bamba came in and begged her to change into something more conservative. Sophia refused, telling her that such fashions were all the rage in London and Paris and should certainly be good enough for Lahore. As Joe darted in between their legs, Bamba continued to argue that her décolletage was unsuitable for the function ahead and eventually Sophia agreed to make alterations to her neckline: 'B insisted on making my pink dress higher for fear of shocking Indians.'[24] In reality it was not the judgement of Indians that Bamba was worried about but the cruel tongues of British socialites. Even though the sisters could disagree passionately, Bamba was at heart a protective older sister.

When they reached the ball, Sophia realised that she and her sister were the only brown faces on the guest list: 'It might have been an English ball to look at the room, full of people – about 500 I should say and all English.'[25] The sisters felt at once conspicuous and ignored as they descended the steps to the main ballroom. Bamba had been tense from the moment they left the house and very soon Sophia too wished she had not come. Nobody asked her to dance and very few people came to speak to them. Their coldness hurt Sophia deeply, since she had encountered some of the guests socially before back in England. Seeing the princesses lurking forlornly in the corner while the others waltzed around them, one man eventually took pity and asked Sophia for a dance later in the evening. He never came back to fulfil the promise.

Sophia was also stung by the absence of Lady Rivaz. Protocol dictated that she should have been there to look after the princesses. An excuse had been made on her behalf, which Sophia did not believe – taking her absence as a direct snub. 'Lady R was not there at all, not being well they said,' she told her journal, 'all sorts of things probably invented.'[26] Sir Charles behaved no better. Visiting dignitaries were always presented to the Lieutenant Governor, but despite waiting all night for an introduction, none was made. Then Rivaz's aide-de-camp came to speak to her and badly mispronounced her name: he asked, 'If I was Princess Ha Ha Ha'.[27] She left it to another to explain the correct way to say her uncomplicated name.

All night Sophia felt as if hands were steering her away from guests of any importance. The goddaughter of Queen Victoria had never felt so insulted: 'I was taken in corners . . . I never spoke to the LG at all that evening except to say howdy and good bye.'[28] The worst moment of the whole night was realising the extent of the whispering behind her older sister's back: 'I did not ask the question as to what people had been saying about B.'[29] Already deeply unhappy at the evening's events, the final straw came when the guests were led into the banquet. Sophia's royal status and her relationship with Queen Victoria should have dictated that she was one of the first to go in, escorted by a high-ranking officer. However 'it was the accountant general I believe who took me into supper but I did not catch his name and do not care'.[30] Just one taste of the treatment Bamba received on a regular basis in India sent Sophia into a rage: 'I was furious about the supper and intend to complain about it. It was very stupid . . . and I should have refused to go into supper.'[31]

A few days later Sophia wrote a blistering letter of complaint to the most senior British official on Indian soil,[32] the new Viceroy, Lord Minto, who had succeeded Curzon just a year before. Sophia's letter pulled few punches. Minto wanted to avoid any diplomatic ugliness and assured the princess that he would look into the matter. She was still regarded by the British as 'a traveller of position', he reassured her, worthy of all the respect such status demanded.[33] In the end nobody from Sir Charles's office offered an apology; nor did Lady Rivaz attempt to defuse the situation by inviting the princesses for tea. A stern word was had with the Jullunder train conductor, but he too remained in his post. Bitterly disappointed, Sophia was beginning to understand her sister's constant agitation.

On 14 January the whole of Lahore was gripped with excitement as a near total eclipse of the sun coincided with a major festival.[34] For Hindus, Vasant Panchami was the celebration of Sarasvati, the goddess of wisdom. For Muslims and Sikhs, Basant was the start of spring. People of all faiths dressed in vivid yellow clothes, like the statues of the goddess herself. The air throbbed with the sound of *dhol* players and their drums; food sellers dragged their carts into the streets, perfuming the air with spices and the smell of molten sugar. The sky was filled with brightly coloured paper kites. Leaving a disappointed Joe at home with the servants, Bamba and Sophia rode out on horseback to the Ravi River, where thousands had congregated to await total darkness.

The push of humanity stopped the sisters from getting near the water's edge where the view would have been most dramatic.[35] Sophia refused to be turned back and, leaving Bamba behind on the bridle path, rode on stubbornly to a nearby bridge. There she tethered her horse and attempted to walk across the mud to get to the water, a protesting servant in tow. However the tide was turning and as the waters rose the crowds retreated, engulfing Sophia in the process. Before she knew it she was caught in the middle of a throng of 'dirty people', splattered with the sludge from the riverbed. Word spread swiftly that Ranjit Singh's granddaughter walked among them. As Sophia and her servant struggled to make it back to Bamba, a phalanx of worshippers pressed in, murmuring the name of the Maharajah: 'a crowd began to collect around us as we walked. I heard lots of people saying who we were.'[36] Despite the surge and the gathering cries of recognition, Sophia was not afraid.

On their quest to discover the Sikh kingdom, the princesses met some of their more humble relatives. Different clans had laid claim to Ranjit Singh's bloodline; the sisters believed their true ancestors were the Sandhawalia family from the village of Raja Sansi, just outside Amritsar.

After the fall of the Sikh Kingdom, life had not been kind to the Raja Sansi cousins. Unlike their other Lahore relatives, this family were living a far from luxurious existence. Sophia recorded her first meeting with them: 'We drove into the village with its narrow streets looking much like other villages, only with some high houses . . . I was most delighted to have seen the home of my ancestors . . . we all sat on the veranda on a velvet cushion which B thought they had put out especially for us.'[37] Two of the male members of the family, Gurdit Singh and Narinder Singh, the sons of Thakur Singh, had been at Elveden when Sophia was little, acting as retainers to her father: 'And oh dear how they are changed poor things, but they have been through so much . . . The youngest having been imprisoned for 5 years for a crime which he never committed – oh dear all these horrid injustices – the older one is quite grey and the young one who was so good looking as a boy and who I fell in love with, cannot have grown an inch since then . . . he is an ugly little shrivelled up man.'[38]

Sophia learned that her father had sent the boys back after a few years. He calculated that they would be more use to him in India. As things turned sour with the British, Duleep had named their father, Thakur Singh Sandhawalia, as his 'prime minister in exile'. He and his sons would be at the very heart of his intrigues, attempting to stir the Punjab in anticipation of the revolt that would never be. As a result the Sandhawalias were forced to flee British territories and settle in the French colony of Pondicherry, where Thakur Singh Sandhawalia eventually died penniless and far away from home. After years of hardship and exile Thakur Singh's sons were finally allowed to make their way back home to the Punjab, where they had been struggling to make ends meet ever since. Sophia was visibly distressed to see their situation, but Bamba was delighted, determined to persuade Sophia to renounce England, as she had.

The next day Bamba had an opportunity to build her case against the British further. The Shalimar Gardens were buzzing with excitement. In tribute to the new season and its colours, thousands of people were flying kites in an anarchic aerial combat lasting as long as daylight. It looked as if a rainbow had shattered in the sky, as men, women and children attempted to cut rival kites with the strings of their own. While watching the display, Sophia and Bamba caught sight of Buta Singh, the servant of the Rajah of Kapurthala. He was the same man who had described Sophia as being a 'first-class' beauty, and had kept up a correspondence with the princess after she had returned to England, even asking her for money when he faced a difficult personal problem. He had no idea he was being watched: 'We saw Buta Singh mounted on a police horse, rather odd, what can it mean!!!'[39] Bamba had long suspected that he was working as a police informant. When later Buta Singh emerged from the crowds on foot to greet them, 'B blew his head off, but it served him right.

He had no business to come up and talk when he knows B will not see him. She called him a traitor and a bad man.'[40]

Bamba suggested that her little sister might want to extend her stay. When Sophia agreed, Bamba was so overjoyed that she decided to throw an enormous 'purdah party' in her little sister's honour. The chosen venue was the Shalimar Gardens and Bamba excitedly wrote to all the most important Indian families in the region. Purdah parties, which took place in the afternoons, were strictly for women only. They were teetotal affairs, where music played in the background, food was served, and distinguished speakers were invited to give improving educational lectures. The absence of men and alcohol made it possible for strictly observant Muslim women to leave their homes with their husbands' blessings.

Bamba and Sophia were determined to make their purdah party the talk of Lahore. Great marquees and elaborate screens were erected to shield guests from unwanted gazes. Entertainers were booked, and cooks hired to cater for every creed and caste. Thanks to Sophia's barracking of a local deputy commissioner on the very morning of the party,[41] the magnificent Mughal fountains were turned on just as they would have been when their father, Duleep Singh, had been a boy. The cascading water created an epic and romantic backdrop for a truly successful event.

There were quieter moments too, when Sophia and Bamba were away from the crowds and only had each other for company. After a long hard ride to Wagah – a village which now lies on the line dividing India and Pakistan – the sisters sat alone by the light of a camp fire: 'We had taken chocolate to drink and heated it up in a saucepan. Just when I had got to the last mugful, B said something which made me laugh and I went into such a choking fit, my mouth quite full of chocolate, I thought I should die. I was laughing all the time I could not breathe.'[42]

Moments of such innocent and private joy were about to become much rarer for the pair. Political turbulence was growing in Lahore, and the Duleep Singh sisters found themselves in the middle of an uprising which was both short-lived and doomed. Sophia soon discovered that her worst fears were true: Bamba's secret friends were fervent nationalists, and her association with them was attracting much unwanted attention for them both.

On 13 February 1907, the sisters were out for a drive, when Sophia suspected that they were being watched: 'followed all the time by a cyclist . . . If it happens again I shall report it . . . we were not out long. I got out and walked with Joe for a little way but the man then followed me.'[43] Returning to The Palms, Sophia and Bamba found a woman waiting on the veranda. Those who were spying on the princesses would have classified their unexpected visitor as a 'person of interest'. In her diary, Sophia described: 'A Bengali lady who is a great worker for the good of her country. She is very good looking and evidently very clever.'[44] Those few lines did their guest little justice. Sophia named the woman only once, calling her 'Mrs Ram Bhuj Datta'. The authorities knew her by a different name. She was Sarla Devi Choudrani, a known revolutionary, and a very dangerous woman.

Born to a family of Bengali intellectuals in Calcutta in 1872, Sarla Devi had always been a spirited girl, well read and unafraid to express her opinions. At the age of twenty-three she caused uproar in her family by informing them of her intention to leave home and teach at a school in Mysore. In India, daughters only left their parents to marry but Sarla Devi could see no reason why women should not be permitted to take jobs and work like the men. Her feminist rebellion did not last long though. After she had been teaching in Mysore for some time, and living happily in the staff accommodation, a prowler broke into her bedroom and terrorised her so badly that she felt she had no choice but to return to the safety of her parental home. Sarla Devi may have lost her personal freedom that night, but it signalled the beginning of her struggle for Indian independence.

Back in Bengal, Sarla Devi took up the editorship of a monthly journal called *Bharathi* ('The Indian'). In the publication she wrote firebrand editorials encouraging Indian men to take to the streets in groups to protect women from sexual molestation by British soldiers. The personnel from the military cantonments had long been criticised for their behaviour towards local women: far away from homes and family, many used prostitutes in the seedier quarters of the city, which grew to sate their appetites; others tried their luck with the brightly dressed housewives, who flitted in and out of the market places. The soldiers' conduct was causing a great deal of disquiet. Sarla named her vigilante group the *antaranga dal* or 'intimate army' and made members swear allegiance to each other and their cause by placing their hands on a map of India. It was not long before members of the *antaranga dal* were promising to sacrifice their lives for the sake of the country's freedom.

No longer satisfied with stirring dissent through her writing alone, in 1902, Sarla Devi began to train people for combat at her father's house. They were taught to fight with sticks and cudgels. Sarla Devi punctuated the physical exertions with a spiritual element of her own invention. After training was over, the group was required to chant the names of nationalist heroes as if they were reciting a prayer. One of those names repeated over and over again was that of Maharajah Ranjit Singh.[45]

Most Bengalis were horrified by her behaviour; one indigenous publication condemned her for 'conduct unworthy of a Hindu woman'. In 1905, at the age of thirty-three, Sarla Devi finally gave in to relentless family pressure and agreed to marry. Her husband, Ram Bhuj Datta, was also an ardent nationalist, and together they moved to Lahore where they began to train an underground Hindu network of rebels. Sophia wrote nothing of this extraordinary life when she referred to the mysterious Mrs Datta sitting on the veranda of The Palms taking tea. Now aware of the British surveillance, Sophia was being more careful about what she committed to paper.

Some episodes however were so noteworthy that Sophia could not help herself. Just days after Sarla Devi's visit to The Palms, on 16 February 1907, the sisters were out riding when 'we met a shut carriage driving hard and 2 mounted police and 1 behind. B said perhaps it's the Punjabi case, so we looked as it passed but we could recognise no one. There was an Englishman and 2 policemen inside and 2 other men . . . We were very curious . . . then thought we would follow to the prison but no one would tell us anything . . . we were returning when we met 2 tongas coming at a furious rate, so B rode after . . . we were told it <u>was</u> the Punjabi case and the editor had got 6 months and the proprietor 2 years rigorous imprisonment.'[46]

The Punjabi Case was the name given to a controversy that had rocked Lahore. It centred on the publication of articles which were critical of the British. The editor and proprietor were charged with sedition, and everyone was waiting to see how harsh the punishment might be. As the princesses found out, the judge had handed out the most severe sentences he could. He condemned the pair to lengthy terms of 'rigorous imprisonment', punishing them with body-breaking hard labour and possible transportation to the dreaded Kala Pani or 'Black Water' prison on the remote Andaman Islands. It lit a touch paper in Lahore. Students walked out of their classes and threatened to take over the streets. In some quarters violent retribution was promised unless there was an immediate release. Tension escalated within a matter of hours and Sophia and Bamba were caught right in the middle of it.

Digging their heels into already glistening flanks, the sisters raced their horses towards the city centre where the crowds were massing: 'As we got into the Mall we heard shouts . . . the students were marching up the Mall to the house of the Prisoners . . . and all along they were shouting Shame Shame to the Europeans they met.'[47] Two Englishmen had stopped alongside Sophia and Bamba, and watched the scene unfold. Sophia overheard one of them: 'he said he would like to get a whip and thank them'.[48]

The comment provoked fury in Sophia: 'My blood was up and I said quite loud, "Yes Shame on the British". I don't know and don't care if they heard. It is such a disgraceful case that no one can quite understand. It is an awful shame on the British.'[49]

Later that same day, while Sophia and her sister attempted to gather their thoughts at home, Rajah Harnam Singh of Kapurthala, and their friend, Gurcharan Singh, came by to make sure the sisters were safe. The day's events hung heavy in the air and Bamba was less cautious than she should have been. Sophia could do nothing to stem her sister's anti-British tirade. After the Rajah had politely taken his leave of them, their friend lingered. His mood was grave. He apologised to the sisters for exposing them to the Rajah, a man he firmly believed was a British informant. Every word they had uttered that afternoon, the Sardar-ji said, would be reported back to the authorities. Sophia struggled to comprehend the allegation, but the Sardar-ji was adamant: 'Harnam Singh spared no one with the British Officials.'[50] The news upset Sophia greatly: 'After all he was an Indian . . . how could he betray them? I <u>cannot</u> believe this of him . . .'[51]

When recording the episode in her diary later that evening, she tried desperately to remember if Bamba had uttered anything that might be considered seditious, reassuring herself that, 'B was rather bitter . . . but nothing serious was said.'[52] Yet even if Harnam Singh did report their unguarded conversation, it would hardly have registered against the backdrop of growing civil disorder.

Students were dragging Englishmen out of tongas and beating them in the street. Dirt had been thrown into the eyes of the district commissioner's horse in an effort to unseat him from his saddle. Gangs of youths were turning on the police all over the city, and the violence threatened to spiral out of control. To make matters worse, rumours were swirling round Lahore that an Indian nationalist leader, whose mere presence could stir cities, was arriving later that very evening.

# 13

# India Awake!

With his plump cheeks, round body and drooping moustache, Gopal Krishna Gokhale looked like a benign, bespectacled clerk; but, despite his appearance, he caused trouble wherever he went. Born in Maharashtra in 1866 to a high-caste yet poor Hindu family, Gokhale had taken minor secretarial jobs in his youth, working for the British. Earning a much-needed wage during the day, his nights were spent devouring works of philosophy and political theory. He became a devotee of the British social reformers, John Stuart Mill and Edmund Burke. As one of the first generation of Indians allowed to attend university under the Raj, Gokhale was frustrated that educated young Indians could play no part in the governance of their own country. Looking for somewhere to vent his disaffection, he joined the Indian National Congress (INC). At the time, it was a modest society founded by Theosophists, but in a matter of years the group grew and became a vociferous political movement. Gokhale was elected chairman in 1905.

It was a meteoric rise for such a softly spoken and unlikely leader. In a different life, Gokhale would have been better suited to the world of academia rather than revolutionary politics, but despite his understated and ponderous delivery, vast crowds would turn up to hear him speak. The sheer numbers caused policing difficulties for the authorities, who would have preferred to have thrown him into prison. However, Gokhale always stopped short of sedition, giving them no excuse. As a passionate moderate, he believed it was possible for the chains to be loosened and for the British and Indians to work together.

Gokhale asked his followers to be patient and steadfast, employing only non-violent means to make their feelings heard. Such was the growing anti-British feeling at the turn of the century that those who could not personally hear him speak pored over his words in articles appearing in the indigenous press. Gokhale's speeches were transcribed and translated with ferocious zeal, and his essays reproduced and disseminated all over India and beyond. Among those who came into contact with Gokhale through his writing was an unknown Gujarati lawyer who had emigrated to South Africa fourteen years before. Slight of build, with prominent ears which would one day support unmistakable round wire spectacles, Mohandas Karamchand Gandhi was mesmerised by the political pamphlets coming from Gokhale's pen.[1] In 1907 Gandhi found himself battling against South Africa's toughening race laws and when it came to colonial resistance, the Indian National Congress was his only template. (The South African Native National Congress – precursor to the ANC – would only come into existence five years later.)

Gokhale's non-violent message appealed to Gandhi's own sensibilities and he was working up the courage to invite his distant mentor to visit him in Durban. Watching with fascination, he waited to see what would happen in faraway Punjab as the Indian nationalist movement flexed its muscles.

In Lahore, on the evening of 16 February, the streets bubbled with civil unrest. After the initial lawlessness of the day, some of which had been witnessed by Sophia and her sister, by sunset the British had finally contained the worst of the violence by a show of brute force. News of Gokhale's imminent arrival spread rapidly through Lahore, causing the local administration to convulse with trepidation. Like most of those around them, Sophia and her sister were desperate to hear Gokhale speak. His arrival that night heralded a carnival atmosphere as students greeted him with noisy joy, unhitching the horses, and pulling his carriage through the streets with their own bodies.² Gokhale was due to deliver his first Lahore lecture the very next day.

All lessons at the university were cancelled as young men poured into Lahore's main lecture theatre to await Gokhale's latest sermon. When the two Duleep Singh princesses arrived they were ushered into the seats reserved for special guests, beside the speaker's lectern. To Sophia's dismay, she and her sister were left facing a packed and boisterous house. As she wrote in her diary that night: 'We were stuck up on the stage and clapping ensued, oh horrors – we knew we were going to have reserved seats and feared this, but the clapping was awful!! However of course it was nice of them to put us up there.'³

When Gokhale slowly shuffled up the steps to take his position before the audience, the sound of cheering and clapping was deafening. Sophia was carried along by the excitement, and clapped with all her might. Then Gokhale turned to where she and Bamba sat, and asked the audience to rise in respect for the granddaughters of the great Maharajah Ranjit Singh. The wave of sound that hit her was like nothing Sophia had experienced before. Such public displays were precisely the type of rabble-rousing the Duleep Singhs had so frequently been warned against. She was left filled with a mixture of dread, embarrassment and intense gratitude.

Sophia described Gokhale's speech as: 'Such an excellent one, full of sense . . . a very wise man.'⁴ Gokhale spoke at length about the tensions in the country, and of his belief that only by granting a degree of Indian self-governance could that tension be dissipated. Sophia noticed that the hall was packed with thousands of people.⁵ Those Indians who had made it into the auditorium absorbed every word, often rising in noisy ovation: 'Every now and then there was a great [clamour] of people and it was quite difficult to get them all to sit down again.'⁶ Hundreds of young Indians had failed to get inside the overspilling hall, and were left standing on the pavement outside, having the words relayed to them in a series of Chinese whispers.

After the lecture, Sophia and Bamba left the theatre with cheers ringing in their ears, but not before they had enjoyed a brief personal audience with Gokhale. Sophia did not note in her diary what he said to them, but it was significant enough to convince both her and Bamba to attend a second lecture, due to be delivered the next day. That night, however, all talk of Gokhale in Lahore was eclipsed by another rumour. It was being whispered throughout the city that Lala Lajpat Rai, a militant nationalist detested by the British, would also be taking to the stage. If Gokhale was a spark that could ignite the powder keg of Punjab, Lala Lajpat Rai was the grenade.

Born just one year earlier than Gokhale in the rural belt of Punjab, at forty-five, Lala Lajpat Rai looked considerably older. Without the chubby, smooth face of his fellow nationalist, Rai appeared careworn and frayed. His thick thatch of hair was whitening prematurely, as was his full, bushy moustache. His peers referred to him as Lala-ji, an honorific used in Punjab by children for their fathers. Among the general public, Lajpat Rai was known as 'Punjab Kesari', or 'Lion of Punjab' – a moniker familiar to Sophia, for her grandfather, Maharajah Ranjit Singh, had been given the same title many years before.

Lajpat Rai, like Gokhale, had been a bright young boy with a thirst for education. His father was an Urdu teacher at a government school, and therefore earned very little. Despite the family's relative poverty, Rai proved to be a natural scholar who, like Gokhale, spent much time self-educating. Eventually gaining entry to Lahore's government college to study law, he came into contact with the Arya Samaj, a highly politicised Hindu sect. The Samaj believed in the authority of the Vedas, the most ancient scripture of the Hindus, and had a strong ethos of social duty. Followers were expected to work for the poor as a mark of their devotion to God. As a result, Lala Lajpat Rai came face to face with terrible suffering during the famines of 1896 and 1900. He travelled around the regions hit by the highest death tolls. With a gift for organisation, Lajpat Rai marshalled young volunteers to distribute food and water, and made provision for the disposal of bodies. He also found homes for the orphans left behind, and is personally credited with rehousing almost 250 children in Lahore.

When the devastating Kangra earthquake of 1905 occurred, Lajpat Rai left immediately for the hills, scene of the worst devastation.[7]

There he worked to the point of exhaustion, pulling the dead and injured from the rubble with his own hands. The experience left him angry and bitter. He accused the British of wilful neglect, insisting survivors had been left to fend for themselves without the means to do so. With all his time taken up by disaster relief, Lajpat Rai abandoned his fledgling legal practice, and resolved to give his life to politics and Indian nationalism.

Like Gokhale, Lajpat Rai swiftly became one of the leading figures in the INC. Unlike Gokhale, he had a natural gift for oratory and soon became known as the party's voice. He told packed audiences that food inflation, high taxes and the import of British goods had crippled the prospects of ordinary Indians for generations to come. Lajpat Rai's speeches were impassioned, simple and often delivered in the audience's native dialect. Time and again he asked why their country, so rich in natural resources, was being forced into poverty. Others within the INC were also losing patience with Gokhale's non-confrontational approach. They begged Lajpat Rai to seize the party's leadership and to take the INC towards a more militant agenda. He refused, believing any internal war within the INC would only weaken it, but his relationship with Gokhale became strained, especially when he saw how the British were prepared to carve up his country.

Back in October 1905, the Viceroy Lord Curzon had decided to partition Bengal, scene of the colony's most active Indian nationalism. The predominantly Muslim eastern part of the province was split from the largely Hindu west, and both sides were swallowed by separate, larger administrations. Curzon's partition immediately created a template for sectarian division and violence. Lajpat Rai believed the British were deliberately manufacturing flashpoints in an attempt to divert the growing calls for autonomy. He and a small cadre within the INC declared that Britain's policy of 'divide and rule' would wreck the country for ever. They began to openly question Gokhale's pacifist approach. Once again, the radicals begged Lajpat Rai to lead a rebel group and once again Lajpat Rai refused. Instead, a triumvirate within the INC, including Lajpat Rai, Bal Gangadhar Tilak, a lawyer from Maharashtra, and Bipin Chandra

Pal, a teacher from Bengal, began to formulate militant strategies of resistance from within, much to Gokhale's disapproval.

Known as the 'Lal-Bal-Pal' trio, the three encouraged lockouts in British-owned factories, and called on Indians to burn the vast number of clothes being imported from England. For years, Indian farmers had been pushed to grow cotton. Their crops were then bought by British companies at forcibly depressed prices and exported to Britain where in places such as Manchester, the buds were turned to cloth and exported back to India.

The Lal-Bal-Pal message was simple. India grows the cotton, India can manufacture the cloth, and Indians will keep the money. Their strikes and smoky picket lines were met with overwhelming force. Lajpat Rai also urged an extension of the clothing boycott to include all goods manufactured in Britain. He argued that if the Raj could not export and sell products to India, its largest market, they could ill afford to maintain troops and civil administration in the colony. Dubbed the 'Swadeshi' or 'Self-sufficiency Movement', nationalists began to follow in ever greater numbers, hoping to put money and power back into the hands of Indians. Lajpat Rai's call to action appealed to young idealists but it frightened many of the educated, older aristocrats in Sophia's circle.

The schism within the Indian National Congress had by now become bitterly acrimonious. Predictably, the chance to see two nationalist rivals on the same stage attracted even bigger crowds. On the second night, 17 February, the police came out in great numbers taking positions in tight lines outside the university's main auditorium. Many of them were mounted and most of them were armed.

Sophia and her sister squeezed through a gauntlet of British police to enter the hall. As they did, they were ushered onto the stage again; however, this time, knowing what to expect, Sophia objected, desperately. The organisers would hear none of it, and she and Bamba had no choice but to resume their places of honour alongside the two empty chairs reserved for Gokhale and Lajpat Rai: 'Up we got amid cheers ... Oh dear we were cockatoos with a vengeance today.'[8]

Gokhale spoke with his customary measured tones, but Sophia and the others were taut with anticipation waiting for his fellow speaker. When Lala Lajpat Rai rose, the crowds inside and outside the auditorium erupted. Sophia, who had been so impressed by Gokhale, was entranced by Lajpat Rai. She described his speech as 'beautiful',[9] as he passionately lamented the fate of his country, rich in natural resources but artificially kept poor by the economic policy of the British. He begged the audience to embrace Swadeshi, telling them that only the total boycott of British goods could revive indigenous manufacturing. As Sophia wrote later in her diary: 'He pointed out how so little land is now cultivated,'[10] comparing it to the days of the Sikh Kingdom, when farms covered Punjab and everyone had enough to eat. He spoke of how 'all the raw material is exported – finished . . . he said that students should work for the common good – go with the villagers to preach union'.[11]

That day, Lala Lajpat Rai became Sophia's hero: 'He is a wonderful speaker. A noble unselfish man.'[12] The speech caused such commotion both inside and out that the police threatened to break up the event by force unless things calmed down. In the midst of the mounting hysteria, the man they called 'Punjab Kesari' turned to face Sophia and Bamba. Addressing the sisters with great deference, he thanked them on behalf of Gokhale and himself, 'for the honour we had done them in coming. I turned crimson,' wrote Sophia, 'and did not know where to look. Then the clapping was too much. He went on to mention us further, Granddaughters of the Lion of the Punjab etc. etc.'[13]

The surge in sound tested the patience of the armed police outside and scuffles broke out between them and students who had not been able to fit in the hall. The organisers had to beg the British commanding officers to let the women out safely before things got too violent. Sophia and Bamba were rushed to a waiting tonga, and the horses sped them away. As Sophia looked back on the crowds closing in behind her she thought: 'Which are friends and which are foes in this country?'[14]

A couple of days later Lala Lajpat Rai and Gokhale put their political differences aside and made a rare and unexpected joint visit to

The Palms. The new Lion of Punjab was particularly keen to meet the progeny of his namesake. Not wishing to attract unwanted police attention, the pair told nobody of their visit, not even the princesses themselves. As a result, Sophia and Bamba were completely unprepared. The house was a mess, the sisters were not dressed for company and the servants were thrown into a whirl of confusion as the two men entered the front door. Seeing her hero again, Sophia acted like a dumbstruck teenager. She stammered with embarrassment, unable to answer the visitors' polite questions: 'I never knew anything so awkward . . . the room was fearfully untidy and I was so shy I could not utter a sound. B did not say much and they soon went. I felt the whole thing had been too awkward for words.'[15]

In the weeks that followed, Sophia pored over the nationalist arguments as unrest in Lahore gathered momentum. Lala Lajpat Rai took his agitation to every corner of the city and beyond. The Raj's Colonisation Bill had been passed the year before and it was causing enormous unrest in the countryside. Under the new law, any farmer who died without a blood heir would have all his fields and property sold to the highest bidder and proceeds would go to the British. Since agricultural villages often operated like extended families where acreage and wealth passed between farmers even when there was no blood tie, the new law was seen as an affront to the Punjabi way of life. Coupled with increasing taxation and bad harvests, rural Punjab had become a tinderbox. Lala Lajpat Rai encouraged farmers to take whatever measures were necessary to resist the unjust laws and taxes. It would not be long before the British moved against the princess's new role model.

Leaving the seething political landscape of Lahore behind them for a while, the princesses set out once again to visit their grandfather's dominion. Very soon it became clear that their new nationalist friendships had earned them even more unwelcome attention. Sophia had first noticed they were being followed when she and Bamba were waiting for a train. Two English officers tailed them closely and conspicuously: 'It was the greatest cheek imaginable – followed us right up and sat beside us on the platform. How they dared!!'[16]

Despite the uninvited entourage, the sisters carried on with their plans. One of their first stops was the princely state of Kapurthala, home of Rajah Harnam Singh, the man they no longer trusted.

His nephew, Maharajah Jagatjit Singh, welcomed them to Kapurthala. A portly man of thirty-five, he greeted them with the latest of his four wives, Maharani Kanari, and invited them to a banquet he was throwing in their honour. Despite his hospitality, during the meal Sophia found that she was growing to dislike Jagatjit Singh intensely. Chiefly, it was his politics that offended her: 'This Raja is very over privileged and loves Europe, especially France. He does not seem to care much for his own country or people!!!'[17] Sophia's opinion of the Maharajah fell further when she learned of his infidelity. 'He has an English woman,'[18] she noted tersely in her diary.

Sophia was right about the affair, but wrong about the mistress's nationality. A Spanish flamenco dancer named Anita Delgado had won the Maharajah's heart and would be the next Maharani of Kapurthala. The Maharajah was hastening the construction of a new palace for her. Designed by a French architect, the magnificent and highly ornate structure would bring a piece of Paris to the Punjab. Sophia found the style and lascivious inspiration behind the building entirely distasteful. Hoping for the worst, she wondered 'whether it will resist an earthquake or not it will be interesting to know'.[19] Anita Delgado would rock the foundations of Jagatjit's world, and cheat on him enthusiastically throughout their marriage.[20]

Sophia was keen to leave the kingdom of Kapurthala far behind her; her low opinion of the Maharajah had made it a stressful excursion. On arrival in the city of Jalandhar, the sisters were invited to a garden party by one of the most important British officials in the city. It was the kind of social occasion Sophia had formerly loved, with music, genteel company and the chance to show off her latest dress; however, the event clashed with a nationalist meeting at which Lajpat Rai was slated to appear, and Sophia was desperate to hear him again. Bamba took so long to get ready that they missed their chance, leaving them free to attend the garden party after all.[21] Sophia hated every minute of it: 'We were the only Indians in the place . . . there were the usual English people, we were taken in and sat down inside and some of the English were brought up and introduced to us. It was killing . . . they were so shy and did not know in the least what to say and we did not help them.'[22] Whether it was because of Bamba's constant anti-British invective, or her own hero-worship of Lajpat Rai, Sophia was changing – but not fast enough for Bamba.

The next day, the sisters took tea with some Indian friends, a Sikh lady called Sardarni Balwant Singh, another called Sardarni Atari Singh and a Bengali lady called Mrs Chatterjee. The subject of the English came up and Sophia and Bamba found themselves disagreeing about the very issue that had united them only twenty-four hours before: '. . . there was a great discussion about English people as to whether or not they could be friends of foreigners including Indians of course'.[23] Sophia argued that it was wrong to tar an entire people because of the misdeeds of a few: 'I say I have a few [English] friends and know I have but B says that can't be.'[24] The two Sikh ladies agreed wholeheartedly with Bamba. Only Mrs Chatterjee would concede weakly, 'there are some nice ones'.[25] Despite being outnumbered Sophia refused to change her opinion and instead the topic changed course awkwardly to Lala Lajpat Rai's latest speech. The next day Sophia and Bamba would be too busy to take up where they left off, for they were embarking on the next leg of their tour which would take them to Ferozepur, Jalalabad and Mamdot.

South of Lahore stood Mamdot, once part of the old city of Kasur. Ranjit Singh had overwhelmed the Muslim rulers in 1807, but when they submitted to him without violence, he allowed them to keep Mamdot as their fiefdom. After a seven-hour train journey, Sophia and Bamba were met at the station by a Major Barton 'and the Nawab of Mamdot (a boy of 10). The Bartons seem very nice people.'[26] The major acted as a kind of substitute parent for the young nawab, and seemed to have a powerful hold over the boy. Barton escorted the princesses to meet the nawab's mother and three sisters, who lived in strict purdah: 'they can only speak Punjabi of course . . . B spoke to them and asked them to bring out their jewels to show us. They own very fine things, most of them very old.'[27]

The following day the princesses were taken by the little nawab and Major Barton to Mamdot's famous horse fair, where Sophia and Bamba again became the focus of attention: 'A crowd had clustered round us everywhere this morning as we walked about the show!! I think they must have known who we were.'[28] Sophia had little time to appreciate the adulation; it was all she could do to stop Joe from being crushed under numerous hooves. Over the next few weeks, the tiny dog's antics would come as welcome light relief. Like a clown he dashed excitedly in and out of the path of regally decorated elephants, almost daring them to step on him. He growled at most strangers, whether they were princes or paupers. Sophia was kept busy trying to keep the Pomeranian from being skewered for his insolence.

Later that night the young nawab, whom Sophia described as a 'fat and funny old boy',[29] threw a formal dinner for his special guests. Bamba and Sophia found themselves seated next to Major Barton and another British officer, Captain Walker, who had travelled from Lahore to attend. The meal turned into an inquisition: 'Oh dear I was catechised. But Major Barton was very nice about it and said it was from interest he asked these questions. But we think it was to know our own special opinion about things.'[30]

Sophia found the relentless questioning unsettling, and the effort to conceal her recent friendships and new political convictions proved too much for her at times: 'I got blocked once . . . not knowing papa's exact age when he was deposed.'[31] The next day at dinner the same thing happened. This time Major Barton sat next to Bamba, 'with a policeman on her other side'. As Sophia noted, 'B said she got well questioned.'[32] Despite the obvious probing, there were moments in the formality that Sophia and her sister found hilarious: 'The Nawab had to make his first speech, it was all written out for him but he was so nervous he could hardly get through it and made so many mistakes in spite of the fact he was being readily prompted on both sides poor boy . . . he *dranked* all the people for having come to his state as guests!!'[33]

In the early hours of the next morning, as the princesses slept, a mysterious Indian came to see them. Given the hour and the surreptitious manner of his calling, the maid, angered at being woken, told him to get out and never to come back. He begged her to call the Duleep Singh princesses, insisting that his father and grandfather had served the family and that he had something important to tell them. But she would hear none of it and chased him away. Sophia never did learn who he was or what he so desperately wished to tell them under cover of darkness, but the experience put the sisters on edge.

The princesses left Mamdot and continued their tour of princely states, returning to Lahore every so often to relax and replenish their luggage. Sometimes, during their Lahore sojourns, they managed to fit in social engagements. On one such occasion at the beginning of March, the ladies of the India Association, a group which raised money for schools for poor children, threw a garden party for Lady Rivaz. Showing solidarity with her sister, Sophia not only wore Indian clothes for the first time (an embroidered silk shirt which reached down below her knees, over the top of tightly fitting pyjamas) but also snubbed the Lieutenant General's wife: 'It was a lovely day, I wore my green kurta and B a yellow sari with a good deal of jewellery . . . Lady Rivaz was there but we did not speak to her.'[34]

The LG had greater issues to worry about than the insolence of the Duleep Singh sisters. Apart from the continuing challenge to his authority from nationalists, plague had come to Punjab, with devastating consequences. Public health reports, which were sent regularly back to London, noted, 'the mortality from plague in the Punjab is increasing at an alarming rate, being about a thousand a week, and more than ten times as large as for the corresponding week last year'.[35] As the days progressed, people the sisters knew started to die. Bamba decided it was time to get out of the city, taking only boiled water and food which had been freshly prepared by her own cooks under her close supervision. Whenever they stopped, Bamba would disinfect the luggage herself. Sophia thought such precautions were excessive. In her opinion, fresh air and exercise were the answer to all of life's ailments, even the plague.

Though their luggage smelt strongly of sulphur and carbolic, Sophia noticed that aspects of their travels were becoming a good deal more pleasant. Guards on the trains rushed to help them with tickets and bags; platform staff seemed more courteous too. 'It was very amusing noting the effect my letter to the Viceroy has had,'[36] wrote Sophia. Their weeks touring the princely states of Punjab were often emotionally charged, however. They saw artefacts from their grandfather's kingdom which had been dispersed by the British as rewards to those who had betrayed his son. They tried on priceless jewels and sumptuous silks in the quarters of ranis, and spoke to men whose families had died fighting for their family. In Gujaranwalla, a district in the northeast which had once been nothing more than a hamlet, Sophia saw the very room where her grandfather had been born. The experience took on an almost spiritual dimension, and Sophia was deeply moved by the humble beginnings of the warrior king.

When the sisters reached Nabha in the south-west of Punjab, Sophia took an immediate and intense dislike to Sir Hira Singh, the Rajah of the princely state. He had a snow-white beard and long bony fingers which held Bamba's hand too long and too tightly for Sophia's liking. Hira Singh had sent his men to fight for the British in most of their frontier campaigns for over three decades, and had been knighted for his loyalty. Whispering conspiratorially, a little too close for Sophia's comfort, he told the sisters that their father had been foolish to defy the Raj, adding sweetly that he thought their brothers Victor and Freddie ought to fight for the English to prove that treason did not run in their blood. ('He thought he gave valuable advice,'[37] Sophia wrote in her diary scornfully.) Sophia held her tongue but as usual Bamba found it impossible to do the same. Sophia noted with suspicion that the Rajah absorbed Bamba's rage mildly. Later that same night, Sophia could not sleep with worry: 'I am sorry that there was so much politics talked and that B gave her views so strongly even if they are not always what she really thinks.' Sophia concluded that the Rajah seemed to be provoking them: 'We have nothing to lose but our lives!'[38]

Unnerved by Rajah Hira Singh, Sophia spent her nights in Nabha trying to teach herself how to write backwards, hoping it might foil anyone who might find her diary and pick the little brass lock. She was surprised at how easily she could master the skill. After politely refusing an invitation to extend their stay in Nabha, the sisters carried on with their journey and made their way to the princely state of Faridkot, a dry plain in the south-west of Punjab. It was here that Sophia noticed that they had a rather hapless spy in tow. Major Barton, the man Sophia and Bamba had dined with only weeks before, was skulking in the shadows, watching them as they changed trains. The major seemed entirely unprepared when the sisters waved at him cheerfully, trying to dip out of sight. Sophia and Bamba shrugged off his odd attempts at covert surveillance, leaving him behind to get on their next train. But when they reached their destination Major Barton had mysteriously materialised again: 'he had been talking to the Indian who came to meet us but as soon as he saw us get out of the carriage he turned his back to the window and read his paper. Too odd for words.'[39]

Wherever the sisters went, they stirred great feelings of Sikh pride; cries of 'Bolo Son Nihal!', the Sikh exultation of triumph, rang in the air. Both women learned to answer with the traditional response 'Sat Sri Akal!' ('God is the ultimate truth!') to the delight of the crowds, some of whom wept with emotion. In the princely state of Ferozepur the welcome was overwhelming: 'When we came out we were pelted with flowers and crowds had collected and lots of women came and touched our feet. This we were not at all prepared for, when we were away and into our carriage, we were still being pelted with flowers. Ah these dear people. What a memory they have. Why should they care for us?'[40]

By April 1907, Sophia had spent six months in India and had witnessed firsthand the growing political turbulence in India. The push for Indian self-determination had seduced her. She felt tremendous loyalty to Bamba too. Nevertheless she had a yearning to go home to England and to find a meaningful existence for herself. Sophia had also decided that although Bamba was spending her time with some dangerous nationalists, and was certainly the subject of surveillance, her life was not in any immediate danger and there was no plot to poison her. Somehow it was not enough to be subsumed in Bamba's own battles; Sophia needed to find ones of her own to fight.

The fear of plague pushed Bamba to reluctantly accept her sister's decision to leave. They seemed now to be surrounded by death as the disease took its toll. As Sophia wrote in her diary, the terror was visceral: 'Lahore is full of plague, in fact the whole of Punjab is full of it. It is too awful for words, in fact it is the worst form there has been in the last 10 years. Everyone is dying of it.'[41] Questions were raised in the House of Commons about the scale of the disaster. The Secretary of State for India, John Morley, confirmed that in April, some 314,000 people had died in Punjab alone.[42]

On the night of 3 April, Sophia found she could not sleep. There was more to her insomnia than the intense heat of the night, or Bamba's fears that she had already been infected. Sophia had a very important duty to perform in the morning and her head was filled with it. For the first time since she had arrived in India, Sophia was going to visit the tomb of her grandfather. It was odd that she had not made such a pilgrimage before; perhaps she was afraid of what feelings the visit would provoke. Whenever she could, Sophia had tried to avoid emotionally difficult situations; her early life had taught her that such pain could be unbearable.

Rising early the next morning, Sophia left The Palms quietly by herself. She returned home later, having visited the flower market, her arms filled with roses to lay on her grandfather's tomb. In her absence, Bamba had decided that she did not have the plague after all and was dressed and ready to leave. The grand mausoleum stood in the heart of old Lahore, and had been built on the spot where the Maharajah had been cremated, and where Sophia's grandmother as a young woman had refused to commit *sati*. Surrounded by flat and dusty parkland, Ranjit Singh's tomb rose up and greeted the early sun's rays, catching the light on its broad white dome and gilded cupolas. The building reflected the old King's rule, and was a meld of Hindu, Muslim and Sikh architecture. The domes and clean white stone spoke of Mughal influence, the ornate golden balustrade had the mark of Sikh ostentation and the front entrance had Hindu deities carved in vivid red sandstone. Sophia passed beneath the round belly of Ganesh, the Hindus' elephant-headed god, and removed her sandals at the entrance.

Stepping on cool smooth stone, she left the heat and dust behind her and entered the cavernous quiet of the *Samadhi* or mausoleum. Small convex mirrors set in white cement reflected her face a thousand times over, as she looked up at the ceiling. In silence she climbed the stairs to the main vault, where it took a while for her pupils to adjust. There before her, in the centre of the silence, stood the urn containing her grandfather's ashes. Even giants of history could be reduced to such containers – no bigger than a lady's handbag. The urn had been carved from marble to look like a lotus flower and was surrounded by thirteen smaller, plainer stone flowers. Each of these held the remains of those who had burned themselves alive on Ranjit's pyre: four wives, seven servant girls and two pigeons (which had inadvertently flown into the high flames). What Sophia felt when she stood before her grandfather's grave she did not share, even with her diary, save to say: 'I am glad to have seen the tomb at last. I was determined I would do that before leaving but had wished to do it when I first came.'[43]

Days before she was due to depart Lahore, Sophia awoke one morning to hear a carriage rattling its way towards the house. Looking out of her bathroom window she saw crates wobbling precariously on the back of a cart with the letters 'PDS' writ large on them. It could mean only one thing: Pauline Duleep Singh. The arrival of her half-sister would turn life upside down for the short time Sophia and Bamba had left together.

Ada had been negotiating the terms of Pauline's visit to India for some months. Bamba had only relented after being pressured by both Sophia and Frederick. The manner of her half-sister's arrival was to typify her stay. Pauline had taken the wrong boat, arrived at the wrong time, and, taking matters into her own hands, then turned up at the house without warning. Sophia watched with slight amusement as her two wilful sisters sized one another up: 'Pauline was looking very well . . . she had a bath and washed and had remained in her dressing gown almost all day . . . she had brought 3 huge boxes and several small . . . I brought enough for 10 years and she has brought enough for 20!!'[44]

Although it had been a chaotic beginning, Sophia was delighted by Pauline's arrival. She felt it was high time Bamba learned to love her half-sisters, just as she had been loved. All seemed well at first: 'B seems favourably impressed with her in every way which is a very good thing. She even thinks her pretty which I couldn't say I quite do, though I think she has a nice face and expressions and a very pretty mouth and chin and is pretty when she is excited and laughing.'[45] For Bamba, however, the novelty wore off remarkably quickly. It became clear that Pauline was not the easiest of people: 'She has eaten nothing all day poor child. She does not appreciate either Indian or English food, it is to be hoped she will soon.'[46]

Food was not the only thing that Pauline complained about. Hardly anything was good enough and her fussiness coupled with her constant exhaustion began to grate on Bamba's nerves. Sophia's twenty-year-old half-sister was always too tired or too hot to venture from the house. She refused Sophia and Bamba's offers to see Lahore's attractions; nor did she wish to be introduced to their friends, preferring to play cards with Pir-ji, or ball games with the servants. Pauline even managed to irritate the usually sanguine Sophia on the very day that should have been one of her happiest in Lahore.

Bamba had written to Lajpat Rai explaining that Sophia was leaving for London soon and had asked him to come one last time to meet her. He had accepted the invitation immediately. Sophia was touched: 'I was rather glad as I wanted to see him to say goodbye. He came alright and we had tea and sat some time and talked.'[47] In the end they did not have much time together as this, unfortunately, was also the day that Pauline decided that she wanted to go out and see Lahore: 'P was such a fidget as she wanted to go out shopping and we did not . . . So she got quite rude and eventually I took her to play tennis cricket, then left her and came back for a few minutes but he soon went . . . He is perhaps going to bring a son of his to England this year . . . I shall hope to have him at Hampton Court.'[48] Her conservative neighbours at the palace would never get the chance to be appalled by her choice of house guest, however. When Sophia said goodbye to Lajpat Rai on that frustrating afternoon, it would be the last time they would see each other.

Although her ship home was not due to set sail until 6 May, Sophia left Lahore on 13 April. The journey to Bombay usually took a week, but Sophia had promised to show Pauline some of India and so planned a number of excursions on the way. She had wanted Bamba to come too, but her sister excused herself, saying that she needed to be at home for some unexpected visitors. Their parting was never going to be easy.

Sophia had barely been away for a day when Bamba had a change of heart. At Rawalpindi, some 200 miles away from Lahore, Sophia found an urgent wire waiting for her. Bamba would be travelling all night on the Bombay Mail, and would be with her the next morning. (Sophia commented wryly in her diary that she was surprised her sister had made the train on time.[49]) When Bamba finally arrived, she walked into a furious row. Pauline had been disparaging about India and Sophia could not tolerate it: 'She said we lived like savages out here. She could not eat the food of course. I was not going to stand that so I said to B she better send her back at once. I said I would not speak to her again. Nor did I for the rest of the day.'[50] Bamba found herself in the unlikely role of peacemaker.

After reconciling, the three women spent the next weeks together slowly edging their way to Bombay and the start of Sophia's journey home. Bamba found it easier to talk about the plague than about her little sister's imminent departure: 'B had seen in the paper that the Bishop of Lahore has said a prayer for the plague to end and has said all the missionaries are to say prayers for it. Which shows how very bad it must be, and probably the English are themselves getting frightened about it.'[51] Sophia entertained Pauline in her hotel room for hours with endless games of cribbage while Bamba excused herself and stayed in her bedroom, claiming to have a headache. Despite the underlying tensions, the next eighteen days were a blur of sightseeing and shopping and it was only on her last night in Bombay on 6 May that Sophia could bring herself to acknowledge her own emotions: 'So this was goodbye to poor India. Shall I ever see her again. I doubt it!! And I leave her with many regrets, especially do I loathe leaving B behind.'⁵²

Her first voyage took her from Bombay to Colombo where she would once more change ships. The SS *Yorck* would take her across the oceans to Bremen in Germany where Catherine would be waiting for her. The sisters had planned to spend some weeks together before Sophia had to make her final journey to England. Sophia longed to hear Catherine's news, even though the two of them had kept up their correspondence during her stay in India.

Catherine's recent letters had not been soothing, and she had alarmed Sophia with talk of a brewing war in Europe. Both Bamba and Sophia had dismissed the idea, unable to believe that such a thing was possible. However, four days into her voyage the *Yorck* passed a German naval warship, the SMS *Condor*. The two vessels were so close at one point that Sophia could see that it was brimming with German sailors, making their way back to Europe.⁵³ It was unusual for the *Condor* to be so far away from its patrol territory in the Pacific Ocean, where it had watched over Germany's island territories for years. Sophia shrugged off the unusual sight and instead studied Urdu in her cabin, wrote letters on the top deck, and delighted the children in first class with Joe's latest tricks.

However, her sense of peace was shattered just a week into her voyage when the ship's purser brought her a letter which had been sent to Aden, their last port of anchor. Bamba's familiar writing was on the envelope. As Sophia opened it a newspaper cutting fell out onto her lap. What she read left her shaking with grief and anger. 'Little did I expect the shock of what it contained . . . oh dear, oh dear poor poor India and the Indians. Lala Lajpat Rai has been arrested . . . and deported promptly from Lahore. Did the poor man expect this . . . Oh death . . . this one man one of India's saviours.'⁵⁴

The inky newspaper cutting told her that Lajpat Rai had been picked up by the police and charged with sedition. The sentence was almost certain to be years of hard labour. Sophia, like many others in Punjab, feared that the punishment would kill him. As she headed back to Europe, she fumed in her diary against the country to which she was returning: 'Oh you wicked English how I long for your downfall. How I loathe you all . . . I am your deadly enemy from hereafter. Such injustice I cannot stand . . . I don't believe he was preaching sedition . . . Ah India awake and free yourself! I am afraid this [is] the end of all hope.'[55]

# The Lost Princess

In London, Sophia kept up to date with Lajpat Rai's worsening situation by way of the British newspapers. It emerged that he had been sentenced without trial to indefinite detention, and had been spirited out of India to be held in solitary confinement in a Burmese prison. While in Mandalay he was denied access to lawyers and refused leave to appeal. In the words of Gokhale, the severity of the sentence had 'literally convulsed the country from one end to the other'.[1]

Swathes of outraged Punjabis flocked to the Home Rule cause like never before. A prominent militant nationalist from Maharashtra, Senpati Bapat, warned that if Lala Lajpat Rai was not released immediately, Bapat would shoot the Secretary of State for India himself. The Indian newspaper *Vande Mataram* wrote in an editorial: 'The hour for speeches and fine writing is past. The bureaucracy has thrown down the gauntlet. We take it up. Men of the Punjab! Race of the lion! Show these men who would stamp you into the dust that for one Lajpat they have taken away, a hundred Lajpats will arise in his place. Let them hear a hundred times louder your war-cry – Jai Hindusthan!'[2]

Sophia was frantic about Lajpat Rai's welfare, as well as that of Bamba and Pauline, still in Lahore. The *Daily Mail* made for disturbing reading: 'Troops of all arms are marching into Lahore from Mianmir in preparation for grave eventualities. Police, mounted and un-mounted are also being drafted from all parts of the province . . . Sir Denzil Ibbetson [the new LG] made a careful inspection of the defences of Lahore fort, and summoned reinforcements for the military.'³ According to the paper, Punjabi thugs were pouring into the city: 'Bodies of stalwart rustics armed with bludgeons are moving into Lahore having been enlisted by seditious leaders. These gangs are now crowding into the native city. The Government has issued a proclamation declaring that all meetings of every kind in Lahore are forbidden and will be seen as unlawful assemblies. They are warning the public not to attend any such meeting.'⁴

Sophia could only pray that Bamba was staying away from politics and that Pauline was safely locked up at home after dark. In reality, however, her sisters were more likely to tear each other apart than become the victims of street battles. From the moment Sophia had left them alone the two women had been at each other's throats. Bamba accused Pauline of being lazy, rude, morose and ungrateful as well as having base morals. She claimed to have caught the young princess flirting with neighbours and accepting expensive gifts from friends: 'I think she is quite incorrigible and she had better go back. She is too vulgar for anything,'⁵ wrote Bamba in one of her regular letters of complaint. Sophia had not bargained for such mutual loathing. In her absence all the old resentments were allowed to fly without censor. Pauline regarded Bamba as overbearing and over-privileged; she was also riled by her half-sister's constant adulation of their father. To Pauline, Duleep Singh had been a shambling old drunk whom she loathed. In turn Bamba lashed out at Pauline's mother, viciously attacking Ada for being little more than a common whore: 'I have told her a good deal about her circumstances for I do not see things should be falsely represented . . . She attributes all that is bad to our father. This was too much for me, so I clearly told her the sort of woman her mother is and told her that she derives all her undesirable qualities from there.'⁶ Sophia had stayed with Bamba for six months, but after just six weeks, Pauline was put on a boat back to France. Bamba hoped never to see her again.

Sophia was far too distracted to mediate between the pair. On her voyage back from India, she had concluded that all the British were uniformly wicked. Now, however, she was witnessing a group of Westminster politicians championing Lajpat Rai's cause with as much passion as any Punjabi in Lahore. A small but vociferous group of cross-party MPs were repeatedly raising the case in Parliament. The Secretary of State was left flailing before his peers; Morley's inadequate answers about Lajpat Rai's arrest were met by scorn and noisy disbelief. On 29 May 1907 the Conservative MP from Liverpool, Dr V. H. Rutherford, once again led the charge against the Secretary of State:

DR RUTHERFORD: I beg to ask the Secretary of State for India whether, in view of the fact that the arrest and deportation of Lala Lajpat Rai without trial has fired the indignation of His Majesty's subjects in India, he will either bring him to trial or release him, and so help to restore law and order and respect for British justice.

MR MORLEY: I am aware that the circumstances mentioned by my hon. friend have been viewed with lively disapproval by some sections of His Majesty's Indian subjects and with lively approval by other sections, and I cannot at all agree with my hon. friend that either the trial or the release of the person detained would by any means help to restore law and order.

DR RUTHERFORD: Will the Secretary of State inform the House on what charge this gentleman had been arrested and deported without trial?

MR MORLEY: Under the regulations of 1818, under which he was arrested, the formulation of a charge can be brought forward and substantiation is not necessary.

DR RUTHERFORD: Has the right honourable gentleman himself received any evidence justifying this serious undertaking on the part of the Indian Government?

MR MORLEY: I have not the least desire to evade any of these questions, but it would be far more convenient if my hon. friend would possess himself in patience for only a week, when it would be my duty and satisfaction to explain to the House the whole of this matter.

MR O'GRADY (Labour MP for Leeds East): I would like to ask the right honourable gentleman a simple question. Is it not a fact that this gentleman was arrested as a result of speaking at a meeting against the increase of the land and irrigation taxes? Does the right honourable gentleman consider that to be sedition? Does it come within the purview of the regulations of 1818?

MR MORLEY: My hon. friend calls that a simple question! To answer it would involve me in complexities which would take at least half an hour.[7]

The cross-party group refused to be put off and thanks to their dogged determination, in September 1907, after he had spent six difficult months in prison, the Indian government was forced to release Lajpat Rai without charge. Not only did they let him go but the Colonisation Bill, against which he had fought so hard, was dropped by the Viceroy. The episode reminded Sophia of a truth she had lost briefly: not all the British were the same; some made very good friends indeed.

In his private papers, Morley, who was later elevated to the House of Lords, admitted that his administration had treated Lajpat Rai abominably. The Secretary of State blamed his colleagues for causing him to lie to Parliament: 'It seems clear from the papers that the Lieutenant-Governor of Burma refused Lajpat's request to see his solicitor. This is in itself, a hateful thing to do, only worthy of Russia, or, say Australia, in her Italian days. But worse still, I was allowed to tell the House of Commons that access to a solicitor would of course be allowed . . . More than that, I was permitted to say that he was allowed to receive letters from his family. It now seems that some 50 such letters were stopped, and I was never told.'[8] Sophia's letters may well have been among those Lajpat Rai never read.

Although in the months that followed Sophia remained passionate about both Lajpat Rai and his Swadeshi movement, her connection with India was becoming remote and unfulfilling. The passage of time and the miles which lay between her and Punjab were not being bridged well by her sister. Bamba's letters dwelt more on her irritations with servants and the weather than on matters Sophia longed to hear of. Apart from Catherine's fleeting visits, and her occasional trips to see Freddie and Victor, Sophia felt more cut off at Faraday House than ever before. She felt useless again, unable to do anything for her friends in India except read about their troubles in the papers. She sent money regularly for the upkeep of Punjabi schools;[9] she sent money to her cousins, the Raja Sansis, and bought shipments of dolls for Bamba to distribute at local orphanages.[10] But these acts did little to fill the void. Before she knew it, Sophia had slipped back into mundane routine. The greyness of London and the pointlessness of her life began to eat at her again. She lost weight and lost interest in all her former hobbies, showing Joe at fewer and fewer dog shows and failing to breed any new champions. Sophia spent almost nothing on new outfits and rarely went out. The newspapers forgot about her and she forgot about most of her friends. It was only a chance meeting with a young woman called Una Dugdale that re-infused her life with meaning.

A few years younger than Sophia, Una Dugdale, the daughter of a naval commander, had much in common with the Indian princess. She too was a headstrong debutante and, like Sophia, she had been apolitical for most of her life. Educated at Cheltenham Ladies' College and Paris, where she studied singing, Una moved in influential circles and counted the London elite as her friends. She had first heard about the suffragettes and their cause from her friend, Frank Rutter, the art critic for the *Sunday Times*.[11] However, it was not until she heard Christabel Pankhurst speak that she pledged her life to their cause.

While Sophia was being converted to nationalism by the oratory of Lala Lajpat Rai, Una was being seduced by the words of Emmeline Pankhurst's eldest daughter. In the summer of 1907 Una had attended an open air rally in London's Hyde Park. She watched as Christabel roared and gestured like a woman possessed, denouncing injustices perpetrated against women and children by an uncaring patriarchy. Women must have the vote and they were willing to fight for it. Her words electrified the crowds and the press soon took to calling her the 'Queen of the Mob'.

From that moment Una Dugdale became a willing member of that mob,[12] and she was but one of a growing number. On 4 February, under the banner of Millicent Fawcett's National Union of Women's Suffrage Societies, more than 3,000 women marched in the cold, wet streets of London. More than forty disparate organisations representing factory workers, titled women, academics and temperance activists, came together to demand a place for women at the ballot box. In unremitting drizzle, under the persistent tramp of their boots, the ground turned to sludge. As Millicent Fawcett later recalled: 'The London weather did its worst against us; mud, mud, mud was its prominent feature.' The protest became known as the Mud March. For the first time the men in power heard a cohesive female voice demanding the right to decide how they should be governed. It was an echo of the cry Sophia had heard so frequently in India from the likes of Lajpat Rai and Gokhale.

Just nine days later, Emmeline Pankhurst led a charge on Westminster itself. On 13 February, the Women's Society for Social and Political Union convened the first ever 'Women's Parliament' in Caxton Hall near St James's Park. They then marched on the Houses of Parliament with the intention of handing in a petition to the politicians sitting inside the chamber. When they reached the gates, however, the women were told to disperse with immediate effect and police on horseback were sent charging into the crowd. Scuffles broke out and more than fifty suffragettes were arrested. The heavy-handed police reaction succeeded in galvanising the WSPU. Emmeline Pankhurst declared that the time for talking was over and that 'Deeds not Words' would change history.

When Sophia's path crossed with Una Dugdale in 1908, the latter was already a prominent member of the WSPU. (Dugdale would later become the first woman in England to refuse to use the word 'obey' in her wedding vows.) They met at a social event held at the Dugdale family home.[13] Since Una hailed from one of the wealthier families in Warwickshire and, like Sophia, regularly travelled around the country for 'the season', it was surprising that the two women

The streets of Lahore, *c.* 1900. Against the wishes of the British government, Sophia travelled to India. There she was confronted with Indian poverty and gained an understanding of what had been taken from her family by the British. The experience radicalised her thinking.

The villages of the Punjab were a world away from the opulence of Sophia's life in London. She was astonished to find that wherever she went the name of her grandfather, Ranjit Singh, was still venerated.

Famine ravaged India at the turn of the century. Many blamed the British for an inadequate response, which they insisted prolonged the humanitarian disaster.

Lord Curzon, Viceroy of India, was despised by the Duleep Singh sisters.

The 1903 Delhi Durbar. Curzon orchestrated an overwhelming display of British might. As punishment for her defiance in travelling to India, Sophia was prohibited from taking her place in the Punjab camp. She was also shunned by British dignitaries and officials.

Sophia driving the suffragette press carts through London in 1911. Her high-profile support embarrassed both the government and the Crown.

Caxton Hall on Black Friday, 18 November 1910. Sophia (*circled*) would later lead the march to Parliament alongside Emmeline Pankhurst and a group of 'celebrity suffragettes'. They expected trouble, but nothing on the scale of the violence they would face.

# The Daily Mirror

THE MORNINQ JOURNAL WITH THE SECOND LARGEST NET SALE

No. 2,205.   Registered at the G. P. O. as a Newspaper.   SATURDAY, NOVEMBER 19, 1910   One Halfpenny.

## VIOLENT SCENES AT WESTMINSTER, WHERE MANY SUFFRAGETTES WERE ARRESTED WHILE TRYING TO FORCE THEIR WAY INTO THE HOUSE OF COMMONS.

While forcibly endeavouring yesterday to enter the Houses of Parliament, great numbers of suffragettes used more frantic methods than ever before. Above is illustrated one of yesterday's incidents. A woman has fallen down while struggling, and she is in a fainting condition. The photograph shows how far women will go for the vote,

The brutality of Black Friday, as reported on the front page of the *Daily Mirror*, shocked the nation. Sophia's friend Ada Wright is pictured lying semi-conscious on the ground. Sophia was herself arrested for her part in the clashes between suffragettes and the police.

In her best handwriting, in vibrant blue ink, Sophia defaced her 1911 census paper with the protest 'No vote, no census'. 'As women do not count, they refuse to be counted, and I have a conscientious objection to filling in this form.'

Sophia sells copies of *The Suffragette* outside Hampton Court. Her actions sent King George V into a rage, prompting the Palace to ask 'if anything could be done to stop her?'

had not met before. No record of Sophia's feelings on that day survive, and it is only thanks to the meticulous record-keeping of another leading suffragette, Mary Blathwayt, that we know Sophia was captivated by Una's passion.[14] When Una spoke of the WSPU, her lilting voice grew high-pitched and animated. She rolled her Rs like an actor relating a soliloquy in the spotlight of a major theatre.[15] To the softly spoken princess, Una seemed wildly exciting, as did her colourful descriptions of suffragist skirmishes with police. Sophia signed up as a member of the WSPU that very afternoon, pledging a lifetime commitment to the cause of women's rights. In the absence of Catherine, Bamba and Eddie, very quickly the WSPU became Sophia's new family.

Had she not become obsessed with the suffragettes in 1909, Sophia might have ended up with a more conventional family of her own. That same year, she received a desperate letter from one of her Raja Sansi cousins in Punjab. Gurdit Singh had recently lost his wife and wrote begging Sophia for help, telling her that he had two sons, aged fifteen and ten, and one daughter aged five who needed the love of a mother and the prospect of a decent future, neither of which he felt he could provide. Gurdit Singh reminded the princess of the hardships his family had endured for her father's sake. His English may have been strained but his message was clear: 'The calamities and troubles which I faced during my life are too many . . . I am unable to support and educate my children. Therefore I must respectfully and humbly request and pray for so benign affectionate cousin that is you, that you like to keep with you one of my three children in England.'[16]

Gurdit Singh's desperation caused him to ramble in the letter, sometimes he begged Sophia to keep one of his children, sometimes just the boys and sometimes all three. He wanted them to receive a good education so that their life might be easier than his own. He had reason to hope for a positive response, for two years before, Sophia had put the idea into his head herself: 'I will be more than happy to have either of your sons . . . I cannot speak Urdu or Punjabi, so he will have to learn to speak English . . . of course you realise that having anything to do with us, will not gain him any high posts in India, in fact it will probably do the opposite thing, as the government are not fond of us.'[17]

In other letters Gurdit Singh, referring to himself as her 'unfortunate cousin', confessed to Sophia that hardship was driving him to very dark thoughts: 'I consider it will be better if god give me an early death, because I do not like to alive further in the separation of my so beloved wife. It is too much sorrow for me . . . Kindly excuse me that I repeatedly trouble you, because I am assured that there is no anyone else to sympathise with me besides you in this transitory world. Your this kindness I will never forget as long as we live in this world. I shall ever pray for your long life and prosperity.'[18]

Sophia now had the chance of becoming an adoptive mother to three children who were her own flesh and blood. But the opportunity, which once she might have leapt at, had come too late. Sophia had already committed herself. She wrote back to her cousin declining the offer but promising to send whatever money she could whenever she could.

Sophia was just finding her feet within the women's suffrage movement when, in February 1909, her sister Catherine proposed a visit from Germany. The two of them had not seen each other for months and Sophia hoped to take Catherine to watch the state opening of Parliament. Her respect for politicians had grown since she had seen some of them fighting for the rights of her mentor Lajpat Rai, and been shaken again thanks to the denouncements of the suffragettes, who accused them of maliciously denying women the vote. She wanted to see them with her own eyes and to have Catherine's considered opinion.

The Lord Chamberlain, Earl Spencer the Viscount of Althorpe, would ordinarily have granted Sophia's wish without question. However he must have heard something disconcerting, a rumour serious enough to warrant further inquiry. It fell to Sir William Hutt Curzon Wyllie of the India Office to respond to the Lord Chamberlain's letter. As aide-de-camp to the Secretary of State, he had access to all the relevant classified files on the Duleep Singh princesses. Sophia may have left Indian politics behind, but her brief dalliance had followed her.

Curzon Wyllie and his colleague, William Lee Warner, at the Political and Secret Department, were the repositories of all surveillance that took place on behalf of the Indian government. This made them detested by Indians: the pair were described by one native publication as, 'Old unrepentant foes of India who have fattened on the misery of the Indian peasant every [day] since they began their career'.[19]

Despite his reputation, and her past associations, Curzon Wyllie did not deem Sophia to be a particular threat:

> Sir in reference to your letter of the 20th instant I am directed to state for the information of the Lord Great Chamberlain that the Princesses Catherine and Sophia Duleep Singh are the daughters of the late highness the Maharajah Duleep Singh, GCSI of the Punjab, and sisters of Prince Victor Duleep Singh . . . They are received at Court as Princess Catherine and Princess Sophia Duleep Singh . . . They have no recognised status in India and are to all intents and purposes British Crown subjects. Their present request to the Lord Great Chamberlain would appear deserving of favourable consideration.[20]

In an additional note, pinned to the same file, Curzon Wyllie added greater detail both about Sophia's family history and her recent trip to India. Negative reports seemed to have been associated only with Bamba. Sophia's elder sister was regarded as the corrupting influence in her life. The criticism was not entirely without foundation. Bamba had always ruled over her little sister, and it had been she who had led Sophia into the cause of Indian nationalism. However, the suffragette movement was something all of her own.

Sophia's local branch of the WSPU was situated in Kingston-upon-Thames, just a few miles away from Hampton Court. Although it stood at the heart of affluent and leafy suburbia, Kingston, together with neighbouring Richmond, made up two of the most active hotbeds of militant suffragette activity in the country. In 1909, Sophia's local WSPU leader was a striking young Irish woman called Norah Dacre Fox.[21] With her detonative personality, Norah bore more than a passing resemblance to Christabel Pankhurst. Like her leader, she could pass for a much younger woman, and often chose to exploit the fact, wearing her flyaway blonde hair in girlish coils on either side of her head. The image did not fit the message, because sweet-faced Norah believed suffragettes should use any means necessary to achieve their aims. Vandalism and arson were acceptable strategies in her opinion. In the course of her life, she would go to prison three times for acting on those beliefs.[22] Not since Sophia sat in a room with the revolutionary Sarla Devi in Lahore had she been in the company of such a dangerous woman.

As well as her devotion to the WSPU, Dacre Fox was also an ardent anti-vivisectionist, which could only have endeared her more to the animal-loving princess. Soon Sophia was devoting all her time to the cause. At first she turned her attention to the movement's finances, throwing herself into fundraising. She helped organise bazaars and the suffragettes gleefully advertised jams and cakes 'made by the Princess herself', although it was highly unlikely that Sophia even knew how to light an oven let alone how to bake a cake.

Not satisfied with raising funds for the effort, Sophia asked if she could do more. Only too happy to give her the chance, the suffragettes asked the princess to appear at numerous suffragette 'At Homes' – afternoons of parlour politics where women were recruited or pressed for money in genteel surroundings. Sophia's celebrity proved to be very useful as many women came as much to see an Indian princess as to hear about the suffragettes. In no time, Sophia's efforts came to the attention of the WSPU leadership. Intrigued, Emmeline Pankhurst asked to meet her and quickly Sophia gained access to the inner circle of the union. Her status and close history with Queen Victoria's family made her newsworthy and the Pankhursts began to think of ways to utilise their royal rebel. Sophia awaited their instructions, anxious to be of service. The princess's new group of friends included Emmeline Pethick Lawrence, Ethel Smyth and Annie Kenny. Together they were the most vilified women in England, and Sophia delighted in their company.

She was not the only Indian being seduced by the suffragettes. Gandhi had travelled to England in 1906 in an effort to convince the

British authorities to repeal the most contentious legislation in his country, the Asiatic Law Amendment Ordinance of 1906. Because of it, Indians in South Africa were being fingerprinted like common criminals and forced to carry papers, as if they were aliens in their own country. The British were treating them even worse than the Boers they had defeated. Failure to produce the required pass documents resulted in arrest and even deportation without trial. The law also rendered Indian marriages illegal and therefore all children born to them illegitimate. Moreover, the police were using their powers of stop and search to harass Indians at will. Gandhi believed that a British failure to address his community's concerns would lead to bloodshed on the streets of the Transvaal, something he wanted to avoid at all cost.

The meetings did not go well, and Gandhi despondently prepared for his return to Durban. Just as he was about to leave, he saw one of the first protests of the WSPU break upon Westminster. Writing for his journal *Indian Opinion*, under the headline, 'Deeds Better Than Words', Gandhi described the suffragettes' actions: 'They have sent petitions, written letters, delivered speeches and tried many other means. Last Wednesday they went to the House of Commons as soon as it opened and demanded the right to vote; they caused some damage also, for which they were prosecuted and sentenced to furnish a security of £5 each. On their refusing to do so, they were sentenced to imprisonment and they are now in gaol. Most of the women have got three months. All of them come from respectable families and some are very well educated.'[23]

Gandhi spent considerable time describing one particular suffragette, Annie Cobden Sanderson (whom George Bernard Shaw would describe in *The Times* as 'one of the nicest women in England').[24] Gandhi quoted the speech she gave from the dock: 'I shall never obey any law in the making of which I have had not hand; I will not accept the authority of the court executing those laws; if you send me to gaol, I will go there, but I shall on no account pay a fine. I will not furnish any security either.'[25] She was sent to Holloway Prison.

Gandhi was exhilarated by those words and resolved to use suffragette strategy when he went home to South Africa. Arrest, defiance and a refusal to pay fines were to become his first acts of civil disobedience. Later, he would also come to be inspired by the suffragettes' willingness to go on hunger strike. As he wrote in a newspaper editorial in 1906, the suffragettes had come up with a method that no state, no matter how powerful, could resist: 'It is no wonder that a people which produces such daughters and mothers should hold the sceptre . . . People do not have much faith in articles and speeches. Anyone can do that, they call for no courage. Deeds after all are better than words. All other things are unavailing and no one is afraid of them. The only way therefore is to sacrifice oneself and take the plunge.'[26]

Not only did the suffragettes provide Gandhi with inspiration, they also challenged his preconceptions about women. Gandhi had married his wife, Kasturba, when the two of them were just thirteen and fourteen years of age. She had been the epitome of subservience, putting up with his long absences and vow of chastity with uncomplaining stoicism. The British women he saw throwing themselves at the hooves of charging police horses forced Gandhi to revaluate his opinions: 'If even women display such courage, will the Transvaal Indians fail in their duty and be afraid of gaol? Or would they rather consider the gaol a palace and readily go there?' Suffragette defiance caused him to think of the future of colonial rule elsewhere in the world. 'When that time comes,' he wrote, 'India's bonds will snap of themselves.'[27]

In the summer of 1909, the WSPU decided that a campaign of stone-throwing and destruction of government property were legitimate strategies. Gandhi, with his non-violent sensibilities, found the shattering glass and increased willingness to brawl with police distasteful. While he now sought to put distance between himself and the suffragettes, others were not finding the WSPU's decision to embrace militancy nearly so hard to comprehend. While Emmeline Pankhurst and her followers were targeting the windows of Westminster, a group of Indian nationalists set their sights on the men who sat behind them. Their activities centred on a residential address in north London, some twenty miles away from Hampton Court.

*    *    *

Halfway up Highgate Hill, 65 Cromwell Avenue was a large Victorian mansion, hidden from the road behind tall linden trees. With its redbrick façade and cheery white-framed windows, it was an unlikely hub of political discontent. Purchased a few years earlier, it served as a hostel for some twenty-five foreign students. Thanks to the brown faces which were seen regularly entering and leaving the house, in no time locals took to calling the place 'India House'. It became a well-known landmark although very little was known about number 65's mysterious owner.

Shyamji Krishnavarma was a rich man who had acquired his wealth by marrying the daughter of a successful Bombay merchant. Impeccably dressed with a closely cropped salt-and-pepper beard, receding hairline and small, pebble spectacles, he seemed the epitome of a comfortable middle-class Indian. However, Krishnavarma was a radical nationalist with murder on his mind.

In his youth he had been a brilliant Sanskrit scholar, with great ambitions. Winning scholarships from two Oxford colleges to study Eastern languages, he seemed well on the way to realising his dreams. Like Gandhi, he had trained as a lawyer, but unlike him, Krishnavarma became bitter when he found himself barred from the high office he felt his intellect warranted. Resentment gave way to thoughts of violence after India's plague of 1897. In his home city of Bombay and neighbouring Poona, the British had forced tens of thousands from their homes and into makeshift camps in an effort to contain the epidemic. Many Indians felt corralled like animals, left to suffer and die away from their loved ones. As the government blocked thousands of terrified residents from fleeing the cities, panic spread almost as quickly as the disease. Soldiers made the hysteria worse by conducting heavy-handed house-to-house searches, looking for the infected.

Krishnavarma blamed the British for treating his countrymen with a lack of humanity. He blamed them for reducing Indians to second-class status in their own country and for smothering the language and culture that he loved with their own. He decided to punish them for all their transgressions.

When he bought the imposing north London mansion on Highgate Hill, Krishnavarma let it be known that he had done so to help his fellow countrymen. The capital's landlords were reluctant to rent to brown-skinned foreigners, no matter how well they spoke. As well as providing a much-needed roof over their heads, he handed out scholarships to bright young Indians who wished to attend English universities but who were too poor to do so. His work made him a hero in the eyes of many impressionable young men. Biding his time, Krishnavarma waited for the right people to walk through his doors.[28]

It was not long before 65 Cromwell Avenue began to attract exactly the kind of people he was looking for. Disgruntled Indians, Irish nationalists, Russians, and an assortment of continental radicals all gathered at the house for weekly lectures and study groups. Although they placed India House under surveillance, the British failed to take the place seriously. They regarded it as a house of hot air more than a threat to national security. However, on 1 July 1909, just after 11 p.m., seven shots rang out in Kensington that confirmed the building's place in history. The gunman's target was Sir William Hutt Curzon Wyllie, ADC to the Secretary of State for India, and the very man who had, just six months before, prepared detailed but magnanimous files on Sophia Duleep Singh.

Curzon Wyllie had been attending a formal event at the Imperial Institute as a guest of the National Indian Association, a benign body which followed the Gokhale school of moderate nationalism. The evening had been convivial, with most people arriving at eight, eating canapés and drinking wine until the arrival of the guest of honour. Curzon Wyllie and his wife arrived just after ten, and the atmosphere was merry as he took to the dais, praising the successful partnership in India between the Raj and the ruled. Guests of both nationalities applauded his speech, raising their glasses to a mutually beneficial future. Musical entertainment followed and people mingled happily. Then at about eleven, Sir William's wife indicated it was time to leave.[29]

The couple said their goodbyes, Lady Curzon Wyllie walking ahead, while her husband was accosted by numerous guests keen to shake his hand. It was then that a tall, wiry young Indian in a Western suit and tie came out of the crowd and stood in Curzon Wyllie's path. Twenty-six-year-old Madhan Lal Dhingra had been studying engineering at University College London and had previously lived at India House. As a legitimate member of the National Indian Association he drew little attention. That night, as well as wearing his smartest suit, which hung loose on his slight frame, he also wore a light blue turban, tied in the style of a Punjabi farmer. Curzon Wyllie smiled broadly and put out his hand in warm greeting, having no reason to suspect Dhingra. He had a passing acquaintance with the young man through his father, a respected physician and supporter of British India.[30]

As he got close enough to touch him, Dhingra pulled out a gun and fired multiple rounds at close range into Curzon Wyllie's face. The lieutenant colonel crumpled into the arms of a Parsee doctor, Cowasji Lalkaka, who had been escorting him to the door. Other bullets which had been intended for Curzon Wyllie hit the doctor in the upper body as he attempted to cradle the fallen man in his arms. Amid piercing screams, Lalkaka fell at Curzon Wyllie's side, their blood pooling together on the floor.[31]

Dhingra had come to the party that night armed with a revolver, two pistols and two knives, hidden in the pockets of his suit. He attempted to shoot himself at the scene, but was prevented from doing so when fellow guests, coming to their senses, leapt to restrain him. The police arrived swiftly and after a brief struggle Madhan Lal Dhingra was led quietly away. The investigation that followed revealed India House for what it was: a training camp for radical young Indians. The outhouse of the mansion was found to contain chemicals, bomb-making manuals and a printing press which produced piles of virulently anti-British pamphlets. India House became arguably the first foreign terrorist cell on English soil.[32]

Madhan Lal Dhingra was tried for the murder of Curzon Wyllie and the Parsee doctor on 23 July 1909 at the Old Bailey. He refused to recognise the court, and would only give one statement in the dock: 'I maintain that if it is patriotic in an Englishman to fight against the Germans if they were to occupy this country, it is much more justifiable and patriotic in my case to fight against the English. I hold the English people responsible for the murder of 80 millions of Indian people in the last fifty years, and they are also responsible for taking away £100,000,000 every year from India to this country. I also hold them responsible for the hanging and deportation of my patriotic countrymen.'[33]

Dhingra had no feelings of remorse: 'I am surprised at the terrible hypocrisy, the farce, and the mockery of the English people. They pose as the champions of oppressed humanity – the peoples of the Congo and the people of Russia – when there is terrible oppression and horrible atrocities committed in India; for example, the killing of two millions of people every year and the outraging of our women ... I make this statement, not because I wish to plead for mercy or anything of that kind. I wish that English people should sentence me to death, for in that case the vengeance of my countrymen will be all the more keen ...'[34]

Madhan Lal Dhingra went to the gallows on 17 August at five past ten in the morning. His family had disowned him and the state refused to cremate him according to his Hindu faith. Dhingra's body lay buried in an anonymous plot, under English soil, for decades.

# The Hampton Court Harridan

Quite apart from the assassination of Curzon Wyllie, the summer of 1909 proved to be wretched for King Edward VII's government. Two miles from India House, an artist called Marion Wallace-Dunlop started a chain of events which shook the British penal system to its foundations. On 5 July, as inmates at Holloway Prison in north London were counted, and preparations made for the first meal of the day, Marion informed her guards that she would not be eating her 'boiled egg, thin toast and tea'.[1] She then went on to refuse her lunch and evening meal, vowing to continue in this manner until the governor recognised her as a political prisoner. So began the first suffragette hunger strike in history, and a long and relentless headache for the state.

In her mid-forties, Marion Wallace Dunlop was a tall, slim woman, with a sharp face and look of perpetual determination on her pursed, thin lips. Her father had been decorated for distinguished service during the Indian Mutiny; however Marion better identified with older ancestors, describing herself as 'a direct descendant of the mother of William Wallace',[2] the Scottish rebel who defeated the English army in 1297. Marion was in prison because ten days earlier she had walked up to the gates of the House of Commons and produced a large ink stamp from her handbag. Pushing it calmly onto the great block of stone outside the main entrance, she left a black, indelible calling card. It read: 'Women's Deputation. June 29. Bill of Rights. It is the right of the subjects to petition the King, and all commitments and prosecutions for such petitioning are illegal.'[3] Making no attempt to hide her act, committed right under the noses of the policemen stationed at St Stephen's Gate, the entrance to the House of Commons, Marion was promptly arrested.

Her inked message pre-empted a planned WSPU march, due to take place three days later. Emmeline Pankhurst was going to present the prime minister, Herbert Henry Asquith, with a petition calling for the vote for women. Only male householders over the age of twenty-one were entitled to vote in Britain at the time, and the calls for greater enfranchisement were getting louder. If she could garner enough signatures the country's Bill of Rights granted the suffragette leader permission to take her case to the King. With hundreds of followers in tow, on the evening of the 29th, Pankhurst approached the gates of the House of Commons and demanded to speak to the prime minister. When he would neither see her nor accept her petition, scuffles broke out in Parliament Square. Suffragettes began to smash the windows of the House of Commons, showering MPs inside with glass. The sound of falling shards provoked a roar of noise below, and battle commenced. There began, as Emmeline put it, 'that old miserable business of refusing to leave, of being forced backward, and returning again and again until arrested'.[4] Politicians clambered out onto the railings of Palace Yard to get a better look as suffragettes were lifted off their feet and thrown backwards. The women got up again and again and pushed against the uniformed men, attempting to reach the gates. Some managed to get close while others were dragged away punching and kicking. The police and the suffragettes flailed at one another in full view of the press and the public. Some women were slapped, others pinned to the walls of the palace. Silk hats and helmets littered the road under Big Ben. Emmeline Pankhurst herself struck an officer twice in a deliberate attempt to get arrested. She was lifted off the pavement, a policeman holding her under each arm.

Una Dugdale, the suffragette who had converted Princess Sophia to the cause just weeks before, was among the 107 women and eight men who were also hauled off to the police station. Una had struggled with two police officers outside the Stranger's Entrance and had been punched repeatedly about the head. If Princess Sophia had seen her new friend in the days that followed, she would barely have recognised her, such were her injuries. Her complaints of police brutality were ignored and, like many of her companions that day, Una was given a one-month sentence at Holloway Prison, charged with assaulting a police officer.[5]

In the wake of the press interest that followed, Marion Wallace-Dunlop, who was already in custody for her 'graffiti', was swiftly tried, found guilty and fined for 'doing damage to the value of 10s'. When she refused to pay, the judge ruled that she too should be sent to prison for a month. It was not Marion's first brush with the law. In 1908 she had been arrested for throwing stones at the windows of 10 Downing Street. She had been sent to prison then too and had been appalled by the treatment of suffragettes behind bars. Despite being arrested for what they insisted were political crimes, she and her fellow campaigners were held with thieves and murderers in the lower divisions. By classifying their acts as criminal, the justice system was debasing the suffragette cause. Marion vowed never to submit to such treatment again.

In 1909, after her 'defacement of Parliament', Marion once again demanded to be classed as a political prisoner. She informed Holloway staff that not only would she refuse to submit to the lower division regime, she would also not wear the black-and-white arrowhead prison uniform. When her transfer request was refused, Marion stopped eating. No matter how she was cajoled by the wardens, she refused to let any food and barely any water pass her lips. Holloway was in uproar as news of her defiance spread. Her hunger strike threw the guards into a panic, and caused a sensation among sympathisers: one summed up the feelings of many when he wrote to Marion, praising her for her sacrifice: 'Nothing has moved me so much – stirred me to the depths of my being – as your heroic action.'[6]

Wallace-Dunlop never did get her wish to become a first-division prisoner. After only ninety-one hours of hunger strike, the governor set her free, realising he might have a dead suffragette on his hands if he did not. Almost immediately other suffragettes up and down the country followed Marion's example. As a result they too were released, and brass bands comprised of rapturous women set up outside the gates of their prisons, ready to welcome them like heroes. The loud and impromptu parties made a mockery of the courts, the wardens, the home secretary and ultimately the prime minister himself.

There was one prison, however, which took a stand. The governor at Birmingham's Winson Green decided that women who refused food would have nourishment forced into their bodies. The government gave nervous assent as Winson Green became a test ground for a new and uncompromising strategy. Women found their jaws prised apart by metal vices and had rubber hosepipes forced down their throats. Doctors then poured a starchy liquid through a funnel at one end. Guards held down thrashing bodies of women who felt like they were drowning. Others checked pulses to ensure they were not straining the prisoners to the point of cardiac failure. Where Winson Green led the way other prisons quickly followed. Reports of force-feeding spread throughout the country and detailed accounts from the prisoners brought a deluge of complaints.

One of the first suffragettes to be force-fed was Laura Ainsworth. She told Marion Wallace Dunlop, and a journalist, Henry Noel Brailsford, what she had been through. Four women wardens had entered her cell, grabbing Laura and pinning her to the bed: 'One doctor (with a towel round his neck) kneels at the back of your right shoulder and forces your head back, there is a wardress at the back to help him, he forces your mouth and the other doctor (who faces you) pushes the tube down your mouth about 18 inches; while this is being done you first have a very great tickling sensation, then a choking feeling, and then you feel quite stunned; when the tube has gone down the required distance the gag (a cork one) is forced down between your teeth.'[7]

The feed, a white liquid called Benger's Food, was sludge-like and cloying and often ended up being vomited after bouts of choking. Widely available on grocers' shelves, it was marketed as a food supplement for children with 'stomach troubles'. Under a picture of a silhouetted mother with her two frolicking children, the marketing material for the product read: 'Watch your children during their growing period. Those who are not fully enjoying fair "happy days" should have a cup of Benger's Food between meals and just before bedtime.'

If too much liquid came back up after force-feeding, the prison staff held the woman down for a second feed. The ritual often left women physically and emotionally broken. They spoke of having the insides of their mouths ripped and of being bloodied by the struggle to get the pipe down. Others spoke of having tubes forced into their nostrils and rectums in order to administer feed. The horror was often described in terms akin to rape. Henry Brailsford was so sickened by the practice that he resigned from his newspaper, the *Daily News*, when it came out in support of force-feeding.

For many outside the suffragette fold, it seemed as if Britain in 1909 was in the grip of mania. Daughters of perfectly respectable households appeared to have gone mad, smashing windows and chaining themselves to government buildings, while the upholders of law and order responded like barbarians. The WSPU marched, harried politicians in the street, and no longer restricted their targets to government buildings, smashing the windows of London's gentlemen's clubs too. One suffragette, Muriel Matters, commandeered an airship and dropped hundreds of 'Votes for Women' leaflets over the Houses of Parliament. Others urged even more incendiary responses.[8]

In October 1909 a new suffragette organisation, the Women's Tax Resistance League, was born. Based on the American Independence battle cry: 'No taxation without representation', the league decided to hit the government where it hurt most: in the Exchequer. Suffragette tax resisters refused to declare their incomes, tore up letters from the tax office and slammed their doors in the faces of inspectors. The courts warned the women that if they refused to pay, they risked the enforced seizure and sale of their property and the worst offenders would be sent to prison. Despite all the attendant horrors that custodial sentences represented at this time, Princess Sophia immediately signed up as a tax resister. She did so against a backdrop of increasing activism and lawlessness.

Suffragettes were turning their ire on politicians everywhere. Speeches were disrupted, nails thrown under tyres and placards thrust in faces. Police forces often responded violently and neither side showed any sign of backing down. To add to the sense of chaos, the government itself looked like it might fall. The Tory-dominated House of Lords had rejected the Liberal government's so-called People's Budget, a radical set of reforms in social welfare. By doing so they made it inevitable that Asquith would have to call a general election three years early to prove he still had the mandate of the people. It was a particularly poisonous time in Parliament, with Liberals and Conservatives at loggerheads. The country braced itself for weeks of febrile electioneering at a point where the British people were feeling more insecure than ever. The polls were set to open on 15 January 1910, and in the flux that preceded them, the suffragettes saw their chance to take their campaign right into the heart of democracy.

At hustings all around Britain, suffragettes harried Liberal MPs, shouting and ringing noisy hand bells to drown them out. They plastered the walls of speaking venues with images of force-feeding, and hid in cupboards and behind church organs so that they might leap out and disrupt unfriendly politicians mid-flow. Suffragettes canvassed for candidates opposing sitting Liberal MPs, and denounced Asquith's front bench with inexhaustible zeal. Their constant interference with his campaign drove the prime minister to demand that suffragettes be kept well away from him at all times. As Emmeline Pankhurst wrote gleefully in her memoirs, 'Mr Asquith travelled from one constituency to another accompanied by a bodyguard of detectives and official "chuckers out", whose sole duty it was to eject women, and men as well, who interrupted his meetings on the question of Votes for Women.'[9]

Asquith was wise to engage special suffragette-repelling bodyguards. In November 1909, a woman called Therese Gurnett, described by the papers as being 'modishly dressed', broke through the police lines at Brighton station, ran up to the Liberal candidate, Winston Churchill, and proceeded to thrash him repeatedly with a dog whip. Newspapers across the globe devoured the story. The

*New York Times* reported: 'The astounded statesman seized his pettycoated assailant, who fought like a tiger cat, and after a sharp tussle, during which the two barely escaped falling from the platform to the tracks below, succeeded in wrenching the weapon from her hands.'[10]

Churchill managed to disarm the suffragette with the help of two police officers, but not before she landed blows. Only his hat saved him from worse injury. 'The Lash curled about his face and left a red mark. When the police got hold of the woman she pointed scornfully at the minister's dented headpiece and while her face flushed with excitement, cried: "That's what you've got and you'll get more of the same from British women".'[11]

The Liberals' constant skirmishes with women made them easy targets for opposition mockery. The Tories characterised them as weak and feeble, unable to deal with the 'fairer sex'. The Labour Party painted them as reactionary old fools. In January 1910, when the votes were finally counted, Asquith's party was returned to power, but his majority was in tatters. The Liberals could only rule with the support of the Labour Party and the Irish nationalists. Asquith never forgave the suffragettes for wrecking his election.

Asquith was a peculiar mix of contradictions. A plain-speaking Yorkshire-born barrister with a remarkably forensic mind, he had acquired a fearsome reputation as a social reformer. But where women's suffrage was concerned, Asquith had a blind spot. Some have blamed his aggressively anti-suffragette stance on a life spent in some of England's most elitist male-dominated institutions, or even as an embittered reaction to his second wife, Margot Tennant – a wildly indiscreet woman who could not be trusted with political pillow talk. Either way, the man described by his predecessor as 'the sledgehammer' for his debating power in the Commons was implacably hostile to Emmeline Pankhurst and all who followed her.

Despite Asquith retaining his position as prime minister, the period after the general election brought with it a lull in hostilities. The government set up a committee to look into the possibilities of extending the vote to women. Chaired by the Earl of Lytton, whose own sister was a leading suffragette, the committee consisted of twenty-five Liberals, seventeen Conservatives, six Irish nationalists and six members of the Labour Party. The cross-party participation was encouraging and the men worked hard to find compromise legislation which might be palatable to all their disparate political ideologies but at the same time satisfy the suffragettes. After much wrangling, the 'Conciliation Bill' was drafted. It was a watered-down version of what Emmeline Pankhurst and her followers wanted, since it only granted the vote to women householders and to women occupiers of business premises paying £10 or more in rental. But sensing that it was the best deal they could get, the suffragettes of the WSPU reluctantly accepted the offer. After years of struggle, they finally seemed to be getting somewhere.

On 6 May 1910, King Edward VII died during the night. With his death, the Duleep Singhs lost their last real benefactor at Buckingham Palace. The King, like his mother and father before him, had genuine affection for Sophia's family. In contrast, Edward's son and successor, George V, had little, if any memory of the Maharajah and cared less about his progeny. Edward's demise was sudden but should have come as no surprise. He had been a voracious smoker most of his life, with a twelve-cigar-a-day habit to add to his numerous cigarettes. The day before he died, Edward suffered several heart attacks which left him weak and extremely short of breath. Ignoring the advice of his physician and family, he refused to go to bed, saying: 'No I shall not give in; I shall go on; I shall work to the end.'[12] The next night he slipped into unconsciousness and was declared dead just before midnight.

Despite King Edward's death, the business of government continued. A month later, on 14 June 1910, the Conciliation Bill was introduced to the House of Commons by David Shackleton. A large-bellied MP with a full black beard and rumbling laugh, Shackleton was the ideal candidate to push through the bill. One of only a handful of Labour MPs in the house, he had grown up in the industrialised north and had first-hand knowledge of the issues championed by social reformers and suffragettes. Born to a poor family in the small hamlet of Cloughfold in Lancashire, Shackleton found himself working in a weaving shed by the age of nine; by twelve, he was running three large looms himself.[13] Around him, men and boys aged rapidly with their back-breaking work. Many turned to alcohol, drinking their wages away and leaving their wives to scrape for money to feed the children. Sometimes the alcohol led to domestic violence. Shackleton had been determined to escape the cycle of poverty and was a staunch teetotaller. From the age of twelve, he walked to evening classes in Accrington after his long and exhausting days in the factories. By twenty, he had become an ardent trade unionist and in 1902, he was elected MP for Clitheroe. The Conciliation Bill appeared to be in safe hands.

The passage of any bill through Parliament can be a long and tortuous process. Proposed legislation is debated, amended and batted between the House of Lords and the House of Commons, until Parliament agrees that it is fit to receive Royal Assent and become law. Before the Parliament Act of 1911, legislation was even more fragile than it is today. Peers could vote to veto a bill, killing it dead in its tracks, and thwarting the will of the elected house in the process. Shackleton's bill therefore had to run the gauntlet before it could pass into law. In 1910 all the signs seemed to suggest that the Conciliation Bill would make its way smoothly through. After sailing through the first stage, the government set aside 11 and 12 July for the second reading, leaving plenty of time for the bill to complete its journey before the end of the parliamentary session. To the suffragettes' delight, the Conciliation Bill then went through its second reading with a majority of 109 votes. Their joy was short-lived, however. Asquith suddenly decided to change the rules declaring that all franchise bills should now go to a 'Committee of the Whole House', thereby immediately lengthening the time needed for the legislation to pass. It could, in theory, still get through, but it would almost certainly need extra time to accommodate the added layers of debate and scrutiny.

Alarmed by the prime minister's manoeuvre, and anxious to press upon the politicians the importance of haste, the suffragettes swiftly organised a huge demonstration in support of the bill. On 23 July half a square mile of space was cleared in Hyde Park for forty large, makeshift platforms. One hundred and fifty prominent supporters were booked to speak and bands from all over the country promised to come and play. Two mammoth processions, representing suffragettes from all parts of the political spectrum, converged on the site at 5.30 p.m. Dressed in whites, they snaked their way through opposite sides of the park, cutting a pale river through banks of spectating men in their dark suits and hats.

The march from the west was organised by the Women's Freedom League and had a Roman theme. Women carried centurion-like standards declaring where they had come from or what they had come for. The words 'Justice' and 'Victory' hovered over their heads. The procession from the east was organised by the Women's Society for Social and Political Union and had an Oriental theme. Colourful bonnets and sashes brought splashes of colour to their otherwise snow-white attire. Not for the first time, East and West collided in Sophia's politics, as the space in Hyde Park filled with some 20,000 protesters. Stages were decorated in purple, green and white suffragette colours, and banners were raised with such slogans as 'The Bill Must Go Through', and 'Where There's A Bill There's A Way!' Their efforts were doomed from the start. On the very evening of the Hyde Park demonstration, Herbert Asquith wrote privately to Lord Lytton, the chairman of the Conciliation Bill committee, and told him he would not allow any more time for the bill during that session of Parliament. He was in effect smothering the legislation in its infancy.

When news of Asquith's letter leaked out, it was met by a tidal wave of rage. In desperation, supportive MPs begged the suffragettes to keep faith, assuring them that they could still squeeze the bill through in the autumn, despite the prime minister's wrecking tactics. Emmeline Pankhurst did not believe them. On 10 November, just days before the autumn session was due to commence, Pankhurst called a meeting at the Albert Hall. It was filled to the rafters with angry suffragettes. Princess Sophia, in her liveried carriage, accompanied by her gleaming footmen, swept up to the entrance of the Albert Hall to hear what her suffragette sisters were planning next. Every seat was filled, and suffragettes crowded into the standing areas in the soaring heights of the auditorium. From the speeches alone it seemed as if they were on the brink of war. Emmeline was in thunderous form: 'This is the last constitutional effort of the Women's Social and Political Union to secure passage of the bill into law. If the bill, in spite of our efforts, is killed by the government, then first of all, I have to say there is an end of the truce.'[14] The noise threatened to raise the Albert Hall's great domed roof.

If Asquith had indeed killed the bill by depriving it of the time it needed to pass, Emmeline declared she would go to the House of Commons and batter down the doors. As she later recalled in her memoirs: 'Instantly, all over the hall, women sprang to their feet crying out, "Mrs Pankhurst, I will go with you!" "I will go!" "I will go!" And I knew our brave women were as ever ready to give themselves, their very lives, if need be, for the cause of freedom.'[15] One of the first to step forward was Sophia Duleep Singh. Emmeline embraced her offer warmly and asked the princess if she would lead the suffragettes with her, walking at her side and in full view of the watching world. Sophia did not hesitate. She would do whatever was required of her.

The plan set for 18 November, the date Parliament was due to return, was a simple one. First the women would gather at Caxton Hall, Westminster. They would then divide themselves into contingents not more than a dozen strong. Emmeline would depart first, with her hand-picked deputation marching in a tight knot around her. The rest of her supporters would leave the hall at intervals of five to ten minutes. The suffragettes aimed to march in this way, group by group, through the winter streets, to the gates of the House of Commons. Turning up in small divisions meant they would break no laws of public order, giving the police no excuse to arrest them. Their chants would build in volume as their numbers grew, making it impossible for those sitting inside the House of Commons to ignore them.

It was a cold, grey, wet Friday morning when Sophia and the others gathered at Caxton Hall. Although suffragettes had met there many times before, this felt different, as if the whole battle for women's votes might be won or lost in the next few hours. The sense of agitation built to a climax as the time to leave approached. After a rousing recital of their battle song 'March of the Women', at half past eleven, the scrape of chairs and the rustle of more than 300 skirts marked the moment when Sophia and her fellow suffragettes rose to do battle. Rumours of an increased police presence rumbled through their ranks, and the women speculated as to how extreme the police response might be.

The new home secretary, the youngest holder of that office Britain had ever known, was the charismatic forty-five-year-old Winston Churchill. Still with a full head of strawberry blond hair in 1910, he had an impressive record of military service and a well-established reputation for swaggering self-confidence. Aware that his fellow politicians were watching him closely, Churchill was determined not to be bettered by a group of noisy women. Although he would later deny it, according to the Metropolitan Police Commissioner, Churchill ordered his men to keep Pankhurst and her followers away from the prime minister at all costs, and without making any arrests. Churchill reckoned that if the police could just push the suffragettes back for long enough, they would tire and go home. He wanted to avoid messy trials and even messier hunger strikes. He was about to make a catastrophic miscalculation.

Sophia, at thirty-four, was by far the youngest suffragette in Emmeline Pankhurst's nine-woman-strong vanguard. Her breath turned to vapour on the cold autumnal air as she attempted to keep up with the taller women and their longer strides. Although Sophia was used to the company of royalty, she felt awed by her companions that day. Pulling expensive furs tightly around her, Sophia took in her group. Emmeline had prepared her companions for the possibility of arrest, and personally relished the prospect. Knowing the press would be there to capture the image of her being carried or dragged from the scene, Emmeline had dressed with panache, wearing a full-length fur coat and elaborate hat, complete with tall black feathers.

England's first woman doctor and also its first woman mayor, Elizabeth Garrett Anderson, walked in step with Emmeline. Hiding her shock of snow-white hair beneath a tidy black bonnet, her over-coat was sober and practical. At seventy-four, she walked stiffly but quickly through the chill, leaning on Emmeline's arm from time to time. Close behind, Elizabeth's daughter Louisa Garrett Anderson moved silently like a protective shadow. Described by the *Votes for Women* magazine as 'pale, calm and quiet', even in the midst of a riot, Louisa provided everyone with a sense of reassurance. She too was a qualified doctor, and more experienced women knew her services might be needed that day. From beneath a cloud of black frizzy hair, Hertha Ayrton looked tense. At fifty-six years of age, she was a distinguished and brilliant physicist and the first woman to be accepted into the Institute of Electrical Engineers. With her broad frame and close-set, intensely green eyes, Ayrton, like the princess, could not help but stand out in a crowd. When the British press falsely attributed the discovery of radium to Marie Curie's husband, she complained bitterly. The Nobel Prize committee was just as guilty as the newspapers of snubbing the true discoverer of 'radioac-tive bodies'. At first it named Curie's husband and male research partner for the award instead of the rightful winner herself. Only after Monsieur Pierre Curie's bitter remonstration was Marie included in the prize. She would only ever receive a quarter of the award. Ayrton made it her life's mission to rectify the injustice and sent scathing letters to editors: 'Errors are notoriously hard to kill,' she wrote. 'But an error that ascribes to a man what was actually the work of a woman has more lives than a cat.'[16]

Another chosen by Pankhurst to be in the vanguard was Annie Cobden Sanderson, the suffragette who had first inspired Gandhi. At fifty-seven, she was one of the best-connected women in Britain: a close friend of George Bernard Shaw and William Morris, she had also recently been a guest at Winston Churchill's wedding. Despite her smiling features and soft, bosomy body, Sanderson was one of the most hardened suffragettes who walked with Sophia.

The eldest suffragette in the Pankhurst group, Dorinda Neligan, was a seventy-seven-year-old headmistress from Croydon who had spent much of her life fighting for girls' education rights. Fragile on her feet, she was accompanied by the slightly more robust sixty-six-year-old Georgina Solomon, widow of the Cape Town statesman Saul Solomon. The Solomons were almost as well known throughout the colonies as Sophia. They had long held uncompromising and unfashionable views, standing against the tide of public opinion, and arguing for racial and religious equality in South Africa.

Riding close behind them, sitting ramrod straight on her thoroughbred horse, was the striking figure of the Hon. Evelina Haverfield; crop in hand, she looked intently at the road ahead, taut with expectation. The twice-married aristocrat and mother of two had been arrested with Emmeline Pankhurst in front of the House of Commons before. She and the older women knew how dangerous confrontations with the police could be and so scanned the route intently, ready for trouble.

At first, their vigilance seemed unnecessary. All seemed to go well and Sophia and the others reached Parliament Square just before noon. The approach to the Palace of Westminster was unusually busy, and almost as soon as they caught sight of their destination, the atmosphere began to prickle. As well as the police, crowds of civilian men filled the square, attracted by press speculation over what might happen if the suffragettes turned up en masse for the opening of Parliament. A contingent of US Navy sailors on shore leave had also travelled to Westminster expecting some kind of show. The police were visible in great numbers and closed in on Sophia and the others, letting them pass but jostling them as they did. Murmuring words of encouragement to each other the suffragettes pushed slowly ahead towards St Stephen's Gate.

Emmeline, Sophia and the other younger members of the deputation took special care to shield Dorinda, Georgina and Elizabeth. Hertha Ayrton later admitted that she had been terrified of what might happen to them and only Louisa Garrett Anderson's reassurances calmed her enough to carry on putting one foot in front of the other. Though she blanched with fear,[17] the collective stature of the women seemed to protect them. Emmeline even believed that the gathered public were on her side. She claimed in her memoirs that 'the crowds proved remarkably friendly. They pushed and struggled to make a clear pathway for us, and in spite of the efforts of the police, my small deputation actually succeeded in reaching the doors of the Stranger's Entrance. We mounted the steps to the enthusiastic cheers of the multitudes that filled the streets.'[18]

Either she misread the situation, or the atmosphere turned on the head of a pin. Within minutes, as the next detachment neared the gate, the chimes of Big Ben were suddenly drowned out by screaming.

Police closed in and Sophia and the others found themselves pressed up against the gates to Parliament, which remained closed. A line of officers formed between them and the rest of the square, trapping them at St Stephen's Gate. Unable to move, Sophia was forced to watch as friends, arriving steadily in their interval groups, were met with extreme violence just feet away. 'We stood there for hours gazing down on a scene which I hope never to look upon again,' wrote Emmeline Pankhurst.[19] Women were tossed like rag dolls between groups of men as police and onlookers jeered. As more and more women arrived, so too did police reinforcements. Horses charged into the crowd, knocking women to the ground. Other suffragettes were slapped about the face or shoved with enough force to lift them off their feet. Fighting back, women pushed, scratched and kicked at the men. Small groups of suffragettes tried to pull mounted police from their horses; others attempted to seize reins in order to stop the beasts from trampling their fallen comrades. A number of officers swung their helmets at the suffragettes like clubs. To anyone watching, the scene looked less like a police operation and more like a late-night fight after pub closing time.

Suffragettes were repeatedly thrown to the ground by police in an effort to exhaust them. Some were badly hurt and others were knocked unconscious. One would later complain that she had been hurled into the path of an oncoming vehicle, narrowly avoiding having her head crushed under its wheels. Suffragettes were grabbed about the breasts, had their clothes ripped and skirts raised high to reveal their undergarments. Some would later describe officers ramming knees between their legs. Molestation and abuse rained down upon them, initiated by the men in uniform, who encouraged the crowds to join in.

Even Winston Churchill, no friend of the suffragettes or their methods, was appalled by the excesses of his force that day. In the many hours of recriminations that followed, the Metropolitan Police Commissioner insisted that his officers had been forced into an impossible situation by the home secretary, Winston Churchill, who had not wanted the women anywhere near the House of Commons but did not want them arrested either. In the absence of any clear instruction, the police believed it was their job to use any means necessary to deter the women from reaching Parliament. Since the women refused to give up, the situation had escalated out of control.

Eyewitness accounts from the women painted a picture of state-sponsored violence that went on well into the afternoon: 'For hours I was beaten about the body, thrown backwards and forwards from one to another, until one felt dazed with the horror of it . . . Often seized by the coat collar, dragged out of the crowd, only to be pushed helplessly along in front of one's tormentor into a side street . . . he beat one up and down one's spine until cramp seized one's legs, when he would then release one with a vicious shove, and with insulting speeches, such as "I will teach you a lesson. I will teach you not to come back any more. I will punish you, you —, you —".'[20]

Some bystanders, appalled by what they were seeing and hearing, tried to help by pulling some of the suffragettes out of the way of charging horses, or stemming their bleeding cuts with handkerchiefs. Others goaded each other to grope and fondle cornered women. It was suspected by the WSPU that the civilians who showed most enthusiasm for the sexual assault were in fact plain-clothes police-men. Sophia was forced to watch it all, trapped at St Stephen's. With the tall uniformed men surrounding her, she looked small and help-less. Emmeline Pankhurst was screaming at her side, demanding that the police stop the violence and make arrests. Her voice was drowned out by the noise. Unable to contain herself, or be contained any longer, Evelina Haverfield, still on horseback, barged through the line, charging at the police. Cutting through the crowds, she swung her crop in the faces of the officers, knocking many down as she rode into the densest parts of the square. When she was finally pulled from her saddle Evelina punched one officer in the mouth. As she was dragged away she was heard to lament that she had not hit him hard enough. Next time, she swore, she would bring a revolver.

Evelina had created a break in the police line and Sophia slipped through it. Her small figure bobbed, pushed and weaved its way into the midst of the fighting. The plight of one particular woman had moved her from paralysed horror to action. She saw a suffragette struggling with a police officer for what seemed an age. Every time he pushed her down, she rose up again. The policeman was getting more frustrated and violent and the woman was finding it harder to get back on her feet. After one particularly brutal throw, it seemed she was on the verge of losing consciousness. Sophia watched as 'she fell onto her hands and knees and when she got up, he took hold of her most roughly'.[21]

It was too much for the princess, who elbowed her way through the seething mass and forced herself between the woman and the policeman. She pushed against him trying to get him to release his hold, while in a high-pitched, clipped voice she screamed at him to back off. Faced by the tiny, brown-faced, raging figure, the officer was shocked enough to step away. Letting the limp creature in his hands fall to the pavement he turned and disappeared into the crowd. After seeing that the woman was not badly hurt, Sophia followed the officer into the riot. She repeatedly screamed for him to stop and face her. She kept on his heels, demanding his name and the name of his senior officer. At last catching sight of his identification number, she repeated it to herself again and again until she had committed it to memory. She had no intention of letting Constable V700 get away with his behaviour that day.

It seemed that no matter how many times they were thrown down, assaulted or shoved back from the gates, the suffragettes continued to pick themselves up and push forward. Ada Wright, a suffragette who would become a friend of Sophia, described the events in her memoirs: 'It was a terrible day, and we were battered by the police all day long. The police rode at us with their horses, so I caught hold of the reins and would not let go. A policeman caught hold of my arm, and twisted it round and round, until I felt the bone almost breaking.'[22] Although

Churchill tried to stop it, the *Daily Mirror* ran a picture of Ada on their front page the following morning, lying semi-conscious on the ground, clutching her head, while a police officer loomed over her. The events of 'Black Friday' would shock the world.

Henry Brailsford, the journalist who had resigned his job over the issue of force-feeding, collected suffragist accounts from that day. They made for difficult reading, even for the most vociferous critics of the WSPU. Delia MacDermott was one of many to lodge official complaints against the police: 'The constable R21 almost choked me . . . by putting his arm round my neck and pressing the back of his hand on my throat.'[23] Her breast had been 'gripped and pounded', and she had been 'lifted right up by the waist and flung into the crowd by Constable R21 who told her "It is no good taking our numbers today"'.[24]

By Westminster Bridge, the aged Georgina Solomon was violently sexually assaulted by an officer who encouraged bystanders to do what they wished with her.[25] Another suffragette, Elizabeth Freeman, gave evidence about the attack on Annie Cobden Sanderson, one of the women who had led the march with Sophia: 'My attention was drawn to a policeman thumping a woman in the small of the back with doubled fist. Recognising the woman as Mrs Cobden Sanderson I spoke to her, calling her by name, thinking the policeman would desist when he knew who she was, but he did not.' With her protestations she attracted the attention of another officer who said, 'Remember you are a man today.' He then rained oaths upon her while his colleague continued to hit Annie. According to Elizabeth, he 'had the leader of the deputation by the throat, pushing her head backward'. When Elizabeth tried to pull his hand away from Annie's neck, he 'addressed his attention to me, giving my arm and hand a sudden twist and turning his own arm down, so that I found myself on my knees and was kicked in the abdomen, and also in the back by those at the back of me'.[26]

Compared to her friends, Sophia had been lucky. In her attempt to stop and then follow Constable V700 through the crowds, she had sustained some bruising to her arms which she shrugged off. Writing to Winston Churchill a week later on her distinctive blue paper with its five-pointed coronet, she described the assault on the suffragette she had tried to help. Referring to herself in the third person she told the home secretary: 'The policeman was unnecessarily and brutally rough and Princess Sophia hopes he will be suitably punished. Princess Sophia Duleep Singh was herself on the Deputation on the 18th and received several bruises on her arm, but she did not find that in her case the police were rougher than necessary.'[27] Sophia failed to mention that she had been arrested later that same day, along with 115 women and four men.

After almost six long hours of struggle on the streets of Westminster, the police had finally changed their tactics and rounded up the suffragettes for arrest. Bow Street police station became a scene of bedlam with the arrival of so many suffragettes. Police officers wearily noted down particulars as the stream of arrested crammed into the entrance. It had been a long day for them too and many suspected that some of the women were giving them false identities to make their jobs even more difficult. At least the officer who processed Princess Duleep Singh of Hampton Court Palace knew she was not telling lies. Sophia was charged with obstructing the police in their duties and told, like the rest of the protesters, that she was bailed until the morning when she would have to return to Bow Street magistrates' court and hear her fate.

Sophia's name was added to a fat Home Office ledger containing the names of hundreds of suffragettes who had found themselves placed under arrest. Handwritten and annotated with references to other police files and surveillance records, the book was a record of some of the most troublesome and politically organised women in Britain. Under the date Friday 18 November 1910, nestled between 'Alice Singer' and 'Margaret Skewing', Sophia's name – incorrectly recorded as 'Singh Princess A Duleep' – sat incongruously. Scrawled tightly beneath her entry is the line 'complains of police conduct'.[28] Sophia returned to Hampton Court to spend an unsettled few hours, plagued by images she had witnessed that day.

When the women turned up at Bow Street magistrates' court in the morning, they found all charges against them had been dropped. Emmeline Pankhurst claimed fear of their testimony lay behind the leniency. Though they were denied their day in court, the sworn statements given by suffragettes to the likes of Henry Brailsford in the days that followed continued to cause shock and disgust. In particular, sexual brutality was highlighted again and again: 'Several times constables and plain-clothes men who were in the crowd passed their arms around me from the back and clutched hold of my breasts in as public a manner as possible, and men in the crowd followed their example. I was also pummelled on the chest, and my breast was clutched by one constable from the front. As a consequence, three days later, I had to receive medical attention ... my breasts were discoloured and very painful ... My skirt was lifted up as high as possible, and the constable attempted to lift me off the ground by raising his knee. This he could not do, so he threw me into the crowd and incited the men to treat me as they wished. Consequently several men who, I believe, were policemen in plain clothes, also endeavoured to lift my dress.'[29]

It was widely believed at the turn of the century that blows to the breasts caused cancer, so many of the women spent the next few months racked with worry. Although nobody was killed on Black Friday itself, two women died in the weeks that followed from injuries sustained that day. One was Emmeline Pankhurst's sister Mary Clarke, the other a suffragette from Upminster, Henria Williams.

Brailsford demanded a government inquiry, blaming Churchill's order to avoid arrest for the excessive violence. Notwithstanding the offending instruction, Brailsford was stunned by 'the frequency of torture and indecency' and 'the more obviously unprovoked acts of violence which many of the men committed. A man acting under this order might feel he was justified in flinging a woman back with some violence when she attempted to pass the cordon. But this order alone would not suggest to him that he should run forward and fell her with a blow on the mouth, or twist her arms, or bend her thumb, or manipulate her breasts.'[30] In Brailsford's opinion, the home secretary had allowed the police to feel themselves above the law that day.

Despite his accusations, Churchill refused an official inquiry. He also refused to act on Sophia's letter of complaint. Instead, Churchill directed her handwritten note to the Metropolitan Police

Commissioner, who in turn forwarded it to Constable V700's section head for investigation. Some in the commissioner's department were trying to discredit the complaints. On one Home Office file, which had been opened solely to deal with Sophia's allegations, a senior officer had written: '? Put up,'[31] suggesting that he thought Sophia had been coached into making the complaint.

After three weeks of paper-shuffling, the Police Commissioner ruled in favour of officer V700, stating that he had not used 'more force than necessary to repel the attempts made by suffragette ladies'.[32]

Sophia refused to accept the verdict and harried the commissioner with further questions. On 17 December 1910, Winston Churchill personally annotated her file with the terse comment: 'Send no further reply to her'.[33] He signed off with his initials 'WSC', and the case was closed.

To Sophia, it was reminiscent of her time in the Punjab, when her complaints had gone unheeded. She would soon discover that some of the same figures who had loomed large then, were playing a prominent role in her current struggle too.

# A Familiar Enemy

George Nathaniel Curzon, 1st Marquis Curzon of Kedleston, and former Viceroy of India, was back in Britain, watching the events of Black Friday in horror. It confirmed what he had always thought: some women were simply out of control and had to be reminded of their place. While Sophia and the others regrouped, Curzon set up 'The National League for Opposing Woman Suffrage'. It was an influential organisation which would try and block any attempt to grant votes to women. By his actions, Curzon became one of the most detested figures among Sophia's friends. The princess's feelings, however, had much deeper roots.

In 1902, Sophia and her sisters had blamed Curzon for the indignity of being shut out of the Punjab camp while everyone they knew watched the durbar from prominent VIP seats. The Viceroy had enjoyed the status of a god while they had been forced to make their way to their father's former empire in nervous anonymity. Sophia's fury had not diminished over time. In India, Curzon had seemed omnipotent. It had taken one of Britain's most ruthless soldiers to bring him down off his pedestal.

Horatio Herbert Kitchener was a decorated war hero with an imposing moustache and a formidable reputation. At the turn of the century he was enjoying a similar deified status to the Viceroy himself. While Curzon had nawabs and maharajahs bowing before him, Kitchener's military successes in Egypt and Sudan, against armies much larger than his own, gave him an air of invincibility. When, in November 1902, Kitchener was appointed Curzon's commander-in-chief, ripples of excitement ran through the Raj. Two giants of British colonial rule were going to work together. India would be led by an unassailable team.

Outwardly, the men had much in common. Like Curzon, Kitchener was well over six feet tall and able to intimidate people just by walking into a room. The general, then in his early fifties, carried himself with the straight-back discipline of a lifelong army man. Curzon, almost ten years younger, walked with a similarly formal and erect bearing. The Viceroy, who had never served in the military, could thank a metal corset for his gait. After he sustained a serious spinal injury from a boyhood riding accident, the contraption had been wrapped around his torso every day of his life. Constantly in pain, Curzon often found it hard to sleep, and was frequently irascible. Yet there was another, more sinister comparison which bound them to each other. Nationalists blamed Curzon for mishandling relief efforts during the Indian famine of 1899–1900, thereby causing a far greater loss of life. Kitchener too stood accused of starving men, women and children to death. The difference was that Curzon had been dealing with the aftermath of a natural disaster and Kitchener's South African famine was all his own work.

Before India, Kitchener had proved himself a ferocious champion of empire in another continent. The invasion, colonisation and annexation of African territory by European powers during the nineteenth century had left the region unstable for decades. Descendants of Dutch and Huguenot colonists clashed with the British in South Africa leading to the First Boer War in 1880. Fighting was fierce but brief, lasting only a year. After the signing of treaties, a fragile peace held for almost two decades. However, the inexorable spread of Queen Victoria's empire pushed the region to the brink once more. War was declared by the Boers on 11 October 1899, and having taken the initiative, the Dutch-speaking farmers proved to be surprisingly successful. British garrisons were left beleaguered and stranded. In response, the Empire called for their best military man to crush the threat once and for all. They called for Kitchener and the tide began to turn. The Boers lost battles and thousands became disheartened and surrendered; only 20,000 'bitter-enders' refused to give up. They knew the land better than the British soldiers, and kept the fight going for two further years using guerrilla tactics.

Kitchener responded with two strategies which would gain international notoriety for decades. 'Scorched earth' and 'concentration camps' were unfamiliar tactics until his devastating use of both. First Kitchener ordered his men to set fire to Boer fields, farms and storehouses, killing crops and livestock. He wanted to hobble the Afrikaners' means of food production for years to come. With the camps, his ambitions were more far-reaching. They were designed to break the spirit of the Boer rebels for ever.

Male prisoners of war were captured and sent to overseas prison camps in St Helena and Ceylon. Women, children, the elderly and infirm were also rounded up and marched for miles to forty-five internment camps. Black South Africans found themselves herded into sixty-four separate, racially segregated camps. They had nothing to do with the war, but were simply farm labourers whom Kitchener wanted to keep out of the fields. Any harvests that escaped his flames would be left to rot in the soil.

Regardless of skin colour, when prisoners (or rather 'the interned') arrived at their respective camps, they found disease-ridden pits of despair. All had been hastily constructed and were badly managed. Without adequate rations or sanitary provision, and with scant shelter from the elements, infants were the first to die. Nursing mothers found they made no milk to breastfeed. The children were next; emaciated by their tiny rations they were too weak to fight infections. Their deaths were often painful and drawn out. Little wrapped bodies were removed from the camps on a daily basis.

Despite Kitchener's best efforts, rumours of the enormous suffering in his camps began to seep out, causing much disquiet in Westminster. The Secretary of State for War, Sir William St John Freemantle Broderick, was forced to calm critics in England by insisting that all the interned Boers were 'contented and comfortable'. His words, however, were exposed as lies by the most unlikely of characters. Emily Hobhouse, a rector's daughter from the tiny parish of St Ive near Liskeard in Cornwall, had a very different story to tell.

Born in 1860, Emily was handsome but highly strung, which made her shun attention. Victorian England had failed to give her an education commensurate with her intelligence, so instead she busied herself with social work around her father's church. Her mother died young, and her father became grievously ill soon after, leaving Emily to act as his sole nurse and companion. She tended him with enormous dedication for many years; however when he too died in 1895, Emily was left bereft. Church work was no longer fulfilling and, audaciously, Emily decided to leave England. Travelling to America, she settled in a region of Minnesota, where many Cornish miner emigrants lived. There, just as she had at home, Emily helped the poorest families, distributing food and clothing among the most needy, and working to combat prostitution and drunkenness. In the course of her charitable endeavours Emily fell in love. Unfortunately, she also had her heart broken.

Although Emily Hobhouse never did say why the engagement to an American businessman, John Carr Jackson, ended as abruptly as it did, contemporaries believed he had given her plenty of reason to call the marriage off. His worst transgressions involved excessive drinking, but he also managed to squander much of her meagre fortune on disastrous land speculations. After she separated from him, Emily moved back to London to find her country preparing for war in South Africa. She saw young men, clearly unfit to fight, signing up at recruitment offices. They came from poor backgrounds and many had rickets or other obvious signs of malnutrition and sickness. These men were accepted by the army, put into uniforms and shipped off. Emily was outraged and became an ardent pacifist. Around 22,000 British and colonial soldiers would die during the Second Boer War, the vast majority losing their lives to typhoid and dysentery, too feeble to resist contagion.[1]

Under the watchful eye of her uncle, the Liberal politician, Henry Hobhouse, Emily found herself appointed Secretary of the Women's

Branch of the South African Conciliation Committee. It was not long before news of atrocities in the concentration camps began to trickle through to her. She wanted to see for herself what was being done in Britain's name, and packed her bags for the long voyage to South Africa. When later asked why she had decided to take such a step, Emily declared that the suffering of her fellow women compelled her: 'I came quite naturally, in obedience to the feeling of unity or oneness of womanhood . . . it is when the community is shaken to its foundations, that abysmal depths of privation call to each other and that a deeper unity of humanity evinces itself.'[2] As her words suggest, Emily was a suffragette.

Alongside her pacifist commitments she had pledged loyalty to the Adult Suffrage League, a radical group that believed all women, regardless of their social and financial status, deserved to be given the vote. From the moment Emily Hobhouse arrived in South Africa she set about collecting food and clothing for those interred in the camps. Armed only with letters of recommendation from a couple of influential Liberal politicians, she demanded that they opened the gates and let her see what was going on inside.

Kitchener despised Emily's meddling. He took to referring to her as 'that bloody woman',[3] and barred her from seeing most of his concentration camps. Nevertheless the ones she was able to visit uncovered a picture far worse than any she might have imagined. Typhoid, measles and dysentery were running wild among the ragged and starving. Children were dying in startling numbers, and those who survived were skeletal shadows, unable to support the weight of their own bodies. Emily saw lips pulled back with malnutrition and hollow shadows around vacant, rheumy eyes. It is estimated that almost 30,000 Boers died of starvation and disease in the camps during the Second Boer War. Children accounted for more than 22,000 of those deaths.

Appalled, Emily Hobhouse stepped up her relief efforts, hiring trucks, filling them with provisions paid for with money she had raised in London, and attempting to deliver to as many of the internees as she could reach. Emily also collected testimonies and photographic evidence of life in the camps. She used these to produce a blistering report which she intended to put before Parliament on her return to England: 'I call this camp system a wholesale cruelty . . . To keep these Camps going is murder to the children . . . The women are wonderful. They cry very little and never complain. The very magnitude of their sufferings, their indignities, loss and anxiety seems to lift them beyond tears . . . only when it cuts afresh at them through their children do their feelings flash out . . . I can't describe what it is to see these children lying about in a state of collapse. It's just exactly like faded flowers thrown away. And one has to stand and look on at such misery, and be able to do almost nothing.'[4]

Emily's report, a 'Visit to the Camps of Women and Children in the Cape and Orange River Colonies', was delivered to Westminster in June 1901. So seismic were her revelations that just weeks later the British government established a commission, headed by the moderate suffragette leader Millicent Fawcett. She visited South Africa and confirmed Emily's damning evidence of neglect, disease and cruelty. Despite the commission's findings and the horror with which they were greeted, Kitchener was not censured by his superiors. Rather, his career rocketed and he was promoted in 1902 to the rank of general, given the title 'Viscount Kitchener of Khartoum and of the Vaal in the Colony of Transvaal and of Aspall in the County of Suffolk' and sent, with all honours, to serve alongside the Viceroy of India.

Due to his early experiences with women such as Hobhouse and Fawcett, Kitchener loathed the suffragettes. He would later describe himself as 'disgusted' when he found out that his own niece, Franny Parker, turned out to be one of the most militant, hunger-striking members of the WSPU. Under the alias of 'Janet Arthur', Franny would be imprisoned on several occasions for causing damage to property and, most notably, for trying to blow up the cottage of Scotland's greatest poet, Robbie Burns.[5]

After his arrival in India, Kitchener managed to work effectively with Curzon for a while. Charged with reorganising the Indian Army, the general did so with great speed and efficiency, much to the delight of the government in London. However, it was not in

Curzon's nature to share the limelight for long, and soon the growing praise for Kitchener began to grate. The Viceroy taunted his general constantly, even taking issue with the way Kitchener signed his letters 'Lord Kitchener of Khartoum'. Knowing how much it would irritate him, Curzon told him that his signature took up too much space on the page and too much time to read. He suggested that he simply sign off as 'Kitchener' instead.

The underlying accusation of narcissism from one as conceited as Curzon was too much to bear. From his time at Balliol College, Oxford, Curzon had been mocked for his vanity in prose and verse. One particular piece of undergraduate doggerel followed him all his life:

> My name is George Nathaniel Curzon,
> I am a most superior person.
> My cheeks are pink, my hair is sleek,
> I dine at Blenheim once a week.[6]

In an indignant blaze, Kitchener set about undermining his Viceroy with ruthless efficiency. By August 1905 the two were in furious deadlock over who should be in charge of military supplies. The standoff between the two silverbacks spilled over the frontiers of the Raj. The Secretary of State for India found himself having to arbitrate between his two most senior men from his seat in Whitehall. He was the same William St John Fremantle Broderick who had attempted to explain away concerns over Kitchener's concentration camps in South Africa. Once again, he backed Kitchener to the hilt.

Humiliated, Curzon had no choice but to step down, and did so in a cloud of resentment. His undignified exit from India in 1905 delighted the Duleep Singh sisters. Writing to Sophia, Catherine expressed her unconcealed glee: 'What do you say to Lord Curzon really having resigned. I think it too perfect a joke!'[7]

On his return to England, the suffragettes quickly became the target of the former Viceroy's ire. Curzon began to formulate in speeches and publications his 'Fifteen Good Reasons Against the Grant of Female Suffrage'; the resulting list would become the mantra for Curzon's National League for Opposing Woman Suffrage, and for anti-suffragists generally. The vote, he claimed, would turn women against motherhood ('their proper sphere and highest duty'); their innate emotionalism caused women to make unpredictable decisions at times of crisis; moreover, women simply were not intellectually up to the complexities of politics. In essence, 'women have not as a sex, or a class, the calmness of temperament with a balance of mind, nor have they the training, necessary to qualify them to exercise a weighty judgment in political affairs'.

None of these arguments was new to the WSPU; however Curzon introduced an additional international dimension to his opposition. He argued that giving women the vote would jeopardise the very foundation of His Majesty's Empire: 'the presence of a large female factor in the constituencies returning a British government to power would tend to weaken Great Britain in the estimation of foreign powers'. Critically, Curzon drew attention to the effects equal franchise would have on the most precious 'jewel in the Crown'. 'It would be gravely misunderstood and would become a source of weakness in India.'[8]

The suffragist newspaper, *The Vote*, turned a torrent of vitriol towards the fallen Viceroy. Referring to Curzon's 'cloven hoof', in their Christmas Eve edition in 1910, the editorial thundered: 'He seems to forget that the worship of the Female is by far the most popular cult in India, and that for one prayer put up to a god there are five thousand to a goddess.' The paper went on: 'He also ignores – if, indeed, he ever grasped, since few Indian officials do – the enormous influence which women wield in the present unrest. The Feminist movement is intimately associated with the aspirations of Young India.'[9] Suffragette magazines and pamphlets began to lampoon Curzon regularly. Sophia watched and relished the mockery of her old foe by her new friends. Eager to prove herself worthy of their sorority, Sophia threw herself, quite literally, into WSPU activities with a new vigour.

The WSPU chose the day of the King's speech to Parliament, on 6 February 1911, to stage a coordinated protest. George V was expected to sweep his way from Buckingham Palace towards Parliament in a gilded carriage, with his wife, Queen Mary, by his side. Troops had been drilling for weeks so that they might march in tight, pristine formation, as the King's escort. The regalia and marching bands were sure to attract crowds, and the police prepared themselves for a huge turnout. With their bunting and flags, supporters woke early, and made their way to London, all vying for the best spot to wave at their new king. The suffragettes rose earlier still.

At dawn, small groups of WSPU women made for the homes of the most prominent Cabinet ministers in the country. Armed with banners and posters, they wanted their slogans to be the first thing ministers saw on their way to Parliament. Princess Sophia, who could have watched the King's speech from the VIP seats in the spectators' gallery at the House of Lords, made her way up Whitehall instead. Accompanied by one other suffragette, her destination was a plain black door in an elegant cream frame, with a bright, white '10' nailed to the front.

The police officers stationed outside Downing Street saw Sophia, but failed to register any threat. Quite possibly they assumed that the finely dressed lady with the wide-brimmed hat tipped low over her face was one of a number who had come to wave Herbert Asquith on his way. Sophia and her silent companion waited patiently and unobtrusively until the prime minister emerged, a phalanx of civil servants and policeman around him. As he got into the chauffeur-driven car which would take him the short distance to the House of Commons, the princess squeezed her way between them. Brandishing a poster concealed in her expensive fur muff, she ran into the road and hurled herself at the car, shouting suffragette slogans and pressing herself against the prime minister's closed window. Asquith fumed as Sophia gestured wildly at the banner held in her hands. Policemen moved to grab her, while the chauffeur tried to manoeuvre the huge lumbering vehicle around the princess. As she was physically lifted out of the way, the green and white banner fluttered out of her hands. It bore one simple line: 'Give women the vote!'

The prospect of having Queen Victoria's goddaughter arrested on the day of her grandson's speech proved too embarrassing. After being detained briefly, Sophia was released without charge.

Newspapers throughout the Empire reported Princess Sophia's deeds that day. The *Sheffield Daily Telegraph* detailed her breakaway actions under the headline 'Princess As Picket', whilst the Jamaican broadsheet *The Gleaner* described how, 'Princess Sophia Duleep Singh awaited outside the government offices in Downing Street for the departure of Premier Asquith. When the Prime Minister appeared the Princess stepped in front of his automobile and pulled out from her muff a banner . . . She endeavoured to stop the progress of the Premier, but was removed by a policeman.'[10]

Weeks later Sophia dared the authorities to arrest her again. The census of 1911 was set to be the most comprehensive ever. Men with ledgers and bundles of questionnaires were dispatched all over the country. Individual households, institutions, workhouses, even naval and merchant vessels in British waters would be included; officials were charged with looking under boxes and in alleyways in order to count the number of homeless on the streets. It was a chance for world-famous British bureaucracy to show its mettle. It was also a chance for the suffragettes to launch their most coordinated act of civil disobedience to date.

The count was scheduled for the night of Sunday 2 April. The suffragist women set out to wreck the operation in any way they could. Adopting the slogan, 'If women don't count, neither should they be counted', they risked fines and imprisonment in their efforts to evade the enumerators. Suffragettes spoiled their papers by scrawling political messages where their answers should have been. Others spent census night away from home so they could not be counted at all. In London, women gathered in numbers at Trafalgar Square and around a skating rink in Aldwych; they spent all night walking in circles and singing songs to keep themselves warm. Others donned their thickest coats and hid out in attics, sheds and barns. They did these things so that when the statistical snapshot was taken, a slice of Britain would simply appear to have vanished.

The most celebrated census dodge on 2 April came from Emily Wilding Davison. On the night in question she hid in a broom cupboard at the Houses of Parliament, right under the noses of politicians and police. Sustained by meat lozenges and lime juice, she remained undiscovered for forty-six hours. Her efforts were in vain. Discovered by a cleaner the morning after, the Clerk of Works at the House of Commons informed the census officials of her where-abouts. Even though the deadline for counting had passed, her address was listed on the census papers as 'Found Hiding in Crypt of Westminster Hall Westminster'.

Princess Sophia preferred to express her dissent in more comfortable surroundings. From her home at Hampton Court, she awaited the census papers and when the time came to fill them in, she left the boxes blank. Instead, in uncharacteristically neat handwriting she wrote: 'No Vote, No Census',[11] diagonally across the paper. Having left her slogan, Sophia went on to elaborate underneath, stating the motto of the anti-census movement: 'As women do not count, they refuse to be counted.'[12] She chose vivid blue ink to stand out against the black and white of the official printed page. Signing her defiance with a curling flourish, she waited to see what the state would do next.

All the women who dodged the census fully expected legal repercussions. In the event however, none were prosecuted. Emmeline Pankhurst claimed their numbers were too many, and the government was wary of risking further hunger strikes in prisons. Newspaper editorials on the other hand were apoplectic. One letter to *The Times* described the boycott as a 'crime against science'. The magazine *Punch* saw the lighter side, quipping: 'The suffragettes have definitely taken leave of their census.'[13]

After witnessing her conduct on Black Friday and her commitment to the census boycott, the suffragettes believed that their royal recruit might be willing to take a more high-profile role still. They begged Sophia to give keynote speeches at public events. As loyal as she was to the cause, the prospect filled the princess with dread. She became her mother's daughter once more: embarrassed, awkward and desperate to avoid attention.

The local branch of the WSPU in Kingston-upon-Thames was particularly keen to harness her celebrity on a more public platform, but Sophia felt ill at the thought: 'Dear Madam, I am so sorry, I really cannot take the chair at your meeting, I am quite useless for that sort of thing. Please forgive me for refusing. I feel very unkind. If I am here when you have it I will try and come over to the meeting and help in any way I can, only not to speak or take the chair.'[14]

Sometimes it was impossible to say no. In April 1911, her friend, hero and Black Friday companion, Elizabeth Garrett Anderson, was invited to speak in Richmond. Also on the bill was the outspoken English playwright, Laurence Houseman. It was to be a major event in the suffragist calendar, and would include a celebrity auction, to which the wife of writer Thomas Hardy had contributed one of her own dresses – 'an old-style brocade dress to use as they want'.[15] The organisers wanted Sophia to complete the impressive billing, but she begged them to find somebody else. Unable to dissuade them, she agreed to take part but warned that her appearance would be a letdown to all concerned: 'I will come on the 9th to the meeting with pleasure. I hope you have found someone else to support the resolution, If not I will do so, but very much prefer not to and I shall only say about 5 words!'[16]

Even though she was to be one of their VIP guests, Sophia insisted on paying for her own tickets. Not wanting to detract from the guests of honour, she also decided not to travel to the venue in her usual liveried carriage, opting for the train instead. The only problem was, Sophia did not know very much about public transport or how it worked: 'I shall hope to bring some people over from home with me. Is it a ticket meeting, if so how much are they please? And can you tell me if the train goes anywhere near the rooms.'[17] How her sisters would have taunted her if they knew how she humbled herself before her suffragette friends. She signed off her deferential letter with, 'Please forgive me for bothering you . . . Yours truly SDS.'[18]

Although uncomfortable speaking in front of an audience, Sophia had no problem with goading the police and the courts. The princess had been a dedicated member of the Women's Tax Resistance League from the start, donating money to its war chest. Small but fiercely committed, the organisation spent 1911 producing booklets advising their almost 200-strong membership to stop paying tax and explaining what would happen to them when they did. Advice started from the moment the tax collector would come to their doors: 'He will most probably beg you to pay, and emphasise the fact that he person-ally is not answerable for this injustice to women, drawing your attention to the fact that the non-payment of your tax involves him (an innocent factor) in very great difficulties. All this you must harden your heart to.'[19] Women were taught how to barricade them-selves in their houses to escape the arrival of the bailiffs who might follow. Those who wished to could nail their front doors shut, or block them with heavy furniture. Diagrams of pulley systems and drop baskets were also available for those preparing longer terms of self-imposed incarceration.

Unimpressed by the tactics, by the middle of 1911 the Inland Revenue began to pursue tax resisters energetically. One of their first targets was a suffragette called Emma Lloyd. Born in West Bromwich in 1867, she was one of seven children. Her father had been prone to bouts of heavy drinking and she had watched as her mother strug-gled to support her large and hungry family. As a result of their dire poverty, Emma was forced to leave school at the age of eight. She found work as a coal picker, earning pennies by gathering lumps from the pit mounds. At the age of twelve, Emma entered domestic service, starting with the lowliest of jobs. She gradually worked her way up to a full-time position as a maid-of-all-works, counting herself lucky, despite the back-breaking work and long hours. However, after just a few years, Emma lost her job and her income when her employer's brother made a sexual advance towards her. Sacked without even a reference to her name she was forced to move far away in search of work and a life free of scandal.

Emma moved to Lancashire, where she finally found employment again. In the few hours she was not scraping together an income, she taught at the local Sunday school and it was here that Emma became involved with the church debating society. To her surprise, she found that she was quite good at it. The church gave her the ability to speak publicly, but it was Princess Sophia's old nemesis, Lord Curzon, who gave Emma the subject matter. The former Viceroy had been touring Lancashire, appearing before public meetings speaking of the glories of the British Empire. It was at one such event that Curzon steadfastly ignored a particular raised hand in his audience. No matter how much she tried, Emma Lloyd could not get Curzon to pick her amidst the raft of questions taken from the floor. As she later noted, he had refused to answer her question because 'she was a woman and did not have the vote'.[20]

From the moment Curzon dismissed and humiliated her, Emma became a committed suffragette, vowing never to be rendered voiceless in public again. With fighting spirit renewing her, Emma decided to take control of the rest of her life. First she made a defiant return to Wolverhampton, the scene of her 'disgrace'. She had saved just enough money to purchase a small business for her mother to run with her help. When not working at the shop, which also served as the front room of their house, Emma spent her time volunteering for the Independent Labour Party. Keir Hardie was more disposed to the question of female enfranchisement than any other leader and his party welcomed Emma Lloyd and put her talents to use.

She was regularly booked to speak at political rallies, and charmed crowds with her zeal and ability to deal with hecklers. It was during her time with the ILP that she met and then married Frank Sproson, a postman who also served as the secretary of the Wolverhampton branch of the ILP. Frank worshipped Emma for her passion and her spirit of rebellion. When asked later why he had found her qualities so attractive, Frank would answer: 'I admire the rebel against injustice, man or woman, because I know that it is to them that all real progress is due.'[21]

It was not long before Emma's path crossed with that of Emmeline Pankhurst, since the WSPU and the ILP often shared platforms. Immediately the two women sensed a kindred spirit and became close friends, with Emmeline staying at the Sproson family home when she visited Wolverhampton. However, before long the relationship began to sour. Emma grew tired of Pankhurst's autocratic style of leadership. She left the WSPU and threw her efforts into tax resistance instead.

On 23 May 1911, Emma Sproson caused a storm of controversy when she was sentenced to a term in prison for keeping a dog without a licence. She had refused to pay for her family pet, insisting that she would not accept taxation without representation. She had barely been released from Stafford Prison when Emma found herself in the dock once again for her continual refusal to pay. On 20 June she was sentenced to a month in prison and her husband was also given a week's custodial sentence for aiding and abetting her. Frank Sproson insisted that his only crime was that he had not cracked the whip at home, bringing his wife into line: 'In the eyes of the law, I was lord and master, so that my offence, therefore, was not that I did anything, but rather that I did not do anything. I did not assert my authority, I did not force my wife into subjection, and however legal the magistrate's decision may have been, it certainly was not just.' [22]

Emma Sproson went on hunger strike, fighting for and eventually winning the right to be treated as a political prisoner. Her case received widespread media attention; Winston Churchill was questioned repeatedly in the House of Commons about the legality of trying and punishing her twice for the same offence, and for dragging her husband into the matter. Churchill was unrepentant. The message the government wished to send was a clear one. Pay your dues or go to gaol.

Princess Sophia stopped paying for the licences for her dogs as soon as Emma Sproson was sent to prison. In an effort to goad the authorities to come for her too, she also refused to pay the charges associated with keeping servants and refused to pay the licence for her carriage with its armorial bearings. None of these liabilities were large, but they were deeply symbolic. At first the letters asking for payment were polite; gradually they took on a more hectoring tone. But still the princess refused to pay. After the final demands went unheeded, Sophia was sent a letter by the courts informing her that she now faced fines and a court hearing. She politely wrote back that she had no intention of paying either the taxes or the penalties and they could take her to court if they liked. A summons was issued calling Sophia to appear before Spelthorne Petty Sessions Court in Middlesex. Courteously Sophia wrote back telling the court she had no intention of attending but would send her lawyer, Leon Castello, instead.

On 22 June, Castello admitted seven of the offences with which the princess had been charged, but informed the court that even though she acknowledged she was breaking the law, regrettably she would not be paying the fine.[23] Instead Sophia asked him to read a long statement on her behalf. It spoke of the injustice of making women pay tax when they had been given no voice in the governing of the country. She, and others like her, had no intention of contributing until the situation was rectified.

The judge listened impatiently to the lecture, and then informed Castello that the court was not in the least bit interested in the princess's political essay. Bringing down his gavel he fined her one pound for the dog licences, one pound for the servants, and one pound for the carriage.[24] Castello was unsurprised by the judgment and nodded sympathetically as he heard the details of the fine. When the judge finished speaking, the princess's lawyer informed him that his client would not be paying a penny of the tax due or the fine just imposed. The court bristled with excitement as everyone realised they were witnessing the birth of a scandal. Just how far would Princess Duleep Singh take this? Would she be prepared to go to gaol like Emma Sproson?

Again, the authorities were reluctant to endure the storm of publicity which would follow the princess's imprisonment, so instead they decided to try and force Sophia to pay the fines. Two weeks after her non-appearance at Spelthorne Court, bailiffs for the County of Middlesex arrived at Faraday House with a warrant. They informed the housekeeper that if the bill for the outstanding licences and the court penalties was not paid immediately, they would have no choice but to enter the property and seize goods for sale. Alarmed, Margaret Mayes disappeared for some minutes to confer with her mistress. When she returned, she told the men on her doorstep that Princess Sophia had a counter-offer to make. She would gladly pay them as soon as the prime minister ensured she had the right to vote. Unimpressed, the men barged past and entered the house. Experienced as they were, they made their way immediately to where a lady might keep her jewellery, and took a seven-stone diamond ring from Sophia's vanity case.[25] The ring was worth considerably more than the fines and court costs combined.

When the item came up for sale in July at an auction house in Ashford in Kent, almost all the seats were taken up by women bedecked in the colours of the suffragettes. They waited patiently for the princess's ring to come under the hammer, and when it did not one of them raised their hands to bid, nor in the midst of their considerable clamour could any other attendee place a bid on Sophia's jewels. As this went on, the auctioneer was forced to repeatedly drop his starting bid to kick-start the sale. It was not until he reached the sum of £10, that one woman calmly raised her hand and the hammer fell.[26]

The buyer was Louise Jopling Rowe, one of the most prominent women artists of the Victorian era, and confidante of the painter James Whistler and playwright Oscar Wilde. She was also a passionate suffragette. Upon winning her lot she graciously returned the ring to Sophia amidst hearty applause from the other women.[27] The suffragettes then unfurled banners in the auction rooms and proceeded to hold a noisy rally. With bemused staff looking on, the women congratulated Sophia for making her stand and risking prison for their cause. As she turned the ring over in the palm of her hand, she may have reflected on the last time diamonds had been taken from her family by the state. They had been considerably bigger then, and nobody had tried or even wanted to give them back.

# We Have No Hold

Sophia's dedication to the cause in 1911 endeared her to the most influential woman in the country, the WSPU leader Emmeline Pankhurst. In October, Emmeline had decided to embark on a tour of North America, hoping to encourage the suffragettes across the Atlantic. The Americans and Canadians would pay handsomely to hear her speak, and since her personal funds had been severely depleted over her years of suffragette campaigning, the tour made financial and political sense. On 2 October 1911, two days before she was set to leave, the suffragettes of the WSPU gave her a rousing farewell at the London Pavilion theatre. It was a raucous and packed affair, and Emmeline responded with her usual gusto. However, the moment of her departure was altogether more intimate.

Two days later she was met by a small party of her closest friends at Waterloo station. From here she would make her way by train to Southampton and board the White Star liner RMS *Oceanic*. Lady Constance Lytton, Annie Kenny and Emily Wilding Davison were waiting for her, as were Mabel Tuke, Kitty and Alfred Marshal and Victor Duval, the husband of Una Dugdale. With them was Princess Sophia Duleep Singh.[1] As she waved her leader farewell, Sophia's place at the heart of the movement was confirmed, as was its place in her own heart.

On her return from North America four months later, Emmeline Pankhurst seemed even more fired up than before. On 16 February

1912 she declared that 'the argument of the broken pane of glass is the most valuable argument in modern politics'.[2] It was fair warning for what was to follow for, less than a month later, her organisation entered the most violent stage of coordinated militancy to date.

On 1 March, a group of around 150 women were summoned to WSPU headquarters at Lincoln's Inn for a special operation. There, just across the road from the Royal Courts of Justice, they were issued with detailed instructions, maps and timings. Little toffee hammers, usually found in confectioners' shops, were also handed out. Folding their papers away, and tucking their hammers into sleeves, the specially selected suffragettes left in small groups, heading off in different directions. They aroused no suspicion in the bustling streets, having left all their suffragette paraphernalia at home. To all intents and purposes, they were just well-heeled ladies out for an afternoon of shopping. Nobody seemed to notice that although they looked at the window displays for long periods of time, they seemed to take no interest in the items for sale.

At exactly 5.45 p.m., with calm calculation, each woman took her hammer from its hiding place and struck out at any large window before her. The suffragettes had learnt about the weakest points in glass, and how to hit in such a way as to give maximum time to retreat from falling shards. Windows came crashing down all over the capital. The suffragettes had set out to target some of London's most famous commercial giants: Liberty, Marshall & Snelgrove and Burberry were among the biggest department stores in the world. Passers-by were left gaping as cascades of jagged glass came down. Messrs Stewart Dawson and Co. on the Strand, an international watchmakers and jewellers, with the motto: 'There is no new thing under the sun', struggled to grasp the novelty of what had happened to them. Their windows had been smashed but no attempt had been made to grab any of the valuable jewels on display. Bemused pedestrians ground the transparent splinters into sparkling dust underfoot as police pushed them back from the scene.

The suffragettes struck art dealerships too, including the highly respected Duveen Brothers. With art galleries in London, New York and Paris dating back to the 1860s, Duveen's had thought themselves above the vagaries of common politics; however nobody was immune that day. International corporations in large imposing buildings found themselves on the suffragette lists too. The Canadian Pacific Railway Company and Norddeutscher Lloyd, the most important German shipping company, as well as Sophia's own beloved American Eastman Kodak store, all had their London headquarters targeted by the tap of the toffee hammer. If the suffragettes had sought to embarrass their government before the eyes of the world, they succeeded.

Emmeline Pankhurst not only orchestrated the window smashing, she took part personally. The WSPU leader had set her sights on Asquith himself, and that day she travelled to the prime minister's residence, where she smashed four of Downing Street's windows. Promptly arrested by the police, she managed to wrench her arm free from a constable's grasp and broke a Cabinet Office window in the time it took for them to take hold of her again. Collectively, the suffragettes caused thousands of pounds worth of damage; carpenters were busy through the night, boarding up around the city. Never before had the women embarked on such a large-scale, destructive demonstration. The day of window smashing marked a dramatic change in tactics. It was the beginning of the full-skirted 'guerillists'.

More than 120 women were arrested on 1 March, but that did not stop the WSPU from proceeding with a similar protest three days later. With their leader behind bars, the guerillists organised another sizeable demonstration in Parliament Square. It too ended in shattered glass. Suffragettes hurled rocks at the windows of any government building they could get close to. In response, the police raided WSPU headquarters in London's Kingsway, rounding up anyone they could find. It was a deliberate show of force, during which police overturned furniture and ransacked offices. Although they managed to arrest most of the people in Lincoln's Inn House, one important figure managed to evade them. According to the *Thames Valley Times*,[3] a militant suffragette adopting a disguise managed to slip out of the building, escaping right from under the noses of the raiding police. The newspaper for the Richmond and Twickenham area[4] gave more colourful details, reporting that

Christabel Pankhurst was the fugitive. According to the paper, she had calmly walked out of Lincoln's Inn House after letting down her long hair, putting on a short skirt and school hat. After giving police the slip, the schoolgirl-suffragette had made her way to their local area and was now hiding somewhere between Richmond Bridge and Hampton Court, aided by 'local sympathisers'. Everybody in the area was aware of their most high-profile local suffragette; suspicion would invariably have fallen on the dark princess at the palace.

In reality, Sophia had nothing to do with Christabel's escape. Not only were the reports of Christabel's whereabouts untrue, they had been deliberately seeded in the press to throw police off her trail. Emmeline's daughter had in fact left the country the day after her escape from Lincoln's Inn, and was now in Paris, far out of the reach of the law. Notwithstanding the truth, when it eventually emerged, Sophia's neighbours had even more reason to regard her with suspicion and animosity.

Some politicians were trying desperately to push another Conciliation Bill through Parliament. Like its predecessor, it too had success at second reading. However, against the backdrop of escalating suffragette violence, MPs who had once been sympathetic to the cause found it impossible to support the bill. The legislation was defeated and the WSPU responded by ratcheting up their campaign further. Window-smashing continued while the suffragettes also turned their attention to the places where Cabinet ministers liked to relax. They carved up golf courses and interrupted operas and plays. In the early hours of 13 July, police arrested two women outside the country residence of Lewis Harcourt, one of the leading anti-suffragists in Parliament. When the women were searched, a constable found cans of flammable oil, matches, firelighters, a hammer, tools to pick a lock, a torch, and 'a piece of American cloth smeared over with some sticky substance'.[5]

Less than a week later, Mary Leigh, a suffragette who had already been arrested nine times for acts of militancy, threw a small axe into a carriage in which the prime minister was travelling during a tour of Ireland. Asquith was unhurt and Mary managed to escape, only to appear later that same evening at the Theatre Royal in Dublin where she set fire to the curtains behind a box and threw a flaming chair into the orchestra. Together with her accomplice, she then attempted to set off small homemade bombs made out of tin cans. When the police came to arrest them, Mary made no attempt to escape. Her arson attempt had succeeded in its aim. It had terrified Herbert Asquith once more, who only a short time before had been watching a play in the same theatre.

The headlines shocked the public. However it was the suffragettes' assault on His Majesty's Royal Mail which turned their anxiety into rage. Common people were now caught up in the crossfire. In October, letters in a pillar box outside Kew Green post office were found to be soaked in a concentrated solution of potassium permanganate; the letters inside were completely ruined.[6] Uncorked bottles, which once contained the offending chemical, had been posted in the same box. To ensure everyone knew who was responsible, they were placed in a large envelope marked 'Votes for Women'.

The letter-spoiling campaign got even closer to Sophia's home four weeks later, when pillar boxes in Richmond were attacked with bottles of ink, tar and burning rags.[7] During this time, many high-profile members of the suffragette movement condemned the violence and left the WSPU. They abhorred the way the movement's campaign was now impacting on the life of law-abiding citizens. Sophia was not merely uncritical of the organisation's methods, she actively supported them. Continuing as a prominent member of her local Kingston branch, she also went out of her way to be seen at the much-maligned Richmond and Kew branches, epicentres of the postal outrages. Moreover, even though her shyness of public-speaking made it difficult, she accepted more invitations to appear on stage with the most hated women in the country.

Early in February 1913, two of the orchid houses at Kew Gardens were broken into and exotic plants pulled from their pots and trampled into the ground.[8] Sophia and her sisters had loved Kew, as had their father before them. If she felt any personal pain at the destruction, Sophia recorded none, unlike the newspapers who gave full vent to their anger. There was something peculiarly outrageous in the eyes of the male-dominated press about the damaging of flowers. It had been argued many times that women were built to love and nurture living things. In the minds of the anti-suffragists, women who destroyed flowers were somehow 'unnatural', and capable of any depravity. *The Times* commented on the 'wanton character' of those responsible. To taunt them further, the vandals had left a calling card near the broken and shredded plants, on which was written: 'orchids can be destroyed, but not a woman's honour'. [9]

Two days later. Emmeline Pankhurst made a speech in which she deliberately drew audience attention to a large bouquet of orchids left casually on the table in front of her. She also acknowledged that the recent suffragette tactics might be causing the general public much inconvenience: 'We are not destroying Orchid Houses, breaking windows, cutting telegraph wires, injuring golf greens, in order to win the approval of the people who were attacked. If the general public were pleased with what we are doing, that would be a proof that our warfare is ineffective. We don't intend that you should be pleased.'[10]

The suffragettes were becoming more ambitious as the weeks passed by. Returning to Kew Gardens just a couple of weeks later, two suffragettes soaked the rustic Tea Pavilion with paraffin and set it alight. As the building burned to the ground, firemen, who had come too late to save the place, found calling cards strewn nearby. One read: 'Peace on earth and goodwill to men, when women get the vote.'[11]

Arson was fast becoming the favoured weapon in Pankhurst's guerrilla war. At 6.10 a.m. on the morning of 18 February, Emily Wilding Davison, the same suffragette who had hidden from the census in a cupboard at the House of Commons, together with willing accomplices, fire-bombed a partly built house in Surrey. The house belonged to the Chancellor of the Exchequer, David Lloyd George. Although he was far away at the time, all politicians were shaken by the fact that suffragettes were now targeting them individually, and their attacks were becoming potentially life-threatening.

Personal animosity did not always dictate the target. On 26 April the suffragettes decided they would set fire to an empty commuter train. The 9.15 from Waterloo to Teddington had been shunted into a siding in preparation for the next day's journeys. Sometime around three in the morning, a local policeman called in a report of seeing flames rising from the carriages. The fire took hold with surprising speed and ferocity. According to staff working for South Western Railways: 'it seemed as if the whole train was doomed to destruction as a strong wind was blowing, which carried the flames from one compartment to another. In less than a quarter of an hour the entire compartment of the second-class coach burnt out from the floor to the roof.'[12]

The plans had been both ambitious and meticulously planned. Suffragettes had entered by a siding, 'removing a paling from a fence nearly six-foot high'.[13] Squeezing through the small gap, they had made their way in total darkness, across uneven ground to the stationary train. Small footprints were found in the dirt leading from the rails to the road, suggesting two women might have been involved in the attack. When police combed the wreckage at dawn, they found a large number of partially burnt candles, four cans of petrol, three of which had been emptied, and a basket filled with cotton wool. It was doubtful that whoever lit the fires was new to the art of arson. Just as at Kew's orchid houses, the women left calling cards. Suffragette literature and a number of postcards addressed to 'dishonourable MPs' were found scattered around the charred remains of the carriage.[14]

Sir Robert Anderson, formerly the head of the Criminal Investigation Department at Scotland Yard, reacted with fury and suggested that a bill should be put forward in Parliament which would declare all window-smashers and fire-starters 'criminal lunatics', therefore allowing them to be sent directly to asylums when caught.[15] Although his response was extreme, much of the country was beginning to agree with a more hard-line approach. All were on edge, waiting to see where the women might strike next. Conjecture ran wild: the *Standard* reported that the suffragettes were planning to kidnap members of the Cabinet. The government was taking no chances and special measures were put in place. Detectives were attached to every prominent member of the front bench and they followed them like shadows.

Pankhurst's guerillist campaign was causing nationwide chaos, and increasing numbers of Sophia's suffragette friends found it impossible to justify the climate of fear being created. Emmeline Pethick-Lawrence, the Pankhursts' most loyal lieutenant, began to openly question the arson campaign. Evelina Haverfield, who had ridden into the crowds during Black Friday brandishing her whip, withdrew from active WSPU service altogether. Elizabeth Garrett Anderson also backed away, warning her daughter to do the same. She withdrew much-needed funding from the organisation, as did Hertha Ayrton, the engineer and ardent defender of Marie Curie who had risked the blows of policemen as she walked beside Sophia two years before. Even the most committed supporters of women's franchise found they could no longer call themselves WSPU suffragettes.

The Blathwayt family, who had recorded Sophia's conversion to the suffragette cause in their journals and had financially supported and physically cared for leading suffragettes for years, also stopped giving money to the WSPU. Theirs was a particularly painful separation from the cause since they had loved one of the most prominent WSPU suffragettes, Annie Kenny. Mr Blathwayt had even named the summer house on his estate 'Suffragette's Rest', because he wanted it to be a haven for women recovering from force-feeding. However when a house near the family was fire-bombed, it rattled them all. Emily Blathwayt wrote in her diaries: 'I am glad to say Mary is writing to resign membership with the W.S.P.U. Now they have begun burning houses in the neighbourhood I feel more than ever ashamed to be connected with them.'[16]

Sophia steadfastly refused to distance herself from her WSPU friends. Instead she ramped up her contributions to the organisation, giving a colossal £30 in 1913,[17] when the average pledge amounted to just a few shillings. Unlike the Blathwayts, when trouble came to her own doorstep, she stayed true to Emmeline and the WSPU. Reading the cuttings Sophia sent with her letters, Catherine and Bamba must have wondered just how far the suffragettes would have to go before they alienated their little sister.

*    *    *

The police were out in force at Bow Street magistrates' court on 9 May for one of the most sensational trials of the decade. Supporters and detractors were turned away in droves and only a handful of suffragettes were allowed in to the courtroom. They were searched for banners, missiles or pamphlets, and police were stationed close to where they sat in the public gallery. The authorities did not want a repeat of past hearings where noisy women had disrupted proceedings with noise and the throwing of boots, heavy books and rotten fruit. They were taking no chances this time.

Newspaper reports focused on two high-profile aristocrats sitting in court, supporting their friends, the accused: 'Among the women present were Muriel, Countess de la Warr and Princess Sophia Duleep Singh.'[18] Their attendance alone condemned them as women who sympathised with the militant extremists. Annie Kenney, Edwy Godwin Clayton, Flora Drummond, Beatrice Sanders, Rachel Barrett, Geraldine Lennox, Agnes Lake, Harriet Kerr and Andrew Drew were all charged with conspiracy under the Malicious Damage to Property Act. The name of the law did little to live up to the police case against the accused. The nine had been charged with planning arson attacks on locations in Trafalgar Square, St Martin's Lane, Charing Cross Road, Oxford Street, Bloomsbury, Westminster, and the head office of the British telephone system. The prosecution argued that their campaign of terror, had it not been foiled, would also have brought chaos to the north of England, where they were intending to firebomb cotton mills and timber yards.

Incriminating documents had been found during a police raid of Annie Kenney's flat. These included a letter from Edwy Clayton, who was an analytical chemist by trade, apologising to Kenney for the delay in supplying the materials she had asked for: 'by next week I shall be able to manage the exact proportion . . . I will let you have the results as soon as I think them good enough.'[19] Clayton lamented his failure to produce a good enough compound for the suffragette's needs.[20] The sign-off Clayton used in his letter would be one of the prosecution's most damning pieces of evidence: 'Please burn this . . .'[21] It seems that Annie Kenney had forgotten to do so, and had tucked the letter away, along with other papers, in a book called *Bristol Riots, 1851*.

The case against the nine was strong. In another handwritten note, police found a list marked 'various suggestions'. The first proposed 'a scheme of simultaneously smashing a considerable number of street fire alarms. This appears to me to be an especially good idea. It will cause tremendous confusion and excitement, and should be at once, easier and less risky than some other operations.'[22] In another communication read by the prosecutor, one of the accused was said to have written: 'on the ground floor of the building is a series of rooms with seven or eight closed windows half covered with green blinds . . . I do not doubt that it will be easy to smash the closed windows and escape. After having broken the windows benzoline and methylated spirits might be thrown in.'[23]

The case dominated the news and the coverage was heady and dramatic, with headlines such as 'A Bomb at St Pauls', and 'Diabolical Suffragist Plot', alongside descriptions of a 'fiendish plot' to disrupt plays around the capital, under the banner 'Sneezing Powder for London Audiences'.[24] The public, alarmed by the news reports, began to turn against the suffragettes and those who supported them. Sitting quietly in the Bow Street courtroom, Sophia did not care. She would not desert her sisters. Others were willing to go further still.

Of all the militant suffragettes in the WSPU, there were few, if any, who could match the zeal of Emily Wilding Davison. Emily, formerly a teacher, was described by Sylvia Pankhurst as 'tall and slender, with unusually long arms, a small narrow head and red hair. Her illusive, whimsical green eyes and thin, half-smiling mouth, bore often the mocking expression of the Mona Lisa.'[25] She had been a member of the WSPU since 1906, and almost from the start had displayed a willingness to go to extremes for the cause.

Emily had been imprisoned eight times for offences including obstruction, assault, throwing stones at politicians, smashing windows and setting fire to letter boxes. Every time she was locked up, she demanded to be treated as a political prisoner and was refused. Emily would then go on hunger strike and the authorities would feed her by force. It took a terrible toll, both physically and psychologically. On

22 June, the latest attempt to feed her via a pipe down her throat had been so painful that Emily threw herself from a balcony in protest. It was only the netting three floors below which stopped her from being killed. When questioned by prison staff, Emily told them 'the tragedy was wanted'. A year passed until she was a free woman again, planning her next big gesture for the cause. It would be her last.

The Epsom Derby on 4 June 1913 was a cause of particular excitement. It was more than a horse race, it was an event of national celebration and seen as the greatest sporting carnival in the world; Disraeli once described it as 'an epitome of human life, with its comedy and tragedy, its irony and pathos, and its revelation of the whole range of man's passions and emotions'. Commoners had the chance to rub shoulders with aristocrats. It was traditional for the royal family to attend, and to enter their horses for the races. King George V was due to be there with his wife, Queen Mary, and their handsome bay colt, Anmer. Named after a village on the Sandringham Estate, Anmer was causing some frisson at the bookmakers.

Emily Davison travelled to Epsom on the day with two large suffragette banners folded and pinned to the inside back of her coat. Carried by the tide of spectators pushing their way to the course, Emily seemed to know exactly where she wanted to be. She forced her way to the railings at Tattenham Corner, a sharp bend on the flats, and waited patiently. While nobody was watching, she retrieved her banners and held them in her hands, out of sight till the horses thundered into view. As the front runners passed, Emily ducked under the barrier and ran out onto the course, right in front of Anmer. The jockey, Herbert Jones, was sent flying from his saddle as the horse hit Emily with full force, knocking her body several feet in the air and somersaulting in the process. Emily landed heavily on the ground, limp and bleeding, as the crowds converged. She lay there on the racecourse surrounded by spectators furious at her audacity and she slipped into a coma from which she never regained consciousness. Emily died four days later at Epsom Cottage Hospital. Doctors confirmed that her skull had been fractured and she had suffered significant internal injuries.

Emily Wilding Davison became the first martyr of the suffragette cause and news of her death was met by an outpouring of grief. A momentous funeral was hastily arranged and suffragettes planned to travel from all over the country to pay their respects. Just hours after she was declared dead by physicians, the suffragettes showed how hotly their rage was burning.

About a mile away from Hampton Court Palace stood Hurst Park racecourse in East Molesey. On 9 June, shortly after midnight, a police officer on his bicycle saw an unusual glow coming from the grandstand of the racecourse. As he dismounted and wheeled his bike over to take a closer look, he saw the seats in the 'King's stand' burst into flames. The local fire brigade was quick to react and firemen arrived within minutes, but their steam pump was no match for the inferno which took hold of the timber construction. Flames leapt so high, they could be seen from Carshalton, twelve miles away.

By morning, nothing was left but a twisted skeleton of iron, the remnants of the stand. The fire had burned so ferociously that even the glass in the nearby buildings had melted. Among the debris, police found suffragettes' calling cards. The arsonists had also placed a placard near the scene, which read, 'Give the Women the Franchise'.[26]

Emily Wilding Davison's funeral took place on 14 June 1913. Even those who felt uncomfortable with recent militancy turned out in great numbers. The guard of honour, suffragettes wearing white dresses and black sashes, escorted her body from Epsom to St George's church in Bloomsbury, central London. Thousands had come from all over the British Isles, and wreaths had been sent from all over the world. The outpouring of emotion was overwhelming, particularly as the suffragettes prepared to move Emily's coffin onto the train which would take her remains north, to her family burial plot in Morpeth, Northumberland.

The sight of her coffin galvanised many to continue in their own acts of militancy, and the police were kept busy with numerous outbreaks of violence and vandalism over the weeks that followed. The galleries of Hampton Court were closed after police received a tip-off that militants were going to strike, though nobody knew whether the threat was one of arson, paint-throwing or window-smashing.

Instead of distancing herself from the cause, as the Blathwayts had when militancy began to impact on their home, Sophia once again decided to show the world her support for the WSPU and their tactics. She had dabbled with selling the WSPU newspaper *The Suffragette* during the spring. Now she began to sell it regularly, and right outside the gates of Hampton Court Palace. The sight of the Indian princess in her expensive furs with a satchel strapped across her body, sandwich board by her side, waving around a paper and shouting 'Votes for Women' caused a scandal at the very highest levels.

William Carrington, Keeper of the Privy Purse and sometime sounding board for the sovereign's private rages, was forced to take to his writing desk. Carefully cutting out a picture from the most recent copy of *The Suffragette*, he dropped the smudged picture of Sophia selling her papers into an envelope. Before sealing it, he also dropped in a compliment slip bearing the crest of Buckingham Palace. No words needed to be written, the recipient would know what was expected.[27]

The note was conveyed directly to the Marquis of Crewe, Secretary of State for India. He had already heard a barrage of complaints from the Palace about the woman in the picture. This last act of hers had pushed the King over the edge and he wanted her thrown out of Hampton Court. Crewe circulated the note to his senior civil servants, noting that he had already spoken to George V's private secretary about Princess Duleep Singh. He did not think it was up to the India Office to do the King's bidding: 'I have shown this to Lord Strathfordham who thinks the Lord Chamberlain is the person to warn the lady that she must not make herself compromised at H Court, or in the immediate neighbourhood. Inform Sir W Carrington of this and of our inability to help,'[28] and he signed off the letter with his customary 'C'. After sealing his response, Crewe placed the photo of Sophia, still attached to the Palace stationery, in the file held on the princess by the Political and Secret Department. He also wrote a letter to his private secretary and most trusted aide, Sir

Arthur Hirtzel, apprising him of his response. Crewe had been grateful for his guidance.

Hirtzel had already warned the Secretary of State about the oncoming tirade from Buckingham Palace. 'Lord Crewe, Sir William Carrington telephoned me about this picture which appeared in this week's *Suffragette*. He asked "If anything could be done to 'stop her'?" We have no financial hold over the Dhuleep Singh princesses, but of course it is for the King to say whether her conduct is such as should call for her eviction from the lodging she now enjoys in Hampton Court by his Majesty's favour. May I so reply to Sir W Carrington?'[29]

The King had no desire to personally sanction Sophia's eviction. The headlines which undoubtedly would have followed if he acted were too ghastly to contemplate. Sophia was his own grandmother's ward, and since Queen Victoria had given Faraday House to her, George V felt in no position to take it away. Instead, an even closer watch was kept on the troublesome princess, while the King and his courtiers fumed over her ingratitude.

Sophia became used to fury. She was now surrounded by it every time she left her house. The picture galleries at Hampton Court remained closed for months; all the while Sophia continued to sell her newspaper outside the palace. The loss of visitors to the tourist attraction was crippling local businesses, especially the restaurants and nearby hotels. Traders begged Hampton Court to reopen or else they feared bankruptcy. Sophia with her sandwich board was a constant reminder of the money they were losing and the reason they were losing it.

If Buckingham Palace and the residents of East Molesey had hoped Christmas would bring them some respite from Sophia's antics, they were wrong. The *Daily Mail* published a graphic account of her latest suffragette activities on 30 December. They even sent a photographer to capture the moment when the princess, swathed in expensive black furs with an ornate feather hat on her head, left Feltham police court. She was not there to support her friends. It was Sophia's turn to take her place in the dock. Although she had been arrested before, this was the first time she had found herself facing prosecution.

In an article headlined 'Princess's Unpaid Taxes. Fines Upon Four Summonses', the *Mail* gave details of the charges against her:[30]

> The Princess Sophia Duleep Singh, residing at Hampton Road, Hampton Court, attended at Feltham Police Court yesterday upon summonses for refusing to pay taxes . . . She employed a groom without a licence, and also kept two dogs and a carriage without payment of the necessary licence. She came to court wearing the badge and medal of the Tax Resistance League and was accompanied by six other ladies including the secretary of the league, Mrs Kineton Parkes.

After the Inland Revenue presented its evidence, her lawyer Leon Castello rose to his feet. Having conferred briefly with his client, Castello informed the judge that on this occasion, the princess would be speaking for herself. When Sophia rose, her voice was steady, although the piece of foolscap paper in her hands trembled a little. The *Daily Mail* journalist reported two lines of what she said to the court: 'When the women of England are enfranchised and the State acknowledges me as a citizen, I shall, of course, pay my share willingly to its upkeep . . . I don't say I will pay these fines either.'[31] Other newspapers, including *The Times*, printed her speech in full:

> I am unable conscientiously to pay money to the state, as I am not allowed to exercise any control over its expenditure, neither am I allowed any voice in the choosing of members of Parliament, whose salaries I have to help to pay. This is very unjustified. When the women of England are enfranchised and the State acknowledges me as a citizen, I shall, of course, pay my share willingly towards its upkeep, if I am not a fit person for the purposes of representation, why should I be a fit person for taxation?[32]

The judge told her he had no interest in her politics and that she risked prison if she continued her refusal. 'Mr White (supervisor of taxes) helpfully informed the judge that the princess was convicted of a similar offence in May 1911.' With that, the judge brought down his gavel and fined the princess £12 10s for the unpaid taxes, and gave her until the first week of the new year to pay her dues. When she calmly told him she had no intention of paying now or in the new year she was told to expect the bailiffs.

A collection of newspaper cuttings about Sophia's day in court found their way to the desk of the Secretary of State for India again. In one from the *Daily Mail*, the princess's words had been underlined in blue pencil. Sighing, Lord Crewe wrote a note to his private secretary: 'Dear Hirtzel, Buck Pal will probably write here again full of rage and grief. They read the *Mail* assiduously there . . . ,'[33] and with that, he added the papers to Sophia's file.

# Indian Clubs

The bailiffs barged their way into Faraday House early on 6 January 1914. They rifled through drawers and cupboards until they found what they were looking for: a necklace comprising 131 pearls, and a diamond-and-pearl-studded gold bangle with a heart-shaped diamond talisman.

With the housekeeper's protests ringing in their ears, they took the goods and slated them for auction at Twickenham town hall in March. Once again, when the day arrived, suffragettes flooded the sale room. Sophia swept in imperiously and took a seat at the front of the hall, locking her dark and furious eyes with those of the auctioneer. As he cleared his throat to announce the start of the sale, Sophia rose to her feet, turned her back on him and facing the seated bidders in the hall announced: 'I protest against this sale, seeing it is most unjust to women that they should be compelled to pay unjust taxes, when they have no voice in the government of the country.'[1] Having made her declaration, to loud applause, she took her seat again, placed her hands in her lap and waited.

The auctioneer, Henry Alaway, was forced to lower his starting bid again and again before anyone would raise their hand. The atmosphere was tense, and Sophia, sitting sphinx-like and fixing him with her narrow stare, made his job even more difficult. Bidding was cripplingly slow and only two people raised their hands, one of whom was a particularly formidable woman who glowered her competitor into submission. Alaway brought down his hammer, relieved to have the business over and done with. For a fraction of its true value, the Secretary of the Women's Tax Resistance League, Gertrude Eaton, had won the lot.[2]

Gertrude was well known in the women's movement. For years she had been teaching suffragettes how to overcome nerves and speak in public. Giving free lessons to WSPU members, she showed them how to project to the back of large halls without losing control of their voices, or their tempers. As Gertrude handed over £10 for the necklace and £7 for the bangle,[3] she knew her gesture was worth more than any speech she could ever give. She had experience of bailiffs herself. Two years before, men had forced their way into her Kensington home, seizing all her silverware for her own unpaid fines.[4] Accepting Gertrude's gift gratefully, Sophia vowed that as long as women were kept from the ballot box, nobody would ever be able to force her to pay her taxes.

Less than two months later, Sophia was in court again, for the same offence. Such flagrant and repeated disregard for the law ought to have put Sophia in prison. Women who owed far less had been given custodial sentences; however the law treated aristocratic women and commoners very differently. Never was that more clearly illustrated than in the case of Lady Constance Lytton, daughter of a former Viceroy of India. The Earl of Lytton had held the post during the reign of Queen Victoria. It was he who had declared her Empress before the rajahs and nawabs. Constance's mother, a lady-in-waiting to the Queen, was a powerful force in the royal court; the Lyttons therefore led a life of extreme privilege. Constance had never been particularly wilful and had only discovered politics, like Sophia, in mid-life. Her induction came quite by chance when she donated money to a local dance troupe of working-class girls. Through them she heard the plight of suffragettes in prison. The stories of starvation and force-feeding horrified her, and swept up by outrage, in 1909, at the age of thirty-seven, Constance joined the militant wing of the WSPU.

During a deputation to Parliament on 24 February, things turned violent and Constance was arrested. Before setting off, she had prepared her mother for just such an eventuality: 'If you ever see this letter it will mean that after joining the deputation I have been arrested and shall not see you again until I have been to Holloway . . . What maternity there lurks in me has for years past been gradually awakening over the fate of prisoners, the deliberate, cruel harm that is done to them, their souls and bodies, the ignorant, exasperating waste of good opportunities in connection with them, till now the thought of them, the yearning after them, turns in me and tugs at me as vitally and irrepressibly as ever a physical child can call upon its mother.'[5]

Though many of her companions in the deputation had been sent to gaol for their part in the affray, the authorities had different plans for Constance. The magistrate 'bound her over', offering her the chance to go free if she would promise to refrain from suffragette activities in the future. Constance flatly refused, leaving him no choice but to sentence her to one month in prison.

In Holloway, despite her protestations, she spent most of her time in the comfort of the prison's hospital wing. Constance knew she was being accorded special treatment because of her family background and demanded to be treated like any other suffragette. The prison governor's refusal made her even more determined. One night she took a needle and a piece of broken enamel from her hatpin and carved a 'V' deep into the flesh of her breast, just over her heart. The prison medic was horrified and news of Constance's self-mutilation spread quickly. She later confessed that her intention had been to carve 'Votes for Women' from her heart, across her torso up towards her neck, until the last letters reached her cheek. Only the intervention of medical staff prevented her.

By October 1909, Constance Lytton and Emily Wilding Davison had joined forces. Together, they threw stones at a car in which they believed the Chancellor of the Exchequer David Lloyd George was travelling. As it turned out, he was not in the car, but they were arrested. When the case came to court the authorities again tried everything they could to avoid convicting Lady Lytton. The prosecution seemed to be doing the job of the defence, arguing that she must have been led astray by other dark forces. Constance was furious and made a fiery speech from the dock, insisting that she had known exactly what she was doing, that she was sorry it had not been Lloyd George in the car, and that she would do the same again. She was sentenced to one month in prison.

To her dismay, Constance was given preferential treatment once more. The authorities used her mild congenital heart condition as an excuse to free her on medical grounds after only a few days. Deeply ashamed, Constance decided that the next time she was arrested, she would hide her true identity. In January 1910 she travelled to Liverpool and took part in the WSPU's campaign against Liberals standing at the general election. She disguised herself as one plain 'Jane Warton', and in her words, made herself as ugly as possible, for 'I had noticed several times while I was in prison that prisoners of unprepossessing appearance obtained least favour'.[6]

It was while she was in Liverpool that 'Jane Warton' was arrested for marching on Walton gaol, a sprawling Victorian prison spread over twenty-two acres of land. Suffragettes being held on remand at Walton were frequently force-fed. She was apprehended outside the governor's house and sentenced to two weeks' imprisonment. Believing her to be a working-class woman, the authorities did not give Constance the mandatory medical examination which would have revealed her heart defect. Unlike her previous sentences, this time when Lady Lytton refused to eat, she was not released by a sheepish warden. Instead, Constance was held down and had a pipe pushed down her throat into her stomach. Even though she experienced a level of brutality which almost killed her, Lady Lytton never revealed her true identity.

The force-feeding made her dangerously ill, however, and Constance was only released on medical grounds when rumours of her true identity reached the Press Association. Her subsequent accounts of the prison and feeding regime were eviscerating, and heaped embarrassment on the prison service and home secretary. If the daughter of an earl could cause such a stink, the government had no appetite to see what the Queen's godchild and daughter of the Maharajah of the Punjab could do. Sophia remained at large, despite her frequent and enthusiastic attempts to get arrested. It was not as easy for her to hide her identity as it had been for 'Jane Warton'.

The Prisoners' Temporary Discharge of Ill Health Act finally ended the practice of force-feeding. The legislation came about partly as a result of the outcry which followed testimonials such as those of Lady Lytton. The law stated that suffragettes would now be allowed to refuse food if they wished until such time as a prison doctor regarded their lives to be at risk. At such a point, prisoners would be released under strict licence, giving them time to recover. When fit enough to complete their sentences, the police would re-arrest them.

Suffragette women released under the provision of the new law became experts at evading the police. They received training in counter-surveillance techniques, and had a network of safe houses throughout the British Isles. Suffragettes such as Anne Kenney would travel with a rope ladder in case they were discovered on the higher floors of one of their hiding places and had to flee.[7] The police were made to look comically inept as colourful accounts of daring escapes hit the headlines. Soon the Temporary Discharge of Ill Health Act became more popularly known as the 'Cat and Mouse Act'. The police were the 'cats' and the suffragette 'mice' ran rings around them.

Emmeline Pankhurst had been playing cat and mouse with the government long before they even enacted their new legislation. On the occasions from 1912 that she was arrested, she refused food, became dangerously ill and then had to be released. The authorities were terrified that she might die in prison, and had learned the hard way that they could not force her to eat. They had tried once, at which point she grabbed a heavy clay jug from her cell and threatened to smash it over her own head if they so much as touched her. One of Emmeline's most punishing hunger strikes lasted nine days, during which time she lost two stone in weight, developed jaundice and eventually lapsed into unconsciousness, before being set free.

In 1914, Emmeline was out on licence, this time for the crime of inciting the arson on Lloyd George's newly built house in Walton on the Hill, Surrey. Sentenced to three years, she had always denied the

charge, although she freely admitted she was delighted by the resulting inferno. In prison she had once again starved herself to the point
of death, and Holloway had been forced to let her go. Under the
terms of the Cat and Mouse law, she was to be tended by her nurse
and doctor until such time as she was well enough to finish her
sentence. She was to stay at one address, where she would be guarded
around the clock by police stationed outside. Emmeline was explic-
itly forbidden from public speaking, meeting other suffragettes, or
travelling anywhere in a motor car. Failure to adhere to these terms
would lead to her immediate arrest and incarceration, whether she
was well enough or not to face the rest of her sentence.

On 8 February 1914, while she was meant to be recovering in bed,
Emmeline gave her guards the slip. Two nights later a notice was
published in the press; it said Emmeline would be speaking at her
friend's house in central London later that night, and all were
welcome to attend. The announcement was a 'catch me if you can'
taunt to the authorities, and later that day they flooded the square
with officers.

The residence at 2 Campden Hill Square was a handsome townhouse with tall windows and a balcony on the first floor which
looked out onto a manicured square of garden, exclusively for the
use of the well-heeled people living on the street. Georgina
Brackenbury, who lived at the house with her mother and father, was
a leading suffragette who frequently opened her doors to women
recovering from their hunger strikes. The address was soon known
as 'Mouse Castle' because it had felt like a safe haven for those recu-
perating or hiding from the police.

By seven that evening the square was filled with more than a thousand people. The newspaper advertisement had done its work, as
both pro- and anti-suffragists crammed into the area outside number
2, all waiting to see what Emmeline would say, and how far the police
would go to get her. At 8 o'clock, a frail figure, dressed completely in
black, appeared at the first-floor window. To a cacophony of cheers
and boos, the mysterious woman stepped out onto the balcony. She
looked like Emmeline but nobody could be sure. The figure high
above them wore a hat with a veil drawn over her face. As the crowds

jostled to get a better look, the police began to close in. With dramatic and deliberate flourish the woman on the balcony lifted her veil. It was indeed Emmeline, her taut cheeks flushed with passion: 'I have reached London tonight in spite of armies of police. I am here tonight and not a man is going to protect me, because this is a woman's fight, and we are going to protect ourselves! I am coming out amongst you in a few minutes and I challenge the government to re-arrest me!'[8]

The officers surged towards the door, but the sheer numbers of people slowed them down and in the crucial minutes it took for officers to push their way towards the front door, a group of around a dozen women emerged from the house. In their midst was a diminutive, veiled figure, who the suffragettes were determined to escort out of the square, right under the noses of the police.

Emmeline was going to make a run for it. Her suffragette companions – many of whom had been trained in the martial art of ju-jitsu[9] – formed a tight protective circle around her as the hordes tried to swallow them up. To keep their leader free as long as possible, as well as to protect them against violence from the general public, the WSPU had created a secret group known as 'The Bodyguard' – two dozen or so women who were charged with providing security at suffragette rallies throughout Britain. They had been trained in secret locations by Edith Garrud, who was among the very first professional ju-jitsu instructors in the Western world.

Linking arms, the Bodyguard pushed and shoved through the seething mass. As they called out to other suffragettes in the square to join them, an outer ring formed. Princess Sophia and Ada Wright both stepped forward to help fortify the second ring. They and the others who joined them pushed back against the crowds, attempting to clear a path to the road. Shouts of encouragement rang out as the women fought to stay on their feet and hold the perimeter. 'It's Mrs. Pankhurst, friends! Don't let her be arrested!' screamed one of the suffragettes, as the police closed in. No sooner had the words left Katherine Willoughby Marshall's lips than punches began to fly.

Police grappled with the women, wrenching them apart, trying to reach the veiled figure. As the officers brandished their truncheons, a few of the suffragette Bodyguard pulled out Indian clubs from the folds of their long dresses: made of hardwood and shaped like bowling pins, the clubs were almost two feet long and weighted at the bulbous end. Though traditionally used in callisthenic exercise classes, that night they were bludgeons, and the fight became bloody very quickly. Without a club to swing, Ada Wright used her body to block the police from reaching their leader. Sophia, who was also unarmed, clung to Ada's side, pushing back those who tried to outflank them. The women were no match for the volume of police deployed. One officer knocked Sophia and Ada to the floor, and arrested them both.

The circle was now broken and the police were able to reach their quarry. One policeman struck the woman on the head with a truncheon; several others held her down, causing her to black out. Still unconscious, veil flapping around her face, the silent and motionless figure was lifted out of the crowds and carried out at shoulder height by six police officers. Fighting off the suffragettes the whole time, the police managed to convey the limp figure all the way to Ladbroke Grove police station. It was only then that they realised their mistake. The dazed woman in their custody wasn't Emmeline at all. When they lifted her veil to charge her, they saw they had fallen for a decoy. Florence Evelyn Smith was the same height and build as the WSPU leader. While she and her suffragette colleagues had been distracting the police, Emmeline had escaped, and was long gone. The mouse was on the run again and would next be seen inciting a riot in Glasgow.

Many women were arrested that evening, but only seven were charged. One of them was Ada Wright. Even though she had escaped prison yet again, Sophia was in court for the duration of the trial and sat prominently where the press could see her. When the case against Ada Wright was heard, Sophia took the stand and swore on oath that her friend had done nothing wrong, but rather had been the victim of police violence. According to the princess's evidence, they had both been arrested on false pretences: 'On behalf of Ada Wright it was pleaded that she was only arrested after asking Princess Sophia Duleep Singh, who was beside her, to take the Constable's number . . .'[10]

Sophia's testimony did Ada little good. Although the case against her was flimsy, when the court heard that she had five previous convictions for suffragette affray, she was found guilty. The judge gave her the choice between fourteen days imprisonment or a fine of twenty shillings. Unsurprisingly, Ada took the prison sentence. While she waited in her cell, mentally preparing herself for the moment the police would arrive to take her to Holloway Prison, an inexplicable thing happened: as she would later recall, 'the door was flung open and she was told her fine had been paid by the Princess'.[11]

Like Constance Lytton, perhaps Sophia could not stand the idea that she was free, while her friend was being sent to gaol for essentially the same crime. Like all members of the WSPU, the princess knew the payment of fines was a contentious issue. Most suffragettes felt that only through their suffering in prison would public opinion be moved in their favour. However, on this occasion Sophia felt compelled to break the code. Secretly, and filled with shame, she paid the fine.

Tortured by the idea that Ada and the others would hate what she had done, Sophia increased her donations to the WSPU considerably: in 1914 she gave £51 of her £600 annual income to the Pankhurst war chest.[12] It was the largest donation from an individual that year, and it came at a time of greatest need, when the authorities were pressing the WSPU harder than ever. The sum was not the round figure of £50 which would have been more natural to most people. Sophia, however, had India on her mind. Numbers ending with '1' are deemed to be auspicious in Indian culture (which is why even today at weddings people usually give gifts of £11, £51 or £101). Sophia was not just giving her friends money; she was sending them good fortune.

Sophia was not the only Duleep Singh to give money to the suffragettes in 1914. Princess Pauline Duleep Singh, whom Bamba had once described as 'too vulgar for anything', had donated the sum of one shilling to the WSPU coffers.[13] Sophia was succeeding where others had failed. In small steps, she was teaching Ada's daughter to care about someone other than herself.

Pauline had spent the years after her visit to India feeling lost and lonely. Even though she had been warmly welcomed by Sophia on trips to London, and had spent a few Christmases with Prince Freddy at Old Buckenham Hall, she still felt disconnected from her family. Bamba had made no secret of her animosity, Catherine was indifferent, and Victor cared more for her mother than for her. Her younger sister, Irene, meanwhile, desperate for some stability after a peripatetic childhood, had married the first man who had asked her. At the age of twenty-one, she hid her royal title, cut her ties with her family, and put all her faith in Pierre Marie Alexandre Villemant – a man who would eventually leave her.[14]

Now, at the height of her own suffragette activities, Sophia stepped into Pauline's life again and decided to introduce the twenty-three-year-old to her beloved WSPU. It was a place where Sophia had never felt alone, and she hoped her half-sister might feel the same way. The suffragettes proved no comfort to Pauline, however, and before the year was out she had met and married Lieutenant John Torry, a rector's son from Sussex.[15]

Sophia continued to plough her time and money into the WSPU. She had failed to convert Pauline, but she had more success with Catherine. Her sister gave small amounts to the suffragettes regularly, though she preferred to be affiliated with Millicent Fawcett's moderates. At her home in Germany, women's suffrage was not her main priority. Catherine feared that a war involving the main Western powers was imminent, and that the conflict might put her and the rest of the family on opposing sides.

While Europe edged towards the brink, Sophia continued to wave her placards, sell *The Suffragette*, speak at meetings, and behave provocatively. She drove 'press carts' through the city of London[16] – open horse-drawn carriages piled high with campaign newspapers and covered in suffragette posters and ribbons. Travelling in convoy with her friends, and dressed impeccably for the long and dirty journeys, Sophia always made sure that she was positioned in the first carriage to attract as much attention as possible.

Even in June, with international tensions at breaking point, such attention was forthcoming when the *New York Times* published an article listing prominent suffragettes who were giving money to the WSPU. The individuals named included a handful of aristocrats, and several members of the clergy. Foremost among the 'named and shamed' were Princess Sophia and her sister Catherine. 'Do Princess Sophia Duleep Singh, Princess Catherine Duleep Singh, and Lady Wolsey, all of whom have enjoyed the hospitality of the King at Hampton Court Palace, approve of the burning of that historic residence, which has been marked for destruction for some time?' the paper asked. 'Princess Sophia Duleep Singh and Princess Catherine Duleep Singh are housed as the King's guests at Hampton Court Palace, yet the Princess has given £51 and collected £6 pounds and 7s in the last year to aid a union many members of which intend to burn Hampton Court Palace at the first opportunity.'[17]

The list was enough to provoke the Palace authorities again. And it might have proved the final straw for King George V had not the outbreak of the First World War brought all matters suffragette to a sudden and complete halt.

As soon as war was declared Emmeline Pankhurst sent a circular to Sophia and the other members of the WSPU. In it she asked them to put down their rocks and matches: 'It was inevitable that Great Britain should take part in the war, and with that patriotism, which has served women to endure endless torture in prison cells for the national good, we ardently desire that our country shall be victorious.'[18] For the suffragettes, the militant campaign was over, but for Sophia, a different kind of battle had already begun. She had to get Catherine out of Germany, and she had to do it fast.

# PART III

## *War And Peace, 1914–1948*

# The Lady Vanishes

From the moment war was declared on 4 August 1914, Sophia could think only of her sister Catherine. She was stuck on the wrong side of enemy lines and, more worryingly, neither her brother Freddie, who was still a serving officer in the British Army, nor Victor, great friends with the exceedingly wealthy and well connected, had the power to get her out.

As luck would have it, Sir James Dunlop Smith, the Viceroy of India's private secretary, was in London for the summer. As soon as Sophia became aware of his presence, she wrote asking for and then demanding an urgent meeting. Exasperated and sick with worry, Sophia turned up at the India Office in person on 7 August. Of all the Viceroy's senior advisers, Sir James was the most sympathetic to Indian royalty. He had worked closely with Lord Curzon as the first British political agent to the Phulkian states of the Punjab – the collection of independent Sikh principalities which had sworn allegiance to the Raj. All of them had been hostile to British meddling at first, but Dunlop Smith's quiet respect and earnest interest in their culture earned him many royal friendships. Sophia was counting on that same regard when she begged him for help.

Sir James diligently recorded notes from their meeting and sent them to his superiors, with a request for advice on how to respond. Copies were also sent to the War Office and for filing with the

Political and Secret Department. Summarising her predicament, Dunlop Smith wrote: 'Princess Sophia Duleep Singh has just called to ask if anything can be done for her sister, Princess Katherine. When they last heard she was in Willhelmschone Cassel Prussia . . . The last letter they received was dated the 23rd. Since then all efforts to communicate with her have failed. She was living with a German lady, an intimate friend, and her sister is not at all clear whether she (Pr Katherine) wishes to leave Germany. All the family wish to get in communication with her.'[1]

The note was passed around the highest levels, but the answer, when it came just twenty-four hours later, brought Sophia no relief. Under instructions from his superiors, Sir James told the princess that many similar applications had been made to the Foreign Office and all were being told the same thing, that it was 'quite impossible for them to assist the enquiries to communicate with friends'.[2] He could only suggest that she approached the American embassy for information; they still had a diplomatic presence in Germany, though, he cautioned, 'the FO won't advise this course officially'.[3]

Sophia read Sir James's reply despondently, dismayed by the government's indifference. Only one thing gave her comfort. Despite what she had told Dunlop Smith, Sophia knew full well that Catherine was safe, for now at least. The letter of 23 July had not been the last communication from her sister. Catherine had written once more, immediately after the declaration of war. The British War Office knew it too. Letters to and from Faraday House had been intercepted at the post office and Catherine's last missive had been sent directly to the War Office for further investigation. The reason for their interest, and Sophia's reluctance to share the letter with Dunlop Smith, was its treacherous contents:

Dear Soph,
    It is awful. Having no news of you all – we are going to
Switzerland in November. If it is possible, then, and from there,
of course, we can communicate – I am perfectly all right here,
you must not be anxious in any way, it is just the same as in times
of peace, perfect order everywhere, and no sort of restrictions for

me . . . There have been no murders or disturbances by Germans in Germany and the destruction of property, et cetera in their enemies countries has simply been the just punishment of civilians who have taken part in the war. I implore ☆ to have nothing to do with this unjust war against Germany. Please pay the remainder on Harrods when do you and any bills etc. Much love to all, especially B who, I fear, may have been worrying.

Your loving sister, Catherine.[4]

The line 'unjust war against Germany' had been underlined in red pencil by the interceptor. Catherine had also used a childish code in the letter, which further provoked interest; the star with the 'S' inside it was interpreted by the Foreign Office to mean Victor. Unaware that she had condemned herself by her own hand, Catherine ended her letter with the practical postscript: 'I enclose a letter to Coutts, authorising them to allow you to act on my account.'[5]

Copies of the damning letter shuttled between the War Office and Sir Percy Cox, Secretary to the Government of India. Notes on Catherine and Sophia were urgently requested and shared between departments, as was a detailed history of the family. Ultimately, after some consideration, it was concluded that Catherine was 'decidedly pro-German in her sentiments',[6] but was not a threat of any serious kind. She could be left in Germany as far as the India and War Office were concerned. A closer eye would have to be kept on the sister at Hampton Court though.

While Sophia continued to fret about Catherine, with whom she now had no contact, there was some good news regarding her WSPU friends at least. Six days after the start of the war, the government released all suffragette prisoners. Emmeline Pankhurst and Prime Minister Asquith had struck a deal. For the duration of the war all acts of militancy would cease. In exchange for his positive reconsideration of the franchise question, Emmeline assured Asquith that her women would not only stop the violence, they would also get behind the war effort.

Some of the more fiery members of the movement were appalled by her actions. Among them was Kitty Marion, one of the WSPU's most committed arsonists. She had endured 232 force-feedings while on hunger strike during a prison term of fourteen weeks and two days.[7] She was not about to drop the struggle just because Emmeline willed it. Kitty vowed to continue alone if necessary and eventually left Britain for the United States, helping to invigorate the suffragette movement there. Undeterred by criticism, Emmeline, together with her daughter Christabel, began to work in earnest for the war effort.

Both of them spoke passionately at rallies, urging young men to enlist and fight valiantly for their country. Emmeline was even given a £2,000 grant by the government to organise a morale-boosting parade though the capital the following year.

Thousands of miles away in India, more than 40,000 men were preparing to be deployed in Europe, the first wave of a million-man force that would eventually leave India. The Viceroy had committed his entire army as soon as war was declared. Two infantry divisions, the 3rd Lahore and the 7th Meerut, were the first to be mobilised. They set sail for Egypt, dressed in light khaki drill uniforms, clothes suited to the hot climate and offering little protection for what lay ahead. Disembarking on 10 October in Marseilles, they found France was already gripped by frost. As the men stood shivering, waiting for their orders, their commander-in-chief, Lieutenant General Sir James Wilcox, attempted to warm his cold and dejected troops with words: 'You are the descendants of the men who have been mighty rulers and great warriors for many centuries. You will never forget this. You will recall the glories of your race. Hindu and Mohammedan will be fighting side-by-side with British soldiers and our gallant French allies. You will be helping to make history. You will be the first Indian soldiers of the King Emperor, who will have the honour of showing Europe that the sons of India have lost none of their ancient martial instincts.'[8]

The men were told to think of their gods as they marched to the Western front, a deep scar of trenches that was eventually gouged into the land all the way from the North Sea to the Swiss frontier. On either side, armies dug in. Fighting was at close quarters, ruthless, and ultimately advanced neither side by more than a few feet. The ground beneath the soldiers' boots was wet and cold. They only had thin soles and flimsy socks and their overcoats failed to protect them from the freezing conditions. Pneumonia and frostbite wreaked havoc, but still the Indian troops marched onwards, trudging every mile while their bones ached. Across the Channel, civilians mobilised by knitting gloves, scarves and undershirts 'for the brave Indian men on the front'.

The British high command was feeding its Indian troops piecemeal into some of the fiercest fighting around Ypres. Losses were devastating. Indian battalions usually comprised a complement of 764 men. In less than a month, the 47th Sikhs of the Lahore Infantry Division were left with just over half that number. One despairing sepoy wrote home to his family: 'This is not war; it is the ending of the world,'[9] and described the deaths of his comrades in arms like 'the grinding of corn in a mill'.[10]

By December, temperatures plummeted even further. Just outside the village of Gorre, north of the Somme, trenches had become so clogged with filthy, flowing icy water that orders were given to evacuate. As one British officer, Captain Roly Grimshaw of the 34th Poon Horse, sat in the mud, waiting with his men for rations, he watched a seemingly endless stream of wounded pass him by. They were like the animated dead, silent, save for the occasional moan from a stretcher: 'the state of the wounded beggars all description. Little Gurkhas sloping through the freezing mud ... Tommies with no caps, and plastered in blood and mud from head to foot; Sikhs with their hair all down ... Pathans more dirty and untidy than usual; all limping, all reeling along like drunken men, some helping an almost foundered comrade. In most cases, misery depicted on their faces.'[11]

Those who died on the front were buried quickly and notes were made of names and causes of death. Although burial was acceptable for Muslims, it created a matter of great spiritual difficulty for the Hindus and Sikhs. According to their religious beliefs, the very ones that Lt General Wilcox had stirred in them in Marseilles, only fire could free their souls from their bodies. However, in the trenches, where the dim glow of a lit cigarette could attract the attention of a German sniper, cremations were out of the question.

The Indian wounded began to flow back to England within a matter of weeks and their numbers quickly overwhelmed such provision as had been laid aside for them. The steady stream of broken Indians turned into a flood and three stationary hospital ships were commandeered in the port of Southampton. It was not long before the *Sicilia*, *Glengorm Castle* and *Goorkha* were also overwhelmed. The sleepy market town of New Milton in Hampshire had one of its grandest buildings turned into a convalescent home; in the seaside resort of Bournemouth a large hotel was commandeered and filled with medical equipment. The buildings, although quickly found, were difficult to staff and supply, such was the disparate spread of locations. Civil servants looked for one single town that might become the hub for Indian wounded. It had to be large, sophisticated and willing to accept wave upon wave of foreigners from the front.

Brighton had long been a place associated with convalescence. Elegant Regency-style terraces stretched up wide streets with sea views and the cheery promenade was often filled with London's most fashionable people. The rich and exhausted had been coming to the town since the time of its greatest patron, the playboy Prince Regent, later to become King George IV. He spent so much time in the town, escaping the political machinations of his father's court, that he asked the architect John Nash to create a palace for him by the sea. The resulting Royal Pavilion was an embodiment of the prince's exotic and extravagant taste. The town now offered its largest buildings to the war effort, including the Pavilion. With its domes, carved stone lattice work, towers and minarets, it looked more like a palace fit for a Maharajah than the holiday home of a future King of England.

An old workhouse was also handed over, filled with 2,000 beds, and named the Kitchener Hospital, after the man who now held the position of Secretary of State for War. Although it looked like any other military hospital, wards were separated in line with caste and religion. Nine separate kitchens had to be built in order to cater for the complex dietary requirements of the Indian men with their diverse faiths. Staff were taught how to ritually slaughter animals and about the importance of keeping food for the high-caste Hindus securely and separately stored from all the rest. Sacks of rice and lentils were ordered, and cooks were sought who might know what to do with them.[12] There were separate taps for Hindus and Muslims, and on the lawns of the Pavilion itself, a makeshift Sikh temple was erected. Schools in York Place, a street near Brighton's main station, were gutted and refitted in record time.[13] These were to be hospitals of intensive care for critically wounded men evacuated from the Western front.

Just days before Christmas 1914, the first Indian casualties were brought in. As the local paper reported, they made a pitiful sight: 'They arrived under rather mournful conditions. A drab day, rain-storms and a fierce sea running in the Channel, mud-laden streets, and a vista of dripping umbrellas and mackintoshes. That was the first impression the Warriors got of Brighton, and it was rather chilling ... The hundred stretcher cases in the first train that reached the terminus on Monday afternoon, constituted perhaps the most distressing of the many pathetic sights seen on similar occasions during the past four months. Something akin to a feeling of awe was created by the silence.'[14] The Viceroy of India, Sir Charles Hardinge, made it clear that it was not his practice to employ white women in hospitals meant for Indian soldiers. Since this was also the view of General Wilcox, only a handful of English women were ever permitted to work in Brighton's Indian hospitals and then only in supervisory roles.[15] Male orderlies filled the roles that ordinarily would have been carried out by nurses. The message was clear and colonial: it was not desirable for British women to touch brown patients.

Nevertheless, the soldiers were grateful for the care they received, as Isher Singh, a solder from the Sikh 59th Rifles, and a survivor of the battle of Neuve Chapelle, wrote from his bed: 'Do not be anxious about me. We are very well looked after. White soldiers are always besides our bed – day and night. We get very good food four times a day. We also get milk. Our hospital is in the place where the King used to have his throne. Every man is washed once in hot water. The King has given strict order that no trouble be given to any black man in hospital. Men in hospital are tended like flowers and the King and Queen sometimes comes to visit them.'[16]

For a while the city, dubbed Dr Brighton for its healing role, coped well enough with the incoming Indian wounded, but by the beginning of 1915 it became clear that more medical provision was needed. Individuals with Raj connections rallied around to raise money. At the same time, the War Office cast around for a suitable site for a possible private hospital that might supplement their own offerings. Brockenhurst, some eighty miles along the coast, west of Brighton, proved to be the best location. It had already been temporarily used as a treatment centre for wounded Indians at the start of the war and was close to the port of Southampton with good railway connections. Overnight, the Lady Hardinge Hospital sprang up in the form of tents and sturdy galvanised huts.[17] Named in honour of the Viceroy's late wife, the Lady Hardinge had a capacity for 500 beds. Because of the corrugated appearance of the wards, to the locals it was known simply as 'Tin Town'.

Tin Town itself may have been a metallic sprawl, but it looked out upon picturesque vistas. The site had been donated to the war effort by Mrs Edward Morant, a redoubtable matriarch who lived at Brockenhurst Park, a grand mansion with its own lakes and sculpted grounds. A descendant of one of eighteenth-century England's richest plantation owners, Mrs Morant was not just wealthy, she was well connected too. Up until the outbreak of war, she had used all her influence and energy to oppose the suffragettes. Morant was one of a number of women recruited by Lord Curzon to show the world that 'right-minded women' did not need or want the vote. She served as the President of the Lymington Anti-Suffrage League and was the type of woman Sophia and her friends despised.

Since the Lady Hardinge was not a government hospital and therefore received no state funding, donations were desperately sought for its upkeep. Men who had once served with the Indian Army or civil service contributed funds, but the lion's share came from the 'Indian Soldiers' Fund Sub-Committee of the Ladies' Committee of the Order of St John of Jerusalem'.

Despite its big name, the charity had small beginnings. At the outbreak of war, members raised just enough money to buy religious artefacts for soldiers at the front. Crates filled with Korans,

Brahminical threads and copies of the Sikh holy book were sent to the trenches. However by 1915, when it became clear that Brighton was struggling with the influx of wounded, the fund turned its attention from the soldiers' spiritual needs to the corporeal. Donating more than £10,000, the charity paid for equipment and vital medical supplies for Brockenhurst and also for a small convalescent home in nearby Milford-on-Sea.[18]

Because it was privately run, the Lady Hardinge could ignore many of the rules slavishly followed by state hospitals. The ban on female nurses was the first regulation to go. Lady Hardinge ran under the hawkish eye of its matron, Edith McCall Anderson. One of the most highly regarded nurses in the country, Anderson was a sturdy woman with experience of military hospitals dating back to the Boer War.[19] With a love of order and discipline, she commanded a contingent of female staff, all of whom were volunteers. These included 'seventeen Sisters, all of whom speak Hindustani'. The 'bi-linguals' had spent their lives in India, either supporting their husbands, or working for the Raj in their own right. They were able to share memories with the men, comfort them in their own language and generally lift their spirits better than anyone else.

Officers in the Indian Army were accorded special privileges at the hospital. They were dressed in rich blue pyjamas and gowns with red piping. The clothes had been donated by one of the richest women in the world, Lady Rothschild, and the men 'looked very smart as well as warm'.[20] Even the hospital bedding and the men's underclothes had been sent by well-wishers. As a reporter for the *British Journal of Nursing* noted, some soldiers had found a new use for the knitted scarves that were sent: 'ingeniously worn in more than one instance as turbans'. The same journalist was particularly impressed by the aesthetic merits of the wards, noting that they had 'quilts of Turkey twill which suit the dark faces above them'.[21]

In 1915, the hospital received the royal seal of approval when King George V toured its wards. Although he met the matron and many members of her staff, it is unlikely that His Majesty was introduced to one particular nurse. Sophia Duleep Singh was now a member of Matron McCall Anderson's caring army. She had not been content with merely visiting the Indian soldiers at Brighton and had swapped her civilian clothes for a Red Cross nurse's uniform in 1915. She spent much of the year tending to the broken sons of the Punjab. In many ways it felt like coming home for Sophia, who had spent the most stable part of her childhood in Brighton under the care of the Oliphants.

It was the first time many of the men had seen an Indian woman in months, though Sophia was a mystery to them at first. She may have looked like the women they had left at home but she spoke hardly a word of Hindustani and most of the white nurses could communicate better than she could. When they found out who Sophia really was, their confusion turned to awe. The soldiers could not believe that the granddaughter of Ranjit Singh sat by their bedsides in a nurse's uniform. Of all the Indians at Lady Hardinge Hospital and Milford, the Punjabi soldiers were the most affected by Sophia's presence. Hardened Sikh fighters were bashful and tongue-tied. When they could muster the courage, they begged the princess for signed photographs so that they could prove to their families that they had truly met a Duleep Singh. Sophia gave them pictures of herself, but felt they deserved something better. Somehow, despite wartime restrictions, Sophia managed to get little ivory shaving mirrors made up for the soldiers in her care. These were flat compacts which could be folded and slipped into pockets. The exotic little luxuries were made all the more precious to the men when she wrote personal messages on the back.[22] Soldiers such as Kartar Singh of the 15th Sikhs wrote to his family in Punjab bursting with pride: 'My friends this is a photo of our King's granddaughter – he who was King of the Sikhs, Ranjit Singh.'[23]

Kartar Singh had been the kind of soldier the British high command dreamt of. He obeyed orders efficiently and without question, fought valiantly, and was grateful for every kindness shown to him by the English. There were many like him, young men from the old Sikh kingdom who had left their homes and families, perhaps even their villages for the very first time. They had signed up to fight a foreign war with allies who did not speak the same language as them, against an enemy who posed no threat to their country.

However, not every Punjabi was as loyal as Kartar Singh. Some soldiers in the Indian Army were not only refusing to fight in the Great War, but were also encouraging fellow soldiers to rise up and slit the throats of their British commanding officers. They were members of the Ghadar party (from the Urdu 'revolt'), and while the British were fully engaged in Europe, they found themselves fighting an enemy that had sprung up within their own ranks too.

The movement was founded in the United States in 1913 by a small group of newly settled Indians. They included Lala Har Dayal, a brilliant Punjabi academic who had moved to America to escape British colonial rule. In his youth in Delhi, Har Dayal had been poor but clever. The sixth of seven children, Har Dayal distinguished himself at school, showing particular aptitude for the ancient Indian language of Sanskrit. He excelled in his degree at the Punjab University, and received scholarships to study at Oxford. However, once in England, Har Dayal became frustrated with the limitations placed on his future. Despite his intellect the best he could hope for on his return was a life as a mid-level bureaucrat in the Indian Civil Service, pushing papers for the British. It was not enough.

Har Dayal began to make visits to India House in Highgate. There, in Krishnavarma's nest of radicals, he met many young men who hated colonialism as much as he did. Their anti-British speeches made sense to him and he gave up his place at St John's College, Oxford, returning to India where he wrote fiery anti-colonial articles in the indigenous press. When the Raj banned his writings in 1908, Har Dayal was advised by his great friend (and Sophia's mentor) Lala Lajpat Rai that arrest was imminent and he should leave India immediately. Heeding his words, he packed and left, not knowing if he would ever return.

Har Dayal travelled around Europe for months before eventually settling in France where he discovered a vibrant anarchist movement. Their belief that any power could be toppled inspired him and he became the editor of a radical Indian newspaper, *Vande Mataram* ('I bow to the Motherland'). It was a nationalist publication, written in English, which openly praised men who defied the Raj. Madhan Lal Dhingra, the killer of Curzon Wyllie, was celebrated on the paper's front pages on the day he was hanged. In a stinging editorial, Har Dayal himself wrote: 'Dhingra has behaved at each stage of his trial like a hero of ancient times, he has reminded us of the history of medieval Rajputs and Sikhs who loved death like a bride. England thinks she killed Dhingra, in reality he lives forever, and has given the deathblow to English sovereignty in India.'[24]

Though he had found his political voice, Paris was not for Har Dayal. Listless, he decided to move again, this time setting his sights on California. In 1911, life in the United States was filled with promise and opportunity. As well as becoming heavily involved in the trade union movement in San Francisco, Har Dayal took up the post of lecturer in Indian philosophy and Sanskrit at Stanford University. He was fired when the administration found out about his anti-British writing.

Without a job, living in cramped, rented accommodation near the University of California in Berkeley, Har Dayal's sense of dispossession and rage became volcanic. Wanting desperately to go home, but knowing he faced immediate arrest if he did, in 1913, Har Dayal began to plan an uprising. With a group of Indian ex-pat friends, he founded the Ghadar movement.

Punjabis had been coming to America and Canada for years, some to escape arrest, but most to work as labourers on the farms stretching from California's central valley all the way up to British Columbia. Gurdwaras sprang up in Stockton, then one of California's largest cities, and Abbotsford and Vancouver in British Columbia. These places of Sikh worship contributed vast sums for Har Dayal's revolution.

At the beginning, the movement's most powerful weapon was its newspaper. The *Ghadar* carried the standard '*Anghrezi Raj ka Dushman*' under its masthead. Translated, the motto meant 'Enemies of the British', and the first line in the very first issue read: 'Today there begins "Ghadar" in foreign lands, but in our country's tongue, a war against the British Raj.'

The articles were incendiary: 'What is our name? Ghadar. What is our work? Ghadar. Where will be the revolution? In India. The time will soon come when rifles and blood will take the place of pens and ink.'[25] The Ghadar revolutionaries saw the Great War as an opportunity to agitate while the British were vulnerable. Ghadars urged Indian soldiers to rise up in mutiny against their over-stretched commanding officers. From their headquarters in California, they were successful in inciting soldiers in the Hong Kong regiments and in Singapore. Ringleaders were arrested, court-martialled and either hanged or deported to India for trial. Still the rebellion spread. Just outside Singapore city, in February 1915, the worst mutiny of Indian sepoys occurred as the 130th Baluchi Regiment revolted against their officers. Up to half of the 850 soldiers stormed the barracks at Tanglin, and attempted to free the German prisoners of war held there. Most of the Germans refused to join them, despite being offered rifles. Even without their help, the mutiny dragged on for seven days, as the British struggled to take back control. Eventually Allied warships were redirected towards Singapore, and the mutiny was put down, but not before forty-seven British soldiers and local civilians had been killed. In the aftermath of the Singapore mutiny, four Indian soldiers were hanged, sixty-nine were given life imprisonment and 126 were punished with lengthy terms of imprisonment with hard labour.

Despite the punishments, the Ghadar message continued to spread, causing smaller army uprisings as far as Iran and Iraq. Each time the Ghadar sepoys mutinied, they were crushed by superior British fire-power. However, the movement had flexed its muscles enough to frighten the Raj. Contagion needed to be stopped before it reached India, where the British might lose control of their empire for ever.

By 1916 a million copies of their weekly newsletter were being published and circulated around the world. The revolutionary message was most enthusiastically received in the Punjab, from where, at the outbreak of the Great War, half the Indian Army had been drawn. Realising the dangers, the British clamped down hard; hundreds of Ghadar sympathisers were rounded up and charged with sedition. According to one Indian estimate, 145 were hanged, and 308 were given sentences longer than fourteen years. The harsher the sentences, the more young Punjabis flocked to the Ghadar flag.

Though she sympathised, Sophia could not bring herself to aban-don the Indian soldiers on the Western front. Their pitiful state moved her to search for new ways in which to help them. Just as she did with the suffragettes and the lascars before them, Sophia decided the best thing she could do was raise money.

The British Red Cross's forty-sixth anniversary on 4 August 1916 gave Sophia her first opportunity. A nationwide event known as 'Our Day' was staged across the Empire. Men and women were asked to pay generous sums for the privilege of wearing Red Cross flag badges in their lapels, with proceeds earmarked for a soldiers' welfare fund. Sophia commandeered the effort for India, and together with a small group of Indian women, part of the first trickle of immigration into Georgian England, set up stalls in front of a well-known whisky merchant in London's Haymarket. In front of Dewar House, the Indian women, along with British friends dressed in Eastern silks, enthusiastically harangued passers-by for money to be spent specifically on sepoys at the front. Sophia, who led their efforts, wore a sober black skirt suit with a hat and patent court shoes. Many such fundraising events took place up and down the country, but despite her dress, Sophia's stood out for its colour and exuberance. *The Times* gave her campaign prominent coverage and, for a change, their about article about Sophia did not condemn or criticise: 'Haymarket was made gay by the Princess's Indian stall, which she had draped with Indian silks and gleaming embroideries. By her were Lady Beecham and Mrs Drummond-Wolff in Punjabi dress, whilst many Indian ladies and children and a large number of retired Anglo-Indians found their way to the stall and a little Hindustani was exchanged with goodly sums.'[26]

Buoyed by her success, Sophia decided to do more. On 17 April 1917, she wrote to New Scotland Yard, asking for a licence to hold substantial street collections throughout the capital. The YMCA had planned a similar event for Indian soldiers earlier in the year but had lost interest in the venture. Sophia picked up the reins and decided to carry on without them. In her application, she informed the Metropolitan Police that all money raised would go towards buying decent waterproof shoes, warm clothes, chocolate and cigarettes for the soldiers. Her request seemed uncontroversial and, under normal circumstances, such a licence would have been granted without difficulty. Sophia's letter however was immediately forwarded to the India Office for the attention of the Secretary of State himself. The police did not feel able to act without higher authority.

A flurry of communications followed between the commissioner, the India Office's Political and Secret Department and the Secretary of State for India. After some deliberation it was decided that the princess ought to be dissuaded. The idea that the ungrateful suffragette from Hampton Court might receive plaudits for her war efforts was troubling to the Home Office. The India Office too had its own reasons to say no. While the Ghadars were agitating within the army, the last thing they needed was the granddaughter of Ranjit Singh to be lauded as a saviour of the very men they were sending to fight and die at the front. But how could they say no to such a laudable ambition without looking ridiculous?

A memo from the Political and Secret Department explained the dilemma and weighed up the dangers: 'The original scheme, which was to have been worked by the YMCA, has evidently dropped. I don't think the project, if it ever comes off, will be a success, but I don't see how the Secretary of State can do anything, but "concur". If there were any suspicion that the India Office looked askance at the proposals, the results would be serious.'[27]

But still the politicians and civil servants could not bring themselves to give Sophia the go-ahead. On 20 August, a further memo was sent to the police giving them possible grounds to turn her down: 'Sir, in reply to your letter of the 16th inst GR 249504, regarding an application made on behalf of Princess Sophia Duleep Singh for permission to hold a street collection throughout London for the benefit of Indian troops, I am directed by the Secretary of State for India to say that it appears to him undesirable that such collection should be undertaken on the initiative of private persons. If it is decided to hold one for the purpose in question, he would prefer that the arrangements should be made by the committee of the Indian Soldiers' Fund.'[28]

There were also rumours coming from Whitehall that the new Viceroy, Lord Chelmsford, had already given his blessing to Sophia's plans. If he had, then London was caught in a trap, and there was potential for great embarrassment, with the Secretary of State saying one thing and the Viceroy of India another. An urgent telegram was fired off to Delhi by Lord Wimborne, the Lord Lieutenant of Ireland. He asked the Viceroy to think very carefully about what he may and may not have said about Sophia's scheme: 'has Princess Sophia Dileep [sic] Singh's proposed Indian flag day [received] official approval? And asked to interest Viceroy of India in scheme (?) Please wire reply.'[29]

Days later, the Political and Secret Department found to its horror that it was not tacit approval from the Viceroy they had to worry about. Sir Arthur Hirtzel read with gloom that his own Secretary of State in London, the very man who was most against Sophia getting the credit for her fundraising plan, had himself praised her idea in a letter to a third party months before. The matter had entirely slipped his mind.

If the Secretary of State thought the idea had merit before Sophia's name had been attached to it, and had wished it every success, he could not very well turn it down now. A new strategy had to be found quickly. Arthur Hirtzel drafted another letter to the head of the Metropolitan Police: 'Sir, in reply to your letter, 16 August 1917, No GR 249504, I am directed to inform you that the Secretary of State for India in Council cannot support officially proposals of the kind indicated, for the benefit of Indian troops, but he does not wish to raise any objection to a collection being held by the YMCA, provided that it is clear that it is a private enterprise of that association and in no way connected with the India Office. The YMCA has already been acquainted informally with the Secretary of State's views on the subject.'[30]

Suddenly, without explanation, the YMCA was again interested in plans it had rejected months before, and invited Sophia to be the honourable secretary of the venture. Oblivious to the machinations going on behind her back, she accepted and then got on with the business of organising her event. There were badges to make, tins and trays to be sourced and ranks of enthusiastic volunteers to enlist. She was happy because she felt useful. Activity took her out of the dreariness of Hampton Court and distracted her from the depression which often haunted her when she had time on her hands. The government too was pleased. The fundraising event for Indian soldiers would go ahead without the whiff of a Duleep Singh name about it. Sophia's name would disappear in a long list of committee members. That was the plan anyway.

The date of the event was set for 20 September 1918 and was to take the form of a flag day. Since the outbreak of war, flag days had been a successful method of collecting money from the general public. Little metal badges with pictures of soldiers, or names of causes, were produced in their thousands. Collecting tins were issued to men, women and children, and they were dispatched, often wearing patriotic fancy dress, to rattle metal boxes under the noses of the general public. Vast sums of money had been raised already for specific regiments and for prisoners of war and Sophia hoped to replicate such success with her India Day. In addition to shoes, chocolate and warm clothes, the princess had higher ambitions for her event. She wanted huts for the sepoys to sleep in, for many were still struggling against the elements.

Sophia spent the next few months working with the YMCA committee, happy to be busy in a flurry of planning and preparation. A knock at the door of her home on 8 June threatened to bring everything to a halt.

Since the first days of the war, Sophia had dreaded the telegram that would bring bad news about Catherine. As she opened the envelope she realised with horror that she had been worrying about the wrong sibling. Victor, her eldest brother, was dead, killed by a massive coronary heart attack the previous day in Paris.

Victor and Anne had moved into their apartment at 40 Avenue du Trocadero[31] in 1912, when the stigma of bankruptcy had become too much to bear in England. They had been able to enjoy life in France without suffering the ignominy of gossip. War, however, trapped them there and they had spent the last four years waiting for a ceasefire that never came. The telegram informed Sophia that Victor would be buried in three days' time, at an Anglican cemetery high up on a hillside above his beloved Monte Carlo. With war raging and travel forbidden, none of the family would be able to say a last farewell. The realisation broke his youngest sister's heart.

There was little opportunity for Sophia to mourn: there were too many preparations to be made and too many soldiers counting on her. India Day may just have saved the princess from months of crippling despair.

A week before the event, just as her little metal flags and badges arrived, Sophia received correspondence so momentous, it made her forget her fury at the police who – churlishly in her view – had refused to grant permission for 'real live elephants' to march with her India Day collectors through London.[32] The freshly delivered papers not only gave her a great morale boost, but also reduced to tatters the British government's attempts to untangle her name from the charity.

Field Marshal Lord John French, commander-in-chief of the British Expeditionary Force, had written an open letter to Sophia thanking her for her efforts. He praised the Indian troops under his command, describing their 'fine fighting qualities, tenacity and endurance' during the first battle of Ypres.[33] 'I have no hesitation in saying,' Lord French continued, 'that they splendidly upheld the glorious fighting traditions of the Indian Army . . . It will always be a source of pride and happiness to me that I have been associated in the field with these gallant troops.'[34]

On 14 September, under the headline 'Gallant Indian Troops', *The Times* ran a prominent article which began with the very words that the India Office had not wanted to read: 'Princess Sophia Duleep Singh, who is organising the "India Day" celebrations in London next Friday, September 20, has received a letter from Lord French in which he pays tribute to the services rendered by India's fighting men on the Western Front during the years 1914 and 1915 . . .'[35] The paper then reproduced the field marshal's praise-laden letter in full. No mention at all was made of the YMCA.

Lord French's stirring words, printed in Britain's newspaper of record, created terrific publicity and helped to make Sophia's fundraiser a resounding success. India Day raised enough money to buy 50,000 huts for sepoys garrisoned all over the world.

Sophia's was one of the last great wartime fundraising efforts. Armistice Day on 11 November 1918 marked victory for the allies

Indian soldiers in the trenches during the First World War – more than a million would eventually serve. One despairing sepoy wrote, 'This is not a war; it is the ending of the world', and described the deaths of his comrades-in-arms as 'the grinding of corn in a mill'.

Sophia took up the cause of the Indian soldiers. Some of the worst casualties from the Western Front came from the old Sikh kingdom of her grandfather.

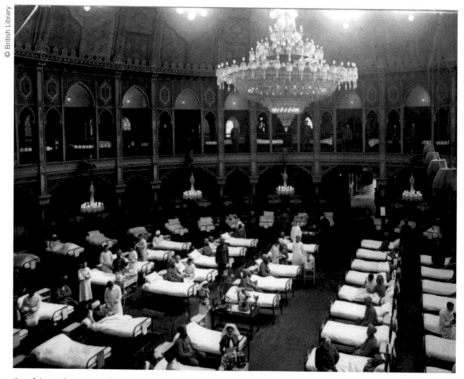

Sophia volunteered as a nurse, working with the flood of wounded Indian soldiers pouring into Britain from the Front. Brighton Pavilion (*above*) became one of many makeshift hospitals which sprang up overnight.

Sophia (*third from left*) with a group of her fellow volunteer nurses. All were British and some, who had served the Raj in India, spoke the language of the soldiers better than she did.

Punjabi patients could not believe they were being treated by their princess.

As well as nursing the troops, Sophia (*fourth from left*) threw herself into raising funds for warm clothes and huts for Indian soldiers. Her efforts won the praise of Field Marshal Lord French, and scuppered the government's plan to suppress her involvement.

Despite her activism, Sophia retained the keys to Hampton Court Palace, opposite her own grace-and-favour lodgings at Faraday House. She regularly walked her dogs in the grounds.

The Snell sisters, Ethel (*left*) and Margaret (*middle*), both maids and later friends of Sophia, and the redoubtable Margaret Mayes (*right*), housekeeper at Faraday House.

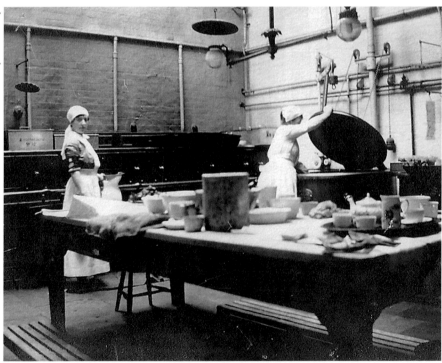

The kitchens at Faraday House. With war declared and the threat of Hitler's Blitz looming, Sophia reluctantly let go most of her staff and prepared to evacuate to Penn in Buckinghamshire.

Sophia retained Lane, her driver, and her feisty new housekeeper, Bosie – the only woman who seemed able to stand up to the increasingly irascible princess.

Lane and Bosie married and their child Catherine became the centre of Sophia's world. As her godmother, she even renamed the child 'Drovna', a fragment of her own unorthodox middle name.

Sophia's house, Rathenrea, a sprawling bungalow in Penn. It became a haven for her new family and for three children, the Sarbutts, evacuated from London.

All three Sarbutt children, (*left to right*) Shirley, John and Michael, the 'little pickle'.

Bamba, the self-styled Queen of
Punjab. The servants loathed her.

Catherine with her beloved
Lina Schaeffer, separated only
by death in 1938.

Sophia in the garden of Rathenrea, with her ancient, bad-tempered parrot, Akbar.
She had finally found contentment surrounded by her children and her animals.

Sophia guarded Drovna and the Sarbutt children like a lioness, often sending the chauffeur to collect them from school. She once lavished an entire fortnight's sugar ration on cakes and treats.

Sophia (*left*) and Catherine at a suffragette dinner in 1937. When Catherine died in 1942 it was Sophia who found her body. It broke her. 'It completely stunned and stupefied me – and I couldn't shake myself up to ordinary things again.'

Sophia and her beloved god-daughter Drovna. The princess was determined to raise the housekeeper's daughter as a lady and revelled in her maternal role.

and complete defeat for the Germans. While millions took to the streets to celebrate the end of a four-year nightmare, Sophia pushed her way through the cheering crowds, heavy with anxiety. The reports from vanquished Germany were not good. A successful British naval blockade had stopped food from getting in to the country for some time and there was no sign of a swift re-estab-lishment of supply lines. Thousands were starving to death in the cold, and influenza was sweeping through the weakened popula-tion. Sophia needed to get Catherine out before disease or hunger took her.

On the very day that peace broke out, the Dutch legation* in Berlin received an urgent and imperious request for a new passport for one Princess Duleep Singh, an Indian princess trapped in Germany. Struck by Sophia's royal title on the letter, the Dutch bureaucrat spent a little longer at his desk than he may have wanted to on Armistice Day. He wired his British counterparts asking if there would be any objection if they were to grant Catherine travel documents, 'with the request that it may be informed whether this lady will be permitted to land in England if she obtains permission from the German authorities to leave Germany'.[36]

Despite the Dutchman's urgent action, it took more than a month for the paperwork to reach the relevant desk in Britain. Sophia could not stand the delay and wrote again on 12 December. This time she addressed her letter to the Prisoners of War Department at the Foreign Office. Catherine had finally been in touch and, as Sophia feared, she was facing a desperate situation. Lina Schaeffer was seriously ill and weak from hunger. Catherine wanted to get out of Germany but at the same time could not bear to leave Lina's side.

Although her sister was vacillating about the best course of action, Sophia was in no doubt about what she should do. Without a passport, Catherine was trapped, so Sophia decided to escalate matters. Writing directly to Lord Newton, one of the most senior men at the Foreign Office with special responsibility for Prisoners

---

* The Dutch were charged with taking care of the interests of British subjects during the war.

of War, Sophia's letter was blunt and to the point. He simply had to help her sister: get her a Dutch passport or a British one, Sophia did not care. The princess could not countenance continued delay. Whether Newton knew Sophia personally or not, he took the letter seriously. Passing it on to the India Office immediately, he dictated an accompanying memo which strongly suggested that the India Office might want to get on with it: 'I am directed by Lord Newton to transmit herewith, for the information of Mr Secretary Montagu, a copy of a note from the Netherland Legation at Berlin regarding the issue of a British passport to enable the Princess Catherine Duleep Singh to return to this country. I am also to enclose a copy of a letter from Princess Sophia Duleep Singh in regard to the same matter, and am to request that Lord Newton may be favoured at as early a date as possible with an expression of Mr Montagu's opinion as to whether a passport or other facilities to leave Germany may be granted to Princess Catherine Duleep Singh.'[37]

On Christmas Eve a bundle of papers marked urgent made it on to the desks of the War Office. The timing was bad, for most government ministries were winding up for the first peacetime Christmas in years. However by now, Sophia's letter had garnered some important attention. Seeing the names tagged to the file, the War Office immediately hand-delivered the papers to Sir Edwin Samuel Montagu, the Secretary of State for India. He read them and noted Lord Newton's suggestion that they give him an answer 'at as early a date as possible'. Despite the nudge, the Secretary of State was in no mood to let Duleep Singh's offspring hold him back from Christmas with his family. He left the papers where they lay with a view to returning to them after Boxing Day.

On 27 December, full of Christmas cheer, Montagu dictated a secret memo to colleagues. He had decided that Catherine could be granted a British passport, observing dryly: 'I hardly think that we are in a position to make difficulties. Quite early in the war (Sept 1914) we intercepted a foolish pro-German letter from Princess Catherine; but so far as I know, nothing has been heard of her since. It may be hoped that she has found occasion to modify her views. In any case, there seems to be no sufficient evidence for treating her as an "enemy".'[38]

Catherine was coming home. The war was over at last, and despite the government's best efforts, Sophia had managed to help her Indian soldiers and get the credit. She could not have hoped for a better start to 1919.

# Such Troublesome Times

The turmoil of the Great War had repercussions far beyond the battle-fields of Europe. Although the British had worried about the impact, news of Sophia's charity work was entirely lost on India. The general noise of dissent had grown deafening. Nationalist politicians did not need to use dispossessed monarchs to stir up anti-British feelings. The Great War had taken a visible toll on India's young men and the same question was being asked all over the country: 'Why have we sent our sons to die for those who oppress us?' Rebellion spread from the ranks and into the civilian population as episodes of lawlessness increased. In an effort to restore order, in 1919 the Raj passed a set of draconian laws.

Under the aegis of the Rowlatt Act, Indians could be arrested without warrant. They could be detained without trial for an indefinite period of time and political prisoners would be tried *in camera*. They could be denied the right to know what evidence was held against them, or indeed who was accusing them. Public meetings were made illegal, and any journalist writing critical articles could be charged with sedition and incarcerated for long terms with hard labour. The Rowlatt laws were so extreme that they managed to offend even moderate nationalists.

Gandhi had made the ocean crossing from Cape Town to Bombay just before the start of the war. In July 1914 he had decided to make

India his home once again, after successfully defying the government of South Africa. Through a series of strikes and marches between 1906 and 1914, he had forced the legislators to overturn many of the country's worst anti-Indian laws. The victory was all the more impressive when one considered who his main adversary had been. The Minister of the Interior, General Jan Christiaan Smuts, was a dedicated believer in racial segregation and the natural superiority of whites. He was also a battle-hardened Afrikaner soldier. Nevertheless Smuts had not come across an opponent like Gandhi.

Refusing to carry the pass papers,[*] when arrested, Gandhi never lifted a hand to fend off the inevitable blows from the police. When he appeared before magistrates, he always asked for the most severe sentences, even though sometimes the judge was minded to be lenient. When they sent him to prison, he said he was enjoying 'free hospitality' at 'His Majesty's hotel'.[1] He told prison governors that he looked forward to coming back and always broke the law as soon as he was released.

The man drove Smuts to distraction, publicly burning his identity papers and those of hundreds of other Indians. Every time he spoke hundreds more would follow him. At one point, over 2,000 people defied the Black Act in the Transvaal and went to prison en masse. Despite increasingly severe sentences, harsh prison conditions, confiscation of property and deportations, Gandhi's popularity and power grew. Inspired by the suffragettes, he invited women to join him in his dissent. His wife Kasturba had been among the first to go to prison, leading hundreds of other women to do the same. Gandhi's ambitions grew, as he led more than 2,000 people over forty miles in a protest march. Ultimately, the little Indian lawyer would call a nationwide strike, crippling plantations, factories and mines. The South African government was running out of officers to enforce the law and prison places for those who broke it.

In June 1914, Smuts was forced to repeal his Black Act, and found that even though Gandhi had got the better of him, he had grown fond of his irritating rebel. The two men could never be friends but Gandhi's charming guile had earned grudging respect. Personal

---

[*] In South Africa, people of Indian origin were obliged to carry identity documents at all times.

feelings notwithstanding, Smuts was very glad when he found out the Indian troublemaker was planning to leave South Africa for India. The Raj was welcome to him, and Smuts wondered if the British had any idea what was in store for them. Before setting sail, Gandhi presented Smuts with a leaving present: a pair of sandals made by his own hands. It was a strange gift to give, and it took a lifetime for Smuts to understand its value. Twenty-five years later, Smuts would return the sandals to Gandhi with a note: 'I have worn these sandals for many a summer, even though I may feel that I am not worthy to stand in the shoes of so great a man.'

Gandhi returned to India in 1914 a hero. Princess Sophia's friend Gokhale was particularly excited by his return. He urged Congress to make him their new and unifying leader. The popularity of the extreme wing of 'Lal-Bal-Pal' terrified him and only Gandhi had the power to provide nationalists with an alternative. Gokhale was convinced of this after travelling to South Africa in 1912. He had admired his wily understanding of the law and his non-violent methods of breaking it. Despite Gokhale's enthusiasm, Gandhi seemed reluctant to throw his lot in with the nationalists at first. He explained that he needed time to reacquaint himself with India, a home he had left when just a fresh-faced young man in his early twenties. More than two decades had passed and Gandhi insisted that he needed time to think and learn before he would lift a finger to help.

Gandhi's political epiphany took place on the railway tracks laid by the British. They spread like a spider's web across the country and on them he travelled the length and breadth of India. From Lahore to Madras and Karachi to Calcutta, Gandhi chose the foetid and over-crowded compartments of third class. Sitting with the poorest, he shared food and stories with India's most downtrodden people. From the grimy windows, he saw with his own eyes the rampant poverty among India's peasants and the obscene prosperity of the Raj. It made him angry. It also made him change his mind about joining the nationalists.

When Gandhi returned from his long pilgrimage he was transformed. He now insisted on dressing like a peasant, wearing only the rough white *khadi*, or homespun cotton which was the uniform of the poor. He shaved his head, leaving just a lock of black hair high on the back of his skull, a sign of orthodox Hinduism, which also informed the world of his vow of celibacy or *Brahmacharya*. Gandhi believed that a man's potency was wasted when he spilled his seed, and he wanted to have all his human strength for the fight ahead.

His appearance and odd manner made many feel uncomfortable. Like him, other leading nationalists had studied at the bar in London. They could not understand his desire to look like a beggar rather than a barrister and worried that the British would never take such a man seriously. Gandhi was unperturbed. From the top of his stubbled head, down to the cheap sandals on his feet, when he beat the British he wanted to do so as an Indian. At first he tried quiet diplomacy, writing letters and requesting meetings with government officials. When the British failed to respond he decided to employ other means of persuasion.

In 1917 farmers in the north Indian state of Bihar were being forced by the Raj to grow indigo instead of edible crops. The blue pigment was vital for British textile production but useless to the families producing it. It leached the soil and could fill nobody's belly. Bihar teetered on the brink of famine and to make matters worse, when harvested, the indigo was purchased for a fraction of its value by British buyers, the only people who wanted it. Struggling to make ends meet, the peasant farmers were being crushed both by their forced harvests and by ever-increasing government land taxes. Desperate for help, they sent word for the one man who they thought might understand.

When Gandhi made his way to the rural district of Champeran in April 1917, large parts of Bihar were already gripped by starvation. He had intended to stay only for a couple of days, to get a feel for the farmers' problems and return to the capital to lobby on their behalf, but from the moment his train pulled in on the platform he felt his commitment to the people and the place galvanise.

The excitement his anticipated visit had caused alarmed the authorities. The station platform and surrounding area were filled with Indians bristling with enthusiasm hours before his arrival. They waited in the blistering sun, carrying garlands that wilted in their hands. When the train finally wheezed its way to a halt at the station, the place erupted. Hundreds rushed to greet Gandhi as he descended from the third-class compartment, hands pressed together in humble greeting. The senior policeman, sent to watch his arrival that day, was alarmed. Never had he seen such upheaval in his district and he knew there were too few police stationed at Champeran to subdue the crowds if things got out of hand. He had no choice but to let Gandhi go on his way.

What was meant to be a two-day visit ended up lasting more than six months. During that time Gandhi collected dossiers of evidence against the British and set up an ashram to feed and care for the most destitute. He also led marches against the worst tenant landlords, calling for strikes until the Raj saw sense. Such coordinated, mass civil disobedience forced the British to re-negotiate contracts and end revenue collections until the famine had passed. Gandhi had won his first victory and not one single shot had been fired. It was around this time that the people of Champeran began to refer to Gandhi as *Mahatma*, the great soul, and as *Bapu*, father.

In 1919, Rowlatt's threat to political and personal freedom outraged Gandhi more than anything that had gone before. It was perhaps the Raj's willingness to subvert their own system of jurisprudence that most offended the lawyer in him. Others in his movement were talking of armed struggle but Gandhi begged them to wait. He was sure he could kill Rowlatt without incurring any loss of human life.

His plan came to him in a dream. He would do nothing. More accurately, Gandhi would encourage the whole of India to do nothing with him. Under Rowlatt strikes were illegal, so instead Gandhi called for a day of national prayer on 7 April 1919. Shopkeepers, factory workers, office clerks, teachers, students and civil servants were encouraged to stay at home and spend their time 'meditating and fasting'. It was to be a day of spiritual cleansing.

At first the British did not take Gandhi seriously, but when the day itself dawned, the whole country was blanketed by an unearthly silence. Streets were empty, shops were closed and factory gates remained locked. The railway and telegraph systems snarled up and froze as operators, coal shifters, coolies, engineers and guards stayed away. For twenty-four hours the Raj was thrown into paralysed chaos. For the first time, one man had united the nation in a coordinated act of resistance and shown the British how tenuous their hold on a country of more than 250 million people could be.

A scattering of violent incidents marred Gandhi's wholesale triumph. The most serious of these occurred in Punjab's Amritsar, where youths chose to mark the day with a march that ended in brutal clashes with the police. The Punjab government, terrified of the spread of lawlessness, responded ferociously with baton charges and gunfire, while the courts put the main cities in lockdown. Duleep Singh's old kingdom was simmering once again.

The boiling point came when two of Punjab's leading nationalists, Dr Saif-ud-Din Kitchlew, a Cambridge-educated Muslim lawyer, and Dr Satyapal, a middle-class Hindu who had held the King's commission during the Great War, were invited to meet with the deputy commissioner, Miles Irving, about an edict banning them from speaking in public. The two men were keen to reverse the decision and so entered Irving's home prepared for a legal showdown. To their shock, almost as soon as they set foot inside, they were arrested and spirited away for immediate deportation to Nepal. Their friends, who had been asked to wait on the veranda outside, had no idea why the meeting was taking so long. It was only when a British officer came and told them to leave without Satyapal and Kitchlew that the truth became known.

The streets erupted in fury as news of the betrayal and subsequent arrests spread. Crowds gathered, screaming 'Habeas corpus' at the British soldiers who nervously held them back, trying to stop them from marching on Irving's home. At one particular standoff, on a railway footbridge in the middle of the city, crowds surged forward and soldiers opened fire. A handful of people were shot and killed. Word went out that the British were now firing on unarmed men. Mobs of Indian vigilantes armed with long sticks began to target the *Angrez* (English) wherever they could find them. A terrified bank manager who greeted an angry group with gunshots was subsequently battered to death, his body burnt with his office furniture. Post offices, railway stations and offices were set alight; soldiers responded with more bullets and more killing. Rumours were being fanned along with the flames. It was said a British female doctor had laughed in the desperate faces of Indians bleeding to death from bullet wounds inflicted at the bridge.

Hoping to punish her for her heartlessness, a mob found a missionary school teacher instead and mistaking her for the doctor, dragged the young woman from her bicycle and beat her savagely, leaving her for dead in the dirt. When later the assailants found out she had in fact survived, crawling into a neighbourhood house on her hands and knees, they returned to finish her off. It was only thanks to the courage and quick thinking of a local Indian woman that the missionary survived, hiding in her house with her benefactor's young children, while the mob was directed elsewhere. After two days of lawlessness, when it became clear that nothing could be done to get the nationalist leaders back from Nepal, the rage on the streets seemed to subside into miserable resignation. The British, however, had been left shaken. Sir Michael Francis O'Dwyer, the Lieutenant General in the region, believed a short, sharp shock was needed to remind the people of Punjab who was in charge.

On 13 April 1919, a large public meeting was called by nationalists in Amritsar's Jallianwallah Bagh, to discuss the arrests of Satyapal and Kitchlew and hear from those who might take their place. Since the two men had been non-violent Gandhians, like most of their followers, no trouble was expected. Jallianwallah Bagh was an open area nestled between tall tenement buildings in the heart of the city. It lay just a short distance from the Golden Temple, the most holy shrine of the Sikhs. Then, as now, there was only one entrance to the Bagh. This alleyway is narrow enough to make it difficult for three people to walk through side by side. Emerging from the gloom, visitors are met by seven flat, open acres, disturbed only by the sight of a squat, wide well at its centre.

Organisers had promised a peaceful meeting. All were invited and many drifted in and out during the course of the day. The atmosphere was convivial, lazy even. Though they knew they were breaking the recently enacted Rowlatt laws by meeting in such numbers, the Bagh was still filled with men, women and children and a cheery atmosphere prevailed. Their carefree attitude might have had something to do with Vaisakhi, the most joyous festival in Punjab's calendar, a celebration of the spring harvest. In full swing, every street corner was taken by somebody trying to sell something to the tide of humanity passing by. Men with colourful turbans ladled great dollops of spiced chickpeas onto hot and oily flat breads. Swirls of sugary syrup bubbled in vats of oil. Smells and sounds writhed around each other as snake charmers filled the air with reedy music, and pedlars shouted loudly, jangling their rainbow-coloured glass bangles.

By about half past three, around 15,000 people had crammed into the gardens. Some listened to the speeches, others stretched out and dozed; many read newspapers or simply had picnics with their loved ones. The open space made a pleasant change from the hectic streets outside. While they lazed, elsewhere in the city a column of men led by Amritsar's martial law commander, Brigadier Reginald Dyer, was in a state of high alert. By 3.40 he was marching 150 men from the Gurkha regiment towards the Bagh. Two armoured cars mounted with heavy machine guns brought up the rear.

At the street entrance to the gardens, Dyer ordered his men to drive the vehicles into the Bagh, but the alley was too narrow. Instead, rifles on their shoulders, the soldiers marched through in single file. Once through to the Bagh, Dyer ordered his men to quick-march into position, as far as they could stretch around the perimeter. People in the gardens looked on at the sudden activity in confusion. Expecting an imminent order to disperse, some started to pack up their picnic things. Those closest to the exit even tried to leave, but soldiers had blocked the only way out.

Suddenly and without any warning, Dyer commanded his men to open fire on the thickest parts of the crowd. Gurkhas swivelled to follow swarms of terrified, screaming Indians as they ran for cover that did not exist. Women wailed for their children, and bodies began to pile up as families tried to shield one another from the hail of bullets. The firing lasted for between six and ten minutes; in all the soldiers fired over 1,500 rounds of ammunition, killing or wounding over 1,500 people.[2] If he had been able to get them through to the gardens, Dyer later confirmed, he would have turned his machine guns on the unarmed civilians too.

When the ringing silence eventually descended, the smell of cordite hung heavy over the Bagh like an acrid, choking veil. Curfew had already been called in the city, and nobody was allowed to remove bodies, or take the wounded for medical attention. People stayed where they fell, and remained there all night. Those who survived cradled the dying, comforting them as best they could, as the brown dust of Jallianwallah Bagh turned black with blood in the first shadows of the long night ahead.

At dawn the sound of wailing filled the city and spread throughout Punjab like a torrent of pain. One hundred and twenty bodies were retrieved from the well alone. Estimates of fatalities have been hotly disputed. An official British investigation at the time put the figure at 379, but Indians insist that the figure is closer to a thousand dead. Dyer was unrepentant and at a formal enquiry following the massacre insisted that he had 'done a jolly good thing'. The Lieutenant General of the Punjab also endorsed Dyer's actions that day, describing them as 'quite correct' under the circumstances.

While the authorities were attempting to teach the people of the Punjab a lesson, others were attempting to do the same to Sophia and her family. India had changed during the war years and a new breed of men had become the icons of the country. Nationalists took the places on pedestals vacated by rajahs and nawabs; they lived among the common people, spoke like them, and in Gandhi's case, even dressed and ate like them.

A telegram from the Viceroy to the Secretary of State of India in April 1919 reveals the official thinking about the Duleep Singh family at this time: 'In Punjab Dhuleep Singh family is almost forgotten and generous treatment need not therefore be advocated on general political grounds. General policy is to make substantial reduction in political pensions on successions.'[3] The idea of

throwing Sophia out of Hampton Court had already been considered and dismissed, but she and the rest of the family could be
financially squeezed instead.

Frederick, the only male heir left in the Duleep Singh line, would
continue to receive the stipend promised to him after his father's
death; Victor's widow, however, saw her income slashed to the bone.
Anne wrote to the India Office numerous times after her husband's
death, begging the bureaucrats to show some understanding: she was
sinking under tax demands and her late husband's gambling debts,
but they refused to back down.

Duleep's second wife, Ada, who had once been the toast of
Monte Carlo, was in an even more parlous state. In 1914 she had
volunteered for the French Red Cross at Limoges and as part of
the ambulance corps had tended to soldiers in the dressing stations
behind the lines at Verdun, the longest and bloodiest battle of the
war. Ada returned to London in 1919, never wanting to see France
again. With debts of over £17,000 and nowhere to call home, she
was desperate.[4] Freddie showed his stepmother great kindness,
giving her money, sometimes anonymously, and the promise of a
room at his home. However, Ada wanted independence, and
showing the same pragmatic determination as the girl who had
clawed her way out of Lambeth, she offered the India Office a
deal. If they helped her get a small house, and perhaps a hat shop
of her own, she would support herself and would not bother them
for funds again.

Ada's daughter Pauline was also in financial trouble. Her
husband had been killed among the clouds of poison gas at the
battle of Loos in September 1915, and she had been left bereft.[5]
Pauline once again drifted towards Sophia for comfort and became
a frequent guest at both her home and Freddie's. Although Sophia
was glad to help her half-sister, the truth was, she was not faring
too well herself.

At the end of the war, as the nation rejoiced and even though she
had ensured Catherine's safe passage out of Germany, Sophia was
slipping into melancholia again. She needed companionship as well
as something useful to do. Catherine was now back in Germany

nursing Lina. The suffragettes only met occasionally and tales of their past triumphs did little to sustain her. From time to time the princess would invite Indian soldiers, barracked at Hampton Court, into her home, but the visits were merely temporary and fleeting diversions;[6] the Indian soldiers soon went home to their own families, leaving Sophia to brood on her lack of one.

Bamba was no help at all. She wrote less frequently and refused to discuss a return to England. As well as the volatile political situation in Punjab, which absorbed her completely, Bamba had another reason to stay. During the war, when Sophia was busy nursing soldiers in Brighton, Bamba had got married.[7]

Her husband, Lieutenant Colonel David Waters Sutherland, was a professor of pathology at Lahore Medical College and a principal at the city's prestigious King Edward College. Having served in the Indian Army, Sutherland had risen through the ranks to hold the position of Honorary Surgeon to the Viceroy of India.[8] In the midst of the Great War, in 1915, and without warning, Bamba sent telegrams to her family letting them know she should now be addressed as 'Princess Bamba Sutherland'. It was a typically dramatic and unpredictable announcement.

The family was stunned, and no one more so than Sophia who had met Sutherland briefly in 1907. He had made so little impression on her then that she barely mentioned him in her diary. Everyone could see he had next to nothing in common with their sister, except perhaps a shared love of medicine, and even that common ground was problematic. Sutherland's success was a constant reminder of Bamba's failure in the field. As those close to her knew, the princess did not handle such reminders well. The most glaring obstacle to the marriage's credibility was the fact that David was white. Bamba had only ever expressed a romantic attraction to Indian men and her disdain for English people made her wedding all the more implausible. The wedding ceremony, which nobody had been able to attend, had been perfunctory rather than joyous, not that Bamba seemed to mind. Her attitude added fuel to speculation that the relationship with Sutherland was less to do with love than money. According to the terms of their inheritance, both Catherine and Bamba stood to gain dowries of £10,000 upon their marriages.

Real or not, her sister's marriage threw Sophia's own loneliness into even sharper focus. Now in her forties, she rattled about the large house at Hampton Court without anyone to share her life. Her beloved Joe was long dead and no other dog would ever replace him in the princess's affections. There were no suitors to divert her, and friends were all busy rebuilding their own lives after the war. To add to her misery, the bills were mounting and she was struggling to make ends meet. The only brief respite came in August 1919, when Sophia had the opportunity to do one final, simultaneous service for the suffragettes and for India.

In response to increasing unrest, the Secretary of State for India, Edwin Montagu and his Viceroy, Lord Chelmsford, decided to frame a new Act of Parliament. They proposed a dual form of governance, or 'dyarchy', to appease the nationalists. It would allow around ten per cent of Indian men to vote for a newly created stratum of local government. Indian politicians could stand for these provincial bodies and have a say in issues such as health, education, sanitation and agriculture. However the Viceroy, and by extension the British, would still wield ultimate power in the important matters of state, such as policing, taxation, the military, foreign affairs and trade.

As the Government of India Bill started its journey through the House of Commons, groups were invited to give evidence before a Parliamentary Joint Select Committee. One of the first to book passage to London was the Women's Indian Association. The association had lobbied for equal rights since its creation two years before and was outraged that women had been entirely left out of the proposed new democratisation. Three were chosen to represent the interests of around 125 million Indian women as the men in Westminster shaped their law.

One of them was Annie Besant, who at seventy-two had lost none of her vigour or conviction. She had been elected President of the Indian National Congress in 1917, and had become close to Gandhi, although they often clashed over his methods. Annie was an ardent constitutionalist, and disliked his 'clever' circumvention of the law. Their difference in opinion did not stop Annie from devoting her whole life to his cause of Indian Home Rule. She spoke at rallies, produced pamphlets and regularly wrote articles in her Theosophist magazines savaging the Raj. Just weeks before she set sail for London, Annie had been fighting the Madras government in the courts over its decision to seize her printing presses.

By Annie's side was Sarojini Naidu, who at forty was already regarded as a national treasure in India. Commonly known as Bharatya Kokila ('The Nightingale of India'), her hugely popular poetry spoke of love and longing. Her politics in contrast was blistering and uncompromising. Sarojini was one of the youngest and brightest stars in the Congress movement, able to hold huge crowds in the palm of her hand. She had been a child prodigy, winning a place at university at the age of twelve. At sixteen, she had won scholarships to study first at King's College, London, and later at Girton College, Cambridge, where she attended lectures and published volumes of poetry at the same time.

Sarojini returned to India just as Bengal was being ripped apart by Curzon's partition. She joined the nationalists and rose through the ranks at lightning speed. Not only was she a favourite disciple of Gandhi and Rabindranath Tagore, the Nobel laureate, she also became a close friend of an up-and-coming Congress politician, Jawaharlal Nehru. Her looks and personality were at odds with her formidable reputation. Girlish and giggly, Sarojini had a gift for cheekiness which charmed when it could easily have offended. While others genuflected before Gandhi, she teased him, poking fun at his prominent ears, and later would playfully call him her 'Mickey Mouse'. The two would be devoted to one another all of their lives.

Herabai Tata had neither the fame of Sarojini Naidu nor the reputation of Annie Besant; however as honorary secretary of the Women's Indian Association in Bombay, she was one of the most powerful people in India's women's movement. She came from a family of wealthy industrialists, and was, thanks to Sophia Duleep

Singh, the only one of the three who would proudly describe herself as a suffragette.

Born in 1879, Herabai had been married off at sixteen, became pregnant immediately and had her first child a year later. It was not until Herabai met Sophia, on holiday in Kashmir in 1911, that she became political. Her daughter, Mithun Lam, who was just thirteen at the time, recalled the women's first meeting. At first it was something Sophia was wearing that piqued her interest: 'She always wore a small green, white and yellow badge with "Votes for Women" inscribed on it. Naturally, my mother's attention was drawn to it, and as we got friendly, she informed us that she was a member of the Women's League for Peace and Freedom . . . Thus her talks with Princess Sophie [sic] and the literature she sent immediately aroused my mother's interest.'9 This was the year that Sophia had thrown herself at the prime minister's car as it exited Downing Street, spoiled her census form and appeared in court charged with the non-payment of taxes. With her evangelical zeal, the princess managed to cast a spell on them both. After meeting her, Herabai and Mithun devoted their lives to getting Indian women the vote.

In 1919 the Government of India Act consultation was not going well. As Sarojini Naidu wrote to Gandhi late one night from her hotel room, 'There is not much to report except that the evidence before the Joint Committee has begun and all our deputation will be called to give their evidence after the official witnesses have finished . . . Several attempts have been made to find common ground for all the deputations, but in vain so far.'10

Sarojini was not the only one feeling dispirited. Many delegations had come to believe that the British were going to do what they wanted, no matter what Indians felt. She wrote: 'I see a woeful and even wilful ignorance and indifference about India in England – it is so precious to us, so rotten and valueless a thing to them, except as enriching their coffers.'11

In a final push, the Women's Indian Association decided to bolster its argument and its ranks. When the day finally arrived to present evidence, a face familiar to the British press was sitting in the midst of their delegation. Sophia was back among the troublemakers. The reporter for the *Observer* noted archly: 'Facing Mr Montagu, who in spite of the odds against him, is bent upon putting India upon the path of responsible self-government, sat in a long row, Mrs Naidu, the Princess Sophia A. Duleep Singh, Mrs Annie Besant, Mrs P. L. Roy, Mrs Kotwal, Mrs N. C. Sen, Mrs B. Bhola Naath and Mrs Dube.'[12]

The women argued their case passionately, warning the British government that if they made no provision for women's votes, they would be introducing gender inequality to India deliberately and catastrophically. Before the Raj, all had been equally disenfranchised. Now that a system of democracy was being mooted, it made no sense to leave women out. The Secretary of State listened patiently but refused to change his bill. He would leave it to the provincial assemblies to decide if they wanted to give women the vote. Two years later, only some of them took up the opportunity. The decision would have felt like failure for the already downhearted Princess Sophia.

In March 1920, on the same heavy-gauge blue notepaper upon which she had once bullied Winston Churchill, Sophia wrote an uncharacteristically humble letter to the Secretary of State for India. She begged him for financial help: 'Dear Mr Montagu, the great rise in prices, taxes and rates, and the ever increasing difficulty of making two ends meet, leave me no choice but to write to you to ask for assistance.'[13]

The rooms at Faraday could no longer be heated, and despite her frugality, bills were still threatening to engulf her. Montagu's response was tepid. Sophia was asked to provide proof of hardship and to collect details of all her bank accounts and documents of her spending. It was a humiliating business and ultimately did her only a small amount of good. Finally accepting her argument that the cost of living had gone up thanks to inflation, just under £20 was added to her annual allowance. Three years later, that amount and more would be deducted from her income. When the cuts were made again in 1923, the princess wrote again to the India Office: 'I have received your letter of October 18 with regard to the reduction of the allowance, from £200 – £130.68, a year. As it was not sufficiently adequate in the first place to cover expenses, it will be much less so when reduced . . . I am again obliged to use capital, which will further reduce my income.'[14]

No more money was granted to the princess. The Duleep Singhs were going to be allowed to fade from history, and the comfort in which they did so made little difference to the government. Seeing his sister in such financial straits, Freddie decided to step in, believing he could do something more lasting for his 'Saff' than just pay the odd bill when things became too much. He began to look for somebody sharp and dependable who could manage Sophia's household on its diminishing budget. Margaret Mayes had been with the family since Elveden; she was loyal, dependable, almost maternal to the princesses. Sophia had felt lost when age rendered her too frail to work at Faraday House any more. Replacements came and went, but they were unable to attain the high standards set by Mrs Mayes.

Through his contacts at his club, White's, Freddie had come to hear of a capable young woman working for the Dean of St Paul's and duly poached Janet Ivy Bowden for his sister.[15] At twenty-two 'Bosie' became Faraday's housekeeper, even though she was younger than some of the maids already working there. She had a broad open face and a strong square jaw which she stuck out challengingly when she spoke. At just over five foot, she was 'solid and strong'.[16] The four floors of Faraday House would be no problem for her, and from the moment she took up the position, and despite her youth, Bosie ruled the house 'like a Tatar'.[17] The younger servants feared her but also were agog at the way she seemed able to stand up to their mistress.

In later life, Sophia's depressions could make her cruel. She lashed out at staff in her misery and most knew better than to cross her when 'she was in one of her moods'.[18] Bosie would have none of it and, to the gasps of those around her, would tell the princess to 'stop pouting'.[19] Such insolence would have had most women in her position fired immediately, but somehow it managed to snap Sophia temporarily out of her malaise. Not only did she keep Bosie on, but she pulled her closer into her confidence than any other servant who had gone before or would come after.

Despite the breath of fresh air her new housekeeper had brought to the house, Sophia continued at her lowest ebb for years. As always, when things looked bleakest, she turned to her sisters for solace. Bamba, who had been so little help of late, was the first one to act. She told her sister to pack her bags and come to Lahore immediately. Much to the irritation of the India Office, Sophia did not even request permission, merely informing them of the date of her travel after buying a ticket. As she prepared her escape, Sophia wrote letters to the staff explaining why only a few of them would be kept on for the months she intended to be away. It was then that Sophia found out that Bosie had quite a temper herself.

When she learned of her mistress's plans – and even though she had barely been working at the house a year – Bosie flew into an uncontrollable fit of angry crying. She ran into the bathroom, slammed the door and refused to come out. Attracted by the howling, servants came and giggled by the door, but it took Sophia herself to get the housekeeper to open up. 'What the devil is wrong with you?' she asked incredulously.

'Well I just think it's not fair!' cried Bosie. 'It's just not fair. I want to go to India too! I've always wanted to go . . . I want to see an elephant!' As the sobs rained down on the princess, Sophia seemed amused. Turning on her heel, in the quietest of voices, she said: 'Oh my goodness me. So you shall then.' Despite all her financial worries, Sophia bought a second ticket for the voyage to India.

When she arrived in Lahore, Bamba took one look at her sister and realised that the usual round of social engagements, culinary and musical distractions would not be enough for Sophia. Extreme measures would be needed to stop the downward spiral. Even though Bamba could be self-obsessed and insensitive, she understood her little sister, now aged forty-eight, better than anyone in the world. In an effort to jolt her out of her melancholy, Bamba arranged a pilgrimage to Nasik in Maharashtra. It was a place neither of them had visited before, but on the banks of the Godavari, Bamba felt her sister might find peace.

The two princesses arrived with their arms filled with flowers. This was the place where their grandmother, Jindan, had been cremated in 1864. The Maharajah Duleep Singh had watched her body burn on a *ghat* by the water's edge, and scattered most of her ashes over the ripples. Just a handful of the light grey dust was kept from the current and placed in an urn. Duleep paid for the construction of a small tomb on the banks of the Godavari where he placed Jindan's remains. It was to be a place of pilgrimage for him whenever he next visited India. He did not know then that he would never see the place again.

The thought of Jindan's eternal exile from Punjab had always troubled the daughters of Duleep Singh. Her isolation on the banks of the river, far away from home, touched the great pain of Sophia's own loneliness. Sensing the symbolism of the act, Bamba decided it was time to bring Rani Jindan home. Their grandfather's ashes were interred in the grand mausoleum in the heart of Lahore, surrounded by the remains of other wives and servants. The sisters decided Jindan too should rest in such a place. Before they removed her, prayers had to be said. A distinguished-looking Sikh stood on the banks of the river, his back to the princesses, his hands pressed together in prayer. With eyes fixed on a distant point in the water, his voice rose and fell with the swell. Sophia listened to the words, unable to understand what they meant but knowing that Harbans Singh[20] was singing songs of remembrance for her family. He asked God to cherish Jindan's spirit and those of her descendants. He also praised the infinite wisdom and love of the gurus, and praised their deeds in life, and their nobility in death.

Harbans Singh was more than a link between Sophia and the Sikhism of her family. His grandfather had been General Shyam Singh Attariwala,[21] a legendary soldier in the old Sikh Kingdom. Attariwala had led Sikh warriors into Afghanistan, capturing large tracts of land in the name of Maharajah Ranjit Singh in the 1830s. He had died fighting the British in Jindan's name at the battle of Sobaron in 1846. To have the loyal warrior's descendant reading prayers for her family revived Sophia. By the water's edge she felt the strength flow back into her veins.

After bringing Jindan back to Punjab, Sophia resolved to travel across the old Sikh kingdom one last time. She would do so in a way that would have made her grandmother proud. The British had once again impressed upon the princesses the need for a low profile. They must not flaunt their family name, they must not excite crowds. This time around, however, the injunctions meant nothing to them. In the febrile atmosphere of post-massacre Punjab, word of their presence spread quickly, and crowds of excited people gathered wherever they went. Disobeying all government directives, for the second time in her life Sophia put aside her European travelling clothes and donned the traditional Indian costume she had for so long avoided; she wore a maroon sari made of thin georgette, fringed with gold.[22] She wanted to look like the Indian princess her people wanted her to be.

In heavily embroidered fabric, dripping expensive jewels, she and her sister were quickly surrounded by followers.[23] Such was the excitement they stirred in Lahore that local police were called out in force. At first the officers were careful to keep their distance, but then the princesses refused to take a carriage to the Shalimar Gardens, choosing to walk instead. With something resembling a procession in tow, every step they took attracted more people to their entourage. The fine material of Sophia's sari fluttered around her slender frame as she walked proudly through the press of people. Elder Sikh men wept openly before the sisters: 'We are with you,' they sobbed; 'We will give you the world.'[24] A cry went up from the crowd: 'Behold the daughters of Maharajah Duleep Singh!' Others added to the noise: 'Our Princesses are here!'[25] As Bamba and Sophia pressed forward, the clamour and excitement grew. It was only a matter of time before the situation reached a tipping point. Once Sophia and Bamba were safely in the gardens, uniformed men ordered the crowds to disperse. Those who refused were pushed back by the swing of *lathis*.[26]

Bosie, Sophia's housekeeper, was enthralled by India and her mistress's place in it. Dazzled by everything she saw, including the elephants, she could not help but notice that they were being followed. Wherever they went, British officers, often in civilian clothes, were close behind. It was clear they were there to 'keep an eye on them'.[27] Bosie resented the intrusion every bit as much as Sophia and started to form a very different opinion of the Raj. Like all British youngsters, she had been raised in the thrall of Empire, and had believed India to be a place where natives and their masters existed happily together in palaces filled with gold. The reality shocked her.

The princesses would often give their spies the slip by 'dumping'[28] Bosie at the homes of aristocratic Indians to throw them off the trail. The housekeeper was left to muddle through, sometimes for weeks on end, with the other women in the *zenanas*, most of whom lived in purdah, far from the public gaze. They did not speak the same language, nor could she understand many of their ways, but Bosie adored her time there. She learned how to keep ants off the tables by smearing the legs of furniture in oil, and busied herself in the kitchens, learning curry recipes to take back to Faraday House.[29]

After Lahore, Bosie accompanied the sisters to Amritsar, scene of Brigadier Dyer's massacre. Even though five years had passed since the event, the place was still a tinderbox. The British could not afford to spark further controversy by arresting the heirs of Ranjit Singh; nonetheless Sophia and Bamba were watched very closely as they moved about the scarred city.

In April, after an uneasy few weeks, Bamba and Sophia finally left Punjab for the foothills of Kashmir. Among the icy rivers, crystal lakes and craggy hills of Srinagar, in the gentle rain of a Kashmir spring, Sophia found peace for the first time in years. She wrote letters to friends and family again, and found herself taking an interest in all that went on around her. In the breeze coming in from the Kashmiri waters, Sophia felt better than she had in years. Meanwhile, red-hot waves of hatred flowed over the rest of India.

The communal violence which would ultimately turn Sophia's haven into a war zone was beginning to take hold of the country. In 1923 temples and mosques were burning all over India, as gangs of Sikhs and Hindus fought street battles against gangs of Muslims.

Gandhi's dreams of a united nation were threatened partly because of his own success. For the first time since the British took over the country, the Raj no longer looked invincible. Indians allowed themselves to discuss what would happen after the British left. It was not an easy conversation.

Muslims feared for their place in 'New India'. Greatly outnumbered by Hindus and Sikhs, some believed that they would merely be swapping one type of subjugation for another. Muslim leaders sought assurances that their voting-blocks would be given 'electoral weightage', ensuring parity with the majority faith groups. Hindu leaders accused them of divisiveness and disloyalty. The verbal animosity translated quickly into violence.

To outsiders, the cause of rioting was often perplexing and trivial. Gangs of Hindu and Sikh youths would take noisy brass bands outside mosques and play loudly to disrupt prayers. Muslims would retaliate by throwing stones from the minarets and in seconds the street would be strewn with bodies. During Eid, a sacred festival in the Muslim calendar, some Muslims chose to sacrifice cows instead of goats; since cows were regarded as sacred to the Hindus, the act sparked widespread rioting in the capital.[30] When at last the fighting stopped, sixteen Hindus and one Muslim had been killed, and over a hundred people had been hospitalised of each religion respectively. News of communal violence became almost a daily staple of the newspapers. Congress leaders begged for calm, blaming British policies of 'divide and rule' for the chaos. Gandhi despaired, exclaiming, 'Surely there are sane Hindus and sane Mussalmans enough.'[31]

The worst episode of communal violence took place in Kohat, in the North West Frontier, between 9 and 11 September 1924. There, in the mountainous region where India and Afghanistan rise up to embrace, Muslims slaughtered over a hundred Hindus and Sikhs. The attacks were reprisals for an Arya Samaj pamphlet, 'Rangeela Rasool', which, it was said, had insulted their prophet Mohammed. The subsequent 'ethnic cleansing' that took place shook the Indian National Congress to its core. Hindus and Sikhs fled the region for fear of further violence; reprisals against Muslims elsewhere in the country were vicious.

Gandhi decided on drastic action. He would use the weapon of the suffragettes against his own people. He would go on hunger strike.

While staying at the Delhi house of his great friend, the Muslim leader Mohammed Ali, Gandhi stopped eating on 17 September 1924. He let it be known that he would starve himself to death unless Hindus and Muslims ceased all acts of communal violence. His edict was drowned out by the violence spreading through the country. By the second week of his hunger strike, Gandhi's health was beginning to deteriorate at pace. Doctors were warning of dire consequences if he did not stop immediately. Leaders of Congress gathered by his bedside, and Nehru was said to have wept when he saw Gandhi's physical condition.

Slowly, reports of his ill health began to reach all corners of India. Candlelit vigils were held outside the house where he lay, while visitors left his bedside, ashen-faced with worry. The British had always warned that a withdrawal of their forces would mean communal violence in the country. They appeared to be being proved right, and that made the Indian National Congress feel desperate. Gandhi was their last hope, but he seemed to be fading fast.

Despite the pleas of those who loved him, Gandhi said he would continue his fast until he could be shown a newspaper without a single headline of communal violence inside. With his major organs on the verge of failing, after twenty-one days someone was able finally to show him the paper he was waiting for. All rioting had stopped as India prayed for him in temples, mosques and gurdwaras. Gandhi asked for some orange juice and finally broke his fast. The peace would not last long.

Sophia and Bosie returned to England in early 1925, and though nothing much had changed the princess seemed better able to cope with life. Resigned to her Faraday House existence, she accepted the life of a spinster. She even began to enjoy herself again, visiting long-neglected friends and opening her doors to visitors once more. With money as tight as it was, Sophia no longer had the option of buying new gowns and dresses but luckily, Bosie was an expert seamstress, and the two would stay up late into the night, leafing through fashion magazines and cutting up old dresses in order to cobble them into imitations of the latest Parisian designs.

Sophia also spent her time seeing more of Pauline and her brother Frederick. He now lived at Blo Norton Hall, a sixteenth-century moated house near Thetford. His new home brought the family much-needed joy. It seemed to exist in a bubble, just like Freddie himself, untouched by time, politics or reality. The handsome, timbered house was filled with his collection of Jacobean art and old reclaimed stained glass split the light into rainbows on the heavy wooden furniture. Freddie pottered around the vast gardens and planted his groves with trees. Electricity and the telephone were banished from the main house, but the prince relented for the sake of his sisters, furnishing two of the nearby coach-houses with all modern amenities for their comfort. Sophia found herself idling away for weeks there, and such was the peace at Blo Norton that even Catherine could be lured from Germany for long visits.

Dependable, conservative and much loved by all his friends, time and circumstances changed, but Freddie never seemed to. The past had never haunted him and the prince rarely bore anyone ill will. Unlike his little sister, he never caused the Palace a headache and even went on hunting parties with King George V. Not a whiff of scandal had ever given his influential friends cause to abandon him and dukes and earls, as well as the local inhabitants, loved him. Freddie loved them back, giving generously of his time and money. He donated large sums to establish a museum in Thetford,[32] which he filled with relics of British history and with family memorabilia. He wanted everyone to enjoy his treasures.

With none of the airs and graces of his siblings, Freddie had become part of the fabric of local life. He was a stalwart of the local choir, godfather to many children, and was regularly seen bustling about his business in the village of Blo Norton. Freddie was particularly precious to Sophia because he alone had never judged her. Even though her politics had been an anathema to his Primrose League sensibilities, he had loved her without condition or criticism. His door had always been open.

In the summer of 1926, Britain was gripped by a general strike during which more than 1.5 million workers stopped work for ten days in a dispute over miners' pay. Chaos and rage gripped the nation as strikers closed pits and protested at the threat to their livelihoods. The government wished to reduce miners' pay by thirteen per cent while at the same time increasing their shifts. Bus and train drivers downed tools in sympathy and as a result the transport network was crippled along with the pits. Gas and electricity supplies were at risk as workers marched out of their plants too. The nation was convulsed by panic.

Up and down the country, police and strikers were clashing violently while volunteers who attempted to keep the system moving often found themselves beaten up as 'blacklegs'. The government in response deployed tanks on civilian streets and even sent a warship to Newcastle, where strikers had tipped the iconic train, the *Flying Scotsman*, off its tracks. The state of his beloved country would have caused Freddie great misery; however he was, by this time, too ill to care.

Freddie's health had been fragile for months, a fact he had hidden from friends and family. The prince attended all his usual meetings and kept up with all his commitments despite the toll it was taking on him physically. In mid-May, he finally heeded his doctor's advice and took to his bed. The rest seemed to do him little good, and he was finally forced to ask for help. When his sisters found out about his illness, they each dropped what they were doing and rushed to be with him. Sophia was first by his side as Bamba had to make the long voyage back from India, and Catherine from Germany. Even Pauline put aside her feelings about Bamba and came to sit by Freddie's bed. The only sister who was missing was Irene.

On Thursday 12 August, with his sisters around him, Freddie suffered a massive heart attack.[33] The newspapers reported that the 'Last Prince of Lahore' was on his deathbed.[34] Letters and telegrams poured in, offering help and hopes of a swift recovery. Even King George V sent a telegram to Norfolk enquiring after Freddie's health.[35] For three long days the sisters did their best to make him comfortable,[36] but on a sunny Sunday afternoon at 2.30, with the light streaming through the old and draughty windows, Freddie died. At fifty-eight, he had outlived his father by three years.

The prince's funeral was everything the Maharajah's was not. There was genuine and heartfelt grief at Freddie's passing. Behind St Andrew's church in Blo Norton, Sophia, Bamba, Catherine and Pauline stood in a close huddle by the far western wall of the cemetery. They watched in silence as well-wishers thronged to the graveside. At Duleep Singh's funeral, the aristocracy had sent flowers and proxies; for Freddie, dukes, duchesses and lords attended in person, including the Duke of Grafton, Lord Dawson of Penn, Lord Henniker and the Countess of Albemarle.[37] Floral tributes overran the little church from groups as diverse as London's Carlton Club to the famers from the local villages.

He had never once set foot in India, but as the last male lineal descendant of Ranjit Singh, the legacy of the Sikh kingdom was buried with Frederick Duleep Singh that day. The grave was made up of 400-year-old bricks which he himself had bought from old demolished houses just for the occasion of his burial.[38] Even in death, Freddie seemed reluctant to let the modern world touch him. To the sound of the hymn 'The Strife is Over', earth was piled high upon his grave.

At the time of Freddie's funeral, Irene Duleep Singh, who had been conspicuous by her absence, was convinced she was losing her mind. In the view of many of those closest to her, she had been teetering on the edge for many years. Prone to serious mood swings all her life, the end of her marriage to the Frenchman Pierre Villemant, after only a few years, seemed to have tipped her into mania. Three years before, she had suffered a similar crisis, gripped by anxiety attacks and relentless depression. Then, Irene had admitted herself to a nursing home where doctors diagnosed her with 'neurasthenia',[39] a condition which, according to the celebrated psychiatrist Sigmund Freud, was the result of unfulfilled sexual stimulation or 'non-completed coitus'.[40] The cure for neurasthenia was commonly electroshock therapy.

'Cured', Irene moved back to her Parisian apartment on the Avenue Hoche. It was an elegant and expensive street and for a while

Irene seemed happy enough. She took up painting, saw friends and dined out; however the return to France was secretly gnawing away at her. Estranged from her family yet close to all the places which reminded her of her miserable childhood, she began to lose touch with reality. After barely a year, Irene climbed to the top of her building and threw herself from the window.[41] The fall broke her body, but she failed to kill herself. The story of the suicidal Indian princess appeared in French newspapers and the subsequent attention did little to calm Irene's nerves. In great physical and mental torment she withdrew from the world entirely, and lived like a recluse. Not even her sister Pauline could break through.

Less than two months after Freddie's funeral, Sophia received a devastating telegram from France. On 8 October 1926, a fisherman had dragged a woman's body out of the waters off the Riviera. She was wearing expensive clothes and was believed to be in her mid-thirties. Irene had left a note on a nearby rock, explaining who she was, and what she had done.[42] In the hours before she walked into the water, Irene had also written to her lawyer and friend Lancelot Smith. Her letter to him contained a more detailed account of what led her to take such irrevocable action: 'Nobody will ever hear of me again, as I am going to commit suicide this afternoon . . . I am homeless . . . my nerves have prevented me continuing my studies, but I have grasped my object . . . I have been staying a week at Monte Carlo but here I only play the fool and lose my pocket-money . . . Please forgive me for troubling you in such troublesome times, but it is the last time.'[43]

Somehow *The Times* got hold of the letter and soon everyone came to know of Irene's agony. In the same letter, Irene had asked Lancelot to change the terms of her will. She wanted to leave all that she possessed (an estate worth around £30,000) to Dr Barnardo's Home for Poor and Unwanted Children. The message to her family was clear. She had been unloved and unwanted too.

Irene, who had never had children, achieved a healthy settlement after the end of her marriage. Her sister had been the beneficiary of the estate until Irene changed her mind on the last day of her life. Pauline immediately contested the new will, insisting that her suicidal sister was clearly of unsound mind when she decided to give all her money to charity. Dr Barnardo's vowed to fight back.

Though the affair was distasteful, most people understood why Pauline was taking the charity to court. Nobody however could understand why Bamba decided to contest the will too. Claiming to be the true beneficiary of Irene's estate, she did so with such venom that for the first time in her life, Sophia was forced to distance herself from her sister in shame. In an effort to nullify both her wills, Bamba set out to annihilate Irene's character. If she could prevent Pauline getting her hands on the money, Bamba believed the India Office would split the funds among all of Duleep Singh's surviving heirs equally. Sophia and Catherine quickly ruled themselves out of her suit,[44] leaving Bamba to fight on her own and for herself. She hired one of the most feared barristers in London to tear her dead sister's reputation apart. Sir Ellis Hume-Williams was a King's Counsel, a baronet and a Conservative politician and he tried to convince the court that Irene had been insane for years. Citing epileptic fits which dated back as far as 1915, he revealed Irene's private medical records. Before the judge and reporters he showed that the princess had suffered from delusions since her youth. She had believed herself to be the mother of two babies who had been taken away and hidden by enemies. Sometimes, Irene believed that black blood ran in her veins,[45] and would scratch to get it out. She believed she might be turning into a wild animal, and thrashed on the ground attempting to knock out her evil spirits.[46] When in the throes of her worst manias, she had starved herself, torn out her fingernails and pulled out her hair. The press devoured every sordid detail, dragging the Duleep Singh family before the public gaze again. It was all too much for Sophia, who stayed away from court and refused to give evidence. Bamba, alone at the back of the court, was watched only by Pauline, whose hatred knew no bounds.

After hearing days of vicious testimony and rebuttal, Mr Justice Hill pronounced in favour of Princess Pauline. Not only would she get all of Irene's money, but Bamba would have to pay her court costs on top of those she had incurred for herself.[47] The sum, around £3,600, would never be paid, despite Pauline's repeated attempts to recover the money.[48] She never spoke to Bamba again except through her solicitor, and her relationship with Sophia suffered too as a result of the court case. With Freddie gone, there were no neutral places for them to meet any more and an unbridgeable gulf opened up between the half-sisters. The only occasion when Pauline and Sophia would spend any length of time together again was at Ada's funeral some years later. Neither Catherine nor Bamba would attend. Pauline gave up on her family. She also found herself cutting all ties to England and moved to France. She was never to be heard from again.

# A Solemn Promise

Though the 1920s were marked by sadness and loss for Sophia, there were flashes of joy. The brightest came in February 1928 when 'The Representation of the People (Equal Franchise) Bill' began to make its way through Parliament. Ten years earlier, on 6 February 1918, the first major piece of voting reform had received Royal Assent. It gave women over thirty the parliamentary vote, as long as they were householders. The wives of householders could also cast their ballots, as could those paying rent of not less than £5 per year and university graduates.

The celebrations then had been muted, with suffragette leaders acknowledging that despite their best efforts, only middle-class women would benefit from the change. Years of post-war Depression had pushed the matter to the bottom of all political party agendas, but in 1928, the question of equal suffrage was once again brought before the Houses of Parliament. The legislation being proposed would at last give Sophia and her friends what they had always wanted: equality with men before the ballot box. Even before the bill had passed its second reading there was a real feeling of optimism among the old suffragettes. The Representation of the People (Equal Franchise) Bill 1928 might actually make it this time.

During the two months of debate that followed the bill's introduction, speeches in both houses were often passionate and raw. Some

MPs and members of the House of Lords remained bitterly opposed to the idea of parity; however it was clear that the majority were behind the bill. The Earl of Lytton summed up the feelings of many when he stood before the House of Lords during the second reading on 22 May 1928 and said:

> In listening to the debate that has taken place yesterday and to-day, my mind went back to those days before the War when this subject was so acutely controversial, and to the women who fought the battle for their rights in those far-off and difficult days, some of whom did not live to see the fruits of their labours. I feel that by passing this Bill to-day we are, as it were, placing a wreath on the tomb of those early champions. At least we shall, by passing the Bill, be placing a crown of victory and a seal of finality upon their efforts.[1]

The matter was a particularly charged one for the earl, for it had been his own sister who had carved her 'V' for the vote into her flesh nineteen years before.

Suddenly all caveats were swept away. The years of sacrifice, courage, law-breaking and sheer bloody-mindedness by the suffragettes were about to be rewarded, but neither of the people who had fought so hard over the issue would live to witness the occasion. Both Emmeline Pankhurst and her nemesis Herbert Henry Asquith died in 1928, weeks before the law received Royal Assent on 2 July.[*]

Having suffered a series of strokes, Asquith had become severely paralysed towards the end of his life. Confined to his wheelchair, the former prime minister lived out his last days quietly at his country home in Berkshire. There he mourned the loss of his eldest son, who had been killed at the battle of the Somme in 1916. Compared to most other former prime ministers, Asquith was practically a pauper by the end. Economic depression and loss of income had bitten deep into his finances, and the lavish lifestyle he and Margot had once

---

[*]The year was one filled with loss for Sophia. Her mentor Lala Lajpat Rai died on 17 November 1928. While leading a silent, non-violent march against the Raj he was badly beaten in a *lathi* charge. He later died of his internal injuries.

enjoyed began to catch up with them. Before he died, on 15 February, Asquith's last wish had been that his funeral should not be a public affair. With his family and a few close friends gathered about the grave in a quiet parish church in Oxfordshire's Sutton Courtenay, one would hardly have thought that a former head of state, social reformer, and the scourge of the suffragettes, was being laid to rest. Emmeline Pankhurst's passing would be marked in much grander fashion.

In October 1919, Emmeline decided to leave Britain and travel once more in North America. Accompanied by her faithful nurse, Catherine Pine, she intended to take to the lucrative lecture circuit. Her message was no longer restricted to female empowerment. Emmeline had become terrified of the new world order, and blamed 'Bolshevism' for all post-war woes. Bitterly estranged from her daughter Sylvia, who had thrown in her lot with the communists, Emmeline took any opportunity to condemn the Russian Revolution. At the same time she praised British imperialism, something that confused and hurt Sophia in equal measure.

Although Emmeline had thought she might see out the end of her life in Canada, where 'there seems to be more equality between men and women than in any other country I know', in 1925, the long winters and expense eventually forced her to move back home. In England, she continued to praise the British Empire with increasing enthusiasm: 'Some talk about the Empire and Imperialism as if it were something to decry and something to be ashamed of. [I]t is a great thing to be the inheritors of an empire like ours ... great in territory, great in potential wealth ... If we can only realise and use that potential wealth we can destroy thereby poverty, we can remove and destroy ignorance.'[2]

A year later, Emmeline was selected as a prospective parliamentary candidate for the Conservative Party. She explained to incredulous friends that life experience had moved her from the left to the right of the political spectrum. The same experience had almost destroyed her physically. Thin and fragile, Emmeline was given to bouts of crippling fatigue and caught almost every infection. News that her daughter Sylvia had given birth to a child 'out of wedlock', in April 1928, further weakened her. Regarded as a 'modern' woman,

Emmeline was in many ways a social conservative long before she was a political one. She wept inconsolably for days from grief and disgust, hating Sylvia's disregard for marital convention. Her daughter had brought disgrace on the family as far as Emmeline was concerned, and she refused to have anything to do with her new grandson.

The WSPU leader's health deteriorated quickly after that. In just six weeks she needed round-the-clock care. Christabel moved her mother to a nursing home in Hampstead where doctors took good care of her. Nevertheless, bedbound and anxious, Emmeline begged her daughter to find the doctor who had nursed her back to health after her most debilitating hunger strikes. Christabel did not approve of Dr Chetham Strode's aggressive stomach-pumping treatments, but relented under duress, moving Emmeline to another nursing home in Wimpole Street, to be closer to the new doctor. Finding it hard to breathe, her mother lost the ability to speak. Days later, on 14 June, Emmeline Pankhurst died with Christabel by her side. She was one month away from her seventieth birthday. The cause of death was noted as septicaemia due to influenza.

News of the death reverberated round the world, and obituaries filled foreign papers as well as the British press. Her funeral attracted suffragettes from all over. Women in white dresses, with WSPU sashes, prison badges and other medals of honour, marched behind her coffin in silence. The pallbearers were all women and stalwarts of the WSPU. The *Daily Mail* described the procession as 'like a dead general in the midst of a mourning army'.[3] More than a thousand women followed the funeral cortege to Brompton Cemetery, where they laid their leader to rest.

In the years that followed, Emmeline's friends did what they could to keep her memory alive. The most hardened militants, who had formed the Suffragette Fellowship, met from time to time to compare battle scars and share anecdotes. Made up of women who had broken the law and endured force-feeding as a result, the Fellowship was an exclusive club. It welcomed Sophia into the fold in 1928, even though she had never served a day in prison herself, perhaps realising that it was not for want of trying to get arrested.

Close to the House of Commons, in Victoria Tower Gardens, a

statue of Emmeline was unveiled two years after her death. It showed the WSPU leader elegantly dressed, with one hand casually showing future generations of women the way to Parliament. Hundreds of former suffragettes and national dignitaries gathered for the unveiling on 6 March 1930. The former Prime Minister Stanley Baldwin gave an emotional speech in which he summed up Emmeline's impact on history. As a police band played 'Rise of the Women', Sophia stepped forward and placed large bouquets of flowers at Emmeline's feet. She had been made responsible for the floral tributes that day, and had executed the task with the flair of a princess and the dedication of a true friend.

For the years that followed, Sophia lived quietly at Hampton Court, travelling to Blo Norton regularly to administer Freddie's estate. Her brother had left detailed instructions in his will and it fell to Sophia and Bamba to ensure they were carried out. He had collected so many artefacts in the course of his life that wrapping, cataloguing and crating Freddie's treasures took almost two years. Not since the eviscerating court case had Sophia and Bamba spent so much time together. Shared grief helped them put the past behind them, but things would never go back to the way they once were.

Sophia took responsibility for Freddie's Jacobean collection, taking it to the museum of Inverness, where it remains to this day. Bamba administered almost everything else. Freddie had wanted to leave over a hundred of his East Anglian portraits to the museum he himself had created in Thetford. After supervising delivery and installation, Bamba took it upon herself to ensure the pieces were being well looked after. For months curators dreaded her unannounced visits. She was happy to show them their shortcomings.

With her short temper and long memory for grudges, Bamba had always been a difficult woman. The maids at Faraday House simply referred to her as 'The Bitch',[4] and argued with each other about who should answer the bell when she rang. However, Sophia was also becoming harsher as the years went on. Once known for her kindness, she was now perceived as a grumpy, remote figure by all but her housekeeper. Some of the junior servants disliked her almost as much as her sister.

A change in Bosie's circumstances had also helped to harden Sophia in middle age. While the princess had resigned herself to spinsterhood, her much treasured housekeeper had fallen in love. Bosie's romance with the quiet and unassuming John Lane, the man who worked as the princess's driver, was brief and intense. The two married in 1935, and even though Sophia continued to see her every day, the knowledge that Bosie had someone else to love hurt her.

Lillian Coram was fifteen when she came to work for the princess with her older sister Dorothy. They had lived in Blo Norton village all their lives, but were taken out of school when the family needed extra income. Lillian's mother called on Sophia during one of her many visits to her late brother's home, and asked if the princess might find a position for her girls. Sophia, who always found it hard to say no to people who came to her for help, agreed to take them on as parlour maids, even though she was struggling to pay the servants she already had.

Arriving at Faraday in 1935, Lillian and Dorothy found a house just managing to hang on to its former glory. 'At first there were lots of servants – a cook and a housemaid, the princess's personal maid, the housekeeper and a chauffeur called Lane.'⁵ Dorothy and Lillian settled in, and although the hours were long, and Bosie was terrifying, they enjoyed their time at Faraday. Lillian was captivated by the lavish rugs, and the exotic brass ornaments and silk cushions they had to keep free of dust. In particular, she was attracted to a large portrait of Sophia's father, which hung in the 'Blue Room'. It was a copy of the Winterhalter painting, and the parlour maid, like the former Queen of England, found the young Maharajah's beauty captivating. However, when it came to Sophia, she regarded her merely as a 'bad-tempered old bat'.⁶

Money worries were tormenting Sophia once more and matters reached crisis point soon after Lillian's arrival. Even though she had already dismissed many of her staff, lack of funds forced her to let go half of those who remained. The cheapest of the servants, Lillian and Dorothy, were retained and found themselves 'having to do everything with Mrs Lane on our back all the time'.⁷

Lillian and her sister would often mock their mistress's eccentricities. When Sophia wanted to take the dogs out for a walk, she had a habit of standing in the middle of the great entrance hall at Faraday House, wearing a battered fur coat tied with string, and yelling, 'Houndses, Houndses, where are my Houndses?' at the top of her voice. Lillian and the others found it hilarious and would follow her about mouthing 'Houndses!' and trying not to dissolve into peals of laughter. If the day had been particularly difficult, Lillian took revenge, using one of the princess's beloved pets. 'We often used to hide her wretched tortoise, telling her that we thought it had escaped into the garden. She'd search for it for hours, and finally tell us to stop what we were doing and look about the grounds. She would always be beside herself with worry. It was the best way to get off and chat to the boys by the river. The tortoise was never harmed; it just used to sleep in the laundry quite happily.'[8]

Lillian's only fond memories of Sophia stretched back to the day King Edward VIII abdicated from the throne. On 11 December 1936 the entire household had crammed into the main sitting room at Faraday House to listen to the news on the wireless. Sir John Reith, the first Director General of the BBC, introduced the former King as 'Prince Edward', confirming his decision to give up the throne. While Lillian felt as if their world was turning upside down, she remembered Sophia's still and reassuring presence at the centre of the room: 'She made us feel that things would be alright again.'[9]

There was nothing that even Sophia could say or do to give her sister a similar sense of solace a year later. On 26 August 1938, Lina Schaeffer died at the age of seventy-nine. Catherine and the former governess had spent their lives besotted with one another and even though Lina was gone, Catherine longed to stay in Cassel, in the little house filled with memories. She knew no other home than Germany.

The locals had never understood the presence of the strange Indian lady in their midst. They tolerated her as an exotic eccentricity, and since Lina, a true and patriotic German, had vouched for her good character, Catherine was safe.[10] Even when waves of xenophobia washed over the rest of the country during and after the First World War, the couple remained untroubled. However all that changed when Hitler became leader. Friends began to worry for the odd couple, as reports of Jews and foreigners being beaten up in the streets became more common.

By 1938 the atmosphere had turned pyretic as Germany annexed Austria. All talk was of *Lebensraum*, and the Führer's intention to fight for more land for his German, Aryan people. Dr Fritz Ratig,[11] a resident of Cassel, worried constantly about the sixty-seven-year-old princess. After Lina died, he could not bear the idea of Catherine living alone and unprotected. He begged her to snap out of her grief, warning Catherine to leave the country before it was too late. His words were frightening enough to make her sell everything and leave within the month.

Though resigned to spending the rest of her life in England, Catherine was determined not to swap grief for rage. With no intention of moving into the grace-and-favour house she so detested at Hampton Court, Catherine was wealthy enough to make other arrangements. She and Lina had lived frugally in Cassel and therefore the princess had accumulated substantial savings, which she had asked agents to invest for her over the years. Two of the assets in her portfolio were a smart, six-bedroom manor named Coalhatch House in Penn, Buckinghamshire, and a squat, nine-bedroom, five-bathroom, sprawling bungalow opposite, called Rathenrea.

Catherine chose elegance and moved into Coalhatch House. She set about decorating and furnishing it in the modern European style of her Cassel home. It was a handsome building with generous grounds, ornamental garden and orchard. The rooms were large, with high ceilings and big windows, and it boasted a large library and music room. Coalhatch House had always been one of the smartest houses in Penn, and the locals craned their necks over the high walls to see the 'Indian Queen' they heard had moved in.[12]

Catherine begged her sister to leave London and come and live in the village with her, enticing Sophia with promises of countryside, fresh air and freedom. She even promised to give her Rathenrea as her own private residence. Partly this was an act of great generosity; partly it suited Catherine, who wanted her sister to keep her company but could not bear the idea of Sophia's dogs running their dirty paws all over her clean furnishings. At first Sophia refused, but soon she would have no choice.

A year later, on 1 September 1939, Hitler marched his armies into Poland, seizing the port of Danzig, giving some hint as to the scope of his ambitions. Two days later, at 11.15 a.m., Britain formally declared war on Germany. People listened to the cracking and emotional voice of Chamberlain on the wireless, as he admitted he had failed them: 'You can imagine what a bitter blow it is to me that all my long struggle to win peace has failed. Yet I cannot believe that there is anything more or anything different I could have done and that would have been more successful.'[13]

Everybody knew that London would be one of Hitler's main targets, and that the Luftwaffe possessed enough firepower to devastate the city from the skies. Sophia would rather have stayed on in the capital, despite the threat, just as she had during the first war, but a new addition to her family made that choice impossible. Bosie had given birth to a baby girl at the end of August, and Sophia had fallen in love with her. The tiny fair-haired, chocolate-eyed creature was named Catherine, and the housekeeper, who had never been intimidated by social mores, asked Sophia to be her godmother. The princess agreed instantly.

Sophia dismissed Lillian, Dorothy and the others, and ordered Bosie to take her husband Lane and their baby girl and leave immediately for Rathenrea. She would follow with her menagerie as soon as she could, after winding up her affairs in London.

Elsewhere others were doing the same. The government's evacuation plan, Operation Pied Piper, had already been set in motion. It involved the relocation of more than 3.5 million people from the cities most at risk of aerial bombardment, starting with young children and their mothers and pregnant women. Shirley Sarbutt was a nine-year-old girl at the time. She and her two brothers, eleven-year-old John and seven-year-old Michael, attended the Lamas School in Northfields, west London, where their mother was a teacher.

On Thursday 31 August, members of staff at the school were told that if war was declared, the children would be evacuated at ten the next morning. Coaches were on standby to take them out of the city. As a teacher and a mother of three Mrs Sarbutt had been chosen to go with the convoy and keep the youngest children calm. She would also have to settle them at the other end, although she had no idea where that would be. Each child was given a rucksack filled with emergency rations, a packet of biscuits, a tin of condensed milk and name tags which were to be filled in and tied to a button.[14]

For Shirley and her brothers, the bus journey seemed to take for ever. She woke with a start when the vehicle finally stopped and the children were ushered into an unfamiliar village hall in a village called Penn. 'There were people with lists, calling out our names and then making us stand in different lines to wait for collection. I heard someone shout "Michael Sarbutt", and then mutter 'for the Princess'. Then they did the same for me and John. We were tired and hungry and did not really take much notice. A large woman called Mrs Lane was there to collect us. She had a small baby in her arms and seemed a bit cross.'[15]

Before the coaches had arrived in Penn, Bosie had telephoned Faraday House to tell Sophia of the imminent arrivals. 'Well then. I suppose we really ought to take some,' said the princess. 'Put us down for three or four. We have the room.'[16] The housekeeper, who had not had much sleep with her own new arrival, was not best pleased with her mistress's generosity. Shirley Sarbutt, however, was cock-a-hoop.

'I had never seen a house like Rathenrea before,' she remembered years later. 'It was a huge bungalow ... My mother had one room, my brothers were given another, and I was told to sleep in the lounge. There were two maids in the house already and they had bedrooms. I remember they were dressed in beautiful maroon uniforms, with snow-white aprons and caps. It was like a strange fairy tale, a castle-type thing, only there was hardly any furniture in the house. We were told by Mrs Lane that the Princess was bringing everything from Hampton Court Palace in a few days' time ... I was so confused.'[17]

Ten days later, the trucks started arriving. Shirley watched in awe: 'They were filled with heavy carved things. Beautiful chairs with high backs. Huge ornate tables and little containers for joss sticks. Everything was inlaid and so pretty.'[18] Sophia herself did not arrive for a few days more. It felt like a lifetime for the evacuees, desperate to see the princess.

To keep a sense of normality Shirley and the other evacuees were sent to the local school as soon as they arrived. The Sarbutts, tortured by the idea that they might be stuck doing sums when the princess arrived in her carriage, found it hard to settle: 'We could hardly stand it . . . But one day we came home, and Mrs Lane told us to wash our faces and smarten up. The Princess was in the house and she wanted to meet us. So we lined up and waited.'[19] When Sophia finally arrived, she did not look anything like the fairy tale they had imagined. There was no tiara on her wet and wispy hair and she wore a plain dress, brown cardigan, scruffy jacket and Wellington boots: 'She had just been out with the dogs in the orchard in the pouring rain. I looked at her and thought, "Oh, she's not like a princess at all".'[20]

The children were asked to step forward one by one to be inspected. 'What do you want us to call you?' asked Michael Sarbutt boldly, still somewhat miffed at his first impressions. 'Well,' replied Sophia after a pause, 'You can call me Princess Sophia. That is my name. I am Princess Sophia.'[21] She then turned to Bosie, who had been grumbling about the children all week, referring to them as 'that bleedin' brood'.[22]

'Mrs Lane. These are my three evacuees. Any time they want to come and see me they can . . . If they want to help me walking the dogs I would be delighted, because that way I can get to know them better.'[23] With that, she left to bathe and dress for dinner at Coalhatch House.

Catherine and Sophia quickly fell into a comfortable routine. Each would wake in their respective houses at around noon, take breakfast in bed, and read the papers. Then Catherine tinkered about her large house, while her sister took her numerous dogs for long walks in the fields. Sophia would come home at around four, meet the children, interrogate them about their day at school and then prepare for her evening across the road, taking her two maids with her. There the sisters would eat a formal dinner and spend hours sitting by candlelight. They talked, listened to music and played cards – bridge and whist – until the small hours. When they were both sufficiently exhausted, Sophia would take her leave and return to Rathenrea to sleep.

It was a cosy if uninspiring start to life in Buckinghamshire. Occasionally, to break up the monotony, the sisters called upon neighbours. In particular, Sophia became friendly with Lady Gwendolyn Maclean.[24] Her husband, Sir Donald, had been leader of the Liberal Party until 1920, and had moved to Penn for a quieter pace of life. The couple were cultured and kind and Sophia enjoyed talking about her house full of children and hearing about their sons, one of whom was 'doing very well at the Foreign Office'. Years later, the junior Donald Maclean would be exposed as one of the Cambridge Five agents who had been spying for the Soviet Union.

More than anything, Sophia enjoyed watching Bosie's baby gurgle and flail in her crib. She would pat the child and hum the 'Skye Boat Song', and 'You Are My Sunshine',[25] until she drifted off to sleep. Too awkward to hold her unless someone else placed the child in her arms, Sophia lacked the confidence that went with her maternal feelings. She had very little experience of children – apart from her younger brother Eddie, whom she had loved best of all – and never seemed confident that she was doing the right thing. The princess need not have worried. 'All of us children adored her,'[26] recalled Shirley Sarbutt. 'Every day she would be on the lane as we came home from school, waiting for us with the dogs. They all had their leads off, ready to run about the orchard. She would ask us all about school . . . while we threw balls and made the dogs run and bring them back . . . She once told me I had to tell her everything, leaving no detail out, because she had never gone to school like us, and wanted to know what she had missed.'[27]

In particular, Sophia developed a soft spot for Michael, Shirley's brother, despite his mother cautioning, 'He's a little terror that one!'[28] Michael lived up to his reputation early on during his time with Sophia at Penn. 'He was forever playing tricks on her,' his sister remembered. 'He taught the Princess's Airedale terrier, Peter, how to lie down flat and stay very still. Then he'd go over and say, "Princess, I think Peter's dead." "Dead!" she says in mock horror.'²⁹ Michael used to kill Peter off numerous times a week and Sophia always pretended to believe him. She loved his streak of mischief so much she took to calling him her 'little pickle'. If ever he was out of sight for too long she would say 'where is my little pickle. He's up to no good I don't doubt. Somebody get my little pickle for me.'³⁰

As long as Bosie did not catch them, the children had free run of the house and gardens. Michael would be the only one courageous enough to sneak into Sophia's rooms, to steal cigarettes from the carved teak box on her desk. No matter how hard Bosie tried to stop him, Michael found a way in: 'He's been in there again, that little pickle. He's smoked four of them today. Just wait till I get my hands on him.'³¹ The other children would watch her wander around the garden waving her walking stick as if she was going to give Michael a good hiding: 'She never did of course,'³² remembered Shirley laughing.

Despite the war, large Army & Navy Stores vans still arrived in the village from London with deliveries for the princesses. They brought food, some treats for the baby, and numerous cartons of cigarettes. One afternoon, Catherine made a rare trip across the Hammersley Road, to call upon her sister and see what had arrived in the consignment. The baby was just beginning to crawl, and was entertaining Sophia with her clumsy efforts. All of a sudden, she picked up something from the ground and put it in her mouth. Sophia and Bosie both shouted 'Catherine no!' at the same time, causing Princess Catherine to jump with fright.³³ 'There is only one Catherine in this household and it is I,' the princess muttered as she set down her tea cup and swept out of the house in disgust. Bosie looked at Sophia in panic. 'Don't worry,' replied the princess, calmly watching her sister leave, 'we shall call the baby Drovna. Drovna means daughter. That shall be her name from now on.'³⁴ The child grew up knowing only that name and it was not until years later that she found out that 'Drovna' was a little piece of Sophia's own eccentric middle name.

The children meant everything to Sophia and she would spoil them at any opportunity. When, after a year of living at Rathenrea, Shirley's birthday came round, the ten-year-old asked shyly whether she might have a friend round for tea. The princess insisted that the whole class be invited, and spent the entire sugar ration for a fortnight on cakes and treats for them all. She bought John a pet goat and asked a local farmer to teach him to milk it. When it rained, Sophia sent Lane in 'the motor' to pick up the children, though petrol was in short supply. The arrival of such a grand automobile complete with chauffeur would cause pandemonium at the little village school. Regarding the children as her own, Sophia guarded them like a lioness.

'One time in 1942 I think, we were late back . . . The princess was waiting for us as usual, and demanded to know where we had been,'[35] recalled Shirley. 'We told her a nice old man had stopped us on the way home and wanted to know all about us . . . She was furious. She told us never to talk to strangers again, and got straight on the phone to the local policeman. She must have given him quite the earful because he was off on his bike immediately, huffing and puffing up and down the lane to investigate. It turned out the old man was [the poet] Walter de la Mare, who was staying with his daughter in Penn. He was working on a poem about evacuees. We felt terrible for the trouble we caused for him. Poor man got the fright of his life!'[36]

Thousands of bombs had been dropped on Britain since the start of the war, but despite the Blitz and the horrors that came with it, Sophia had never been more content in her life. Even when in 1942, the Luftwaffe changed tactics and adopted an official bombing policy of targeting civilians, she remained unperturbed. Sophia's air-raid shelter stood at the bottom of her garden, and whenever the siren sounded, she calmly shepherded the children, Bosie, her daughter Drovna and the dogs into the underground Anderson shelter, only to return to the house and sit out the raid smoking angrily out of the window. She was convinced no German bomb would kill her or Catherine. As it turned out, she was right.

On the evening of Sunday 8 November, 1942, Sophia and Catherine had been to watch an amateur dramatic performance in the local village. 'We walked ¾ mile each way,'[37] she would later tell friends. Afterwards they dined at Coalhatch House and played a few hands of whist. Sophia took her leave some time after midnight and Catherine also retired. During the night, the elder princess felt uncomfortable and tried to get up, but the moment she swung her feet to the floor she suffered a heart attack and collapsed. When Princess Catherine failed to ring the bell for her noontime 'breakfast', servants knocked on the door of Rathenrea in alarm. Catherine was always punctilious about her mealtimes.

Sophia ran across the road in panic, darted up the stairs of Coalhatch House to her sister's room and banged on the door. Getting no answer, she ordered the servants to break it down. What she saw brought her to her knees in anguish: 'I found her lying on the floor on her back. It evidently happened when she was getting up. The doctor said it was quite painless and instantaneous and <u>nothing</u> could have been done. A lot of blood on the heart. You can imagine just what an awful shock it was to me.'[38]

Sophia raved in her grief and had to be half-carried, half-dragged from the room. In the days that followed friends begged her to let them help her, but Sophia just wanted to be left alone. As she wrote later: 'It completely stunned and stupefied me – and I couldn't shake myself up to ordinary things again.'[39] She did not even know if her sister in India would read her telegram in time for the funeral. She knew she would be the only member of the Duleep Singh family present to mourn Princess Catherine's passing.

After the funeral, Sophia ordered Catherine's room to be locked and never opened again, but it did little to ease her pain.[40] She could still see Coalhatch House from her windows, and its emptiness proved too horrifying. In an attempt to feel close to her sister still, she renamed Coalhatch 'Hilden Hall' (Catherine's middle name had been Hilda). She became convinced that her dead sister's troubled spirit was haunting the house across the road and would beg the children to go in first and tell her if they could 'feel' anything. Despite Bosie's best efforts, it all became too much for Sophia. Weeks after the funeral, she fled Rathenrea and all those who loved her.

Sophia hid herself away at the country home of one of her Hampton Court friends, Miss Phipps, a fellow grace-and-favour resident. At her isolated house in the New Forest, it took Sophia almost a month to regain enough composure to return to Buckinghamshire.[41] When she did, her thoughts were filled with her own mortality and she started to prepare for her own death. The Sarbutt children were relocated in 1943, moving back with their mother and other relatives, leaving only four-year old Drovna to distract Sophia from the paralysing depression she felt closing in on her.

The little girl was growing up fast, and Sophia threw herself into teaching her everything she knew. As Drovna would later recall: 'One of my earliest memories is of sitting at a table with a ripe peach . . . from our orchard I suppose because rationing made things like that hard to get . . . I could smell it and wanted to eat it so much, but she would make me eat it with a knife and fork. I needed to learn manners you see.'[42] Sophia ordered the finest clothes from the boutiques that had escaped the Blitz and insisted Drovna wear hats and gloves whenever she accompanied her in public. She even presented her with the doll her own godmother had given her. 'Her name is Sophie. She was given to me by a queen,'[43] she told the little girl.

With the advent of peace in 1945, Sophia, like many others, returned to see what the war had left of London. Much of the city-scape was changed beyond recognition, but Hampton Court had been left unscathed. At the start of the war, a few incendiary bombs had been dropped on the palace, but fire wardens managed to kick them away before the old timbers caught fire. Slowly moving back into her old rooms, Sophia had the chance to show Drovna something of her old life. Every day they would venture into the grounds with the dogs, and the princess would make Drovna repeat the names of flowers until she had committed them to memory.[44] She showed her all the Sikh artefacts that still remained in her possession, testing her on what they were and who they had belonged to. Sometimes the flood of information was too much for such a small child. Sophia had a huge box under the stairs, beautifully carved, heavy and old, which she called 'The Elephant Box'. The six-year-old came to believe a real elephant lived inside: 'I thought, poor elephant, no one feeds it. No one ever feeds it. So I used to save things from my tea and leave bits on top so the elephant could have something.' In fact the box contained an exquisite four-foot-tall statue of Maharajah Ranjit Singh riding upon an elephant. Made of the finest solid silver, it depicted Sophia's grandfather in all his splendour, with an attendant at his rear shielding him from the sun with a silk umbrella. Intricate figures carved on the heavy plinth formed the base of the statue: on one side, hunters stalked a deer; on the other, men found themselves stalked by a lioness. The side panels were filled with depictions of Indian and European soldiers, presided over by the one-eyed King. It was a priceless artefact.[45] Although Bosie was not amused when she found the piles of mouldering food on the box, Sophia howled with laughter.[46]

The princess was delighted by everything her little protégé did and said. Apart from the regular gifts, Drovna would be the only child she would attempt to leave her most precious legacy to: 'We'd be walking, and she'd be telling me about the world and elections and how important they were. And then she would kneel down in front of me, looking me right in the eye and say "I want a solemn promise from you" even though I don't think I knew what a solemn promise was at that stage. She would say "You are never, ever not to vote. You must promise me. When you are allowed to vote you are never, ever to fail to do so. You don't realise how far we've come. Promise me." '[47] For the next three years, Sophia made Drovna promise again and again. The ferocity of Sophia's insistence was overwhelming.

Princess Sophia Duleep Singh lived to see India gain its independence. She also saw Partition rip Punjab in two. Great cities she had known and loved were split between irreconcilable new neighbours. Lahore went to Pakistan, Amritsar went to India and a river of blood ran between them, as Hindus, Muslims and Sikhs turned on one another with murderous ferocity. Sophia lived to see the British leave, and mourned what had been left in their wake.

After the war, Bamba was able to travel to England once again, and the two sisters divided their time between Penn and Hampton Court. It was clear that Sophia was not the woman she once was. She moved slowly, and had a constant pain in her eye, which could confine her to her bed for days in agony. Bosie later told her daughter that the princess had been diagnosed with a tumour but had not wanted to worry anyone with the news. The doctors said they could save her life and relieve her pain if they could but remove her eye. Having grown up under canvases depicting her disfigured grandfather, Sophia refused surgery, insisting that fresh air and exercise was all she needed to recover.

Bosie believed Sophia was just too tired to fight any more, and too vain to allow them to destroy her face. Although physically weak, and in almost constant agony, Sophia retained much of her humour right up until the end. On 28 February 1947 she wrote to a former servant, Gwendolyne Edwards, who had been a much-cherished maid at both Rathenrea and Hampton Court. After almost seven years of service, Gwenda had fallen in love with a Spaniard; the pair married, and barely a year later she was expecting twins. Even though she had moved back to her native Wales, Gwenda remained so fond of her former mistress that she wrote regularly and sent her a ham and chocolates for Christmas. It had taken two months for Sophia to gather the strength to thank her in a four-page letter, filled with warmth and little snippets of local news. Penn felt colder than usual, Sophia confessed, and she did not get out as much as she would have liked. Realising that she had painted a sad picture, Sophia attempted to lighten the mood, telling Gwenda she often sat by the fire, holding her aching legs over the flames, 'until they scorched!' Of Gwenda's newborn twin daughters, she joked: 'Babies of that age are all exactly alike, perfectly hideous! Ah well, it's a good thing their mothers never think so!!' Her carefree, teasing tone did not betray her infirmity; however the slope of her trembling handwriting did.[48]

On 22 August 1948, Sophia died peacefully in her sleep at Rathenrea. She was seventy-one years old. Bosie was with her at the end.

# Epilogue

Although she had been a church-going Christian all her life, at the end, Sophia's wish was to have her body cremated like a Sikh, and for her ashes to be scattered in India. Perhaps the country of her ancestors had at last come to feel like 'home'. Maybe she was just honouring her grandmother Jindan, who had made the same journey after death. Perhaps she did not want to leave a cold tombstone for Drovna and others to weep over; Sophia had cried beside too many graves in her youth and would not have wished the same on anyone she loved.

Though she did not explain her decision, it was deliberate and well considered. Protracted illness had given her much time to think about death and her funeral. She asked that, 'A full band shall play Wagner's Funeral March from Götterdammerung' as her body was committed to the flames. Even though it had become unpopular to play Wagner after the Second World War, Sophia did not care. She had listened to the composer frequently with Catherine on creaky gramophone records in Penn.

As the only living Duleep Singh left in the world, it was up to Bamba to fulfil her sister's final wishes. In 1949, at almost eighty years of age, she collected Sophia's ashes and those of their late sister Catherine. An urn of her remains had been lovingly kept at Hilden Hall by Sophia who found comfort in having them near.

Bamba chose to say farewell to Sophia first. Though frail and unwell, she undertook an arduous land and sea route to the city of Lahore, which now stood in the new country of Pakistan. It would have been much easier to take one of the numerous flights that now connected the West to the East. However, as she explained to a cousin, 'I came by land as I brought my darling sisters ashes with me. She did not like flights.'[1] To this day, nobody knows where Bamba scattered Sophia's ashes, or what thoughts passed through her grieving mind.

Weeks later, Bamba made her way back to Europe, stopping briefly in Germany. She arrived one night without warning at the home of one of Lina's relatives, and pressed an urn into his hands. She asked that Catherine's remains be buried next to Lina's. She wanted the women to be together again.[2]

For a while, Bamba took up residence at Hilden Hall, struggling to come to terms with her loss. As always, her emotions found their expression in outbursts of white-hot rage. She accused staff at both Hilden Hall and Rathenrea of stealing from Sophia while she lay dying. One by one they folded up their maroon uniforms and left. Bamba's severest wrath was reserved for Bosie and nine-year-old Drovna. Soon after the funeral, the princess and the housekeeper fought so viciously that Bosie took her family and left Rathenrea in the middle of the night, never to return.[3] Sophia must have expected such difficulties after she was gone, and the memory of Bamba's conduct after Irene's death must have haunted her; yet she still had enough love for her sister to name Bamba as executor of her estate. She was certain Bamba would not betray her trust, and she was right.

Some of the bequests were easy to honour. Beneficiaries included three girls' schools, one Sikh, one Muslim and one Hindu. Though India was riven with division, Sophia was determined that her desire to educate girls would be equal among all the people of the Punjab, irrespective of recent Partition bloodshed. Sophia also left £500 to Battersea Dogs' Home and £450 to the People's Dispensary for Sick Animals, proving that her love for animals matched, and sometimes surpassed, her love for people. A trust fund was also set up for the upkeep of all the family graves in England.

To the friends she cherished most, Miss Phipps in the New Forest and Mrs Mackenzie in Inverness, she opened up her jewellery box. They were invited to choose an item each from among her finest heirlooms. There were pecuniary bequests to cherished individuals from Sophia's past, including 'Sardar Pritam Singh son of the late Sardar Gurdit Singh Sandhawalia of Rajah Sansi Punjab. If he shall be living at my death . . .' He was the same young boy she once could have adopted as her own.

Artworks were left to Indian galleries; her Jacobean pieces, gifts from Freddie, were sent to the same museum in Inverness which had taken his collection, and sums of money were distributed to former servants. Apart from Bamba, who inherited Rathenrea and Hilden Hall, their contents and any remaining items in her jewellery case, the greatest generosity and most personal bequests were left to Bosie, Lane and Drovna. Tellingly, Sophia had left separate amounts to both Bosie and her husband, perhaps believing that it was the only way to ensure financial autonomy for her housekeeper if something went wrong in their marriage. (It never did.) Bosie was left additional items which the princess thought might amuse the woman who had once locked herself in the bathroom because she wanted to see an elephant: 'To Mrs Ivy Janet Lane, my Encyclopaedia, *I See All*, and my books *Famous Pictures* and . . . *Wonders of the Past.*'

Leaving Drovna would always be the most difficult reality to confront. Sophia left the child the entire contents of her Post Office savings account and asked that it be passed to her at the age of twenty-one. However if her parents decided that they needed the money for her during childhood, she gave a caveat to the bequest: 'I authorise my Trustees to apply the whole or any part of the said money to her education, advancement and benefit . . .' Even though she would not be there to see Drovna grow up, she wanted the passage of time to go easy on her goddaughter.

With her duty done, Bamba stripped Rathenrea and Hilden Hall of all their furnishings, selling what she could in local antique shops and disposing of more expensive items through London auctioneers. She then put both houses on the market, bought a ticket for Pakistan and left England for the last time. With Sophia gone, ties to the land of her enemy had at last been severed. Bamba returned to Lahore and lived out the rest of her days with only Pir-ji for company. Till the end, she described herself as 'The Queen of Punjab'. She died in 1957 of a heart attack. Her remains are buried in a graveyard at Lahore's Christian cemetery.

Though she lived through some of the key moments in modern British and Indian history, and took part in some of the most significant struggles for democracy and freedom, surprisingly little has been written about Sophia Duleep Singh. That her family line died with her generation certainly did not help, nor did the fact that she alone took on the mantle of family archivist; although her sisters' and brothers' letters were lovingly collected, Sophia never thought to keep copies of her own correspondence. A few of her letters have turned up in disparate private collections, and Sophia's voice might have been all but lost were it not for the fact that her diary was passed on to the British Library, and three people who knew her well who lived to speak at length and in great detail for the purposes of this book.

Sophia's later prickly relationship with the establishment also helped to bury many traces of her. The princess's name can be found in the Royal Archives, but only if one knows what to ask for. Despite monitoring her every move, and intercepting her letters, the British government's actions contributed the most to wiping Sophia from the official record. They kept her from India as long as they could, and were determined that her presence in England should be inconspicuous. To that end they resorted to underhand methods, as shown by their conduct over her wartime charity efforts. It is ironic that in their enthusiasm to push Sophia out of view, their meticulous bureaucracy has provided an indelible outline of her place in the world.

Historians of British-Sikh origin have done the most to preserve the legacy of Duleep Singh and his children. None more so than the historian Peter Bance, who has diligently collected family ephemera, letters and photographs, all of which are fragments of this exceptional story. The UK Punjab Heritage Association can also be credited with some exemplary work in bringing the story of Maharajah Duleep Singh to a new and enthusiastic generation of Sikhs. In India, although Ranjit Singh and his son are still held in high regard, and much has been written about them, there has been little appetite to celebrate the anglicised family of the deposed Duleep. After independence, India and Pakistan had the likes of Gandhi, Nehru and Jinnah to venerate; politicians now provide the subcontinent with its dynastic drama.

What of the suffragettes who bore her nothing but goodwill – why did they not celebrate Princess Sophia more prominently? The reasons are a little more complicated here. There were so many heroic women who served with Emmeline Pankhurst, but a handful of names eclipse all others. They are the women who risked their very lives in the fight for the vote. Despite her best and repeated efforts, Sophia never managed to be sent to prison, and therefore was denied her chance to go on hunger strike and take her place in the pantheon of WSPU giants. Not even when she threw herself at the prime minister's car would the police and courts punish her as they punished others of lower rank. Thanks to the excellent work of historians such as Elizabeth Crawford, Diane Atkinson and most especially Rozina Visram, and the mainly negative reports of the princess's activities in the international press, clues as to Sophia's part in the movement are there to see. As a suffragette, Sophia was enormously important. It was she who exported the WSPU notion of electoral equality to India, the world's greatest democracy.

All of these sources have helped to tell the story of what Sophia did, but not who she was. That knowledge came from those who knew her personally and were touched by her life. I will be forever grateful to Shirley Phimister, née Sarbutt, for generously sharing her time and recollections with me.

Michael Sarbutt, Sophia's 'little pickle', emigrated to New Zealand in his twenties. He never spoke about his time with Princess Sophia to his own wife or children after he settled there. It was while his family were sorting through his belongings after Michael's death in 2002 that they discovered a mysterious box. Perplexed, they found a letter containing Michael's last wishes along with several black and white photographs that they had never seen before. The pictures appeared to have been taken with a box Brownie and showed a young Michael and his brother and sister playing in an orchard. There were also photographs of an elderly Indian woman. The letter asked that Michael's ashes be scattered on the earth around Sophia's old house. He wanted to go back to the place he had been happiest in his life.[4]

It was left to his sister Shirley to explain the story of Princess Sophia to Michael's grieving family. She also took them back to Buckinghamshire in order to carry out his wishes in 2004. Her brother John had also moved to New Zealand and was in poor health at the time so she alone accompanied Michael's family to the place where they had sheltered during the war. When she reached the place, just off the Hammersley Road, Shirley found that Rathenrea was not as it once was. The building had been modified and expanded, making way for new housing. The family scattered Michael's remains around the orchard, just as he had wanted. Shirley said as she did so, she could almost see the young boy her brother had been, scampering through the trees beside Princess Sophia in her furs and wellington boots, surrounded by dogs. Today, living in west London, she describes her time in Penn as 'magical' and 'the happiest', adding that not a day goes by when she does not think about her beloved princess.[5]

I had almost given up hope of finding Sophia's goddaughter, Drovna. Many months of fruitless searching had yielded nothing. However, one day in July 2012, in response to one of scores of answerphone messages I had left with potential leads, I received a phonecall. 'My name is Drovna – what do you want with my Princess?' she asked in a somewhat challenging tone. We spent almost an hour on the phone, and then Drovna asked me if I would like to come and stay with her. Those days in Pembrokeshire yielded a treasure trove of memories. According to Bosie's daughter, the night Sophia died, part of her mother died too. She suffered a mental collapse in the months that followed and it took many months for her to recover. Even after years had passed, she still found it very difficult to talk about Sophia.[6]

Drovna grew up, got married and had children of her own, one of whom married a Sikh. She still surrounds herself with keepsakes left by Sophia. Drovna could tell me what the princess liked to eat, how she laughed and how she moved and sat. Thanks to her mother's memories which had been passed on to her, she was able to fill in many gaps, even telling me about the time leading up to her death. Sophia had only had days to live when she asked Bosie to keep a few things aside to give to her goddaughter as presents after she had gone. She wanted Drovna to get something every year until she reached the age of majority.[7] The princess had enough time facing her mortality to make such decisions while she lived and elected not to leave these items in her will but to pass them on while she still lived. A small part of her must have worried that Bamba might just contest any legal document and she did not want to put her loved ones through that. Drovna treasures her keepsakes but also remembers her 'solemn vow' to Sophia. At every general election, she makes sure that she goes out to vote. She feels the enormity of the task each and every time.

As far as her place in history is concerned, Sophia was perhaps her own worst enemy. She never sought glory and disliked speaking in public. Before her death, when asked to contribute to her entry in the women's *Who's Who*, Sophia Duleep Singh's was one of the briefest in the book. Under 'interests' she wrote just one line: 'The Advancement of Women'.

# NOTES

## Abbreviations

BDS    Bamba Duleep Singh
BL     British Library
CDS    Catherine Duleep Singh
HC Deb House of Commons Debate
HL Deb House of Lords Debate
HMSO   Her Majesty's Stationery Office
HO     Home Office
IOR    India Office Records
MEPO   Metropolitan Police Records
QVM    Michael Alexander and Sushila Anand, *Queen Victoria's Maharajah, Duleep Singh, 1838–93*, Weidenfeld & Nicolson, London, 1980
RA     Royal Archives
SDS    Sophia Duleep Singh
TNA    The National Archives, Kew

## Prologue

1  The photograph is held in the Suffragette Collection, Museum of London.

## Chapter 1 – Roots of Rebellion

1  State Opening of Parliament, 12 Feb 1876.
2  *The Tablet*, p. 14, 12 Feb 1876.
3  The Battle of the Ten Kings is mentioned in the ancient Hindu text the 'Rig Veda' and also forms the basis of the Mahabharata, one of the most sacred texts in Hinduism.
4  In the spring of 327 BC, Alexander and his army marched into India invading the Punjab. At a brutal battle by the river Hydaspes he lost his beloved horse Bucephalus. Alexander would later be seriously wounded by an arrow which pierced his armour and lodged in his ribcage.
5  The stories of Guru Nanak's childhood are found in the Sikh texts, the *Janamsakhis*, literally translated 'birth stories'. The most influential of these is the *Bhai Bala Janamsakhi*, said to be written by Bala Sandhu, a contemporary of Nanak.
6  Akal Ustat, Verse 85–86.
7  William Dalrymple, *Return of a King: The Battle for Afghanistan*, Bloomsbury, London, 2013, p. 10.

8 Prinsep, James, *History of the Punjab*, Vol. II, W. H. Allen, London, 1846, reprinted Patiala, 1970, p. 174.

9 *The Letters of Queen Victoria,* Project Gutenberg eBook,Vol 2, (1844–1853), Marquis of Dalhousie to Queen Victoria, Simla, 15 May 1850.

10 John Clark Marshman, *The History of India from the Earliest Period to the Close of Lord Dalhousie's Administration in Three Volumes*, Vol. 3, 1867, p. 289.

11 Sir Herbert Benjamin Edwardes and Herman Merivale, *The Life of Sir Henry Lawrence*, Vol. 2, Smith, Elder & Co., London, 1872, p. 91.

12 See www.globalsikhstudies.net

13 Ganda Singh (ed.), *Maharajah Duleep Singh Correspondence*, Patiala, Punjab University, 1972, p. 90.

14 Rani Jindan to J. Lawrence, undated, trans. from Punjabi, in ibid., p. 26.

15 Ibid.

16 Letter from Hardinge to Eliot, 27 Aug 1847, in ibid., p. 32.

17 Hardinge to Lawrence, 14 Aug 1847, Edwardes and Merivale, *Life of Sir Henry Lawrence*, p. 100.

18 Avtar Singh Gill, *Lahore Darbar and Rani Jindan*, Central Publishers, Punjab, 1983, p. 231.

19 G. Singh, *Correspondence*, Rani Jindan to J. Lawrence, 30 Aug 1847, trans. from Punjabi, p. 27.

20 Lady Lena Login, *Sir John Login and Duleep Singh*, W. H. Allen & Co., London, 1890, p. 450.

21 Lady Lena Login: *Lady Login's Recollections, Court Life and Camp Life, 1820–1904*, Smith, Elder & Co., London, 1916, p. 88.

## Chapter 2 – Do Not Be Conspicuous

1 Queen Victoria's Journal, 6 Jul 1854, RA.

2 Login, *Recollections*, p. 116.

3 Peter Bance, *Sovereign, Squire and Rebel: Maharajah Duleep Singh*, Coronet House Publishing Ltd, London, 2009, p. 38; Login, *Sir John Login*, p. 343.

4 Queen Victoria's Journal, 10 Jul 1854, RA.

5 Login, *Recollections*, p. 123.

6 Ibid., p. 124.

7 Ibid.

8 Ibid., p. 125.

9 Ibid.

10 Ibid.

11 Ibid., p. 126.

12 As a comparison the Graf Pink, the most expensive diamond sold in recent history, was sold for $46 million sixty years ago. It is 24.78 carats, compared to the 106 carats of the Koh-I-Noor.

13 *Sheffield Daily Telegraph*, 24 Aug 1857.

14 Jules Verne, *The Demon of Cawnpore*, Scribner, New York, 1881.

15 The meeting is immortalised in Punjabi ballads: 'Dukhiye Ma Putt' by Sohan Singh Sital (in Punjabi).

16 *QVM*, p. 92.

17 Login, *Recollections*, p. 211.

18 Lady Normanby to Lord Mulgrave, 2 Jul 1861, Normanby Archives, *QVM*, p. 93.

19 Letter from Duleep Singh to Login, Jul 1861, Login, *Sir John Login*, p. 463.

20 Christy Campbell, *The Maharajah's Box*, HarperCollins, London, 2001, p. 58.

21 Letter from Duleep Singh to Login, Sep 1861, Login, *Sir John Login*, p. 465.

22 Letter from Sir Charles Phipps to Login, 4 Jan 1862, in ibid., p. 470.

23 *The Times*, 6 Aug 1863.

24 Login, *Recollections*, p. 229.
25 Rena L. Hogg, *A Master-Builder on the Nile: Being a Record of the Life and Aims of John Hogg*, United Presbyterian Board of Publication, Pittsburgh, 1914.
26 Ibid.
27 Letter from Lady Leven to Lady Login, 29 Jul 1864, Login, *Recollections*, p. 240.

## Chapter 3 – The Suffolk Mahal

1 *Ipswich Journal*, 30 May 1863.
2 *The Maharajah Duleep Singh and the Government: A Narrative*, Ballantyne, Hanson & Co., London, 1884.
3 Kelly's Directory for Cambridgeshire, Norfolk and Suffolk, 1883, p. 870.
4 Author interview with Lord Iveagh, owner of Elveden Hall. On the £30,000 for the remodelling, see letter Duleep Singh to Lord Salisbury, undated [Jan 1878], 010/22, RA.
5 See www.census-helper.co.uk/victorian-life
6 The figure of £30,000 equates to around £3.1 million in 2013, according to the Bank of England inflation calculator.
7 *The Field*, No. 2131, 28 Oct 1893.
8 On display at the Victoria & Albert Museum, London.
9 Author interview with Lord Iveagh.
10 Letters from the Maharajah and his wife Bamba, 1864–86, undated, Mss Eur E377/1, Select Materials, BL India Office.
11 *The Field*, No. 2131, 28 Oct 1893.
12 'The Uncle Jack Column', *Newcastle Weekly Courant*, issue 11403, 5 Aug 1893.
13 Letters from Catherine and Bamba to Sophia use both names, Mss Eur E377/4, BL Mss Eur E377/5; see also letters from Prince Albert Edward, Mss Eur 377/9, Select Materials, BL India Office.
14 Mss Eur E377/1.
15 *The Art of Falconry: Being the De Arte Venandi Cum Avibus of Frederick II of Hohenstaufen*, trans. Florence Marjorie Fyfe and Casey A. Wood, Stanford University Press, Stanford, 1969, p. 452.
16 Peter Bance, *The Duleep Singhs: The Photographic Album of Queen Victoria's Maharajah*, Sutton Press, London, 2004, p. 46.
17 Engraved bells from the collection of Catherine Drovna Oxley.
18 Letter from HRH Prince of Wales to R. H. Bob Collins, 6 Dec 1876, private collection of Peter Bance.
19 H. Gladstone, *Record Bags and Shooting Records*, H. F. Whitherby, London, 1930.
20 Author interview with Lord Iveagh.
21 Messrs Coutts and Co. to Duleep Singh, 9 Jan 1878, *QVM*, p. 122.
22 *QVM*, p. 128.
23 Queen Victoria to Duleep Singh, 12 Aug 1878, *QVM*, p. 129.
24 Ibid.

## Chapter 4 – The Fall

1 Queen Victoria to the Marquis of Dalhousie, 24 Nov 1854, *QVM*, p. 64.
2 One of the Old Brigade, *London in the Sixties*, Everett & Co. Ltd, London, 1908, Project Gutenberg eBook, Chapter XV.
3 Ibid.
4 Duleep Singh to Lord Hertford (a shooting friend who claimed to have some influence over Duleep Singh), undated, Hertford Archives.
5 Duleep Singh to Queen Victoria, 13 Sep 1880, *QVM*, p. 138.

6   Queen Victoria to Duleep Singh, 18 Sep 1880, *QVM*, p. 139.
7   Maharajah Duleep Singh and Evans Bell, *The Annexation of the Punjaub*, Trubner & Co., London, 1882.
8   *The Times*, 31 Aug 1882.
9   Duleep Singh to Kimberley, 1 Mar 1883, *QVM*, p. 167.
10  Ibid.
11  Ibid.
12  Kimberly to Duleep Singh, 21 Mar 1883, *QVM*, p. 168.
13  Hertford to Ponsonby, 28 July 1883, *QVM*, p. 169.
14  Ibid.
15  Bill of sale from Philips Son & Neale, Jul 1883, reproduced in *QVM*, p. 171.
16  Ibid.
17  *The Times*, 20 Jul 1883.
18  Duleep Singh to Palace, memo 15 Dec 1883, *QVM*, p. 177.
19  Julian Osgood Field, *Uncensored Recollections*, Eveleigh Nash & Grayson, London, 1924, p. 236.
20  Duleep Singh to Ponsonby, 18 July 1884, *QVM*, p. 178.
21  Ibid.
22  Queen Victoria memo to Ponsonby, 2 Aug 1883, *QVM*, p. 170.
23  Queen Victoria to Duleep Singh, 13 Sep 1884, *QVM*, p. 180.
24  Duleep Singh to Queen Victoria, 16 Sep 1884, *QVM*, p. 182.
25  Author interview with Shirley Sarbutt.
26  Ibid.
27  Osgood Field, *Uncensored,* p. 238.
28  A recurring theme in the letters between the sisters; see IOR Mss Eur E377/4/5/6.
29  IOR Mss Eur E377/10.
30  *The Times*, 23 May 1886.
31  'Abstract of Political Intelligence', Punjab Police, No. 11, 20 Mar 1886, G. Singh, *Correspondence*, p. 330.
32  Record of interview between Lord Kimberley and Duleep Singh, IOR L/P&S 18/D25 (194), 8 Feb 1886.
33  *Standard*, 25 Mar 1886.
34  Duleep Singh to Queen Victoria, 31 Mar 1886, *QVM*, p. 209.

## Chapter 5 – Scramble for India

1   See www.clydesite.co.uk
2   See www.poheritage.com
3   Letters from BDS to Mrs Lansing, 15 Apr 1886, IOR Mss Eur E377/1.
4   Delhi No. II, 1 May 1886, G. Singh, *Correspondence*, p. 301.
5   IOR L/P&S/18/D25.
6   'From Resident Aden to Foreign, Simla', telegram, 21 Apr 1886, G. Singh, *Correspondence*, p. 286.
7   *Lahore Tribune*, 1 May 1887.
8   Queen Victoria to Lord Dufferin, 10 Jun 1886, RA 09/52.
9   Duleep Singh to Dufferin, 12 May 1886, G. Singh, *Correspondence*, p. 341.
10  Lieutenant Governor to Foreign Secretary, Government of India, 14 May 1886, ibid., p. 342.
11  Literally translated it means 'The City of Bliss'.
12  Members of the Sikh brotherhood, or Khalsa, were asked, just as they are today, to follow the 'Five Ks'. The Ks represent Kesh, uncut hair; Kara, the wearing of a steel bracelet; Kanga, the carrying of a wooden comb; Kachha, the wearing of simple cotton undergarments; and Kirpan, the carrying at all times of a blade.

Each of these observances possessed a symbolic significance. The uncut hair signified an acceptance of a simple life free of vanity. The bracelet reminded the wearer that God had no beginning and no end; it was made of steel rather than precious metal to ensure that the rich could never flaunt their wealth through the wearing of it. The comb represented pride in appearance, for the Sikhs believed that a well-groomed man had a well-ordered mind. The Kachha, simple under-shorts that came to the knee, were a reminder that Sikhs should control their sexual desire. Finally all Sikhs were commanded to carry the blade, or Kirpan, which could range in size from a five-inch dagger to a three-foot sword; these weapons were meant to transform the Sikhs into 'soldier saints'. The word Kirpan itself had two roots: Kirpa, meaning 'mercy', and Aan, meaning 'honour'. Whosoever took up the Kirpan was automatically sworn to uphold justice and protect the weak.

13  Campbell, *Box*, pp. 79, 404–6.
14  G. Singh, *Correspondence*, p. 378.
15  *The Times*, 31 Aug 1886.
16  *QVM*, p. 249.
17  Vic Add N2/363 (minute), RA.
18  IOR Foreign DS-Secret, 13 Feb 1887.
19  'AS' to Foreign Department, 23 May 1888, IOR Foreign (Secret 1).
20  See www.royal.gov.uk
21  *The Hindustan*, 6 Oct 1887.
22  *QVM*, p. 249 (memo to the Palace).
23  Ibid.
24  Author interview with Catherine Drovna Oxley.
25  Ibid.
26  Campbell, *Box*, p. 306.
27  *The New York Times*, 16 Feb 1913. Ethel Bury Palliser later became a celebrated tutor of debutantes in America, trading off her association with the Duleep Singh princesses.
28  Edwin Chadwick, *Report on the Sanitary Condition of the Labouring Population of Great Britain*, R. Clowes and Sons, London, 1843.
29  Queen Victoria's Journal, 18 Sep 1887, see www.queenvictoriasjournals.org/home.do
30  Telegram from Duleep Singh to Prince Victor, undated, IOR Mss Eur E377/9.
31  Vic/Add U32, 29 Sep 1887, RA, letter from Queen Victoria to Princess Beatrice, Campbell, *Box*, p. 307.

## Chapter 6 – The Old Nature Rises

1   The gravestone can be found in the churchyard of St Andrew and St Patrick's church, Elveden.
2   Letter from Duleep Singh to Robert Drewitt, Elveden Estate Manager, Vic/Add N2/428, RA.
3   Maharani Bamba's will.
4   Ibid.
5   Arthur Oliphant to Sir Henry Ponsonby, Vic/Main/o/10/74, RA.
6   Ibid.
7   Ibid.
8   Arthur Oliphant to Windsor Castle, 8 Nov 1887, 010/65, Vic/Main/o/10/74, RA.
9   Ibid.
10  The 1891 census shows that Lina Schaeffer even accompanied Princess Catherine out of term time, on a holiday to the Isle of Wight.

11 IOR Mss Eur E377/3/4/5/9.
12 Letter from Prince Edward to Princess Sophia, 8 Feb 1890, IOR Mss Eur E377/9.
13 Letter from Prince Edward to Princess Sophia, 1890, undated, IOR Mss Eur E377/9.
14 School reports for Prince Albert Edward, private collection of Peter Bance.
15 Ibid.
16 Lord Henniker to Queen Victoria, May 1890, *QVM*, p. 289.
17 IOR R/1/1/90.
18 Campbell, *Box*, p. 396.
19 Duleep Singh to Queen Victoria, 18 Jul 1890, *QVM*, p. 288.
20 Cross to Ponsonby, 12 Dec 1890, *QVM*, p. 291.
21 Queen Victoria to Princess Royal, 1 Apr 1891, *QVM*, p. 293.
22 Jagatjit Singh, *My Travels in Europe and America*, Routledge, London, 1895, p. 180.
23 Henniker to Ponsonby, 7 Aug 1891, *QVM*, p. 295.
24 Oliphant to Ponsonby, 9 Aug 1891, *QVM*, p. 295.
25 *British Medical Journal*, 13 Jun 1925, 1(3363): 1112.
26 Letter from Arthur Oliphant to Sir Henry Ponsonby, Jan 1893, *QVM*, p. 296.
27 Ibid.
28 Letter from Arthur Oliphant to Lord Henniker, Windsor, 29 Oct 1893, Campbell, *Box*, p. 424.
29 *QVM*, p. 299.
30 Bance, *Rebel*, p. 93.
31 Ibid.

## Chapter 7 – Polishing the Diamond

1 Osgood Field, *Uncensored*, p. 239.
2 Sir Henry Ponsonby to Her Majesty Queen Victoria, 14 Oct 1889, Vic/Main/0/10/89, RA.
3 Lord Henniker to Lord Ponsonby, Feb 1890, Vic/Addn/2/521, RA.
4 Burne to Ponsonby, 8 Dec 1893, Vic/Addn/2/623, RA.
5 Ibid.
6 Ibid.
7 Oliphant to Ponsonby, 22 Jun 1894, Vic/Addn/2/632, RA.
8 Ibid.
9 Memo on SDS on her concern for CDS, IOR L/PS/11/52.
10 Diary of M. Mayes, private collection of Robert Kybird.
11 Ibid.
12 *Punch*, 11 Jun 1887, p. 277.
13 Sarah E. Parker, *Grace and Favour: A Handbook of Who Lived Where in Hampton Court Palace 1750 to 1950*, www.hrp.org.uk
14 Ibid.
15 Ibid.
16 Ibid.
17 Author interviews with Lillian Coram and Catherine Drovna Oxley.
18 Bills for fuel and maintenance of the Morgan show it was regularly serviced but seldom used, IOR Mss Eur E377/10.
19 Regular bills for Kathleen's grooming and medicine are to be found, ibid.
20 Ibid.
21 Collection of receipts for bills paid to the Revenue, ibid.
22 Author interview with Oxley.
23 Letter to the *New Statesman*, 23 Nov 1917, *New Statesman*, Vol. 10, Statesman Publishing Company, London, 1918, p. 197.

24 Letter from Lord Henniker to Sir Fleetwood I. Edwards, Vic/Addn/2/659, RA.
25 Ibid.
26 Ibid.
27 Vic/Main/QVJ (W), 8 May 1845 (Princess Beatrice's copies).
28 Ibid.
29 *Standard*, 8 May 1895.
30 Ibid.
31 'The Drawing Room', *The Times*, 9 May 1895.
32 Numerous receipts showing Sophia's purchasing extravagance exist in these files, IOR Mss Eur E377/9/10.
33 The Drapers' Record, *The First Moving Staircase in England*, 19 Nov 1898, London, p. 465.
34 *Daily Mail*, 23 Sep 1899.

## Chapter 8 – A Thoroughly English Girl

1 *Lloyds Weekly Newspaper*, 9 Jan 1898.
2 'Unlucky Prince Duleep Singh', *The New York Times*, 2 Dec 1889.
3 'The Indian Prince Has Fled', *The New York Times*, 15 Feb 1890.
4 Bance, *Rebel*, p. 112.
5 *Hackney Express and Shoreditch Observer*, 19 Oct 1895.
6 Bill Strickland (ed.), *The Quotable Cyclist*, Breakaway Books, New York, 1997, p. 324.
7 Peter Zheutlin and Annie Londonderry, *Women on Wheels: The Bicycle and the Women's Movement of the 1890s*, www.annielondonderry.com, p. 4.
8 *The Sketch*, 1896.
9 Ibid.
10 *Wheelwoman*, *The Lady Cyclist*, 16 Jul 1898.
11 Miscellany of receipts from the estate of SDS, IOR Mss Eur E377/9.
12 Ibid.
13 Edward William Jaquet, 'The Kennel Club: A History and Record of Its Work', *Kennel Gazette*, 1905.
14 *Lady's Realm*, Vol. XX, 1901.
15 *The Suburban Sports Woman: The First One Hundred Years of Wimbledon Ladies' Hockey Club*, Trudy Hutchings, published by Wimbledon Ladies' Hockey Club, p. 11.
16 Letters from CDS in India and Europe to SDS, 1900–7, p. 85, IOR Mss Eur E377/4.
17 *Lady's Realm*, Vol. XXI, 1900, p. 558.
18 *The Sketch*, 13 Jan 1904.
19 Loose papers, unnumbered, 1890–1904, IOR Mss Eur E377/9.
20 Charles H. Lane, *Dog Shows and Doggy People*, Hutchinson, London, 1902, pp. 92, 94, 138.
21 Loose papers, unnumbered, 1894–1907, IOR Mss Eur E377/10.
22 Ibid.
23 Letters from CDS in India and Europe to SDS, 1900–7; letter from CDS to SDS, 2 Feb 1900: IOR Mss Eur E377/4.
24 Ibid.
25 Ibid.
26 Ibid.
27 Ibid.
28 Letters from CDS in India and Europe to SDS, 1900–7; letter from CDS to SDS, 9 Feb 1900: IOR Mss Eur E377/4.
29 *Boston Daily Globe*, 17 Jul 1900.

30  Ibid.
31  Ibid.
32  *The New York Times*, Thursday, 14 Nov 1901.
33  *Logansport Pharos Tribune*, 20 Nov 1901.
34  *Oshkosh Daily Northwestern*, 19 Nov 1901.
35  *London Daily Mail*, 25 Dec 1902.
36  *The Church Weekly*, 6 Jun 1902.
37  *The World*, 31 Jan 1902.
38  Ibid.
39  *British Medical Journal*, 1, 287, 1902.

## Chapter 9 – The Cubs Come Home

1  Hansard, House of Commons, 29 Mar 1911, Vol. 23, cc. 1333–4. According to the Bank of England inflation calculator, £250,000 equates to £26.5 million in 2013.
2  Mike Davis, *Late Victorian Holocausts: El Niño Famines and the Making of the Third World*, Verso Books, London, 2002, p. 175.
3  Letter from Foreign Department Simla to R.T.W. Ritchie, Secretary, Political Department, India Office, London, summarising events of 1903, 3 Oct 1906, IOR L/P&S/11/52 P1608.
4  Ibid.
5  *Sheffield Daily Telegraph*, 2 Jan 1903.
6  F. S. Aijazuddin, *Lahore Recollected: An Album*, Sang-e-Meel, Lahore, 2003.
7  Ibid.
8  Letter confirming that no aid would be given to the travelling princesses, IOR L/P&S/11/52 P1608.
9  Mss Eur E377/8, p. 93.
10  H. S. Olcott, 'Constitution and Rules of the Theosophical Society', *The Theosophist* 12 (4), Theosophical Publishing House, Adyar, Jan 1891, pp. 65–72.
11  Emmeline Pankhurst, *My Own Story*, Eveleigh Nash, London, 1914, p. 19.
12  Letter from BDS to SDS, the Braganza Hotel Lahore, 4 Feb 1905, IOR Mss Eur E377/6.
13  Letter from Kedar Natu to SDS, MSS Eur E377/7.
14  Sheo Ram letters, IOR Mss Eur E377/7.
15  Copies of testimonials for Sheo Ram, 1857, IOR MSS Eur E377/7.
16  Ibid.
17  Ibid.
18  Sheo Ram letters, IOR Mss Eur E377/7.

## Chapter 10 – Patron of Lost Souls

1  Arthur Conan Doyle, *Sherlock Holmes: The Man with the Twisted Lip*, Harper & Brothers, New York, 1892, p. 136.
2  Rozina Visram, *Ayahs, Lascars and Princes*, Pluto Press, London, 1986, p. 52.
3  Ibid., p. 35.
4  Joseph Salter, *The Asiatic in England: Sketches of Sixteen Years' Work Among Orientals*, Seely, Jackson & Halliday, London, 1873, pp. 149–51.
5  Visram, *Ayahs*, pp. 35–6.
6  Ibid.
7  IOR/H/MISC/163, pp. 175–85.
8  *Morning Chronicle and London Advertiser*, 26 Dec 1786, as quoted in Visram, *Ayahs*, p. 232.
9  W. Harris et al, *Lascars and Chinese: A Short Address to Young Men of the Several Orthodox Denominations of Christians*, 1814, pp. 3–4, 9–10.

10  Salter, *The Asiatic in England*, pp. 4–5, 149–51.

11  Ibid.

12  Ibid.

13  Rozina Visram, *Asians in Britain: 400 Years of History*, Pluto Press, London, 2002. Sophia together with K. Choudhry and Ratan Tata would open the Lascars' Club at 313 Victoria Dock Road, London, E16 3AA. Her royal connections were invaluable, and she succeeded in getting major funding from both the Maharajah of Burdwan and the Maharajah of Scindia.

14  *Manchester Guardian*, 11 Nov 1904.

15  Author interviews with Lillian Coram and Shirley Sarbutt.

16  *Daily Mail*, 16 Jan 1903, p. 3.

17  Note of deposit and forwarding of 'necklace and rings', 1894–1907, IOR Mss Eur E377/10.

18  Letter from BDS to SDS, 17 Sep 1903, IOR Mss Eur E377/6.

19  Letter from CDS to SDS, 14 Apr 1904, IOR Mss Eur E377/4.

20  Letter from CDS to SDS, 3 Jun 1904, IOR Mss Eur E377/4.

21  Letter from CDS to SDS, 25 Nov 1904, IOR Mss Eur E377/4.

22  Letter from CDS to SDS, 3 Jun 1904, IOR Mss Eur E377/4.

23  Letter from CDS to SDS, 23 Oct 1904, IOR Mss Eur E377/4.

24  Letter from BDS to SDS, 4 Jun 1904, IOR Mss Eur E377/6.

25  Frederick Duleep Singh's diary, 9 Oct 1904, quoted in Bance, *Rebel*, p. 123.

26  See www.primrose-league.leadhoster.com/history.html

27  Bance, *Rebel*, p. 127.

## Chapter 11 – The Princess and the Madman

1  Although the letter is missing from the IOR Mss Eur E377 collection, reference to it is made in SDS Diary, 25 Dec 1906: 'B is quite of the opinion that she was poisoned last winter when she was so ill and it certainly seems suspicious like it confirms what she said . . .'

2  SDS Diary, 5 Nov 1906, IOR Mss Eur E377/8.

3  Ibid.

4  Letter BDS to SDS, The Palms, Lahore, 7 Apr 1905, IOR Mss Eur E377/6.

5  Letter BDS to SDS, The Palms, Lahore, 20 Apr 1905, IOR Mss Eur E377/6.

6  Letter BDS to SDS, Achabad 25 Jul 1905, IOR Mss Eur E377/6.

7  Letter BDS to SDS, The Palms, Lahore, 2 Nov 1905, IOR Mss Eur E377/6.

8  *Choti huzari* is a light meal taken mid-morning.

9  Letter from BDS to SDS, 6 Apr 1905, IOR Mss Eur E377/6.

10  Letter from BDS to SDS, 23 May 1905, IOR Mss Eur E377/6.

11  The *Barbarossa* could accommodate 200 people in first class, 430 in second and 1,935 in steerage. For a history of the ship see www.norwayheritage.com

12  SDS Diary, 27 Nov 1906, IOR Mss Eur E377/8.

13  SDS Diary, 13 Nov 1906, IOR Mss Eur E377/8.

14  Ibid.

15  SDS Diary, entries for 18, 19, 20, 21 Nov 1906, IOR Mss Eur E377/8.

16  SDS Diary, 21 Nov 1906, IOR Mss Eur E377/8.

17  Ibid.

18  SDS Diary, 23 Nov 1906, IOR Mss Eur E377/8.

19  Ibid.

20  Though Sophia never wrote his name, there are only two single men on the ship's manifest who boarded in Southampton and were travelling as far as Ceylon in first class. Her tormenter was either a Mr G. Nicholson or a Mr J. Fitzpatrick, Schedule B Form of Passenger List, *Barbarossa*, 5 Nov 1906, Ship's Master Langreuter.

21  SDS Diary, 28 Nov 1906, IOR Mss Eur E377/8.
22  SDS Diary, 22 Nov 1906, IOR Mss Eur E377/8.
23  SDS Diary, 28 Nov 1906, IOR Mss Eur E377/8.
24  Donald Shaw, One of the Old Brigade, *London in the Sixties*, Everett & Co., London, 1908, p. 261.
25  SDS Diary, 29 Nov 1906, IOR Mss Eur E377/8.
26  SDS Diary, 30 Nov 1906, IOR Mss Eur E377/8.

## Chapter 12 – The Blood is Up

1  SDS Diary, 3 Dec 1906, IOR Mss Eur E377/8.
2  SDS Diary, 15 Dec 1906, IOR Mss Eur E377/8.
3  Ibid.
4  Ibid.
5  SDS Diary, 16 Dec 1906, IOR Mss Eur E377/8.
6  SDS Diary, 17 Dec 1906, IOR Mss Eur E377/8.
7  Ibid.
8  Aijazuddin, *Lahore*, pp. 181–86.
9  SDS Diary, 17 Dec 1906, IOR Mss Eur E377/8.
10  Ibid.
11  SDS Diary, 25 Dec 1906, IOR Mss Eur E377/8.
12  Ibid.
13  Ibid.
14  Ibid.
15  Ibid
16  SDS Diary, 20 Dec 1906, IOR Mss Eur E377/8.
17  Letter from J. R. Dunlop Smith to Lord Knollys, 17 Jan 1907, IOR L/P&S/11/52 P1608.
18  Undated note attached to ibid.
19  Letter J. R. Dunlop Smith to Lord Knollys, 17 Jan 1907, IOR L/P&S/11/52 P1608.
20  SDS Diary, 21 Dec 1906, IOR Mss Eur E377/8.
21  SDS Diary, 28 Dec 1906, IOR Mss Eur E377/8.
22  Ibid.
23  SDS Diary, 31 Dec 1906, IOR Mss Eur E377/8.
24  Ibid.
25  Ibid.
26  Ibid.
27  Ibid.
28  Ibid.
29  Ibid.
30  Ibid.
31  Ibid.
32  Letter SDS to the Viceroy, 11 Jan 1907, IOR Mss Eur E377/7.
33  Reply to SDS from Government House, 17 Jan 1907, IOR Mss Eur E377/7.
34  Animation of the eclipse: www.astro.ukho.gov.uk/eclipse/0111907/Lahore_Pakistan
35  Hindus believed that the eclipse was a time of great evil, and that full immersion in the waters would keep them pure – hence the great crowds that day.
36  SDS Diary, 14 Jan 1907, IOR Mss Eur E377/8.
37  SDS Diary, 16 Jan 1907, IOR Mss Eur E377/8.
38  Ibid.
39  SDS Diary, 18 Jan 1907, IOR Mss Eur E377/8.
40  Ibid.

41 SDS Diary, 2 Feb 1907, IOR Mss Eur E377/8.

42 SDS Diary, 8 Feb 1907, IOR Mss Eur E377/8.

43 SDS Diary, 13 Feb 1907, IOR Mss Eur E377/8.

44 Ibid.

45 Radha Kumar, *The History of Doing: An Illustrated Account of Movements for Women's Rights and Feminism in India*, Kali for Women, 1993, p. 3.

46 SDS Diary, 15 Feb 1907, IOR/Mss Eur E377/8.

47 Ibid.

48 Ibid.

49 Ibid.

50 Ibid.

51 Ibid.

52 Ibid.

## Chapter 13 – India Awake!

1 M. K. Gandhi, *Gokhale: My Political Guru*, Navajivan Publishing House, Ahmedabad, 1955, p. 5.

2 SDS Diary, 16 Feb 1907, IOR Mss Eur E377/8.

3 Ibid.

4 Ibid.

5 Ibid.

6 Ibid.

7 J. S. Grewal and Indu Banga (eds), *Lala Lajpat Rai in Retrospect: Political, Economic, Social, and Cultural Concerns*, Publication Bureau, Panjab University, 2000, pp. 25 and 309.

8 SDS Diary, 17 Feb 1907, IOR Mss Eur E377/8.

9 Ibid.

10 Ibid.

11 Ibid.

12 Ibid.

13 Ibid.

14 Ibid.

15 SDS Diary, 18 Feb 1907, IOR Mss Eur E377/8.

16 Ibid.

17 SDS Diary, 19 Feb 1907, IOR Mss Eur E377/8.

18 Ibid.

19 SDS Diary, 21 Feb 1907, IOR Mss Eur E377/8.

20 Coralie Younger, *Wicked Women of the Raj: European women who broke society's rules and married Indian princes*, HarperCollins, New Delhi, 2011, reprint, p. 74.

21 SDS Diary, 23 Feb 1907, IOR Mss Eur E377/8.

22 Ibid.

23 SDS Diary, 24 Feb 1907, IOR Mss Eur E377/8.

24 Ibid.

25 Ibid.

26 SDS Diary, 27 Feb 1907, IOR Mss Eur E377/8.

27 SDS Diary, 28 Feb 1907, IOR Mss Eur E377/8.

28 Ibid.

29 Ibid.

30 Ibid.

31 Ibid.

32 Ibid.

33 Ibid.

34 SDS Diary, 1 Mar 1907, IOR Mss Eur E377/8.

35 'Outbreak of an Epidemic Disease in India', Acting Assistant Surgeon Eakins reports, 29 Mar 1907, *JSTOR Early Journal Content*, www.jstor.org.
36 SDS Diary, 12 Mar 1907, IOR Mss Eur E377/8.
37 SDS Diary, 19 Mar 1907, IOR Mss Eur E377/8.
38 Ibid.
39 SDS Diary, 20 Mar 1907, IOR Mss Eur E377/8.
40 SDS Diary, 2 Mar 1907, IOR Mss Eur E377/8.
41 SDS Diary, 25 Mar 1907, IOR Mss Eur E377/8.
42 Hansard, HC Deb, 15 May 1907, Vol. 174, c949 949. All Hansard references are available at www.hansard.millbanksystems.com
43 SDS Diary, 4 Apr 1907, IOR Mss Eur E377/8.
44 SDS Diary, 7 Apr 1907, IOR Mss Eur E377/8.
45 Ibid.
46 Ibid.
47 SDS Diary, 11 Apr 1907, IOR Mss Eur E377/8.
48 Ibid.
49 SDS Diary, 13 Apr 1907, IOR Mss Eur E377/8.
50 SDS Diary, 12 Apr 1907, IOR Mss Eur E377/8.
51 SDS Diary, 19 Apr 1907, IOR Mss Eur E377/8.
52 SDS Diary, 6 May 1907, IOR Mss Eur E377/8.
53 SDS Diary, 11 May 1907, IOR Mss Eur E377/8.
54 SDS Diary, 12 May 1907, IOR Mss Eur E377/8.
55 Ibid.

## Chapter 14 – The Lost Princess

1 Letter from Gokhale to Sir William Wedderburn (a Scottish civil servant in India and politician), quoted in J. N. Vajpeyi, *The Extremist Movement in India*, Chugh Publications, Allahabad, 1974, p. 122.
2 *Vande Mataram*, Calcutta, 10 May 1907.
3 *Daily Mail*, 9 May 1907.
4 Ibid.
5 Letter BDS to SDS, 29 Apr 1907, IOR Mss Eur E377/6.
6 Letter BDS to SDS, 2 Jul 1907, IOR Mss Eur E377/6.
7 Hansard, HC Deb, 29 May 1907, Vol. 174, cc1633-4 1633.
8 J. Morley to Minto, 15 Apr 1908, J. Morley Papers, Vol. III, 1905–11, IOR Mss Eur D573.
9 Bills and papers of SDS, IOR Mss Eur E377/10.
10 Ibid.
11 Elizabeth Crawford, *The Women's Suffrage Movement: A Reference Guide 1866-1928*, Routledge, London, 2003, p. 177.
12 Ibid.
13 Ibid.
14 Ibid.
15 Una Duval (née Dugdale) speaking to the BBC in 1955, www.bbc.co.uk/archive/suffragettes
16 Letter from Gurdit Singh Sandhawalia to SDS, undated, Collected Papers of SDS, IOR Mss Eur E377/7.
17 Letter from SDS to Gurdit Singh Sandhawalia, 3 Jul 1907, Sandhawalia family papers, quoted in Bance, *Rebel*, p. 147.
18 Letter from Gurdit Singh Sandhawalia to SDS, undated, collected papers of SDS, IOR Mss Eur E377/7.
19 *Sociologist* (ultra-nationalist Indian publication), Oct 1907.
20 Report from Curzon Wyllie, 26 Jan 1909, IOR L/P&S/ 11/52–P1608.

21  Crawford, *Suffrage*, p. 235

22  G. D. and J. Heath, 'The Women's Suffrage Movement in and around Richmond and Twickenham', 1968 (available at Richmond Museum).

23  Quoted in 'Deeds Better than Words', 26 Oct 1906, from Gandhi's weekly, *Indian Opinion*. Republished (in English, translated from Gujarati) in *The Collected Works of Mahatma Gandhi*, Vol. 6, pp. 29–30.

24  Letter George Bernard Shaw to the Editor, *The Times*, 31 Oct 1906.

25  Quoted in 'Deeds Better than Words', *Collected Works*, pp. 29–30.

26  Ibid.

27  Ibid.

28  Rehana Ahmed and Sumita Mukherjee, *South Asian Resistances in Britain 1858–1947*, Continuum Books, London, 2012, pp. 5–7, 9, 12–13.

29  *The Graphic*, 10 Jul 1909.

30  Ibid.

31  Ibid.

33  The mastermind behind the assassination and other revolutionary activities taking place at India House was Veer Sarvarkar. Arrested in 1910, he was sentenced to two life terms, to be served in the Andaman Islands. The capital's airport in Port Blair now bears his name.

33  Old Bailey proceedings online (www.oldbaileyonline.org, version 7.0, 10 Dec 2012), Jul 1909, trial of DHINGRA, Madhan Lal (25, student) (t19090719-55).

34  Ibid.

## Chapter 15 – The Hampton Court Harridan

1  TNA HO 144/1254/234646.

2  *Votes for Women*, 2 Jul 1909.

3  Constance Lytton, Jane Warton, *Prisons and Prisoners: Some Personal Experiences*, originally printed 1914, reprinted, Cambridge University Press, 2011, p. 200.

4  Pankhurst, *My Own Story*, p. 141.

5  From BBC Home Service, *In Town Tonight*, first broadcast, 29 Jan 1955.

6  Letter from Frederick Pethick Lawrence to Marion Wallace Dunlop, quoted in A. Rosen, *Rise Up, Women! The Militant Campaign of the Women's Social and Political Union, 1903–1914*, Routledge & Kegan Paul, 1974, reprinted 1993, p. 120.

7  Letter from Laura Ainsworth to Marion Wallace Dunlop, quoted in *Votes for Women*, 8 Oct 1909.

8  See BBC Suffragette Archive, www.bbc.co.uk/archive/suffragettes/8315.shtml.

9  Pankhurst, *My Own Story*, p. 163.

10  *The New York Times*, 14 Nov 1909.

11  Ibid.

12  Dana Bentley-Cranch, *Edward VII: Image of an Era 1841–1910*, HMSO, London, 1992, p. 151.

13  Ross Murdoch Martin, *The Lancashire Giant: David Shackleton, Labour Leader and Civil Servant*, Liverpool University Press, Liverpool, 2000.

14  Pankhurst, *My Own Story*, p. 178.

15  Ibid.

16  Julie Des Jardins, *The Madame Curie Complex: The Hidden History of Women in Science*, Feminist Press, New York, 2010, p. 34.

17  TNA MEPO, 3/203/8317586.

18  Pankhurst, *My Own Story*, p. 180.

19  Ibid., and TNA, MEPO 3/203.

20  Memorandum, 'Treatment of the Women's deputation by the Police', TNA,

MEPO 3/203; H. N. Brailsford, Secretary to the Parliamentary Conciliation Committee for Woman Suffrage, p. 6.

21  TNA HO 144/1106/200455.
22  Sophia A. Van Wingerden, *The Women's Suffrage Movement in Britain, 1866–1928*, Palgrave Macmillan, London, 1999, p. 123.
23  TNA MEPO 3/203/8317586.
24  TNA MEPO 3/203/8317586.
25  Georgina Solomon, Letter to the Editor, *The Times*, 3 Mar 1911.
26  TNA MEPO 3/203/8317586.
27  Letter of complaint from SDS to Home Secretary Winston Churchill, 26 Nov 1910, TNA HO/1106/200455.
28  Suffragette Index of Names of Persons Arrested, 1906–14, TNA HO45/24665.
29  TNA MEPO 3/203/8317586.
30  'Treatment of the Women's Deputations by the Police', copy of a memorandum forwarded by the Parliamentary Conciliation Committee for Woman Suffrage to the Home Office, Woman's Press, 1911.
31  Note attached 'To Commissioner of police for observations', TNA HO/1106/200455.
32  Letter from SDS to Home Secretary Winston Churchill, TNA HO/1106/200455.
33  Note attached 'To Commissioner of police for observations', TNA HO/1106/200455.

## Chapter 16 – A Familiar Enemy

1   www.forces-war-records.co.uk/Information/Boer-War-Casualties
2   Emily Hobhouse's letter to the people of South Africa, 1913, Anglo-Boer War Museum, Bloemfontein.
3   John Hall, *That Bloody Woman: The Turbulent Life of Emily Hobhouse*, Truran Publishers, Truro, 2008.
4   'Emily Hobhouse, South African War, 1899–1902', Barbara Harlow and Mia Carter (eds), *Archives of Empire*, Duke University Press, Vol. 2.
5   'Frances Mary Parker (Fanny, alias Janet Arthur) (1875–1924), militant suffragette', Oxford Dictionary of National Biography, Oxford University Press, Oxford.
6   Margaret Baker, *Discovering London Statues and Monuments*, Osprey Publishing, London, 2002, p. 54.
7   Letter from CDS to SDS, 25 Aug 1905, IOR Mss Eur E377.
8   'Lord Curzon's 15 Good Reasons Against the Grant of Female Suffrage', National Library of Scotland, shelfmark 1937.21(82).
9   *The Vote*, 24 Dec 1910.
10  *The Gleaner*, 16 Feb 1911.
11  Census of England and Wales 1911, Public Record Office.
12  Ibid.
13  *Punch*, 22 Mar 1911, Vol. 140, p. 199.
14  Letter to Miss Newsome (9/01/1229); Lady Sophia Duleep Singh to Miss Newsome, Women's Autograph Collection at the Women's Library (9/01/0941 & 9/01/1229).
15  Ibid.
16  Letter to Miss Nancy Grant (regarding a women's suffrage meeting at Richmond), 29 Apr 1911, Women's Autograph Collection at the Women's Library (9/01/0941 & 9/01/1229).
17  Ibid.
18  Ibid.
19  Margaret Kineton Parkes, with Introduction by Laurence Housman, 'The Tax Resistance Movement in Great Britain', Museum of London, Suffragette Collection, 50.82/357.

20 'Emma Sproson (1867–1936)', Oxford Dictionary of National Biography, Oxford University Press, Oxford.
21 Frank Sproson, *The Vote*, 8 Jul 1911.
22 Ibid.
23 *The Times*, 23 May 1911; *Votes for Women*, 26 May 1911.
24 Ibid.
25 SDS's diamond ring seized for non-payment of taxes, Museum of London, Suffragette Collection, 57.57/11.
26 'Report of the Women's Tax Resistance League Activities', *Votes for Women*, 28 Jul 1911.
27 Ibid.

## Chapter 17 – We Have No Hold

1 *Standard*, 5 Oct 1911; *Votes for Women*, 6 Oct 1911.
2 *Votes for Women*, 23 Feb 1912.
3 *Thames Valley Times*, 6 Mar 1912.
4 *Richmond and Twickenham Times*, 13 Apr 1912.
5 *Votes for Women*, 2 Aug 1912, quoting the case for the prosecution, Magisterial Enquiry, Oxford Assize Court, 26 Jul 1912.
6 Heath, 'Women's Suffrage'.
7 Ibid.
8 Ibid.
9 Ibid.
10 Speech by E. Pankhurst at the Pavilion Theatre, 10 Feb 1913, TNA HO 45.231366.
11 Heath, 'Women's Suffrage'.
12 'Teddington Suffragette Attack Remembered 100 Years On', *Richmond and Twickenham Times*, 20 Apr 2013.
13 Ibid.
14 Ibid.
14 *The Suffragette*, 24 Feb 1913, p. 2.
16 Diaries of Emily Blathwayt, Papers of Blathwayt Family of Dyrham, D2659/24, Gloucestershire Archives, Gloucester.
17 Women's Social and Political Union 7th Annual Report, 1913.
18 *The Western Gazette*, 9 May 1913.
19 *The Suffragette*, 12 Dec 1913; *The Western Gazette*, 9 May 1913.
20 Ibid.
21 *The Western Gazette*, 9 May 1913.
22 Ibid.
23 Ibid.
24 Ibid.
25 Sylvia Pankhurst, *The Suffragette Movement*, Longman, London, 1931.
26 Rowland George Martin Baker and Gwendoline F. Baker, *Thameside Molesey – A Towpath Ramble from Hampton Court to Hampton Reach*, Barracuda Press, London 1989, see www.moleseyhistory.co.uk/books/molesey
27 IOR L/PS/11/52.
28 Letter from Lord Crewe, Apr 1913, IOR L/PS/11/52.
29 Memo from Arthur Hirtzel, P 1608 1913, IOR L/PS/11/52.
30 *Daily Mail*, 30 Dec 1913.
31 Ibid.
32 *The Times*, 30 Dec 1913; *Votes for Women*, 2 Jan 1913.
33 Handwritten note attached to newspaper cutting, signed FHL, IOR L/PS/11/52.

## Chapter 18 – Indian Clubs

1   *Adelaide Register*, 5 Mar 1914.
2   *The Times*, 27 Jan 1914.
3   Ibid.
4   *The Vote*, 5 Aug 1911.
5   Lytton and Warton, *Prisons and Prisoners*, p. 33.
6   Ibid., p. 239.
7   Diaries of Mary Blathwayt, D2659, Papers of the Blathwayt family of Dyrham, Gloucestershire Archives, Gloucester.
8   Gretchen Wilson, *With All Her Might: The Life of Gertrude Harding, Militant Suffragette*, Holmes & Meier, New York, 1999, p. 140.
9   See www.bartitsu.org/index.php/2012/07/the-amazons-of-edwardian-london-martial-arts-trained-suffragette-bodyguards
10  'Suffragists' Indian Clubs', *The Times*, 12 Feb 1914.
11  Ada testimony, Museum of London, Suffragette Collection, 57.70–2
12  WSPU 8th Annual Report, 1914, the National Women's Social and Political Union, Annual Reports, Museum of London.
13  Ibid.
14  'Announcement of Marriage of Princess Irene Duleep Singh to Pierre Villemant', *The Times*, 16 Mar 1910.
15  Bance, *Rebel*, p. 101.
16  Diane Atkinson, *The Suffragettes in Pictures*, History Press, London, 2010, p. 56.
17  'Militant Arson Plans', *The New York Times*, 9 Jun 1914.
18  Anne Wiltsher, *Most Dangerous Women: Feminist Peace Campaigners of the Great War*, Pandora Press, Boston, 1985, p. 38.

## Chapter 19 – The Lady Vanishes

1   11/52 Dunlop Smith Memo, 39/10, IOR L/P&S, Political and Secret Department Records.
2   Ibid.
3   Ibid.
4   11/52 intercepted letter from CDS to SDS, 39/10, IOR L/P&S, Political and Secret Department Records.
5   Ibid.
6   11/52 memo to P. Cox, IOR L/P&S, Political and Secret Department Records, India Office.
7   Crawford, *Suffrage*, p. 378.
8   *The Times Documentary History of the War*, Military, Part 1, Times Publishing Company, London, 1918, p. 440.
9   Letter from Mohammed Agim to Subedar Major Firoz Khan, 28 May 1915, IOR L/MIL/5/825/4 f.425.
10  Ibid.
11  George Morton-Jack, *The Indian Army on the Western Front: India's Expeditionary Force to France*, Cambridge University Press, Cambridge, 2014, p. 182.
12  Joyce Collins, *Dr Brighton's Indian Patients December 1914–January 1916*, Brighton Books, Brighton, 1997, p. 7.
13  Ibid.
14  *The Brighton Gazette*, 16 Dec 1914.
15  Collins, *Indian Patients*, p. 21.
16  Letter No. 63, 1 May 1915, David Omissi, *Indian Voices of the Great War: Soldiers' Letters, 1914–1918*, Macmillan, London, 1999.
17  Collins, *Indian Patients*, p. 21.

18 Ibid., p. 23.
19 In 1919 she would receive 'The Bar to the Royal Red Cross', the organisation's highest award for exceptional devotion and bravery. It was presented to her at Buckingham Palace by the King.
20 *British Journal of Nursing*, 6 Mar 1915, p. 6.
21 Ibid., p. 7.
22 Bance, *Rebel*, p. 146.
23 Letter No. 253, 24 Feb 1916, Omissi, *Letters.*
24 Jaywant Joglekar, *Veer Savarkar, Father of Hindu Nationalism*, www.lulu.com, 2006, p. 68.
25 Sat D. Sharma, *India Marching: Reflections from a Nationalistic Perspective*, iUniverse, 2012, www.iuniverse.com, p. 31.
26 *The Times*, 20 Oct 1916.
27 11/52 Notes from Political Department, under heading 'The War', 26 Apr 1918, IOR L/P&S, Political and Secret Department Records.
28 Memo Draft Reply from L/P&S Department to Commissioner of Police, August 1917, IOR L/P&S, Political and Secret Department Records.
29 11/52 In Response to Telegram from Lord Wimborne to the Rt Hon. Secretary of State for India, date missing, IOR L/P&S, Political and Secret Department Records.
30 11/52 Draft Reply to SDS, on Scotland Yard headed paper, undated, IOR L/P&S, Political and Secret Department Records.
31 Bance, *Rebel*, p. 115.
32 *Daily Mirror*, 21 Sep 1928, p. 6.
33 *The Times*, 14 Sep 1918.
34 Ibid.
35 Ibid.
36 11/52 Letter to the British legation in the Hague, 11 Nov 1918, IOR L/P&S, Political and Secret Department Records, India Office.
37 11/52 Prisoners of War Department, Royal Court, House of Lords, London SW1, 24 Dec 1918, IOR L/P&S, Political and Secret Department Records.
38 11/52 Letter to the Secretary of State for India from J. E. Shukhburgh, 27 Dec 1918, IOR L/P&S, Political and Secret Department Records.

## Chapter 20 – Such Troublesome Times

1 See www.mkgandhi.org/articles/gsouthafrica_satyagraha.htm
2 Figures for the dead and wounded are hotly contested even today. The INC quoted casualties of 1,500, with 1,000 killed; the British insisted 1,100 were wounded, 379 killed.
3 Letter from Viceroy, Foreign and Political Department to Secretary of State for India, IOR L/P&S 10/768 DS Family 1918/30.
4 IOR L/P&S 10/768, p. 384.
5 Bance, *Rebel*, p. 97; Torry is Buried in Merville Communal Cemetery, France.
6 Sikhs were stationed at Hampton Court until 1919; Peter Bance, *The Sikhs in Britain*, Coronet House, London, 2012, p. 37.
7 Bance, *Rebel*, p. 154.
8 Ibid.
9 Mithan Lam, *Autumn Leaves*, IOR Mss Eur F 341/147.
10 Letter from Duke's Hotel, 35 St James's Palace, 17 Jul 1919, in Mrinalini Sarabhai (ed.), *The Mahatma and the Poetess*, Sarvoyada International Trust, Bhavan Book University Series, Delhi, 1998.
11 Ibid.
12 'Indian Women and the Franchise', *Observer*, 10 Aug 1919.

13  Letter from SDS to Sec of State, Mar 1920, L/P&S 10/768 DS Family 1918/30.
14  Letter from SDS to Sec of State, Oct 1923, L/P&S 10/768 DS Family 1918/30.
15  Author interview with Oxley.
16  Ibid.
17  Author interview with Coram.
18  Ibid.
19  Author interview with Oxley.
20  Bance, *Rebel,* p. 157.
21  Ibid.
22  Ibid.
23  Campbell, *Box,* pp. 17–18.
24  Ibid.
25  Ibid.
26  Ibid.
27  Author interview with Oxley.
28  Ibid.
29  Ibid.
30  Gene R. Thursby, *Hindu-Muslim Relations in British India: A Study of Controversy, Conflict, and Communal Movements in Northern India 1923– 1928,* Brill, p. 83
31  Stanley Wolpert, *Gandhi's Passion: The Life and Legacy of Mahatma Gandhi,* Oxford University Press, Oxford, 2002, p. 118.
32  The Ancient House Museum, Thetford, remains open today thanks to Freddie's legacy.
33  Bance, *Rebel,* p. 130.
34  *The Times,* 14 Aug 1926.
35  Bance, *Rebel,* p. 130.
36  Ibid.
37  Ibid.
38  Ibid.
39  Bance, *Rebel,* p. 97.
40  Joseph Sandler et al., *Freud's Models of the Mind,* Karnac Books, London, 1997, p. 52.
41  Bance, *Rebel,* p. 97.
42  *The Times,* 28 Nov 1928.
43  Ibid.
44  IOR L/P&S 10/768, legal letter Farrer and Co. Solicitors, 22 Nov 1929, p. 88.
45  *The Times,* 30 Nov 1928.
46  Ibid.
47  IOR L/P&S 10/768, Minutes summarising the case and its outcome for the Political Department, Dec 1929, p. 158.
48  Ibid.

## Chapter 21 – A Solemn Promise

1  HL Deb 22 May 1928, Vol. 71, cc213-56.
2  Quoted in June Purvis, *Emmeline Pankhurst: A Biography,* Routledge, London, 2002, p. 312.
3  *Daily Mail,* 19 Jun 1928.
4  Author interview with Coram.
5  Ibid.
6  Ibid.
7  Ibid.
8  Ibid.

9  Ibid.
10 Bance, *Rebel*, p. 136.
11 Ibid.
12 Author interview with Oxley.
13 From Chamberlain's address to the nation from the Cabinet Room at 10 Downing Street, 3 Sep 1939.
14 Author interview with Shirley Sarbutt.
15 Ibid.
16 Ibid., as told to her by Mrs Lane.
17 Author interview with Sarbutt.
18 Ibid.
19 Ibid.
20 Ibid.
21 Ibid.
22 Ibid.
23 Ibid.
24 Author interview with Oxley.
25 Ibid.
26 Author interview with Sarbutt.
27 Ibid.
28 Ibid.
29 Ibid.
30 Ibid.
31 Ibid.
32 Ibid.
33 Author interview with Oxley.
34 Ibid.
35 Author interview with Sarbutt.
36 Ibid.
37 Private collection of Robert Kybird, Letter to Ethel Snell, 8 Jan 1943; Snell was her old ladies' maid, with whom she stayed in touch until her death.
38 Ibid.
39 Ibid.
40 Author interview with Sarbutt.
41 Letter to Ethel Snell.
42 Author interview with Oxley.
43 Ibid.
44 Ibid.
45 It now resides at the Museum of Hyderabad as part of the Princess Bamba Collection.
46 Ibid.
47 Ibid.
48 Letter, private collection of Peter Bance.

# Epilogue

1 Letter to Pritam Singh Sandhawalia, from the private papers of the Sandhawalia family, quoted in Bance, *Rebel*, p. 159.
2 Ibid., p. 160.
3 Author interview with Oxley.
4 Author interview with Sarbutt.
5 Ibid.
6 Author interview with Oxley.
7 Ibid.

# BIBLIOGRAPHY

Abrams, Fran, *Freedom's Cause: Lives of the Suffragettes*, Profile Books, London, 2003

Ahmed, Rehana and Sumita Mukherjee, *South Asian Resistances in Britain 1858–1947*, Continuum Books, London, 2012

Aijazuddin, F. S., *Lahore Recollected: An Album*, Sang-e-Meel, Lahore, 2003

Alexander, Michael and Sushila Anand, *Queen Victoria's Maharajah, Duleep Singh, 1838–93*, Weidenfeld & Nicolson, London, 1980

Atkinson, Diane, *The Suffragettes in Pictures*, History Press, London, 2010

Baker, Margaret, *Discovering London Statues and Monuments*, Osprey Publishing, London, 2002

Baker, Rowland George Martin and Gwendoline F., *Thameside Molesey – A Towpath Ramble from Hampton Court to Hampton Reach*, Barracuda Press, London, 1989, available at www.moleseyhistory.co.uk/books/molesey

Bance, Peter, *Sovereign, Squire and Rebel: Maharajah Duleep Singh*, Coronet House Publishing Ltd, London, 2009

—, *The Duleep Singhs: The Photographic Album of Queen Victoria's Maharajah*, Sutton Press, London, 2004

—, *The Sikhs in Britain*, Coronet House, London, 2012

Bentley-Cranch, Dana, *Edward VII: Image of an Era 1841–1910*, HMSO, London, 1992

Burke, John and Anthony F Kersting, *Suffolk in Photographs*, Batsford Ltd, London, 1999

Burton, Reginald George, *The First and Second Sikh Wars: An Official British Army History*, Westholme Publishing, Yardley, PA, 2007

Campbell, Christy, *The Maharajah's Box*, HarperCollins, London, 2001

Cannadine, David, *Ornamentalism: How the British Saw Their Empire*, Oxford University Press, Oxford, 2002

Carpenter, Mary Wilson, *Health, Medicine and Society in Victorian England*, Praeger Inc., Santa Barbara, CA, 2009

Chadwick, Edwin, *Report on the Sanitary Condition of the Labouring Population of Great Britain*, R. Clowes and Sons, London, 1843

Chandra, Bipan et al., *India's Struggle for Independence*, Penguin, Delhi, 1989

Collins, Joyce, *Dr Brighton's Indian Patients December 1914–January 1916*, Brighton Books, Brighton, 1997

Conan Doyle, Arthur, *Sherlock Holmes, The Man with the Twisted Lip*, Harper & Brothers, New York, 1892

Crawford, Elizabeth, *The Women's Suffrage Movement: A Reference Guide 1866–1928*, Routledge, London, 2003

Dalrymple, William, *Return of a King: The Battle for Afghanistan*, Bloomsbury, London, 2013

Davis, Mike, *Late Victorian Holocausts: El Niño Famines and the Making of the Third World*, Verso Books, London, 2002

Des Jardins, Julie, *The Madame Curie Complex: The Hidden History of Women in Science*, Feminist Press, New York, 2010

Eakins, Acting Assistant Surgeon, 'Outbreak of an Epidemic Disease in India', 29 Mar 1907, *JSTOR Early Journal Content*, www.jstor.org

Edwardes, Sir Herbert Benjamin and Herman Merivale, *The Life of Sir Henry Lawrence*, Vol. 2, Smith, Elder & Co., London, 1872

'Emma Sproson (1867–1926)', Oxford Dictionary of National Biography, Oxford University Press, Oxford

'Frances Mary Parker (Fanny, alias Janet Arthur) (1875–1924), militant suffragette', *Oxford Dictionary of National Biography*, Oxford University Press, Oxford

Frederick II of Hohenstaufen, *The Art of Falconry: Being the De Arte Venandi Cum Avibus of Frederick II of Hohenstaufen*, trans. and ed. F. Marjorie Fyfe and Casey A. Wood, Stanford University Press, Stanford, 1969

Gandhi, 'Deeds Better than Words', *Indian Opinion*, 26 Oct 1906, republished in *The Collected Works of Mahatma Gandhi*, Vol. 6, www.commons.wikimedia.org

Gandhi, M. K., *Gokhale: My Political Guru*, Navajivan Publishing House, Ahmedabad, 1955

Gill, Avtar Singh, *Lahore Darbar and Rani Jindan*, Central Publishers, Punjab, 1983

Gladstone, H., *Record Bags and Shooting Records*, H. F. Whitherby, London, 1930

Gough, Charles and Arthur D. Innes, *The Sikhs and the Sikh Wars: The Rise, Conquest and Annexation of the Punjab State*, Kaveri Books, Delhi, 2008 (first published 1897)

Grewal, J. S. and Indu Banga (eds), *Lala Lajpat Rai in Retrospect: Political, Economic, Social, and Cultural Concerns*, Publication Bureau, Panjab University, 2000

Hall, John, *That Bloody Woman: The Turbulent Life of Emily Hobhouse*, Truran Publishers, Truro, 2008

Harlow, Barbara and Mia Carter (eds), *Archives of Empire*, Duke University Press

Harris, W. et al, *Lascars and Chinese: A Short Address to Young Men of the Several Orthodox Denominations of Christians*, 1814

Heath, G. D. and J., 'The Women's Suffrage Movement in and around Richmond and Twickenham', 1968, available at Richmond Museum

Hogg, Rena L., *A Master-Builder on the Nile: Being a Record of the Life and Aims of John Hogg*, United Presbyterian Board of Publication, Pittsburgh, 1914

Hutchings, Trudy, *The Suburban Sports Woman: The First One Hundred Years of Wimbledon Ladies' Hockey Club*, published by Wimbledon Ladies' Hockey Club

Jaquet, Edward William, 'The Kennel Club: A History and Record of Its Work', *Kennel Gazette*, 1905

Joglekar, Jaywant, *Veer Savarkar, Father of Hindu Nationalism*, 2006, www.lulu.com

Kumar, Radha, *The History of Doing: An Illustrated Account of Movements for Women's Rights and Feminism in India*, Zubaan, New Delhi, 1997

Lam, Mithan, *Autumn Leaves*, available at IOR Mss Eur F 341/147

Lane, Charles H., *Dog Shows and Doggy People*, Hutchinson, London, 1902

Login, Lady Lena, *Lady Login's Recollections, Court Life and Camp Life, 1820–1904*, Smith, Elder & Co., London, 1916

—, *Sir John Login and Duleep Singh*, W. H. Allen & Co., London, 1890

Lytton, Constance and Jane Warton, *Prisons and Prisoners: Some Personal Experiences*, 1914, reprinted Cambridge University Press, Cambridge, 2011

Madra, Amandeep Singh and Parmjit Singh, *Warrior Saints: Four Centuries of Sikh Military History*, Kashi House, London, 2013 (2nd edn)

Marshman, John Clark, *The History of India from the Earliest Period to the Close of Lord Dalhousie's Administration in Three Volumes*, Vol. 3, original edition 1863–7, full text online www.ibiblio.org

Martin, Ross Murdoch, *The Lancashire Giant: David Shackleton, Labour Leader and Civil Servant*, Liverpool University Press, Liverpool, 2000

Morton-Jack, George, *The Indian Army on the Western Front: India's Expeditionary Force to France*, Cambridge University Press, Cambridge, 2014

Olcott, H. S., 'Constitution and Rules of the Theosophical Society', *The Theosophist*, 12 (4), Theosophical Publishing House, Adyar, 1891

Omissi, David, *Indian Voices of the Great War: Soldiers' Letters, 1914–1918*, Macmillan, London, 1999

One of the Old Brigade, *London in the Sixties*, Everett & Co. Ltd, London, 1908, Project Gutenberg eBook

Osgood Field, Julian, *Uncensored Recollections*, Eveleigh Nash & Grayson, London, 1924

Pankhurst, Emmeline, *My Own Story*, Eveleigh Nash, London, 1914

Pankhurst, Sylvia, *The Suffragette Movement*, Longman, London, 1931

Parker, Sarah E., *Grace and Favour: A Handbook of Who Lived Where in Hampton Court Palace 1750 to 1950*, www.hrp.org.uk

Parkes, Margaret Kineton, with Introduction by Laurence Housman, 'The Tax Resistance Movement in Great Britain', Museum of London Suffragette Collection

Prinsep, James, *History of the Punjab*, Vol. II, W. H. Allen, London, 1846, reprinted Patiala, 1970

Purvis, June, *Emmeline Pankhurst: A Biography*, Routledge, London, 2002

Queen Victoria, *Letters of Queen Victoria, 1844–1853*, Project Gutenberg eBook, Vol. 2

—, *Queen Victoria's Journal*, www.queenvictoriasjournals.org/home.do

Rosen, Andrew, *Rise Up, Women! The Militant Campaign of the Women's Social and Political Union, 1903–1914*, Routledge & Kegan Paul, London and Boston, 1974

Salter, Joseph, *The Asiatic in England: Sketches of Sixteen Years' Work Among Orientals*, Seely, Jackson & Halliday, London, 1873

Sandler, Joseph et al, *Freud's Models of the Mind*, Karnac Books, London, 1997

Sarabhai, Mrinalini (ed.), *The Mahatma and the Poetess*, Sarvoyada International Trust, Bhavan Book University Series, Delhi, 1998

Sharma, Dr Sat D., *India Marching: Reflections from a Nationalistic Perspective*, iUniverse, 2012, www.iuniverse.com

Singh, Ganda (ed.), *Maharajah Duleep Singh Correspondence*, Patiala, Punjab University, 1972

Singh, Jagatjit, *My Travels in Europe and America*, Routledge, London, 1895

Singh, Maharajah Duleep and Evans Bell, *The Annexation of the Punjaub*, Trubner & Co., London, 1882

Singh, Patwant and Jyoti M. Rai, *Empire of the Sikhs: The Life and Times of Maharaja Ranjit Singh*, Peter Owen Ltd, London, 2002 (revised edn)

Strickland, Bill (ed.), *The Quotable Cyclist*, Breakaway Books, New York, 1997

*The Maharajah Duleep Singh and the Government: A Narrative*, Ballantyne, Hanson & Co., London, 1884

*The Times Documentary History of the War*, Times Publishing Company, London, 1918

Thursby, Gene R., *Hindu-Muslim Relations in British India: A Study of Controversy, Conflict, and Communal Movements in Northern India 1923–1928*, Brill, London, 1975

Vajpeyi, J. N., *The Extremist Movement in India*, Chugh Publications, Allahabad, 1974

Van Wingerden, Sophia A., *The Women's Suffrage Movement in Britain, 1866–1928*, Palgrave Macmillan, London, 1999

Verne, Jules, *The Demon of Cawnpore*, Scribner, New York, 1881

Visram, Rozina, *Asians in Britain: 400 Years of History*, Pluto Press, London, 2002
—, *Ayahs, Lascars and Princes*, Pluto Press, London, 1986
Wilson, Gretchen, *With All Her Might: The Life of Gertrude Harding, Militant Suffragette*, Holmes & Meier, New York, 1999
Wiltsher, Anne, *Most Dangerous Women: Feminist Peace Campaigners of the Great War*, Pandora Press, Boston, 1985
Wolpert, Stanley, *Gandhi's Passion: The Life and Legacy of Mahatma Gandhi*, Oxford University Press, Oxford, 2002
Younger, Coralie, *Wicked Women of the Raj: European women who broke society's rules and married Indian princes*, HarperCollins, New Delhi, 2011
Zheutlin, Peter and Annie Londonderry, *Women on Wheels: The Bicycle and the Women's Movement of the 1890s*, www.annielondonderry.com

# ACKNOWLEDGEMENTS

I have had so much help from so many wonderful people, this may take some time. Brace yourselves!

Drovna Oxley and Shirley Phimister (née Sarbutt) are living links to Sophia Duleep Singh. Both knew her and loved her tremendously. They have given me access to their personal archives, and endless cake and hospitality. I am very proud to count these extraordinary women as my friends. Ladies, I hope I did well by your princess.

I was given fantastic insight into the workings of Faraday House by Lillian Coram, who worked as a maid for Sophia, and also Robert Kybird, former mayor of Thetford and present chairman of Breckland District Council. His ancestors include James Mayes (head game-keeper at Elveden), Margaret Mayes (former housekeeper at Faraday House) and Ethel and Maggie Snell (ladies' maids with whom the princess maintained a friendship long after they left her service).

I am also indebted to Ned Guinness, Earl of Iveagh, who kindly opened the doors of Elveden to me. He facilitated a rare and valuable glimpse of the Maharajah's Suffolk palace. He also was good enough to show me the grounds and share some of his family's memories of the Duleep Singhs. Thanks also to his personal assistant Melanie Shuttler, who endured daft queries and even went around the old hall with a measuring tape for me.

The historian and author Peter Bance has been a superstar, nothing less. He has a collection of Duleep Singh family papers and ephemera second to none and has shared his time, expertise and treasures with me. Some of the finest images in this book are drawn from his exten-sive archive. I urge anyone interested in further study to read his books. His wife Satnam kept us fed and watered with the forbearance of a saint while we spent hours poring over documents and photo-graphs. Thank you both: you may now have your lives back!

I am very grateful to Oliver Bone and his staff at the Ancient House Museum in Thetford. I spent happy hours trawling through their extensive archive. Beverly Cook of the Museum of London's Suffragette Collection has also been supremely supportive, always on hand to answer a question or dig out a reference. She was there to share a special moment when I found Sophia peering out of that Black Friday photograph you see in the book. I would also like to thank Ian Franklin at Hampton Court Palace, particularly for pointing me towards the most useful archive material on grace-and-favour homes and their residents.

Amandeep Madra has done so much to educate young British Sikhs about their heritage. He also offered his unstinting help to me right from the start of my research. Poor Amandeep made the mistake of accepting my friendship on a social network. I can only imagine how his heart must have 'soared' as his computer went *ping* for the four-millionth time with yet another *fascinating* question. Thanks, Aman, for never throwing your keyboard out of the window.

Dr Jeevan Deol is a leading expert on Indian history who has taught at SOAS, Oxford and Cambridge. I am privileged to call him a friend and extremely lucky to have been able to draw on his great wealth of knowledge. He has been a generous guide and source of encouragement. Not only that, but he also brought much missing punctuation to the party. I shall never look at a semicolon with suspicion again.

Even before I met the eminent historian Rozina Visram, I was in awe of her work. She has led the field in the study of the Indian diaspora in the UK. Her scholarly works include *Ayahs, Lascars and Princes* – invaluable – and her seminal *Asians in Britain: 400 Years of History* had a great impact on me. She is also a jolly lovely woman who shared her research and experience with an open hand and heart.

Dr Florian Stadtler has published articles and essays on South Asian and British Asian history and literature. He was also my cake-buddy at the British Library. Thanks, Florian, for patiently showing me the ropes. I am also grateful to Penny Brook and Xiao Wei Bond from the Asia Pacific and Africa Collections of the British Library. They have been supremely helpful, allowing me to hold and read Sophia's original documents and diary in my hands.

Thanks also to Dr Mari Takayanagi, Head of Preservation and

Access at the Parliamentary Archives. She has been fantastic at replying to particularly vexing questions thrown up by Hansard. Because of her, I had a thrilling time wandering the vaults deep under Parliament, filled with old scrolls of parchment recording British legislation spanning centuries. For a political journalist it was almost too exciting for words. Alison Derrett of the Royal Archives has also been wonderfully efficient in finding documents and checking references.

Christy Campbell, author of *The Maharajah's Box*, is not just a great author, but a fabulous raconteur – generous with advice. More importantly, he got as excited as I did when I shared new discoveries. For this book I needed to recreate Lahore at the turn of the last century. To that end I must thank historian and former principal of Aitchison College, Fakir Syed Aijazuddin. His writings and guidance were invaluable.

I am also indebted to two friends who have known me for ever and who I love to their brilliant bones. One is Gul Afridi, who not only fact-checked for me in Pakistan but has also been a source of encouragement throughout this process. The other is Sadhana Natali Khan, who read my work in progress and has been an effusive and reassuring presence throughout. Love you girls – you give meaning to the 'sisterhood'. Also I would like to remember my friend Boo Armstrong, who is no longer with us. She, more than anybody I know, embodied the suffragette fighting spirit.

I have been lucky to have some extraordinary viragos in my life. They have shown me what it is to walk to the beat of your own drum: my old teacher Sister Francesca; trailblazing politician Baroness Shreela Flather; firebrand journalist Yasmin Alibhai Brown; and my beloved Maria Birbeck – naughty godmother, deeply missed. Bloody-minded women all – in the most spectacular, beautiful way.

Dr Antoine Sayer has been an amazing help. There are few GPs who would have approached boring and recurring RSI with such good humour and kindness. Fewer still who would have prescribed software for my computer and gone home to fetch his own mouse because mine was 'stupid and evil'. Thanks Doc – I quite literally could not have typed this without you.

Bloomsbury people are the best people. I have been blessed with loveliness thanks to my editor Alexandra Pringle – a publishing legend

– elegance personified – sparkling and hilarious company. As soon as I met her I knew Sophia was in the best hands. Enormous thanks to Anna Simpson, Kate Johnson, Laura Brooke, Helen Flood and Vicky Beddow also of Bloomsbury. They have given amazing support, wise counsel and just made the whole experience fun. They also had names I could spell – unlike Alexandra's exotically named angels, Alexa von Hirschberg, Ianthe Cox-Willmott and Angelique Tran Van Sang. Thanks ladies – you were very helpful but you did give my spellcheck a nervous breakdown.

To my agent, Patrick Walsh, there really are not enough words under 'gratitude' in the thesaurus. You are smart, calm, funny and kind. In short, you rock! I hope you know it.

To my family, Bully, Anup, Christina and the teenies – Mouse and I-man: you have been boundless in your love, patience and understanding. A first book is scary. You have kept me level, you have kept me laughing.

To my mother Shashi Anand – Mum – without you this book just would never have been written. You have looked after Hari and the rest of us when my head has been stuck in a deadline. You never let me down. This book is supposed to be about strong women. I know few who are stronger than you. 'Thank you' seems an inadequate phrase. And to my father – I know you're not here to see this but I bet you'd get a kick out of it. These are the times I miss you most.

To Simon Singh – my much smarter better half. Lovely, clever and kind, you have held my hand from the moment Sophia barged her way into our lives. You have always been interested and constructive and encouraging – even when you had a book on the boil yourself. You aren't just my husband, you are my best mate. And as for Hari – he continues to be a very reliable cuddle generator. Every author needs one.

Finally to my nieces – Mahalia, Nidhi, Richa, Taanya, Nikita, Divya, Shweta, Radhika, Nandni, Ishu and Ridhma – and my goddaughters Eva, Honor and JJ: please make me this solemn vow – even if you don't know what one of those is yet. Whatever happens, you have to vote. Wherever and whenever there is a chance to exercise that right you are to take it. A lot of very fine and brave women risked everything to give you that voice. Never forget what they fought for. Never let anyone take it away.

# INDEX

# A NOTE ON THE AUTHOR

Anita Anand has been a radio and television journalist for almost twenty years. She is the presenter of *Any Answers* on BBC Radio 4. During her career she has also presented *Drive*, *Doubletake* and the *Anita Anand Show* on Radio 5 Live, and *Saturday Live*, *The Westminster Hour*, *Beyond Westminster*, *Midweek* and *Woman's Hour* on Radio 4. On BBC television she has presented *The Daily Politics*, *The Sunday Politics* and *Newsnight*. She lives in west London. This is her first book.

@tweeter_anita

# A NOTE ON THE TYPE

The text of this book is set in Linotype Stempel Garamond, a version of Garamond adapted and first used by the Stempel foundry in 1924. It's one of several versions of Garamond based on the designs of Claude Garamond. It is thought that Garamond based his font on Bembo, cut in 1495 by Francesco Griffo in collaboration with the Italian printer Aldus Manutius. Garamond types were first used in books printed in Paris around 1532. Many of the present-day versions of this type are based on the *Typi Academiae* of Jean Jannon cut in Sedan in 1615.

Claude Garamond was born in Paris in 1480. He learned how to cut type from his father and by the age of fifteen he was able to fashion steel punches the size of a pica with great precision. At the age of sixty he was commissioned by King Francis I to design a Greek alphabet, for this he was given the honourable title of royal type founder. He died in 1561.